W9-CCY-554

GOD BLESS
THE
UNITED STATES
OF
AMERICA

FOUNDING

The Fight for Freedom and

FATHERS

THE BIRTH OF AMERICAN LIBERTY

K. M. KOSTYAL

NATIONAL GEOGRAPHIC

WASHINGTON, D.C.

To my mother, Helen, for so much history

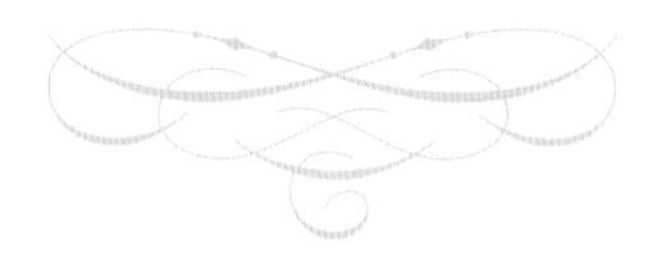

Contents

Page 1: Decorated tobacco box, circa 1795; Pages 2–3: Celebrating the end of an 11-month siege, George Washington parades triumphantly through Boston after the withdrawal of British troops in 1776. Opposite: The lantern used on the night of Paul Revere's ride, April 18, 1775

ANKEE DOODLE
776 Pub. by
J.F. Ryder
VELAND.

{ FOREWORD }

The American Revolution began as a protest against the idea that the British Parliament had the authority to impose taxes and laws on its colonists overseas. For nearly a decade, this protest followed familiar lines of constitutional argument. Americans held that they could not be governed by a legislature in which they had no representatives. British spokesmen replied that the colonists were bound to obey laws passed by Parliament, the highest source of sovereign power in the British Empire. Then, in the spring of 1774, this constitutional dispute exploded into a potential revolution. In response to the Boston Tea Party of December 1773, Parliament enacted a set of measures punishing both Boston and the province of Massachusetts for defying imperial law and policy. The British government hoped to intimidate the other colonies into submission. Instead, the colonies rallied to the cause of Massachusetts, now "suffering in the common cause" of protecting American rights of self-government. Meeting at the First Continental Congress in Philadelphia, delegates from 12 colonies set a joint strategy of resistance. Rather than attempting to negotiate with this new institution, the British government tried to enforce its rule by force of arms. By April 1775, a civil war had begun, first in Massachusetts and then elsewhere. Peace would come eight years later, when Britain formally recognized the independent United States.

The American struggle was revolutionary in many ways. For one, it allowed the colonists to restore legal rule within the states by writing new constitutions, an experience that set critical precedents for the Federal Convention of 1787. But the success of this movement also involved a prolonged war of national liberation. That struggle imposed far greater burdens on the newly forming American people than they had ever known before, and it sorely tried the ability and resources of the new governments they had established. From 1775 until the war's end, the Continental Army was hard-pressed to stay in the field. It faced repeated crises to maintain its strength, dwindling in numbers, frequently lacking adequate supplies, much less pay, yet somehow managing to hold itself together until the victory at Yorktown in 1781 sealed the outcome.

The dominant figure in keeping the army together was George Washington, the wealthy, ambitious, and deeply patriotic Virginia planter who took command in June 1775. In the 21st century as in the 18th, there remains no better way to explain the course of the Revolutionary War than to give Washington the pride of place he eminently earned. Like other generals waging a long war, he committed his share of errors. Yet from the start of the war to its conclusion, and beyond then to the adoption and implementation of the new federal Constitution, he was the nation's leading nationalist. Washington thought of the war as a struggle to create a nation; he treated the army he commanded as a genuinely national institution; and even as he privately grumbled over the decisions of the Continental Congress, he understood that the republic Americans wanted to create required effective civilian, not military, control. Washington's beliefs help us to understand why the American Revolution was truly and admirably revolutionary.

Many of us take that fact for granted, as a given of American patriotism, without fully grasping its significance. The American Revolution is such a well-established part of our history that it is easy to miss its novelty and its surprises. In fact, there were many good reasons why the revolution need not have happened at all, and many ways to imagine how it could have ended differently. Both the British and the Americans found it hard to devise a strategy that would bring decisive victory to their side. It is one of the great strengths of this fast-moving book that it reminds us, as all good history should, of the way in which chance and contingency mingled with deep issues and causes to make the past as surprising to us as it was to the people who made it.

—Jack Rakove

Archibald MacNeal Willard's *famous painting "The Spirit of '76" is also known by the nickname "Yankee Doodle."*

{ INTRODUCTION }

In writing this book, as in all my thinking about the Revolutionary period, I was struck again and again by the improbability of America's very existence. The odds that it ever should have achieved form and function were negligible. And yet history is full of improbabilities and strange, unforeseen turns—trickles of events that suddenly and precipitously swell into floods. This book is about those turns and the men and women who were willing to be swept up into that particular flood of historical change, whatever it cost them.

None of the so-called Founding Fathers possibly could have envisioned in mid-18th-century America how drastically their world, and the world in general, would transform in the next quarter century. As 1760 dawned, most white colonists were proud British subjects, relatively content in the arms of empire. Yet they had grown up with an implicit understanding that risk taking was their heritage. Their great-grandparents or grandparents or even parents had left behind the known, European world to settle in a land an ocean away. If life was often hard in colonial America, it was also filled with possibility—and with hard work, discipline, and strict social codes. Despite these commonalities among the colonies, there were also wide differences.

Surrounded by 13 stars *on a field of blue, a proud eagle adorns an early iteration of the American flag, created circa 1781.*

Massachusetts and Virginia—two of the oldest and most influential colonies—differed in so many ways. The Massachusetts founders traced their ancestry to Puritan stock, and they remained hardy, self-abnegating, pious, and frugal (with the exception of John Hancock, who was as extravagant as his signature). They were mostly farmers, small businessmen, and professionals. The Virginia founders, on the other hand, came from a planter aristocracy fueled by slavery and classism. These "sultans of the South," as one critic called them, were elegant and often pampered, but, like their Massachusetts brethren, they were educated both in the classics and in the ideas of the Enlightenment. Each of the other colonies could claim its own cultural and economic distinctions, which tended to engender competition rather than cooperation with its neighbor colonies.

But as the 17th century moved into its second half and Britain began to put more economic pressure on its American subjects, the colonies increasingly turned to one another. By tradition and historical precedence, the crown and its agents had a right to govern the colonies as they saw fit and for the good of the empire. Yet the Americans refused to be governed against their will and by what they believed were unjust laws. They would not be bullied, as they saw it, into submission with taxes and trade constraints, corrupt officials, and a show of arms. Faced with the colonists' political indignation, Britain could have moderated its American policies in the early 1770s, and the dissension between it and America might have ended as a historical footnote—no more than a scuffle between rulers and ruled. Some British officials in fact argued for moderation, but they lost the argument. Had they won, history may well have taken a different turn, and the world might look very different today—two or three vast empires controlling the globe. Instead, war became inevitable.

Most wars create an initial flush of intoxication, and the "spirit of '76" certainly infected the colonists. But as the long, unremitting struggle dragged on, citizens, politicians, and soldiers alike grew weary of war and its privations. What kept the conflict alive was not the great public zeal for revolution.

Instead, it was a relative handful of men whose ideas, courage, and perseverance shape what America is today. Some we know as founders; others were soldiers who fought on—threadbare, sometimes shoeless, often overmarched and underfed. To them we owe more statues, more books, more recognition.

But it is the larger-than-life Founding Fathers who capture our imagination. There is no official list of them, so each of us must choose our own and come to know and appreciate them in our own time—and with our own predispositions to like some and not others. In writing and researching this book, I gained a greater understanding of them as both humans and heroes. Some I found wanting in one capacity, some in another. Their idiosyncrasies as well as their genius were endlessly captivating. They were all ambitious men, hungry to perform on the grand stage that the Revolution suddenly provided them. As West Indian–born Founding Father Alexander Hamilton freely admitted, "Love of fame, the ruling passion of the noblest minds . . . prompt[s] a man to plan and undertake extensive and arduous enterprises for the public benefit." Hamilton, the visionary and schemer—the one who understood that government requires institutions and that humans require sound government—devoted his life to the public benefit and to his own ambitions. The two complemented each other nicely, as they did in John Adams, whose vanity has become legendary. And yet Adams too gave all he had to the Revolution, and suffered mightily for it. He was away from his beloved wife and most of his children for years at a time, often with little public appreciation for his efforts. His pugnacity, like his vanity, cost him in reputation, and yet his writings show how keenly he understood the struggle—on every level. Adams's letters and writings are more than merely grand insights. They create perhaps the most detailed—and entertaining—account of the founders' actions and interplay that we have.

Hamilton and Adams are just two of the founders covered in the following pages. Whatever else he was, each of the founders was a huge character in his own right and had his own vision for America. Together, they managed to defeat the greatest empire on Earth and then to create a country and government where none existed. They wanted that country to be a unique kind of covenant between people and government—one that allowed unprecedented freedoms and opportunities but provided the armature of civil society. They were by no means in agreement on what that government or that covenant should entail. They debated and connived and sometimes raged against each other as they argued over what the new nation could and should be. Though we now adulate them as the hallowed Founding Fathers, they were never homogeneous or of one mind. But in the end they were willing to compromise on an amorphous idea: America.

Some four score years later, their compromise shattered into another American war—this one waged between the states. In some ways, the Civil War was inevitable—a test of a fragile new concept that had not coalesced into a nation and an indictment of the slavery that persisted. In a farewell letter to the original 13 states at the Revolution's end, George Washington had warned that Americans would decide their own future: "It is in their choice, and depends upon their conduct, whether they will be respectable and prosperous, or contemptable and miserable as a Nation . . ." But he had begun the letter by reminding them of what they had accomplished in their improbable revolt against the mother country: "When we consider the magnitude of the prize we contended for, the doubtful nature of the contest, and the favorable manner in which it has terminated, we shall find the greatest possible reason for gratitude and rejoicing . . . and we shall have equal occasion to felicitate ourselves on the lot which Providence has assigned us." As Washington knew better than anyone else, it had taken more than Providence to win independence and the chance to experiment with democracy. And it will take more than Providence to see the experiment through. ■

CHAPTER 1

America, if she fell, would fall like the strong man. She would . . . pull down the Constitution along with her.

British statesman William Pitt

1763-1774

Commonwealths, Crimes, and Calamities

This is a tale of two peoples, British and American, who in the mid-1700s stood together on the cusp of history. They still saw themselves as one—proud Britons all. Yet in a few short years, the ocean between them would became an ever widening and finally unbridgeable chasm.

No one could have predicted that eventuality as 1763 opened. In some ways, it was the proverbial best of times and worst of times. Great Britain was at the height of its powers, having finally won the sapping Seven Years' War (the Americans called it the French and Indian War), and now its empire was greater than any the West had known since Rome's heyday. Though the mother country was no more than a small clump of islands with its back to Europe, Great Britain's tentacled power stretched to continents around the globe—North America, the West Indies, the Indian subcontinent, the Far East, Africa. It was a far-flung and poorly administered empire, but somehow, despite bribery and inefficiency and what one prime minister called a "salutary neglect," it managed to hold together. Now, though, with the long war with France over, its debts were huge, and it had more territory than ever to administer. The Treaty of Paris of 1763 gave it vast holdings that more than doubled British America: all of Canada and the territories east of the Mississippi

George III *was only 22 when he ascended to the throne of Britain and Ireland in 1760. His poor judgment and poor health would wreak havoc on the empire during his long reign. Preceding pages: In Boston, newly minted patriots gather under the Liberty Tree.*

(except New Orleans), areas claimed by Native Americans who had not been party to the treaty negotiations—and who weren't apt to give up their rights without a fight.

It was obvious that one way to head off trouble was essentially to fence the colonists in and keep them from settling the native lands west of the Appalachian chain. To that end, the Royal Proclamation of 1763 banned westward migration. Unfortunately for some enterprising colonists, their lands were on the wrong side of the proclamation line. Some of these were small landholders, but most were land speculators, among them a Virginia colonel named George Washington, who had served as an officer under the British in the French and Indian War.

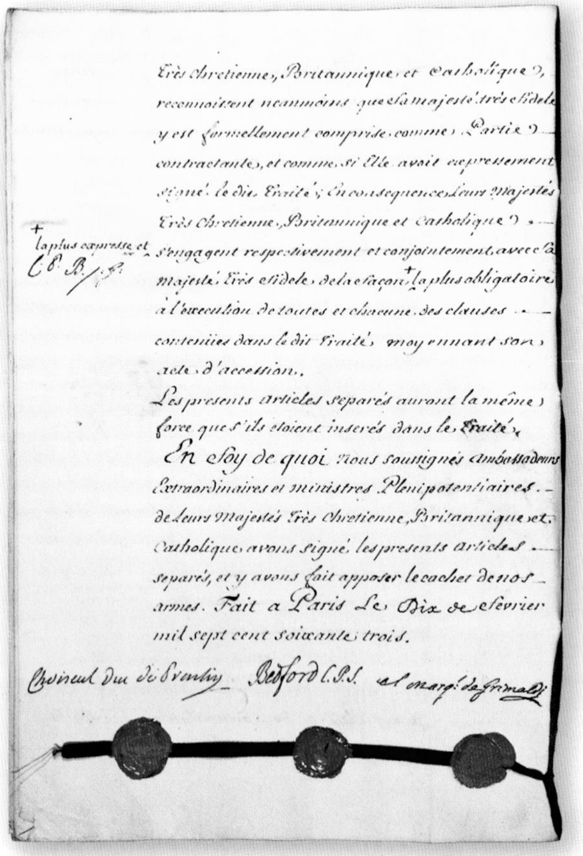
Très chretienne, Britannique et Catholique, reconnoissent neanmoins que sa majesté très fidele y est formellement comprise comme Partie contractante, et comme si Elle avoit expressement signé le dit Traité; En consequence Leurs Majestés Très Chretienne, Britannique et Catholique s'engagent respectivement et conjointement avec Sa majesté Très fidele de la façon + la plus obligatoire à l'execution de toutes et chacune des clauses contenües dans le dit Traité, moyennant son acte d'accession.

+ la plus expresse et

Les presents articles separés auront la même force que s'ils etoient inserés dans le Traité.

En foy de quoi Nous soussignés Ambassadeurs Extraordinaires et ministres Plenipotentiaires de Leurs Majestés Très Chretienne, Britannique et Catholique, avons signé les presents articles separés, et y avons fait apposer le cachet de nos armes. Fait a Paris le Dix de fevrier mil sept cent soixante trois.

Choiseul Duc de Praslin — Bedford C.P.S. — el marq. de Grimaldi

THE 1763 TREATY OF PARIS *ended the Seven Years' War that had pitted France and Spain against Britain. The conflict engulfed territories and empires worldwide, from the Americas to Europe to India and the Philippines. To the British colonists of North America, it was known as the French and Indian War.*

If the British Empire lacked funds for territorial administration, it at least had a powerful military after decades of war with France. Its troops could be dispatched to protect American borders, but supporting the needs of troops in a far-off land was daunting. Solutions would have to be considered, proposed, and debated by the king's ministers and Parliament.

For the past 80 years, since the Glorious Revolution had ousted James II, the king's ministers had increasingly come to hold the reins of government and to exercise quiet but firm control over Parliament. Unquestionably, every Englishman revered his monarch—God save the glorious king—and Americans shared that fealty. And in 1760 it was a relief to see an English-born-and-raised George—George III—take the throne after the previous two weak, German-born Hanoverian monarchs. George, 22 years old at his coronation, was young for the task at hand. Still, as long as government was really in more experienced hands, it seemed all would be well.

But young George had other ideas. He felt an obligation to assert himself, to make sure that peace with other nations was maintained. To that end, he got rid of his powerful, bullying, but brilliant minister William Pitt and gave his own loyal Tory followers prominent positions. They were doing their best to bring some logic to the governance of the empire.

While England was unquestionably the mother country and the colonies her "children"—her "plantations" in a new world—it surely made no sense to force the mother to pick up the entire tab for protecting her children, who were, after all, maturing nicely. The colonists needed to assume a little responsibility on their own instead of flaunting parental authority, as they had done in recent decades. Hadn't Parliament passed the Molasses Act 30 years earlier, in the hope of bringing in a bit of revenue from the New England rum trade? And hadn't the obstreperous New Englanders and some of the middle colonies just ignored it and instead chosen to bribe crown agents to look the other way as they imported the molasses from the Indies to make their rum? Now the time for reckoning, and additional revenues,

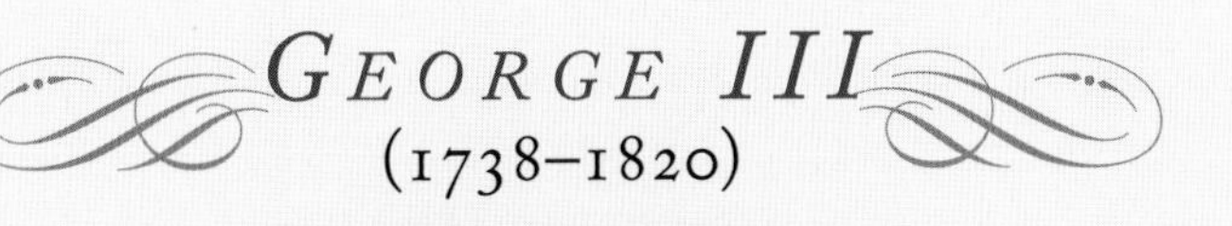

GEORGE III
(1738–1820)

He was only 22 in 1760, when he ascended to the throne of Great Britain and Ireland. His subjects cheered their new young king, "Farmer George," with his quaint interest in agriculture. No one, least of all George, could have imagined then what his future held—that his reign would span 60 years, making him the longest-serving king in English history (and second only to the current Elizabeth as the longest-serving monarch), and that history, far from remembering him affectionately as Farmer George, would instead memorialize him as the "King Who Lost America" and the "Mad King."

His father, Frederick, had been next in line for the throne, but when Frederick died suddenly in 1751, all eyes turned to the 13-year-old George. He was well enough educated but ill prepared both temperamentally and by experience to assume the throne. His parents much preferred their younger son, Edward, and as a consequence, George had become, according to a family friend, "silent, modest, and easily abashed." It didn't help that his mother had isolated her sons and that George had little exposure to children other than his brother. When he suddenly assumed the mantle of heir apparent, his mother tightened her grip and brought in the opinionated Earl of Bute to groom and further educate her son. She even chose George's wife: Charlotte, a German princess. The two didn't meet until their wedding day, and by then, George II had been gone almost a year. Two weeks after the marriage, Britain celebrated George III's official coronation. Among the many proud and well-wishing Britons at the coronation were Benjamin Franklin and John Hancock.

George was determined to be an engaged and diligent monarch. What he wanted first and foremost were peace and a successful end to the Seven Years' War. Two years into his reign, Britain emerged from the long war victorious, but the war's aftermath only led to new turmoil. The taxes that his government hoped to levy on the American colonies to help pay for the war debt and govern the new territory acquired at war's end strained relations to the breaking point. George himself could not levy taxes; Parliament did that. But he did appoint ministers—Tory-leaning ones—to conduct the affairs of state. He had little talent for or understanding of the subtleties of human behavior—let alone backroom politics. His actions and sentiments were often ham-fisted and intractable, and surely his mother's admonition to "Be a King, George! Be a King!" must have informed some of that. In the summer of 1775, he wrote to one of his ministers, "I am of the opinion that when once these rebels have felt a smart blow, they will submit; and no situation can ever change my fixed resolution, either to bring the colonies to due obedience to the legislature of the mother country or to cast them off!" By 1783, they had in fact cast themselves off from the mother country.

Several years later, George fell victim to his first serious bout of "madness." Scholars and scientists generally attribute his condition to a disease called porphyria, but whatever its cause, it would plague him intermittently for the rest of his life. In his last decade insanity overtook him completely, and his son, George, was left to reign as prince regent. Farmer George, the "Royal Brute," the Mad King, died at last in 1820. ■

had come. A reasonable new tax on sugar would replace the Molasses Act—a tax that was something close to the amount the colonists were paying in bribes anyway.

But the new Sugar Act, passed in April 1764, needed a bit of teeth, so it stipulated that ships doing business in the American colonies and merchants in the import/export business would have to jump through additional bureaucratic hoops. Parliament also tacked on stipulations about colonial exports of timber, iron, and a few other goods, which were to be exported exclusively to Britain. Finally, new duties were placed on some imports to the colonies, including coffee and wine.

A MURAL *depicting delegates to the 1754 Albany Congress prominently features William Franklin (far left) and his father, Benjamin (second left), along with several royal governors, including Massachusetts's Thomas Hutchinson (middle). Those three would play memorable roles in the conflict to come. Opposite: In 1763, with the end of the French and Indian War, Britain's holdings in North America vastly increased. Trying to manage the new territories and calm relations with Native American tribes, the crown established the Proclamation Line of 1763, confining settlement in the 13 American colonies to the lands east of the Appalachian spine.*

The Sugar Act of 1764 sailed through Parliament with virtually no resistance. It was just the beginning of what another George—George Grenville, the king's new head of the treasury—had in mind for the colonies.

The Colonial Situation

ACROSS THE WATERS, THE COLONISTS WERE SUFFERING their own economic downturn as the war boom that had fueled a burgeoning consumerism and confidence had tailed off and tobacco, a major export crop, had experienced bumper years of production, driving its prices down. For four years, the American economy had been bleak—though in fact no real "American" anything existed. Instead, British America comprised 13 disparate colonies ruled by 13 little parliaments, each committed to its own culture, economy, and, in some cases, religion. "Fire and water are not more heterogeneous than the different colonies of North America," one British traveler had pronounced. He was probably right, but recent attempts *had* been made to unite that heterogeneity somehow.

In 1754, just as the French and Indian War got under way, colonial notables had met together in New York, at what became known as the Albany Congress. The war, along with general threats from native tribes whose traditional territories were being invaded, had precipitated the historic meeting: The British, who were blundering around in the American wilderness, were ill suited in both temperament and military training to prosecute this war against a more wily and agile enemy. If things didn't improve, the British could lose the conflict, and it hardly helped matters that the 13 colonies were so disinclined to cooperate—they were typically more intent on bickering with each other over territory and petty rivalries than on working against a common enemy. The Albany Congress was called to address this sorry state of disunity, and seven colonies—New York; Pennsylvania; Maryland; and the four New England provinces of Massachusetts, Connecticut, Rhode Island, and New Hampshire—sent representatives.

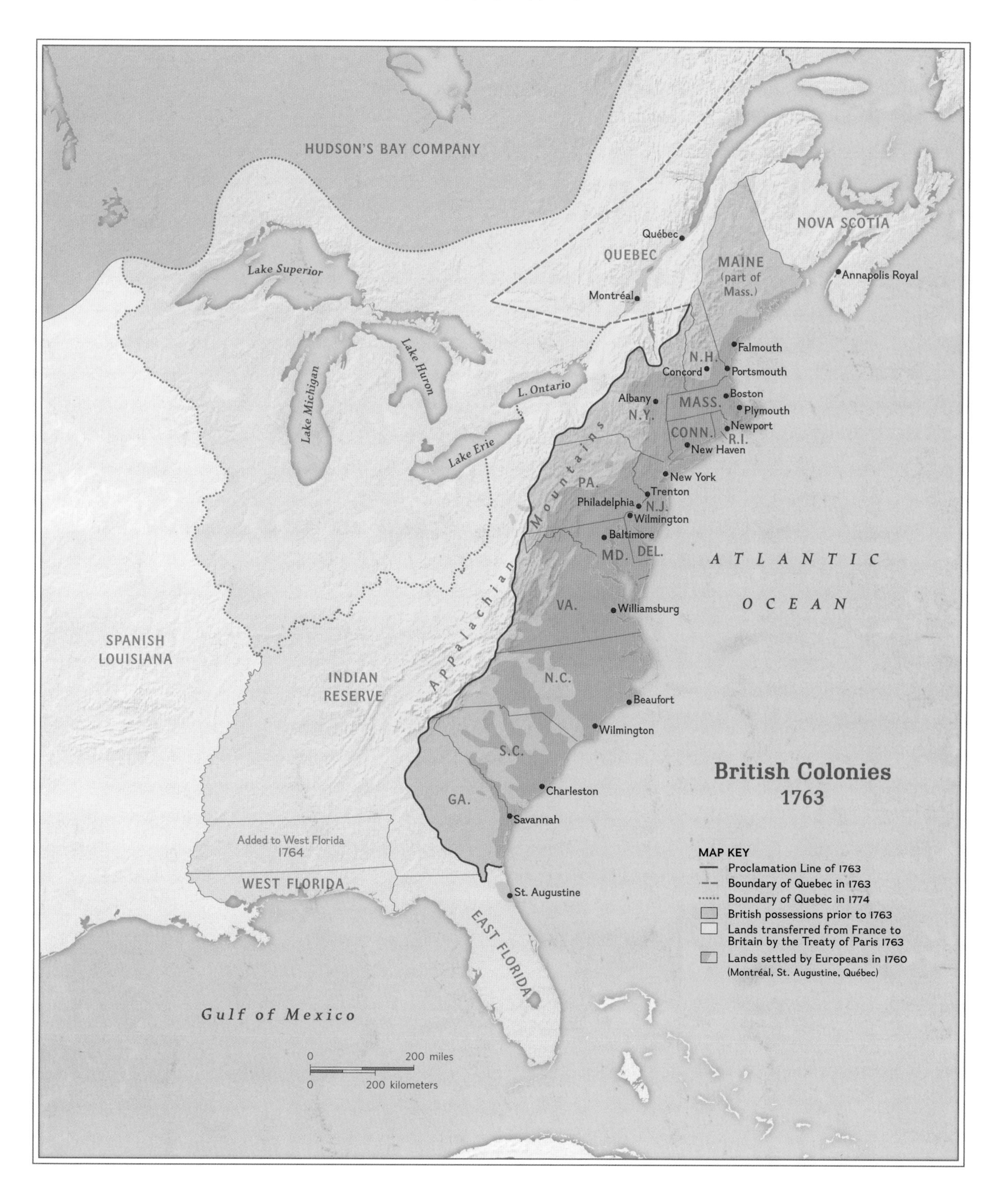
HUDSON'S BAY COMPANY
Lake Superior
Lake Michigan
Lake Huron
L. Ontario
Lake Erie
QUEBEC
Québec
Montréal
NOVA SCOTIA
Annapolis Royal
MAINE
(part of
Mass.)
Falmouth
N.H.
Concord
Portsmouth
Albany
N.Y.
MASS.
Boston
Plymouth
CONN.
Newport
R.I.
New Haven
New York
PA.
Trenton
Philadelphia
N.J.
Wilmington
Baltimore
MD.
DEL.
ATLANTIC
OCEAN
Appalachian Mountains
VA.
Williamsburg
SPANISH
LOUISIANA
INDIAN
RESERVE
N.C.
Beaufort
Wilmington
S.C.
Charleston
GA.
Savannah
British Colonies
1763
Added to West Florida
1764
WEST FLORIDA
St. Augustine
EAST FLORIDA
MAP KEY
Proclamation Line of 1763
Boundary of Quebec in 1763
Boundary of Quebec in 1774
British possessions prior to 1763
Lands transferred from France to Britain by the Treaty of Paris 1763
Lands settled by Europeans in 1760 (Montréal, St. Augustine, Québec)
Gulf of Mexico
0
200 miles
0
200 kilometers

EVERYDAY LIFE IN BOSTON

Colonial box
Leather-covered box from the colonial era

Floral shoes
The shoes of Catharine Greene, wife of Nathanael Greene, who would become a leading general in the Revolution

Leather tankard
A silver-mounted, leather tankard from mid-18th-century Scotland

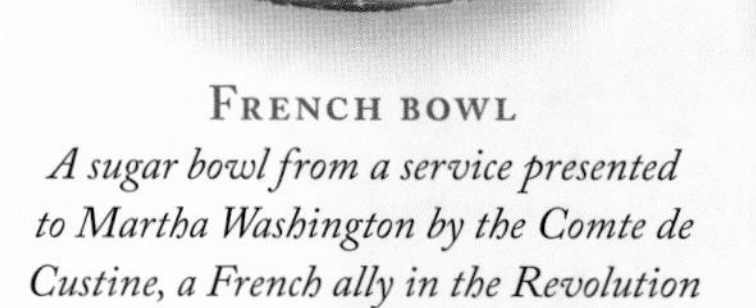

French bowl
A sugar bowl from a service presented to Martha Washington by the Comte de Custine, a French ally in the Revolution

Colonial teapot
A silver teapot designed by versatile craftsman Paul Revere

Embossed wallet
A leather wallet from the period with silver mountings

Tax stamp
A 1765 British tax stamp of the famed Stamp Act

Lady's purse
An American needlework lady's purse dated 1778

The driving force behind the Albany meetings was one of the Pennsylvania delegates, Benjamin Franklin. His resourceful mind was always conjuring schemes for civic betterment, and he firmly believed that the ultimate betterment was a closer union of the colonies. And so he proposed that the colonies be united under a governor-general, appointed by the king and beholden to a grand council that the provincial assemblies would appoint to represent them. The congress, after some debate, approved Franklin's Albany Plan of Union and sent it to the colonies for their approval. The colonies, still deeply provincial and self-interested, did not endorse it.

With a million and a half people, the colonial presence was no more than a thin, fragile line, most of it pressed against the Atlantic, its back to a vast continent, its face to the sea, and for most of its life looking to Britain for unity, commerce, and identity. The colonists had been, and were, proud Britons. But recently things had shifted subtly, as the colonists had begun to identify themselves more and more with their individual, and distinctly New World, aspirations.

For one thing, the overall population of the combined colonies was doubling every 20 years or so, and the five urban centers—Charleston, Philadelphia, New York, Newport, and Boston—were burgeoning. Generally, the colonists were a mixed lot, some long established in America, some recent immigrants, some slaves (in fact, many slaves in the Chesapeake region and far south), and some indentured servants. They weren't as hamstrung by a class system as their mother-country brethren were, though there was a colonial kind of aristocracy, particularly in Virginia and South Carolina, where elite planters held vast territories. Nineteen out of 20 colonists made their living off the land, but there was also an educated professional class and a middling class—merchants, artisans, and maritime traders—and a growing number of poor, among them the indentured servants who, in some southern colonies, were treated abysmally, worse than many slaves. Yet every free white man could move up in this new world—could change his station by dent of thrift, hard work, and moral rectitude. If anyone doubted that, he need only look to the redoubtable Benjamin Franklin to be proved wrong. The American who had famously "tamed" electricity had begun life in penurious circumstances, made a fortune in printing, and become an internationally recognized figure of whom any of the colonies could be proud.

> *Almighty God! I know not what course others may take; but as for me, give me liberty or give me death!"*
>
> PATRICK HENRY, MARCH 1775

The colonies were also proud of their individualized authority. Gradually, they had moved power away from the crown's agents, particularly royal governors, and into the hands of their own elected legislators, who understood and shared their concerns. By and large British Americans had become, in the century and a half since they first had managed to establish a foothold on the continent, a hardworking, provincial, proud, and independent folk. But

NORTH AMERICA
Hudson Bay
Rupert's Land
(Hudson Bay Company)
British possession confirmed 1713
Newfoundland
British possession confirmed, 1713
Louisiana
New France (Canada)
Texas
New Spain (Mexico)
Florida
Bermudas
Bahama Is.
New Orleans
PACIFIC OCEAN
British Isles
England
France
Portugal
Spain
Gibraltar
Azores Is.
Madeira Is.
Canary Is.
Cape Verd Is.
Gambia
Sierra Leone
St. Helena
Angola
AFRI
Area of supply of slave labor
St. Paul de Loanda
Cape Coast Castle
Elmina
Cayenne
Guiana
Surinam
Caracas
New Granada
Peru
SOUTH AMERICA
Brazil
Chile
Falkland Is.
C. Horn
The West Indies (1700 - 1763).
British
Dutch
French
Spanish
Scale 1:50 000 000
Miles
Havana
Cuba
Bahama Is.
Hispaniola
St. Domingue
Jamaica
Porto Rico
Caribbean Sea
Honduras
Yucatan
Baymen
C. Gracias a Dios
Nicaragua
Costa Rica
Porto Bello
Panama
Cartagena
New Granada
Caracas
Valencia
Cumana
Orinoco R.
Curaçao
Grenadines
Grenada
Tobago
Trinidad
Barbados
St. Lucia
Martinique
Dominica
Guadeloupe
Antigua
Barbuda
Montserrat
Nevis
St. Christopher
St. Croix
St. Eustatius
Virgin Is.
Leeward Is.
Windward Is.
British possessions
French
Spanish possessi
Southern boundary of Russian Siber
Abbreviations: Br.-British. F.Fr.-French. Sp.
The dates are those of acquisition by the co
For the expansion of British power in India
see p.137; in North America, p.189.
Scale along the Equator 1:200
20 Meridian 0 of Greenw. 20

A map showing *the territorial claims of the British, French, and Spanish Empires in North America in the middle decades of the 18th century*

part of their pride rested in their defining status as subjects of the king, and they expected the same rights that were accorded to any of his free and loyal subjects.

How, then, could Parliament have enacted a tax on the colonists when in fact they had no representatives to speak on their behalf in that body? Taxes, after all, were a gift of the people to the government, and voted on by legislators who represented the people. The New York General Assembly had explained this in its official protest to the Parliament over the Sugar Act: "An Exemption from the Burthen of ungranted, involuntary Taxes, must be the grand Principle of every free State.—Without such a Right vested in themselves, exclusive of all others, there can be no Liberty, no Happiness, no Security; it is inseparable from the very idea of Property, for who can call that his own, which may be taken away at the Pleasure of another?" And indeed, the colonists had become very attached to their property, something that in the New World they had the liberty to work for, to accrue, and to enjoy.

Nine different colonial legislatures sent protests to Parliament, most of whose members were affronted by such colonial cheek. Charles Townshend expressed the general outrage: "And now will these Americans, Children planted by our care, nourished up by our Indulgence until they are grown to a Degree of Strength and Opulence, and protected by our Arms, will they grudge to contribute their mite to relieve us from the heavy weight of that burden which we lie under?" Col. Isaac Barre, a veteran of the French and Indian War, rose in America's defense: "They planted by your Care? No! your Oppressions planted 'em in America. They fled from your Tyranny to a then uncultivated and unhospitable Country—where they exposed themselves to almost all the hardships to which human Nature is liable . . . remember I this Day told you so, that same Spirit . . . which actuated that people at first will accompany them still." Barre's passionate outburst and prescient warning fell on deaf ears. The Sugar Act held and was quickly followed by the Stamp Act.

This is the Place to affix the STAMP.

THE FAMOUS "JOIN, OR DIE" *snake (bottom) remains the first known American cartoon. Published in 1754 by Benjamin Franklin in the* Pennsylvania Gazette, *it admonishes the colonists to support his plan for union, presented at the Albany Congress. The Emblem of the Effects of the Stamp (top) appeared in the* Pennsylvania Journal *in 1765 as a protest against the hated Stamp Act.*

In truth the Sugar Act mostly affected merchants. They were the ones who had become entangled in the complex weave of trade that had gradually developed: They used the molasses imported from the Indies to make rum, much of which was drunk in New England, but some of which bought African slaves who were sold as so much chattel to the West Indies and the southern colonies (they were more in demand than were indentures, as they weathered the malarial climate better). While the Sugar Act threatened to detangle this intricate import/export weave, the Stamp Act impacted nearly all colonists in their daily lives.

The colonists had heard that this kind of act could be coming their way, and in early May 1765, the rumors were affirmed. From then on, virtually anything written or printed—from deeds to advertisements, from newspapers to playing cards—would have to be produced on special stamped paper issued and taxed by colonial agents of the British government. Most of those agents, handpicked by Grenville, were well-to-do men, just the kind of people likely to raise hackles even further.

In Boston, mobs attacked the homes of one agent, as well as the stately house of Lt. Governor Thomas Hutchinson. Throughout the colonies, boycotts of British goods began, and threats against agents who were appointed to distribute the paper kept it out of circulation, hidden in forts and never off-loaded from British ships. As the months passed, the colonists simply ignored the very idea of such paper. Defiantly going about their business, they created documents on unstamped paper.

A GREAT DEFENDER *of the rights of Americans, Irish colonel Isaac Barre (1726–1802) spoke out for the colonies in Parliament, arguing against the sugar and stamp taxes that had inflamed sentiments across the Atlantic. His phrase "Sons of Liberty" would be adopted by New Englanders and others opposing British taxation without representation.*

In Barre's rousing speech before Parliament, he had called Americans "Sons of Liberty," and now the term became more than mere words. In cities, towns, and villages throughout the colonies, men formed themselves into ad hoc associations that they proudly called Sons of Liberty. A newly elected member of the Virginia House of Burgesses, a young firebrand named Patrick Henry—"a Quaker in religion but the very devil in politics"—took on George III himself in a speech that history has embellished. The actual details of Henry's "Treason Speech" are these: In late May 1765, with only a small group of burgesses in attendance, he made a speech in which he warned the king about other despots who had met a brutal end. While the exact language is in question, history has chosen Henry's words for him: "Caesar had his Brutus, Charles the First his Cromwell, and George the Third . . ." Here, the speaker of the house roundly objected and said Henry was speaking treason, and according to a creditable account, Henry apologized. Legend has put a more histrionic end point on the event, claiming that Henry, rather than reneging, proclaimed, "If this be treason, make the most of it."

Henry had been arguing that a fifth, more incendiary item should be added to the so-called Virginia Resolves, a legalistic list of arguments against taxation without representation and for the rights of citizens. The resolves sounded the "trumpet of sedition" and, coupled with Henry's boldness, fired up patriotic blood. In England, merchants felt the righteous colonial wrath, not in words but in deeds. The American market for English goods ground to a halt, and the British merchants pled their plight with Parliament.

At the same time, Benjamin Franklin pled the colonials' cause. He was in London as an agent representing Pennsylvania's interests and had cultivated friends and allies in the king's government. In February 1766, he went before Parliament and spoke as a representative of all America. He answered almost 175 questions with calm and convincing deference—

but not *too* much deference. He was frank in telling the legislators that the mother country was losing ground with the colonists, and why.

"They submitted willingly to the government of the crown, and paid, in all their courts, obedience to acts of parliament," Franklin said. "Numerous as the people are in the several old provinces, they cost you nothing in forts, citadels, garrisons or armies, to keep them in subjection. They were governed by this country at the expence only of a little pen, ink, and paper. They were led by a thread. They had not only a respect, but an affection for Great Britain, for its laws, its customs and manners, and even a fondness for its fashions, that greatly increased the commerce."

"And what is their temper now?" Franklin was asked. His answer: "Oh, very much altered."

Within the ranks of Parliament, Franklin and America had a powerful ally, as redoubtable in firmness and finesse as Franklin but far less diplomatic. If Franklin made his case with charm and aplomb, William Pitt made his with bombast, cannonading his opponents until they gave way. As secretary of state, he had won the French and Indian War for Britain with steely grit; he had declared, "I know that I can save this country and that no one else can." And he had. Now he was ready once again to champion the cause of the colonists, this time on the floor of Parliament. A month before Franklin appeared, Pitt had made his own defense of colonial rights: "The gentleman asks, 'When were the colonies emancipated?'" Pitt said, referring to another parliamentarian. "I desire to know, when were they made slaves? . . . America, if she fell, would fall like the strong man; she would embrace the pillars of the state, and pull down the Constitution along with her. Is this your boasted peace—not to sheathe the sword in its scabbard, but to sheathe it in the bowels of your countrymen?" Pitt finished by arguing that "the Stamp Act be repealed absolutely, totally, and immediately. That the reason for the repeal be assigned, viz., because it was founded on an erroneous principle . . . At the same time, let the sovereign authority of this country over the colonies be asserted in as strong terms as can be devised."

A TRUE RENAISSANCE MAN, *the self-made Benjamin Franklin turned his intellect to science, civic projects, and diplomacy. His reputation in England made him an effective representative at court, and he served as an agent for several American colonies. Opposite: Like Franklin, William Pitt was a self-made "commoner," in British social terms. Yet he rose to become a member of the king's cabinet and ultimately prime minister (1766–1768). A leader of the populist-leaning Whig Party, he spoke out forcefully on behalf of the American colonists.*

No admirer of Pitt, the king nonetheless was watching American unrest with a wary eye. "I am more and more grieved at the accounts in America," the young, inexperienced George wrote to a cabinet minister. "Where this spirit will end is not to be said."

Franklin had assured his parliamentary inquisitors that America would never submit to the Stamp Act, even if it were moderated, "unless compelled by force of arms." And Britain was not willing—yet—to take up arms against its American children. So less than a year after its passage, it was repealed, and its architect, George Grenville, was gone as prime minister. But the act had raised the hackles of both the English and the Americans, and suspicious feelings lingered between them.

Unlike the British Parliament's *ponderous upper house, the House of Lords—whose members were appointed by the king from the aristocracy—the more boisterous lower house, or House of Commons, was composed of delegates elected by popular vote.*

An Awakening Independence

For the first time, the Americans began to question just who they were and what their status as colonists meant. Of one thing they were sure: They were no longer children needing the firm hand of Mother Britain. So while they celebrated the Stamp Act's repeal in the streets, they also puzzled over the new Declaratory Act that had passed at the same time as the repeal. On the English side of the Atlantic, the political reasons for this new bill were not puzzling: It had been introduced to pacify lawmakers who believed Americans needed to be put in their place. The act decisively declared that Parliament had authority over the colonies "in all cases whatsoever." That was indeed heady authority—and, ironically, it was at odds with King George's own early statement. When he was still Prince of Wales, he had proclaimed, "The pride, the glory of Britain . . . is political liberty."

The colonists agreed with him wholeheartedly, and to that end, they would be the ones who taxed themselves, thank you very much. And that was where matters stood for more than a year, until yet another troublesome minister took the stage—the same Charles Townshend who, a few years earlier, had called Americans "Children planted by our care."

The irrepressible "Champagne Charlie," a sobriquet he earned after delivering a particularly brilliant speech to the House of Commons, had plans for those recalcitrant children—and no hesitation about carrying them out. Parliament, just as out of temper with the colonies, obliged him by passing the Townshend Acts in late June 1767. The first of these acts disbanded the outspoken New York Assembly until its members agreed to uphold the Quartering Act, which decreed that colonists must provide lodging and supplies to British troops quartered in America. The second act put new taxes on some English goods imported to the colonies—things like paint, lead, paper, tea. At the same time, royal governors and other officials were quietly directed to exert the crown's authority and to undercut the power of local legislatures. And more customs officers were dispatched to the colonies, their salaries to be paid out of what they themselves collected in duties. The days of laissez-faire empire were over.

The Americans dug in. They would go without British goods rather than pay new duties. To that end, they set about to make and manufacture more of their own goods, rather than importing them from Britain. In New England, Daughters of Liberty associations sprang up in the countryside, the "daughters" holding spinning bees to produce homespun cloth.

In Philadelphia, John Dickinson became a leading voice against the British after the publication of his *Letters From a Farmer.* The "letters" argued against any kind of tax—internal or external—levied to raise a revenue, and they sounded the alarm at the Quartering Act's strong-arming of the New York legislature:

> The sight of red coats and the hearing of drums would have been most alarming, because people are generally more influenced by their eyes and ears than by their reason," he warned. "But whoever seriously considers the matter must perceive that a dreadful stroke is aimed at the liberty of these colonies. I say of these colonies; for the cause of one is the cause of all. If the Parliament may lawfully deprive New York of any of her rights, it may deprive any or all the other colonies of their rights; and nothing can possibly so much encourage such attempts as a mutual inattention to the interest of each other. To divide and thus to destroy is the first political maxim in attacking those who are powerful by their union. He certainly is not a wise man who folds his arms and reposes himself at home, seeing with unconcern the flames that have invaded his neighbor's house without using any endeavors to extinguish them.

John Dickinson
1732–1808

An early and effective proponent of American rights, John Dickinson began his career as a respected Philadelphia lawyer and colonial legislator. By the mid-1760s, he had begun speaking out against British taxation, and in 1767 he published the first of his dozen *Letters From a Farmer in Pennsylvania.* Arguing against taxation without representation, the letters enjoyed a wide circulation throughout the colonies. Dickinson continued to write well-reasoned documents on American rights in the coming years, but as tensions with Britain reached a breaking point, Dickinson would not endorse a break with the Mother Country. Instead, he was chosen by the Continental Congress to draft the unsuccessful "Olive Branch Petition" to George III. A year later, Dickinson argued against the Declaration of Independence. But once revolution was inevitable, he became an ardent supporter, joining in military campaigns and chairing the committee to write the Articles of Confederation. After the war, he was president of both Delaware and Pennsylvania and a signer of the Constitution.

DURING PROTESTS OVER *the Stamp Act, a large elm shading Boston's South End was christened the Liberty Tree. The Sons of Liberty met under its generous canopy, and in 1766, with the repeal of the act, an obelisk was placed beneath it, engraved with portraits of America's supporters in Britain—among them Isaac Barre, William Pitt, and even George III.*

A VIEW of the OBELISK erected under LIBERTY–TREE in
D
Y–k
M–q–s
R–m
Q
C
K
G III d
O thou whom next to Heav'n we most revere
Fair LIBERTY! thou lovely Goddess hear!
Have we not woo'd thee, won thee, held thee long
Lain in thy Lap, & melted on thy Tongue:
Thro' Deaths & Dangers rugged paths pursu'd
And led thee smiling to this SOLITUDE
Hid thee within our Hearts most golden Cell
And brav'd the Powers of Earth & Powers of Hell
GODDESS! we cannot part, thou must not fly;
Be SLAVES! we dare to scorn it – dare to die
G–l
C––y
L–d
C–l
B–e
W––m
To every Lover of LIBERTY, this Plate is
1 America in distress apprehending the total loss of LIBERTY 2 She implores the

w on the Rejoicings for the Repeal of the —— Stamp-Act 1766
L—d D—h
A—n B—r
L—d D—l
C—s T—d
Boast foul Oppression, boast thy transient Reign
While honest FREEDOM struggles with her Chain
But know the Sons of Virtue, hardy, brave
Disdain to lose thro' mean Dispair to save
Arrouz'd in Thunder, awfull they appear
With proud deliverance stalking in their Rear
While Tyrant-Foes their pallid Fears betray
Shrink from their Arms & give their Vengeance way
See in th'unequal War OPPRESSORS fall
The hate, Contempt and endless Curse of all
L—d G— S—k—e
Mr DeB—t
J—n W—s
L—d C—n
Our FAITH approv'd, our LIBERTY restor'd
Our Hearts bend grateful to our sov'r'gn Lord
Hail darling Monarch! by this act endear'd
Our firm affections are thy best reward
Sh'd Britain's self, against her self divide
And hostile Armies frown on either Side
Sh'd Hosts rebellious shake our Brunswick's Throne
And as they dar'd thy Parent, dare the Son
To this Asylum stretch thine happy Wing
And we'll contend, who best shall love our KING
Paul Revere Sculp
ly dedicated, by her true born SONS, in BOSTON New England
r PATRONS 3. She endures the Conflict for a short Season
4th And has her LIBERTY restor'd by the Royal hand of GEORGE the Third

And certainly the flames were spreading—and they were often thrown by colonial agitators spoiling for a fight. None was so ardent as Samuel Adams. A feisty failed Boston maltster and tax collector with a rigid Puritanical backbone, Adams was a driving force behind the Sons of Liberty and, in 1768, of the now-famous Massachusetts Circular Letter. Sent by the Massachusetts legislatures to other colonial legislatures, the letter proclaimed the recent parliamentary acts unconstitutional. It concluded with a carrot tossed to the king: "This House cannot conclude, without expressing their firm confidence in the King, our common head and father; that the united and dutiful supplications of his distressed American subjects, will meet with his royal and favorable acceptance."

Clear the Land of the Vermin, which are come to devour them.

THE SONS OF LIBERTY

Boston was quickly becoming the hotbed of resistance and a target of the British. In its environs, the newly arrived customs agents, most as corrupt as the old, were busy harassing merchant and fishing vessels, and even the small boats carrying provisions to local markets. Every maritime movement seemed to require a fee for papers; without papers, any vessel stopped by a capricious customs agent could be seized, along with its contents—all of which lined the agent's own pockets. If a colonist objected to having his vessel or cargo seized, he could no longer plead his case in a local court before a jury of his peers. Instead, he had to appear before an admiralty court overseen by British judges.

One merchant not to be cowed by the new regime was another leading Son of Liberty, John Hancock. One of the wealthiest men in the colonies, Hancock had his own shipping business, inherited from the uncle who raised him, and he was engaged in a healthy overseas trade. He knew the British reasonably well, having spent 1760 to 1761 in London on his uncle's business—while there he had attended the king's coronation. When the Stamp Act protests first began, he was disinclined to question Mother Britain, but he soon changed his mind and joined the common cause with Samuel Adams.

Hancock began using his wealth to support the Bostonians' cause, and he publicly disdained the new breed of customs agents at every turn. When two tidesmen, as lower-level customs officials were called, went belowdecks on an unauthorized inspection of his brig *Lydia* in the spring of 1768, Hancock had them unceremoniously removed. The British commissioners, incensed at the incident, were looking to get their own back, so a few months later, after a British warship arrived in Boston Harbor to back up their authority, they seized Hancock's ship *Liberty.* According to Hancock, the ship had followed standard practices by loading its outgoing cargo of tar and whale with the plan to pay the bond on the cargo before leaving port. In the *Liberty*'s case, though, the customs commissioners decided to enforce the letter of the law, which required that Hancock pay before loading.

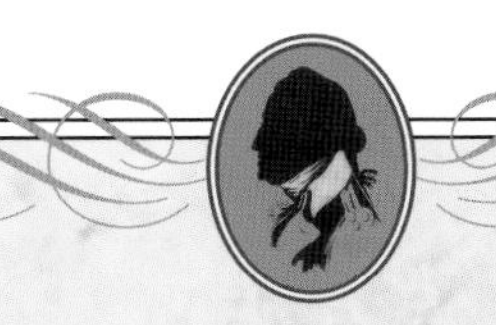

Washington to fellow Virginia patriot George Mason

Mount Vernon 5th April 1769.

Dear sir,

At a time when our lordly Masters in Great Britain will be satisfied with nothing less than the deprivation of American freedom, it seems highly necessary that something shou'd be done to avert the stroke and maintain the liberty which we have derived from our Ancestors; but the manner of doing it to answer the purpose effectually is the point in question.

That no man shou'd scruple, or hesitate a moment to use a[r]ms in defence of so valuable a blessing, on which all the good and evil of life depends; is clearly my opinion; Yet A[r]ms I wou'd beg leave to add, should be the last resource; the de[r]nier resort. Addresses to the Throne, and remonstrances to parliament, we have already, it is said, proved the inefficacy of; how far then their attention to our rights & priviledges is to be awakened or alarmed by starving their Trade & manufactures, remains to be tryed.

George Mason

The northern Colonies, it appears, are endeavouring to adopt this scheme—In my opinion it is a good one; & must be attended with salutary effects, provided it can be carried pretty generally into execution; but how far it is practicable to do so, I will not take upon me to determine. That there will be difficulties attending the execution of it every where, from clashing interests, & selfish designing men (ever attentive to their own gain, & watchful of every turn that can assist their lucrative views, in preference to any other consideration) cannot be denied; but in the Tobacco Colonies where the Trade is so diffused, and in a manner wholly conducted by Factors for their principals at home, these difficulties are certainly enhanced, but I think not insurmountably increased, if the Gentlemen in their several counties wou'd be at some pains to explain matters to the people, & stimulate them to a cordial agreement to purchase none but certain innumerated articles out of any of the Stores after such a period . . .

The more I consider a Scheme of this sort, the more ardently I wish success to it, because I think there are private, as well as public advantages to result from it . . . On the other hand, that the Colonies are considerably indebted to Great Britain, is a truth universally acknowledged. That many families are reduced, almost, if not quite, to penury & want, from the low ebb of their fortunes, and Estates daily selling for the discharge of Debts, the public papers furnish but too many melancholy proofs of . . .

As a June sun set over the harbor, the British man-of-war made for Hancock's dock, planning to haul the *Liberty* out into Boston Harbor. But as if on cue, a crowd had gathered, and British sailors and townsmen went at it. The sailors won, and the *Liberty* was towed away, but the mob wasn't about to give in. Moving on to the homes of other officials, it broke windows and searched for customs agents to beat. The British took their own revenge by declaring that they required more than Hancock's ship and its cargo. They claimed he had off-loaded smuggled cargo when the *Liberty* had first put into port, and they fined him 54,000 pounds sterling.

Hancock, a man known for his generosity to all Bostonians and a favorite son (of both the city and liberty), was no one to tamper with, and the Sons of Liberty declared that they would "clear the Land of the Vermin, which are come to devour them." They met in Liberty Hall—the ground below their designated Liberty Tree, an arching American elm that stood near Boston Common. Liberty was their clarion call, and they would have it, whatever it took—mob violence, defiance of the crown's agents, circular letters, resolutions, and as-yet-unimagined extreme methods. The Sons' tactics were successfully riling the colonists but, understandably, making the British less and less tolerant. The royal governor, his hand forced by London, ordered the Massachusetts legislature to rescind the inflammatory circular letter it had sent to other colonies, but when a vote was taken, 92 members held firm. The letter stood, and the Glorious Ninety-two were immortalized in newspapers and handbills for years to come. In the night of celebration that followed their defiance, some Bostonians claimed to have single-handedly drunk 92 toasts in the men's honor.

JOHN HANCOCK

1737–1793

As extravagant as his famous signature, Hancock reigned as one of the wealthiest men in New England, yet he was a lifelong populist. By the late 1760s he and Samuel Adams had become leading figures in the Sons of Liberty, and at the Second Continental Congress Hancock served as president and the first signer of the Declaration of Independence. With war on the horizon, he hoped he would be made commander in chief of the Continental forces. When that position went to George Washington, Hancock continued as president of the congress for another year, then as a delegate and active supporter of the Revolution, helping to secure supplies and troops for the army. In 1780 he was elected the first governor of Massachusetts, and in the first presidential election his name was entered as one of the candidates. Once again, Washington was chosen over him, yet throughout the early formation of America, the two men complemented and supported each other in the cause of liberty.

BRITISH TROOPS DEPLOY

AS WARM WEATHER HEATED TEMPERS IN THE SUMMER OF 1768, THE Boston patriots grew more restive, their ire aimed at any sign of British authority. More royal troops had been dispatched to Boston from Halifax, Nova Scotia, ostensibly to head off a threat from France, and Boston's citizens, both royal officials and patriots, waited for the troops on tenterhooks, the locals arming themselves against what they claimed, tongue-in-cheek, was a "prevailing apprehension, in the minds of many, of an approaching war with France."

The red-coated troops began arriving in the early fall, with British warships at their back. They disembarked with some ceremony—a show of imperial force—and no one stopped them as they were ferried to the port's Long Wharf and then marched through the streets to the trill of fife and drum. By early 1769, some 4,000 soldiers of the king swarmed the city's streets—nearly a quarter as many troops as residents. They saw the town as a garrison post and acted as soldiers often

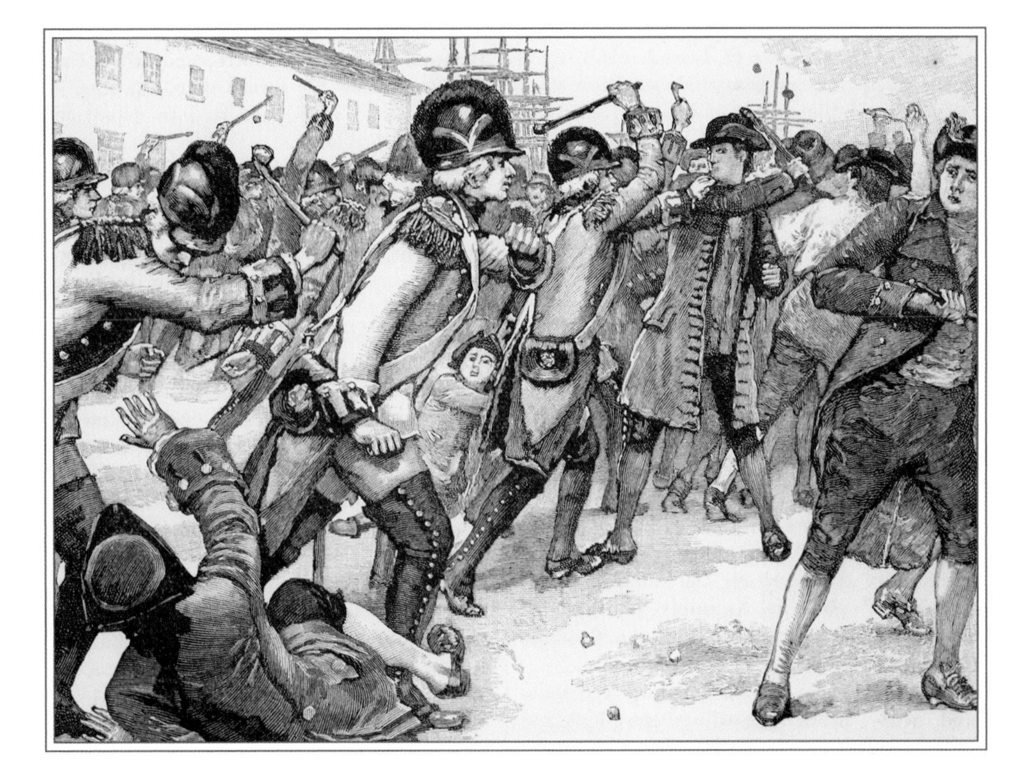

REDCOATS OVERWHELM ROPEMAKERS *in a Boston fray portrayed in* Cassell's Illustrated History of England, *published a century later. The ropemakers resented British soldiers moonlighting and taking work from them.*

did—drinking heartily, occasionally assaulting women, and generally lording it over the locals. Still, most of their first year passed in an uneasy peace with the citizens. But by late summer 1769, tensions were mounting, and the other colonies waited expectantly for more news of the boisterous Bostonians and their fisticuffs with the crown.

The British, for their part, were at a loss about how to proceed. A new prime minister, Lord North, had come to power in January 1770, and he wanted to return relations to some semblance of calm and get trade moving again. To that end, he managed in March 1770 to get the Townshend duties repealed on everything but tea. But it was too late. In Boston, the incendiary moment everyone had anticipated had arrived.

Among the Bostonians' many grievances against the British soldiers was their moonlighting. They were allowed by military authority to take work in local factories and businesses, and they did—at below the going wage. That meant less work for the city's day laborers who needed it. One local ropemaker had approached a soldier in early March and asked if he wanted work. When he said yes, the ropemaker taunted him, saying he could "clean my shithouse." That was enough to set off a brawl between Bostonians and British, and thereafter, bands of both roamed the streets each night and spoiled for a fight.

The Boston Massacre

ON THE EVENING OF MARCH 5 A CROWD BEGAN TO COLLECT IN FRONT OF THE CUSTOMS house, and a young apprentice hurled an insult at the sentry on guard, who in turn clocked

A VIEW OF PART OF THE TOWN OF BOSTON IN NEW-ENGLAND
2
3
4
A
1 Beaver
2 Senegal
3 Martin
4 Glasgow
5 Mermaid
6 Romney
7 Launceston
8 Bonetta
On friday Sept. 30th 1768, the Ships of WAR, armed Schooners, Transports, &c. Came up
a Spring on their Cables, as for a regular Siege. At noon on Saturday October the 1st the
and Train of Artillery, with two peices of Cannon, landed on the Long Wharf; there
playing, and Colours flying, up KING STREET. Each Soldier having received 16 rounds
Col.d by Chr. Remick

BRITTISH SHIPS
OF WAR LANDIN G
THEIR TROOPS! 1768
To the Earl of
Hillsborough, His
Majesty's Secry of State for
America, THIS VIEW of
the only well Plan'd
EXPEDITION, formed for
supporting ye dign
ity of BRITAIN
& chastising ye insolence
of AMERICA, is humy Inscribed.
rbour and Anchored round the TOWN; their Cannon loaded,
enth & twenty-ninth Regiments, a detachment from the 59th Regt.
d and Marched with insolent Parade, Drums beating, Fifes
wder and Ball.
A Long Wharf
B HANCOCK's Wharf
C North Battery
ENGRAVED, PRINTED, & SOLD by PAUL REVERE, BOSTON.

"A View of *Part of the Town of Boston in New-England and Brittish Ships of War Landing Their Troops!*"—*a 1768 propaganda print by colorist Christian Remick— probably inspired the engravings of Paul Revere.*

The BLOODY MASSACRE perpetrated in King-Street BOSTON on March 5th 1770, by a party of the 29th REGT
Engrav'd Printed & Sold by PAUL REVERE BOSTON
hlappy BOSTON! ſee thy Sons deplore,
y hallow'd Walks beſmear'd with guiltleſs Gore:
hile faithleſs P—n and his ſavage Bands,
ith murd'rous Rancour ſtretch their bloody Hands;
ke fierce Barbarians grinning o'er their Prey,
pprove the Camage, and enjoy the Day.
If ſcalding drops from Rage from Anguiſh Wrung
If ſpeechleſs Sorrows lab'ring for a Tongue,
Or if a weeping World can ought appeaſe
The plaintive Ghoſts of Victims ſuch as theſe;
The Patriot's copious Tears for each are ſhed,
A glorious Tribute which embalms the Dead
But know, FATE ſummons to that awful Goal,
Where JUSTICE ſtrips the Murd'rer of his Soul:
Should venal C—ts the ſcandal of the Land,
Snatch the relentleſs Villain from her Hand,
Keen Execrations on this Plate inſcrib'd,
Shall reach a JUDGE who never can be brib'd.
The unhappy Sufferers were Meſs. SAML GRAY, SAML MAVERICK, JAMS CALDWELL, CRISPUS ATTUCKS & PATK CARR
Killed. Six wounded; two of them (CHRISTR MONK & JOHN CLARK) Mortally
Col. by Chr Remick

him for his troubles. The alarm for "fire" then went out, by shout and church bell, and locals—some toting water, others clubs and swords—converged on the customs house. John Adams, distant cousin of the outspoken Sam, later described the crowd as "a motley rabble of saucy boys, negroes and mulattoes, Irish teagues and outlandish Jack tars [sailors]."

When a small, armed contingent of British soldiers marched to the rescue, the mob began hurling snowballs, ice, rubbish, and other missiles at the soldiers. After about 15 minutes, a chunk of ice hit its mark squarely and knocked a soldier off his feet. He recovered himself, scrambled to his feet, and then, probably in anger, fired into the crowd. The other soldiers soon followed suit. When the melee finally abated, the mob had suffered 11 casualties; of those, 3 were dead and 2 others soon died of their wounds.

Ben Franklin had warned the British earlier that they were "putting young soldiers, who are by nature insolent, in the midst of a people who consider themselves threatened and oppressed. It's like setting up a blacksmith's forge in a magazine of gunpowder." Now the gunpowder had exploded. Paul Revere, a local engraver, created a sensational depiction of the Boston "massacre" as an orchestrated British attack, and a pamphlet with the incendiary title "Innocent Blood Crying to God from the Streets of Boston" found wide circulation. The following October, Captain Preston, the officer involved in the massacre, and eight of his soldiers were tried for murder. In his deposition, Preston had reasonably contended, "So bitter and inveterate are many of the malcontents here that they are industriously using every method to fish out evidence to prove it was a concerted scheme to murder the inhabitants. Others are infusing the utmost malice and revenge into the minds of the people who are to be my jurors by false publications . . . While the people's minds are all greatly inflamed, I am, though perfectly innocent, under most unhappy circumstances, having nothing in reason to expect but the loss of life in a very ignominous manner without the interposition of his Majesty's royal goodness."

The *Boston Gazette* *(above) ran this drawing of the coffins of four of the Americans who died in the Boston Massacre, with their initials on top. The fourth, Crispus Attucks, was a man of Native American and African descent. All four, along with a fifth casualty, were buried together in Boston's Granary Burying Ground. Opposite: Paul Revere titled his engraving of the 1770 altercation in Boston between British troops and local belligerents "The Bloody Massacre." History calls it the Boston Massacre. Through his engravings Revere documented a number of the historic moments in his hometown that led up to the Revolution.*

Preston was being represented in court by John Adams, a lawyer by trade and contrarian by nature, not unlike his cousin Samuel. In his final summation on the captain's behalf, Adams reminded the jurors, "The law . . . will preserve a steady undeviating course; it will not bend to the uncertain wishes, imaginations, and wanton tempers of men." Apparently, the jury, which included a few loyalists, agreed with Adams, because despite the wanton tempers then flaring in Boston, the jurors acquitted Preston of the charge that he had given the order to fire. For the rest of his days, Adams was proud of "the Part I took in Defence of Cptn. Preston and the Soldiers," though he admitted that it "procured me Anxiety, and Obloquy enough. It was, however, one of the most gallant, generous, manly and disinterested

Actions of my whole Life, and one of the best Pieces of Service I ever rendered my Country. Judgment of Death against those Soldiers would have been as foul a Stain upon this Country as the Executions of the Quakers or Witches, anciently."

For the two years following the Boston Massacre, relations between the colonies and the mother country remained relatively quiet. Parliament's conciliatory gesture in repealing the hated Townshend Acts had pacified feelings, and the colonies, starting with New York, began to drop their nonimportation stance. As business resumed and coffers refilled, tempers quieted. But now, the colonists looked more to each other than to the mother country. A common enemy had forged a common bond. They had begun to lose faith in what seemed a corrupt system, in which they had no voice and yet were expected to obey. They understood full well what it meant to have troops patrolling their streets, even if, up until then, Boston had borne the brunt of it.

And it was in New England again that the quiet was broken, and again over tension with commissioners. In June 1772, the *Gaspée,* a British ship patrolling the waters of Narragansett Bay in search of colonial smugglers, ran aground. A disgruntled group of colonists boarded the ship, shot and wounded the captain when he attempted to thwart them, removed the rest of the crew, and burned the ship where she lay.

Once more, a local incident incited sympathy far afield. The Virginia House of Burgesses, in its own way as rebellious as New England's Sons of Liberty, appointed a committee of correspondence, charged with communicating with other colonial legislatures about anything and everything that might pose a threat to American rights. Within a year, 12 of the 13 other colonies had formed their own committees, creating a united network of communication. Only Pennsylvania abstained.

NATIVE BOSTONIAN *Thomas Hutchinson (1711–1780) served Massachusetts well in the mid-1700s as speaker of the colonial assembly and lieutenant governor, but as the 1760s progressed, his loyalties to the crown put him in conflict with the growing patriotic fervor. The last colonial governor of Massachusetts, he left for England in 1774 to consult with the king and never returned.*

Throughout these early struggles, Pennsylvania had remained officially quiet because her proprietors, Quaker William Penn's descendants, hoped to gain royal colony status for Pennsylvania. That was not the hope of the citizenry, whose protests, along with those of their elected assembly, were growing louder—both against the Penn proprietary to the colony and against the crown. The fragile thread that, according to Franklin, tied America to British rule was fraying, and Franklin himself was inadvertently about to fray it more.

Still in London, Franklin was now representing Massachusetts as well as other colonial interests. In late 1772, in a letter to Thomas Cushing, speaker of the Massachusetts House of Representatives, Franklin wrote, "There has lately fallen into my hands part of a correspondence I have reason to believe laid the foundation of most if not all our present grievances." The letters, already a few years old by the time Franklin got his hands on them, were from agents of the crown in Massachusetts, including royal governor Thomas Hutchinson, a thorn in the side of the Sons of Liberty. Hutchinson and other letter writers

Rhode Islanders, *disgruntled by crown agents and particularly the rapacious enforcer aboard the* Gaspée, *moved in on the British customs cutter after it ran aground in Narragansett Bay in June 1772. The Americans boarded and burned the ship in a bold act of defiance against British authority.*

made it clear in their correspondence that they held no sympathy for the recent demands of certain American upstarts or for their behavior.

"I doubt whether it is possible to project a system of government in which a colony 3,000 miles distant from the parent state shall enjoy all of the liberty the parent state has," Hutchinson had written in one letter. A few sentences down, he argued for "further restraint of liberty," to avoid a breach in the connection between the colony and its parent state—"For I am sure such a breach must prove the ruin of the colony."

Franklin had insisted that the letters not be published or circulated and that they be returned to him within "some months." Cushing honored Franklin's request for discretion and showed them only to a few members of the Massachusetts House of Representatives, among them probably John Hancock and Samuel Adams. Hutchinson only inflamed tempers more when he made it clear in a January 1773 speech before the Massachusetts General Court that Parliament had jurisdiction over the colonies and that the committees of correspondence should be discontinued. He ended his speech portentously: "I know of no line that can be drawn between the supreme authority of Parliament and the total independence of the colonies." It was becoming increasingly clear that he was right, and as if to

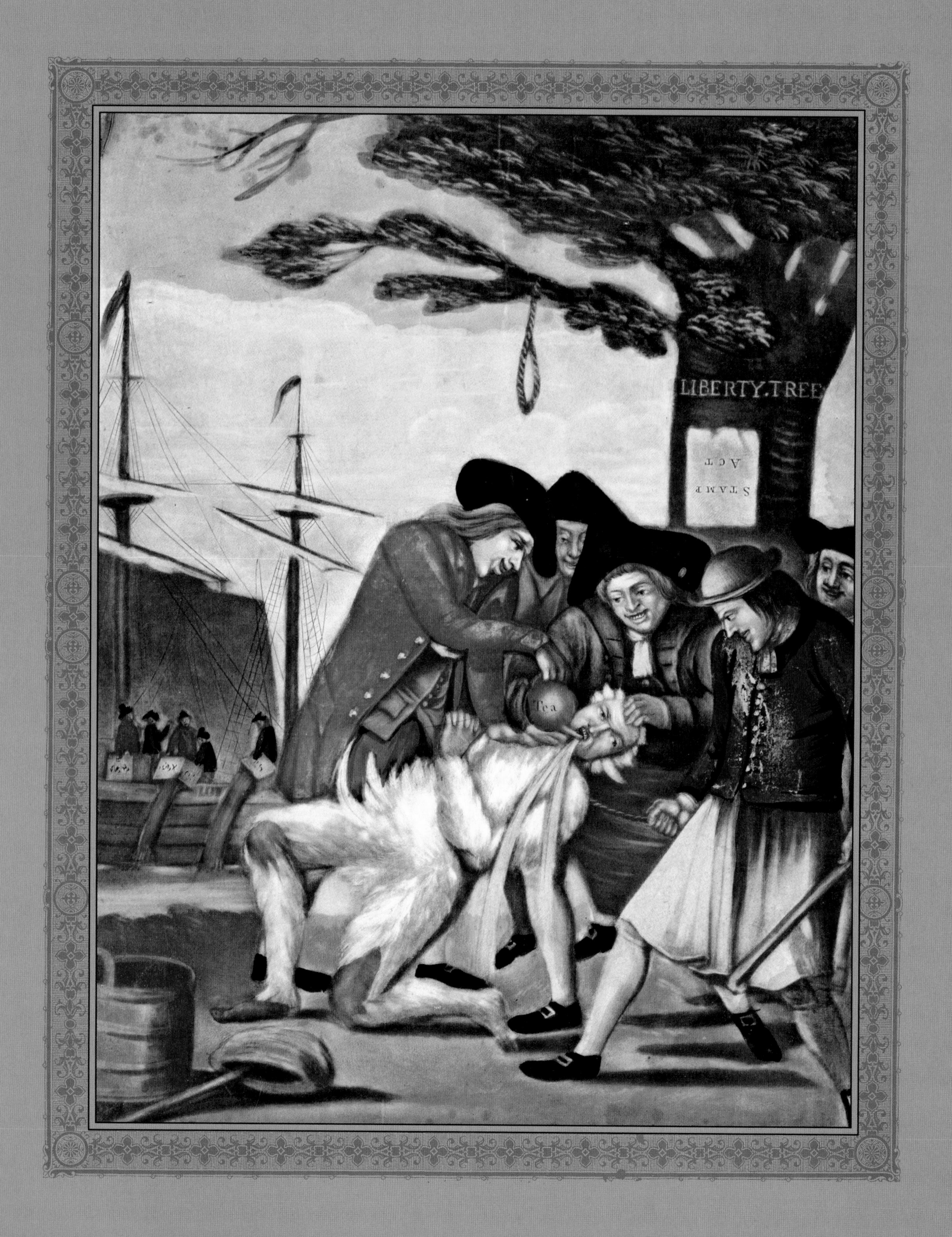
LIBERTY.TREE
STAMP ACT
Tea

hasten things along, Parliament passed yet another act in the spring of 1773: the Tea Act.

Reasonably, Parliament had its eye fixed on the health of the entire British Empire, and the colonies, also reasonably, were fixed on their own health. From Britain's point of view, the Tea Act made perfect sense—as had the Sugar Act, the Stamp Act, the Townshend Acts, the Quartering Act, and all other acts before them. In the case of a tax on tea, it was an obvious enough remedy to the troubles ailing the foundering East India Company. What the company had in abundance was tea, and America was a perfect market for it. Parliament had left a small tax on tea, a leftover from the Townshend Acts, as an affirmation of its authority, and the American colonists had been paying it without complaint. Some smuggling of tea through Holland was also going on, but the new act was not aimed at that. It was aimed at getting rid of the middleman, and that meant American merchants. According to the Tea Act, agents of the East India Company could sell directly to retailers, without paying any of the taxes merchants were required to pay. That would allow them to undercut any competitors' price on tea.

American merchants knew a monopoly in the making when they saw one, and they loudly proclaimed to the public that the British government was bribing them to buy East India tea. Once again, an outcry against taxation without representation, imposed by Parliament, could be heard through the colonies, and it was spread effectively by the committees of correspondence. The match with the mother country was joined again.

Hutchinson's inflammatory secret letters had been released earlier in 1773 and had precipitated the expected public outrage. Mass meetings were held in protest of British bullying and the Tea Act, and the Daughters of Liberty declared, "[R]ather than Freedom, we'll part with our Tea." They tried American-grown herbal substitutes, including boiled basil leaves, which they christened Liberty Tea. In colonial ports, local bands greeted ships laden with tea and forcefully invited them to turn around and go back to wherever they had come from. In some northern colonies, river pilots and sea captains trying to land East India tea were physically threatened. Most of them turned around and sailed away, but in Boston—naturally—the fight became even more heated between Governor Hutchinson and the Sons of Liberty.

TO THE

DELAWARE

PILOTS.

THE Regard we have for your Characters, and our Deſire to promote your future Peace and Safety, are the Occaſion of this Third Addreſs to you.

IN our ſecond Letter we acquainted you, that the Tea Ship was a Three Decker. We are now informed by good Authority, ſhe is not a Three Decker, but an *old black Ship, without a Head,* or *any Ornaments.*

THE *Captain* is a *ſhort fat* Fellow, and a little *obſtinate* withal---So much the worſe for him.---For, ſo ſure as he *rides ruſty*, We ſhall heave him Keel out, ... ---His Upper-Works too, will have an Overhawling----and as it is ſaid, he has a good deal of *Quick Work* about him, We will take particular Care that ſuch Part of him undergoes a thorough Rummaging.

WE have a ſtill *worſe Account* of *his Owner* ;--- for it is ſaid, the Ship POLLY was bought by him on Purpoſe, to make a Penny of us ; and that *he* and Captain *Ayres* were well adviſed of the Riſque they would run, in thus daring to inſult and abuſe us.

Captain Ayres was here in the Time of the Stamp-Act, and ought to have known our People better, than to have expected we would be ſo mean as to ſuffer his *rotten* TEA to be funnel'd down our Throats, with the *Parliament's Duty* mixed with it.

WE know him well, and have calculated to a Gill and a Feather, how much it will require to fit him for an *American Exhibition.* And we hope not one of your Body will behave ſo ill, as to oblige us to clap him in the Cart along Side of the *Captain.*

WE muſt repeat, that the SHIP POLLY is an *old black Ship*, of about Two Hundred and Fifty Tons burthen, *without a Head*, and *without Ornaments*,---and, that CAPTAIN AYRES is a *thick chunky Fellow.*----------As ſuch, TAKE CARE to AVOID THEM.

YOUR OLD FRIENDS,

THE COMMITTEE FOR TARRING AND FEATHERING.

Philadelphia, December 7, 1773.

Monday Morning December 27, 1773.

THE TEA SHIP being arrived, every Inhabitant, who wiſhes to preſerve the Liberty of America, is deſired to meet at the STATE-HOUSE, This Morning, preciſely at TEN o'Clock, to adviſe what is beſt to be done on this alarming Criſis.

FAC-SIMILE OF THE PROCLAMATION ABOUT THE TEA-SHIP.

A 1773 PROCLAMATION *(above) from Philadelphia patriots to Delaware ship pilots warns them not to have dealings with a British tea ship. Opposite: This 1774 British print depicts Bostonians gleefully tarring and feathering a customs commissioner under the Liberty Tree while the famous tea party goes on in the background.*

The governor insisted that the *Dartmouth,* a ship carrying tea and other merchandise, be off-loaded in Boston, where it had already cleared the customs house on November 28. By law the *Dartmouth* had 20 days to pay any duties owed on its cargo, and in those 20 days, local anti-British sentiment boiled. The Americans forced the ship to tie up and put one of their own guards aboard, and a handbill posted throughout the city proclaimed, "Friends! Brethren! Countrymen!—That worst of plagues, the detested tea, shipped for this port by the East India Company, is now arrived in the harbor."

In the following weeks, two more tea-bearing ships tied up beside the *Dartmouth* at Griffin's Wharf: the *Eleanor* and the *Beaver.* As the three ships awaited a determination on the fate of their cargo, Sam Adams and other Sons of Liberty exhorted the crowds that gathered at Boston's Old South Meeting House. John Adams's wife, Abigail, described the charged atmosphere to her friend Mercy Otis Warren, a political satirist who had effectively lampooned the British: "The tea that bainfull weed is arrived. Great and effectual opposition has been made to the landing of it . . . the proceedings of our citizens have been united, spirited and firm. The flame is kindled and like lightening it catches from soul to soul . . ."

The Boston Tea Party

On the morning of December 16, 5,000 souls—a third of Boston's population—thronged to the Old South Meeting House and awaited an answer from Hutchinson. They had sent an emissary to the governor to request that he allow the *Dartmouth* to be sailed safely out of Boston waters, its tea intact and on its way back to England. They didn't get Hutchinson's answer till early evening, and they weren't pleased with it. He had refused. Adams was ready with his own prepared answer to the British: "This meeting can do nothing more to save the country!"

The crowd and the Sons of Liberty had their plan of action already in place, and now they enthusiastically took to the streets. A hundred men or more, some in thinly veiled "disguises" as Mohawk Indians, headed for the three ships tied up at Griffin's Wharf as the crowd followed them. For three hours, the "Mohawk" band threw their own tea party by breaking open almost 350 casks and hoisting some 90,000 pounds of East India tea overboard. By night's end, tea worth roughly 9,000£ sterling by mid-18th-century standards floated or sank beneath the waters of Boston Harbor.

"This destruction of the tea is so bold, so daring, so intrepid and so inflexible, and it must have so important consequences and so lasting that I can't but consider it an epoch in history," John Adams wrote in his journal.

Sometimes called *the headquarters of the Revolution, the Green Dragon public house in Boston's North End was often used by Paul Revere, John Hancock, and other patriots as a meeting place to plan operations against the British.*

Other colonies, inspired by Boston's boldness, staged their own tea parties, and in Britain, the reactions were predictable: frustration, outrage, and determination to teach the colonies once and for all that it was the king and Parliament who governed. Looking for an easy target on which to vent their rage, the British government found one: Benjamin Franklin.

Still in London representing various colonial interests, including those of Massachusetts, Franklin had appeared before the Privy Council just before word of the Boston Tea Party had reached Britain. Franklin planned to use the occasion to argue that Hutchinson be

removed as governor. But the topic was quickly shifted, and Franklin endured a dressing-down by the king's solicitor general on the topic of Hutchinson's purloined letters. Standing silent for most of it, Franklin offered little defense of himself and requested counsel. In the weeks following his appearance, the Boston Tea Party news sent ministerial tempers flaring, and by late January, when Franklin was back in what was known as the Cockpit (as cockfights had been held at the Privy Council in the past), the solicitor general unleashed the full fury of his sharp tongue. Franklin was a "true incendiary" and "prime conductor" of the colonists' bad behavior, and because of the part he played in the Hutchinson letters, said the solicitor general, "He has forfeited the respect of societies and of men." Franklin took the barrage with no show of outward emotion, but with the excoriating attack, the British had themselves forfeited the respect and trust Franklin had put in them and, in so doing, had made a powerful enemy.

The British authorities continued punishing and isolating Massachusetts as an example, showing all the colonies that obedience to the crown was not a request but a requirement. Within a few months Parliament had passed the Boston Port Act, which stated that "WHEREAS dangerous commotions and insurrections have been fomented and raised

BENJAMIN FRANKLIN'S *worst moment in a long and illustrious career probably occurred in the winter of 1774, when British authorities excoriated him at his appearances before the Privy Council in London. Their attacks created a formidable enemy in Franklin, who soon sailed to America and joined the struggle for independence.*

BOARDING BRITISH TEA SHIPS *(preceding pages) docked at Griffin's Wharf, Bostonians, thinly disguised as Native Americans, empty more than 300 chests of East India tea into the sea on December 15, 1774.*

in the town of Boston," the port would be closed "until it shall sufficiently appear to his Majesty that full satisfaction hath been made by or on behalf of the inhabitants of the said town of *Boston* to the united company of merchants of *England* trading to the *East Indies,* for the damage sustained . . ."

The port act was only the beginning. The king and his minister, Lord North, had determined that the colonies would be coerced into obedience, and to that end the so-called Coercive Acts continued. That name was bad enough, but the colonists had another name for them: the Intolerable Acts.

There were five of them in all, and two more, both aimed at Massachusetts, passed in May 1774. The Administration of Justice Act proclaimed that the Massachusetts governor could, at his own discretion, move the trials of royal officials accused of committing capital offenses to England or to another colony. Some colonists called it the Murder Act, because in their minds it meant royal officials could get away with murder—colonists' murders. The second act aimed at Massachusetts stripped its inhabitants of any right at representative government in the council, declaring that as of "August 1, 1774, the council, or court of assistants of the said province for the time being, shall be composed of such [those] nominated and appointed by his Majesty." This effectively changed the colony's royal charter, something that Parliament had never done. Town meetings were banned too.

The other colonies reacted sympathetically to the intolerable treatment ladled out to their Massachusetts brethren, particularly the closing of Boston's port. The Virginia House of Burgesses declared its allegiance and set aside the first day of June as

IN THIS COMPLICATED ALLEGORY, *Britain's Lord North forces tea (the Intolerable Acts) down the throat of a partially clad female figure (America), while two other British lords restrain her; one of them, a notorious womanizer, peeks up her skirt. In the background, a distraught Britannia turns away.*

a day of fasting, humiliation, and prayer; devoutly to implore the Divine interposition, for averting the heavy calamity which threatens destruction to our civil rights, and the evils of civil war; to give us one heart and one mind firmly to oppose, by all just and proper means, every injury to *American* rights; and that the minds of his Majesty and his Parliament may be inspired from above with wisdom, moderation, and justice, to remove from the loyal people of *America* all cause of danger from a continued pursuit of measures pregnant with their ruin.

THOMAS GAGE *served as commander of all British forces in America from 1763 to 1774 and military governor of Massachusetts in 1774–1775. His efforts to quell tensions in the colony failed, and he was recalled in 1775.*

When the royal governor, Lord Dunmore, saw the decree, he dissolved the Virginia House of Burgesses, but they were not easily intimidated. They simply removed themselves down the street and continued to meet in Raleigh Tavern, where they discussed the need for a continental congress with representatives from each colony.

Divine intercession with Parliament apparently did not work, because on June 2, the day following the Day of Fasting and Prayer, it passed the fourth Intolerable Act—the Quartering Act—and this one affected all of the colonies. Henceforth, royal governors could take over private buildings throughout British America for the purpose of quartering troops. Within three weeks, Parliament landed a fifth blow: the Quebec Act. Although this measure was not aimed directly at the 13 colonies, it affected their interests in essential ways.

As a boon to Canadians, the act gave the province of Quebec the land between the Ohio and Mississippi Rivers, some of which had already been settled or purchased by people in the lower 13 colonies. Furthermore, Parliament acknowledged the rights of French Canadians to practice Roman Catholicism. Suddenly, the colonies had "popery" at their doorstep and no doubt creeping ever closer, and they had lost control over their interior borders and their ability to expand westward.

To top off this spring of outrage, the commander in chief of the British army in America, Thomas Gage, had been appointed military governor of Massachusetts. Married to an American heiress, Gage was a conservative man whose integrity had earned him the sobriquet "Honest Tom" when he was a young officer. By 1774, he had his own vested interests in American lands and a great desire to keep the peace. But he also had a deepening dislike of Boston and Bostonians, calling them "the greatest Bullies." In his opinion, "lenient measures and the cautious and legal exertions of . . . government, have served only to render them more daring and licentious." Now he was tasked with bringing those bullies to heel and seeing to it that the Coercive Acts were diligently obeyed.

That wasn't going to happen without a fight. The colonists were becoming increasingly convinced that no rapprochement with the mother country was possible. The king, beloved to them a decade ago, had proved to be a tyrant intent on stripping them of their rights with the help of Parliament. The old colonial British attitude of salutary neglect toward its colonies—or at least its American colonies—was no more. Boston had become an occupied state, and the same could happen to any other place that got out of line.

Throughout the colonies, Americans organized themselves in defiance of royal authority. They formed local associations, committees, and other groups designed to move control of the government and commonweal away from the crown and into local and colonial-wide organizations. In Virginia, delegates held their First Provincial Convention in August. One of the more eloquent young members of the convention, Thomas Jefferson, was too ill to attend but sent instead his "Summary View of the Rights of British America"—"in order that these our rights, as well as the invasions of them, may be laid more fully before his majesty . . ." In his lengthy and logical prose, Jefferson first asserted that "nature has given to all men" the right "of departing from the country in which chance, not choice, has placed them, of going in quest of new habitations, and of there establishing new societies, under such laws and regulations as to them shall seem most likely to promote public happiness." He argued that Parliament had no rights to govern the colonies; only the king had that right—and only a just king deserved it. Jefferson's argument was too inflammatory for the tastes or sentiments of most delegates to the convention, but they were impressed with his prose. They also agreed to form an association forbidding trade with Great Britain. Finally, they voted on delegates to send to the First Continental Congress.

> *In order that these our rights, as well as the invasions of them, may be laid more fully before his majesty.*
>
> THOMAS JEFFERSON, "A SUMMARY VIEW OF THE RIGHTS OF BRITISH AMERICA"

FIRST CONTINENTAL CONGRESS

ON SEPTEMBER 5, 1774, 55 EMINENT MEN REPRESENTING 12 OF THE 13 COLONIES (GEORGIA was missing) met in Philadelphia at Carpenters' Hall. If Philadelphia had been officially reluctant to affront the crown in the previous decade—not because of the city's citizenry but because of its Quaker interests—that reluctance was forgotten. With some 30,000 souls packed into less than a square mile, this was British America's largest city, "capital of the New World," and well situated geographically for an intercolonial meeting.

For seven weeks through that late summer and early fall, the men met with the goal of articulating their grievances clearly to the king, to Parliament, and to the American public. Some delegates attended in the hope of healing the rift between colonies and crown; others, like Sam and John Adams, and Virginians Patrick Henry and Richard Henry Lee, had begun to believe that the time to declare independence was at hand.

The Virginians, most of them well-heeled planters, impressed the other colonists with their elegance in both language and bearing. John Adams described the Virginians as "the

VIRGINIA DELEGATES *Patrick Henry (center) and Richard Henry Lee (right) and George Washington, in his uniform from the French and Indian War, attended the First Continental Congress, held in Philadelphia's Carpenters' Hall in late 1774. Townsfolk (background) gathered at the hall to follow the proceedings.*

©
Clyde O. DeLand
Phila

PHILADELPHIA RANKED AS *the largest city in America and its busiest port by the dawn of the Revolutionary era. Originally established by its Quaker proprietor William Penn in the 1680s as the capital of the colony, it sat at the confluence of the Delaware and Schuylkill Rivers. In this print, the artist takes some liberties, giving it the structures and sophistication of a European city.*

most spirited and consistent, of any." He also confessed in a letter to his wife, Abigail, that in general, "The magnanimity and public spirit which I see here make me blush for the sordid, venal herd which I have seen in my own Province." Peyton Randolph, who had been leader of the Virginia House of Burgesses before it was disbanded and, later, of Virginia's First Provincial Convention, was quickly elected president of the congress.

Despite early enthusiasm, the colonies' particular vested interests began to mar the general magnanimity. The practical problem before the First Continental Congress was how to respond to the Intolerable Acts, and a general trade boycott was the obvious solution. But Virginia's tobacco and South Carolina's rice and indigo needed the British market, and they were unwilling to stop exports until the following year.

Hoping to bridge the trade and economic impasse and move to a broader approach, Pennsylvanian Joseph Galloway, one of the more cautious voices at the congress, put forward a Plan of Union that would unite the colonies but keep them within the empire: They would be governed by a popularly elected Grand Council—the American equivalent of Parliament—charged with overseeing all the colonies, and the king would appoint a president general to represent his interests. Galloway's plan was defeated, probably because before the vote was taken, word of new British oppression reached Philadelphia.

As was often the case, the news came from the Boston area, where His Majesty's troops were fortifying the town. The local population in surrounding Suffolk County had given voice to its grievances in a document called the Suffolk Resolves in mid-September, and a Bostonian named Paul Revere had galloped some 350 miles down the length of the mid-Atlantic to deliver the resolves to the Continental Congress in Philadelphia. An ardent Son of Liberty, silversmith, and engraver, Revere had issued several well-known prints documenting the British "atrocities" in Boston. Now the 40-year-old Revere took on a new role as the deliverer of critical news.

When the Suffolk Resolves reached the Continental Congress, the delegates reiterated their support of Massachusetts by endorsing the document, to the eternal gratitude of John Adams. "This was one of the happiest Days of my Life," he wrote in his diary. "In Congress We had generous, noble Sentiments, and manly Eloquence. This Day convinced me that America will support the Massachusetts or perish with her."

AN ENGLISH ENGRAVER *in the late 18th century created his own imaginative version of the 1774 proceedings of the Continental Congress.*

Before adjourning, the delegates also issued a declaration of the rights granted them "by the immutable laws of nature, the principles of the English constitution, and the several charters or compacts" that had been made. The declaration decorously but emphatically denied Parliament's ability to levy "internal taxes on the colonies" yet stated that the colonies "cheerfully consent to the operation of such acts . . . as are bonfide, restrained to the regulation of our external commerce, for the purpose of securing the commercial advantages of the whole empire to the mother country." It also requested that the king reconsider the Intolerable Acts and the intolerable treatment of Boston.

If the declaration was ambiguous, the success of the First Continental Congress was not. Its crowning achievement was that it happened at all. The delegates representing what had been competing fiefdoms with their own interests and cultures—from the fire-eating Bostonians to the hyper-refined Virginians to the cautionary Pennsylvanians—had come together, taken each other's measure, and found that they could act as one. "The Distinctions between Virginians, Pennsylvanians, New Yorkers and New Englanders, are no more," Adams proclaimed in his diary.

Despite disagreements and some dissension, they had managed to form a protolegislative body. More important, they had agreed to reconvene in Philadelphia in May 1775. And it was at the Second Continental Congress that history truly would be made.

Benjamin Franklin
(1706–1790)

He has been anointed the "First American," and surely the self-made Philadelphian embodies almost everything America admires: ingenuity, common sense, self-reliance, ambition, and sheer guts. Benjamin Franklin lies somewhere between genius and folksy intriguer and squarely in the realm of legend. But who was the man behind the legend?

Herman Melville probably summed him up best: Franklin was a "printer, postmaster, almanac maker, essayist, chemist, orator, tinker, statesman, humorist, philosopher, parlor man, political economist, professor of housewifery, ambassador, projector, maxim-monger, herb-doctor, wit: Jack of all trades, master of each and mastered by none." Melville left out scientist, inventor, avid swimmer, businessman, civic-betterment engineer, and philanderer. In all of these roles (except perhaps the last), Franklin put his stamp on America and its character. But his greatest contribution has to be that he made America possible. Without Benjamin Franklin, the 13 colonies might well have lost the fight with Britain, and their glorious revolution would have ended as a lost cause.

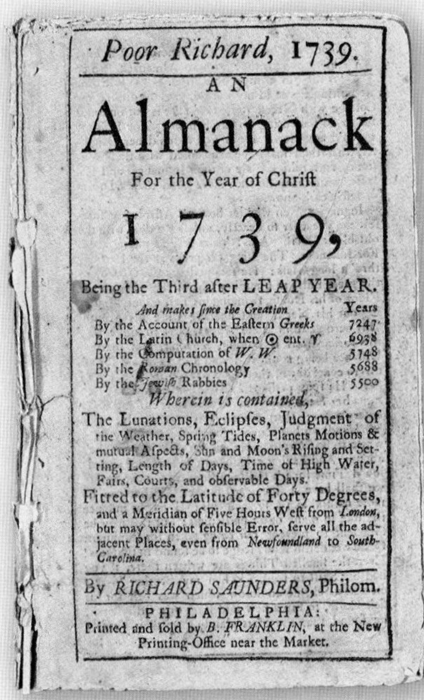

Benjamin Franklin *(shown opposite in a portrait by Joseph-Siffred Duplessis) could as easily sup with European aristocracy as dispense homespun advice to the provincial American public in his wildly popular* Poor Richard's Almanack.

To understand Franklin's quintessential Americanism, you need only look at his early life. The youngest son of 17 children, he grew up in Boston. His father, Josiah, along with his first wife and their three small children, had left England behind and set sail for the burgeoning port city in 1683, when Boston itself was barely 50 years old. The son of a blacksmith, Josiah was an independent thinker, and he took a chance on the New World. Once there, he adopted the trade of tallow chandler and soap maker. He also adopted the ways of Bostonians: frugality, industriousness, and piety. Old South Church, a progressive breakaway from the Puritanism of Boston's founders, became his spiritual bulwark, and he became a prominent member. "His great Excellence lay in a sound Understanding, and solid Judgment in prudential Matters, both in private and public . . ." Ben wrote of his father years later. At the Franklin family table, Ben continued, Josiah "turn'd our Attention to what was good, just, & prudent in the Conduct of Life."

Ben, the third youngest child, had a precocious and questing nature that emerged early in his life: "I do not remember when I could not read," he wrote in his autobiography. Josiah clearly recognized his youngest son's talents. While the other Franklin boys had been apprenticed in various trades, Josiah decided to invest in Ben's future—as a clergyman—and sent the boy to Boston Grammar School (now Boston Latin, and the oldest school in America). Too soon, though, Josiah's own "solid Judgment in prudential Matters" intervened. Given the Franklin family circumstances, the expense of a college education for the boy was out of the question—and anyway, Josiah had noticed "the mean Living many so educated were afterwards able to obtain." He may also have noticed that the boy wasn't really cut from clerical cloth. Whatever the case, after less than a year of school, Ben's formal education came to an end. By the age of ten he was put to work in his father's business.

Franklin's curiosity did not end with his schooling, and he continued to read whatever he could lay hands on. But as he moved toward adolescence, Boston's port atmosphere and the smell of salt air beguiled him into dreams of a life at sea. Those dreams were also cut short when Josiah apprenticed Ben to his older son, Ben's stepbrother James. As James was a printer and Ben, then 12, loved to read, Josiah assumed he had made a good match. And in fact, Ben made the most of his apprenticeship; he wrote a series of popular spoofs under the pseudonym Mrs. Silence Dogood for the paper his brother established, the *New-England Courant.*

But the more Ben began to flex his muscles, the more he chafed at his apprenticeship. He was brawny, physical, ambitious, and full of his own abilities and appetites—intellectual, commercial, sexual. By 16, no longer able to stand being under his brother's thumb, he did what he had dreamed of doing: he sailed away. Ben eventually landed in America's largest city, Philadelphia. He was dirty and hungry, and he had very little with which to sustain himself beyond his own smarts and drive—and the skills he had learned as a printer. It was those skills that kept him going for the next 25 years, as his business prospered and his reputation grew.

Franklin gradually became a self-educated Renaissance man, teaching himself four languages and perfecting his writing skills in everything from learned philosophical pamphlets to the sometimes ribald and always pithy maxims of his popular—and lucrative—*Poor Richard's Almanack,* published annually in the 1730s and 1740s. Among the wisdom it dispensed were the aphorisms "Men and Melons are hard to know"; "She that paints her face, thinks of her Tail"; and "Keep your eyes wide open before marriage, half shut afterwards." The last probably reflected Ben's own marital state. In 1730, after an on-again, off-again courtship, he had taken Deborah Read, the daughter of his first Philadelphia landlord, "to wife." The Franklins had a common-law—not a formal—marriage, because Deborah's first husband had abandoned her and vanished. Months after Ben and Deborah began living together, he presented her with a son, William, whose mother was another woman. Still, in the early decades of their marriage, the two worked side by side to build their family business, and Franklin always wrote of Deborah with deference.

In many ways, deference was Franklin's key to success. He liked to tell a story about his boyhood—that the great Boston Puritan leader Cotton Mather had once been following him down a passageway and had called sharply to him, "Stoop! Stoop!" Suddenly, Franklin's forehead collided with a low beam, and he understood that Mather's advice had been borne of practicality, not piety. But Mather couldn't resist following the boy's collision with an aphorism. "You are young, and have the world before you," he told Franklin. "Stoop as you go through it, and you will miss many hard thumps."

And through the early years of penury and hard work, Franklin had metaphorically stooped—deferred to those above him yet still quietly pursued his omnipresent ambition. That strategy paid off handsomely. By the time he was 42, Franklin was a prosperous man—well-off enough to retire and become a pillar of Philadelphia's intellectual and civic circles. He had served as postmaster of Philadelphia, invented the Franklin

BENJAMIN FRANKLIN *and his common-law wife, Deborah (above), had a tenuous relationship in their later years. Opposite: Noted early American artist Benjamin West's allegorical depiction of Franklin "drawing electricity from the sky"*

Franklin's early career *as a printer has remained enshrined in the American imagination. This image of him in his shop was created in the 1920s, some 130 years after his death.*

stove, and championed a sanitation system for the city and a militia system for the colony (and served as a soldier in the regiment he organized). He anticipated retirement as "a great happiness, leisure to read, study, make experiments, and converse at large with such ingenious and worthy men as are pleased to honour me with their friendship." And many were, on both sides of the Atlantic.

This was the age of Newtonian-inspired science and the Enlightenment and inquiring minds engaged in science. Franklin began his famous experiments on electricity in the early 1750s, and his methodology for proving "whether the clouds that contain that lightning are electrified" quickly earned him international acclaim (and cost one Swedish scientist, whose experiment in a severe storm went awry, his life).

That acclaim, along with Franklin's knowledge of London—he had lived there for a couple of years in his late teens—made him an ideal choice to represent the interests of Pennsylvania in London. His disarming charm and learning ingratiated him with the London elite and powerful, and, as relations heated between the colonies and Parliament, he was well positioned to explain American concerns to those who would listen. At first, Franklin trusted to the beneficence of the British, but he gradually lost that trust. And after a humiliating public dressing-down by the crown's solicitor general in 1774, Franklin set his face against the British and returned to America ready for revolution.

Among the American leaders on the patriotic front lines, Franklin, almost 70 when the first shots were fired, reigned as the elder statesman. Yet in the coming decades, he used his age and experience as a rapier held at the throat of the British. After serving on the committee charged with drafting the Declaration of Independence at the Second Continental

Congress, Franklin sailed for France as an American commissioner to the French court. He took two young grandsons with him. One was the child of his own illegitimate but acknowledged son, William, who had made a success of his life but remained a staunch Loyalist. As Franklin sailed, William was being held prisoner in Connecticut as "a virulent enemy to this country, and a person that may prove dangerous."

Franklin, by contrast, was the person who, through his diplomacy, secured the revolution. The French welcomed him with open arms. "He was not given the title of Monsieur; he was addressed simply as Doctor Franklin, as one would have addressed Plato or Socrates," one Frenchman explained. Using skillful cajoling and charm rather than Socratic reasoning, Franklin helped persuade France to join the American colonists in making common cause against their mutual enemy, Britain. Without France and its skilled officers, gunpowder, troops, and ships, the scant Continental forces—inexperienced, ill equipped, and almost navyless—surely would have succumbed to the British.

Franklin's success in rallying the French probably stemmed from the fact that he enjoyed them and their country—immensely, if the word of John Adams, another commissioner, is to be believed. "The life of Dr. Franklin was a scene of continual dissipation," the puritanical Adams wrote. By American standards of the day, that may have been so. Age had not dampened Franklin's appetites, and Deborah had died in 1775 while Franklin was in London. The French, far from being put off by his flirtations, celebrated him; they even issued medallions engraved with his image. One proclaimed in Latin, "He snatched the lightning from heaven and the scepter from tyrants."

In truth, Franklin had accomplished both things, though he had had help. Along with John Adams and John Jay, he negotiated the Treaty of Paris that ended the war. Adams, resentful of what he saw as his own marginalization in events, predicted, "The history of the Revolution . . . will be *that Dr. Franklin's electrical rod smote the Earth and out sprung General Washington. That Franklin electrified him with his rod and thence forward these two conducted all the policy, negotiations, legislatures and war.*"

Benjamin Franklin suffered no such delusion, and he was disinclined to rest on his laurels. Once independence was achieved, he returned to an America ravaged by war. He, too, was now ravaged by age and illness (gout and kidney stones plagued him), but his voracious intellect was still strong. Asked to serve as President of Pennsylvania, he accepted, because, as he told a friend, "I had not sufficient firmness to refuse." He served in that role for three years, and in the years left to him he continued to invent and to hold forth with his opinions on everything from the Constitution to the need to outlaw slavery.

The culmination of Franklin's long and fruitful life came in 1787, three years before his death. At 81 he attended the Constitutional Convention as its oldest delegate and affixed his signature to the document that finally achieved the union he had lobbied for as long ago as 1754. If the union was less than perfect, Franklin was not overly bothered. He had spent his life cultivating the art of compromise in all things, and he believed in it. But he also had spent his life cultivating the fine art of expression, and now he wanted a last word. The enemies of America had been thirsting, he said, to hear that "our states are on the point separation, only to meet heareafter for the purpose of cutting one another's throat." And yet there they were, representatives of those states meeting relatively amicably and forging a document to govern them all. "I consent, sir," Franklin said, "to this constitution, because I expect no better, and because I am not sure that it is not the best."

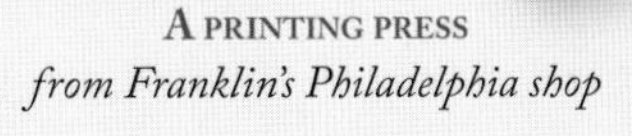

A PRINTING PRESS
from Franklin's Philadelphia shop

BOSTON

CHAPTER 2

Almighty God! I know not what course others may take;
but as for me, give me liberty or give me death!

PATRICK HENRY

1775
LIBERTY OR DEATH

IT HAD TAKEN ONLY A DOZEN SHORT YEARS TO BREED A MOLDERING DISTRUST BETWEEN THE AMERICANS AND the British. By 1775 neither people officially felt much affection or fealty for the other, though there were strong pockets of Loyalists throughout the colonies. In Boston, clandestine associations kept a close eye on both the Loyalists and the redcoats; these secret forces posted watches nightly to be sure no escapades against the colonists were under way. In London, the king and his Tory compatriots were ready to teach the disagreeable colonists a lesson. "Suppose the colonies do abound in men, what does that signify?" Lord Sandwich asked the House of Lords. Then he answered his own question: "They are raw, undisciplined, cowardly men." But the great parliamentarian and political thinker Edmund Burke extolled the colonists' fierce spirit of liberty: "In this character of the Americans, a love of freedom is the predominating feature which marks and distinguishes the whole . . . your colonies become suspicious, restive, and untractable, whenever they see the least attempt to wrest from them by force, or shuffle from them by chicane, what they think the only advantage worth living for."

As Parliament debated the American situation in March 1775, the Second Provincial Convention in Virginia did the same thing across the Atlantic. And again, Patrick Henry became the full-throated voice of

PAUL REVERE, *a Boston silversmith, became an ardent Son of Liberty famous for his nighttime ride. His portraitist, John Singleton Copley, also became famous for his images of prominent American and British subjects. Preceding pages: The British attack on Bunker and Breed's Hills and the burning of Charlestown* rebellion. "Gentlemen may cry, Peace, Peace—but there is no peace," Henry thundered. "The war is actually begun! The next gale that sweeps from the north will bring to our ears the clash of resounding arms! Our brethren are already in the field! Why stand we here idle? . . . Is life so dear, or peace so sweet, as to be purchased at the price of chains and slavery? Forbid it, Almighty God! I know not what course others may take; but as for me, give me liberty or give me death!"

This belief in liberty and the human right to it (if not for slaves) was unprecedented, a new way of conceiving the human condition. For more than a century, it had been growing and maturing in the American ethos, and now the idea of individual freedom was held dear—dear enough to fight for.

In Boston the British commander Thomas Gage understood this. He knew that the town he oversaw, probably along with other colonies, was preparing for a fight. John Hancock had defiantly warned Gage in an open letter that Massachusetts had been "repeatedly alarmed at your Excellency's unusual and warlike Preparations since your Arrival."

Writing for reinforcements, Gage urged his superiors not to underestimate the Americans: "If you think ten thousand men sufficient, send twenty; if one million is thought enough, give two; you save both blood and treasure in the end." His warnings elicited only disdain from his superiors, who, like Lord Sandwich, simply couldn't take the rough colonists seriously. Still, some reinforcements, including several well-regarded officers, were sent his way.

The Americans had no seasoned generals of their own and no military beyond their militias and more elite minutemen, trained to assemble on the double quick. They also had no serious supplies of weaponry or munitions, except what was officially stored in magazines and armories in scattered in towns throughout the colonies. To complicate matters, the crown's secretary of state to the colonies had instructed the royal governors to seize any new munitions coming to the American colonies and to prevent elections for delegates to the Second Continental Congress.

The previous December, the redcoats and the colonists had had a significant dustup over a substantial supply of gunpowder, cannons, and small arms stored in a New Hampshire coastal fort. The colonists had managed to cart the weaponry away, and after that, other New England towns had done the same. "Things now every day grow more and more serious," Lord Percy wrote home in early April. Percy was one of the commanders posted to Boston to serve with General Gage, and he had watched as conditions in the port city grew worse and worse—little food, bad water, and certainly no inclination on the part of the townsfolk

PATRICK HENRY

1736–1799

Energetic, erratic, and persuasive, Patrick Henry was a self-taught lawyer who early on in the struggle with Britain captured the public imagination with his fiery rhetoric. At the First Continental Congress, he declared, "I am not a Virginian, but an American," yet his national role ended after one session of the Second Continental Congress. Returning to Virginia, he continued to press for revolution and military preparedness. In 1776 he became the first elected governor of the state, and over the course of his life served five terms as Virginia governor. After independence, Henry became increasingly wary of a strong central government and the Constitution, calling its objectives "extremely pernicious, impolitic, and dangerous." In the early years of the Republic, he opposed the ideas of Madison, Jefferson, and particularly Hamilton but continued to believe in the union of states. In 1799 he was elected delegate to the state legislature but died at his home, Red Hill, before he could take his seat.

PATRICK HENRY *(opposite) delivering his celebrated but probably apocryphal speech—"If this be treason, make the most of it!"—before the Virginia House of Burgesses in 1765*

ON THE NIGHT of April 18–19, 1775, Paul Revere raced through the countryside from Charlestown to Concord to warn his fellow patriots that the British army was on the move. In Lexington, local militia and redcoats clashed in a shot "heard 'round the world."

to assist the redcoats occupying their town and patrolling their streets. Desertion rose in the British ranks, and Gage ordered several apprehended deserters shot, one on Boston Common. His patience for his men's shortcomings, and particularly for the Bostonians' pranks, was virtually at an end. From London, Gage was encouraged to take some kind of decisive action against the Americans. In mid-April the orders that reached him were more explicit: "Arrest and imprison the principal actors and abettors of the Provincial Congress whose proceedings appear in every light to be acts of treason and rebellion."

The Sons of Liberty got wind of these orders, thanks to their allies in London, and as the weather warmed, they waited and watched. They expected that with the New England cold dissipating, Gage would act.

A cautious man, Gage sent out spies to reconnoiter the surrounding countryside so that he could plan a good target for his first action. By late March, he had it: the town of Concord, less than 20 miles northwest of Boston. His spies and Loyalists within the town itself had assured him it was a storehouse of colonial arms.

PAUL REVERE RIDES

AS THE BRITISH MADE READY TO MARCH, WARY BOSTONIANS WATCHED THE REDCOATS' preparations, listened to their chatter, and soon realized that Concord was the intended target. On April 8, Paul Revere, who had delivered the Suffolk Resolves to the Continental Congress the previous autumn and since had warned other towns of British movements, once again sounded the alarm. This time he rode to Concord and warned town leaders there to "daily expect a Tumult."

But when the tumult did not come, Revere rode the following week to Lexington, where John Hancock, Sam Adams, and other leaders had taken refuge. Lexington lay between Concord and Boston, and Revere wanted Adams and Hancock to be well aware that the British could be headed their way at any time. Still, the British delayed and instead placed their own patrols on the main roads in and out of Boston, making it more difficult for the colonists to issue new warnings. Not to be outdone, Revere and his compatriots came up with a new plan to signal any troop movement—"If the British went out by Water, we would shew two Lanthorns in the North Church Steeple," the highest structure in town, Revere explained. "If by land, one, as a signal, for we were apprehensive it would be difficult to cross the Charles River, or git over Boston neck."

Around ten o'clock the night of April 18, two dim lights appeared in the northwest window of the North Church steeple, just visible to those watching for the signal across the waters in Charlestown. The British would be crossing Boston's bay to Cambridge, and in the meantime, Revere would be quietly ferrying across the Charles to Charlestown in his own small boat, where "a very good horse" was waiting. Outracing a British patrol he encountered, he made for Lexington and roused the militia in several towns along the way. Dutifully, the farmers and shopkeepers left their warm beds behind and prepared to muster as citizen-soldiers.

Revere reached Lexington about midnight and warned a sleeping Hancock and Adams that the British Regulars were coming. After resting briefly, Revere and fellow messenger William Dawes, who had taken a different route to Lexington to sound the alarm in other villages, were off again to deliver the same message to Concord. But before they got there, the British caught them. Delighted to find he had bagged the infernal Paul Revere, their commander "clapped pistol to my head," Revere later recalled, and said "he was agoing to ask me some quesions, and if I did not tell the truth, he would blow my brains out." Revere was undaunted and assured his captor that he was "a man of truth . . . I will tell the truth, for I am not afraid." He warned them away from Lexington, where trouble and colonial forces would be waiting for them. They seemed to believe his warning, particularly when they heard the bells of Lexington ringing in

Samuel Adams

1722–1803

Whatever skills Harvard-educated Samuel Adams lacked as a businessman and Boston maltster he made up for as a political agitator. In 1747, while still in his mid-20s, the puritanical Adams was elected to his first public office. By the time the British imposed the Stamp Act in 1765 he was well positioned to foment local opposition against it. As a delegate to the Massachusetts House he continued his protest of new taxes and duties and later of the British occupation of Boston. In the days preceding the Revolution Adams moved from agitation to action, and he is often credited with playing a leading part in organizing the Boston Tea Party, although historians disagree about his actual role. As a delegate to the First and Second Continental Congresses he signed the Declaration of Independence and helped draft the Articles of Confederation. In 1781 he left Congress and returned to Boston, where he continued to agitate for public virtue in politics.

alarm. Anxious now for their own lives, they released Revere and two other captives and rode away.

Back in Boston, at about the time the signal was posted in Old North Church, a much larger contingent of Regulars had been awakened in their beds and ordered to move out silently through the streets of town. Their mission and destination were not yet revealed. The 800 or 900 troops converged at a small beach on Back Bay, then packed into longboats for the trip across to Cambridge as a full moon lit their way. The overloaded boats ran aground a few feet from shore, and the men were forced to wade through knee-deep, frigid water. The shore itself didn't offer much comfort, as it was no more than marshland. It took several hours before the confused tangle of troops was formed up into companies and ready to march, and by then the men were freezing. The officers urged them forward at a quick march to make up for lost time, but as they passed through the countryside outside Cambridge, word of their movements spread.

If the British went out by Water, we would shew two Lanthorns in the North Church Steeple.

PAUL REVERE

In Lexington some 130 local militiamen had flocked to the town common after hearing Revere's warning. In truth, neither they nor their leader, Capt. John Parker, a veteran of the French and Indian War, knew exactly what they were supposed to do—or whether the alarm had even been real. After a while the chill night soaked into them. Some went home or took refuge in a tavern by the commons; they were under orders to return as soon as they heard the drumbeat. The call to arms sounded as dawn seeped into the cold sky, and there was a confused flurry as men headed for the common, some stopping for ammunition at the meetinghouse.

The British column rounded a bend and swung suddenly into view. The Regulars were hungry, tired, thirsty, and freezing from their night march. They were also probably particularly anxious, because in the previous half hour, they had been able to make out on the hills around them "a vast number of country militia going over the hills with their arms for Lexington." Now, in the gray half-light, they could just make out the Lexington men, about 70 of them, clustered in a corner of the town common a hundred yards from the road. Along the edge of the common were other local men, and as both sides peered into the dawn light, each overestimated the number of the enemy. Without question, though, the colonists were far outnumbered, maybe by as much as ten to one.

The road to Concord led to the left, but a young British marine lieutenant in the forward companies swung his column directly at the militia, rather than having them outflank him. That decision led to the inevitable. The Regulars, their adrenalin flowing, were caught up in the moment, and they unleashed the British battle cry of "Huzza! Huzza! Huzza!"

A British commander cantered toward the Americans and, according to several reports, shouted, "Lay down your arms, you damned rebels!" Some of the Americans began to

BOSTON'S OLD NORTH *(Christ) Church earned a place in history on the night of April 18, 1775, when two sextons hung lanterns from its steeple in a prearranged signal to Paul Revere about British troop movements. Poet Henry Wadsworth Longfellow later immortalized the signal as "One if by land, and two if by sea" in his classic,* Paul Revere's Ride.

AN ENGRAVING *from the mid-18th century titled "A south east view of the great town of Boston in New England in America"*

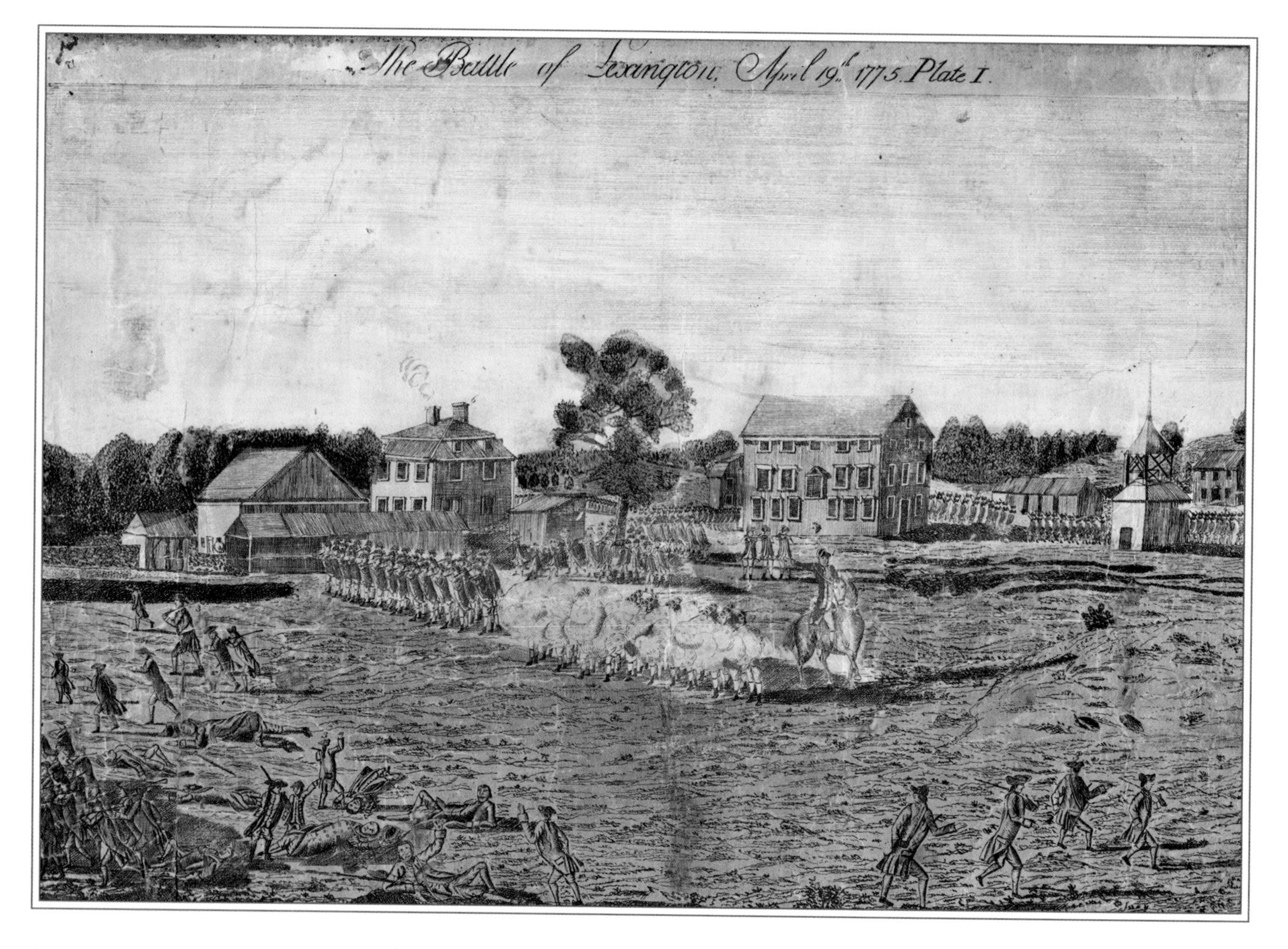

The Battle of Lexington, April 19th 1775. Plate I.

A COLONIAL ENGRAVING *depicts British redcoats firing on American militiamen at the unanticipated Battle of Lexington in the early morning of April 19, 1775.*

barn etc., His Lordship kept the enemy off and brought the troops to Charles Town, from whence they were ferried to Boston."

But Boston, it became clear, was no longer a British stronghold. Word of Lexington and Concord had spread quickly—that the redcoats had "fired without provocation" on Americans, and more luridly, that the Regulars had "engaged in butchering and destroying our brethren there in the most inhuman manner." This would not stand. The battle was not over; it had just begun. Throughout Massachusetts, militiamen set out for the port city, and all through the northern colonies, armies were hastily raised for a siege of Boston. As far away as Georgia, the royal governor reported, "A general rebellion throughout America is coming on suddenly and swiftly."

Most Americans were as unsettled as the Georgia governor at the thought of rebellion. In Virginia, George Washington, a planter and former colonel in the British American forces, wrote to a friend, "The once-happy and peaceful plains of America are either to be drenched with blood or inhabited by a race of slaves. Sad alternative! But can a virtuous man hesitate in his choice?"

In Washington's own Virginia, tensions between the British and the colonists had come to a head just two days after the Lexington and Concord debacle, and for a similar reason: The royal governor, Lord Dunmore, had ordered his troops to remove gunpowder from the Williamsburg magazine early on the morning of April 21. The timing was auspicious, because delegates to the Second Continental Congress were preparing to leave for the long, arduous ride over dirt roads to Philadelphia. To the governor, the fact that the congress was meeting at all was an act of defiance on the part of the Virginians. And now with the uncertain situation in Williamsburg, the capital, those estimable delegates were reluctant to leave—not to mention the fact that most assumed they were on a rumored blacklist of some 30 prominent and rebellious Americans who were soon to be arrested and taken to England for trial.

For his part, Dunmore defended his gunpowder raid rather glibly by relying on another rumor of an upcoming slave insurrection. He claimed he had simply ordered the gunpowder to be taken from the public magazine so that it could be moved to a safer location. But he also warned against any retaliatory violence against his troops: "By the living God if an insult is offered to me or to those who obeyed my orders, I will declare freedom to the slaves and lay the town in ashes." It was not a threat Virginia's white population could take lightly, for unlike the northern colonies, Virginia's citizenry was almost 40 percent enslaved men, women, and children.

Virginia's last royal governor, *Lord Dunmore (1730–1809), inflamed patriotic passions and personally led the fight against the Commonwealth's "rebels" for a year, from mid-1775 to mid-1776. This image of him was painted by Joshua Reynolds, a British artist of his era whose portraits often celebrated military heroes of the empire.*

Dunmore understood the weight that his colony carried. Virginia was the largest by far in both population (roughly half a million) and geographic size (its western borders extended to the Mississippi in the west and the Great Lakes in the north). And he had his hands full with some of the most outspoken and eloquent opponents of British authority. Most of those opponents ultimately let the magazine episode go and instead defied the governor by riding off to join their compatriots in Philadelphia.

For several weeks a watchful and uneasy quiet prevailed. Benjamin Franklin made his heralded return from England in early May, and a broadside proclaimed his sentiments to the colonists: "We have no favours to expect from the Ministry; nothing but submission will satisfy them. They expect little or no opposition will be made to their troops . . ."

On that the ministry was mistaken. The Americans had now taken the offensive, with more militiamen converging on Boston to bolster the siege that had begun after Lexington and Concord. Yet if the patriots' ardor was impressive, their supplies were not. They were critically short of ammunition, and they knew it. To help remedy that problem, two different committees of safety—from Massachusetts and Connecticut—planned a move on

Road from Concord
Road from Lexington
Road from Watertown
Road from Watertown
Road from Malden
Road to Marblehead and Salem
Mystick River
Mystick River
Temple's Farm
Winter Hill
The Left Commanded by General Putnam
Prospect Hill or Mount Pisgah
Charlestown Neck
Bunkers Hill
Breeds Hill
The Center Commanded by General Washington
Lower Fort
Mill Pond
Mill Dam
Willis Creek
Phips Farm
Ruins of Charlestown
Charlestown Point
Ferry
The Common
Cambridge
Main Guard
Lines
Redoubt
Redoubt
Charles River
North End
Bartons Point
Mill Pond
North Battery
Beacon Hill
Long Wharf
The Harbour
South Battery
Windmill Point
The Island
Floating Battery
Dorchester
6 Feet and Dry at Low
4 Feet
Dorchester Hill
Forster Hill
Signal Tree Hill
Boston Neck
Lines
Brookline
Muddy River
Stony Brook
The Right Commanded by General Thomas
Pierpoint's Mill
Bindley's Meadow
Bugles Hill
Circumvallation
Meeting House
George Tavern
Burying Ground
Tan Yard
Roxbury
Roxbury Hill
Road to Dorchester
Road to Dorchester

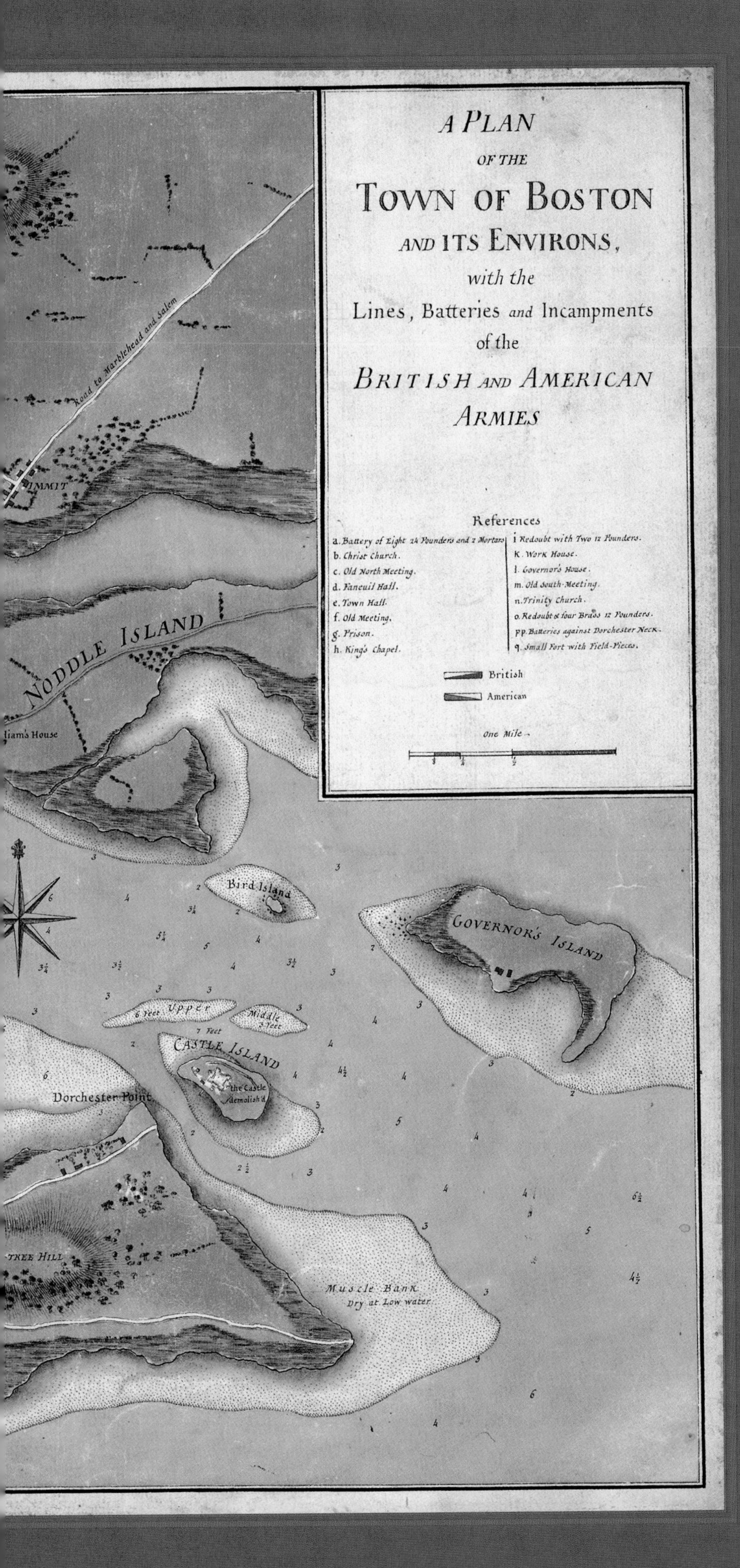

Based on a drawing made in October 1775 by Lt. Richard Williams, a trained engineer and officer in the Royal Welsh Fusiliers, this map concentrates on points of potential military interest in the greater Boston area.

A ROMANTICIZED DEPICTION *of history shows swashbuckling Ethan Allen, leader of Vermont's Green Mountain Boys, taking the British commander of Fort Ticonderoga by surprise and demanding the fort's surrender in the early hours of May 10, 1775.*

Fort Ticonderoga. The dilapidated pile had been built by the French a century earlier on the southwest shore of Lake Champlain to guard the strategic pathway between Canada and New England. Now the fort and its impressive cache of armament were in the hands of a few British troops.

On May 9 the two American contingents—the Connecticut force, made up mostly of Ethan Allen's Green Mountain Boys, and Benedict Arnold from Massachusetts—happened to converge at the same time on the shores of Champlain. The problem was that Arnold had no troops of his own. Allen and Arnold tussled over the command position and came to an uneasy resolution. Before dawn on May 10 they were moving on Ticonderoga.

Taking the garrison by surprise, Allen caught its captain not yet dressed, "with his breeches in his hand," and "ordered him to deliver me the fort instantly . . . In the name of the great Jehovah and the Continental Congress." The captain complied, and the fort and its armament were in American hands before the sun had cleared the horizon. Allen sent his captives off to Connecticut's governor with a note: "I make you a present of a Major, a Captain, and two Lieutenants of the regular Establishment of George the Third."

On the morning of Allen's victory, the Continental Congress was convening for a second time in Philadelphia, and its delegates were only too aware that the colonies were now on the perilous edge of war. To drive that point home, George Washington appeared in his military uniform from the French and Indian War. Suffering from poor health, Virginian Peyton Randolph stepped down as president and was replaced by John Hancock of Massachusetts.

The congress settled down to business. Still anxious to avoid war, the delegates appointed a committee to draft a letter to the king as a last attempt at reconciliation. Several delegates made efforts at the wording. One was a new Virginia delegate, Thomas Jefferson, but his language was considered too harsh. In the end, the final petition came mostly from John Dickinson, who, a decade earlier, had roused the colonists with his *Letters From a Farmer in Pennsylvania.*

In Dickinson's Olive Branch Petition, as it became known, the members of the Continental Congress expressed their loyalty and esteem for the king and at the same time laid out what they saw as the egregious recent oppressions visited on them. Finally, they explained simply, "We ask but for peace, liberty, and safety . . ." In return, they assured him, "Your royal authority over us, and our connection with Great Britain, we shall always carefully and zealously endeavor to support and maintain."

Even Dickinson himself, who was now ardently arguing for reconciliation, doubted the petition would be successful. "While we revere and love our mother country," he told his colleagues, "her sword is opening our veins." And so, while the delegates petitioned the king

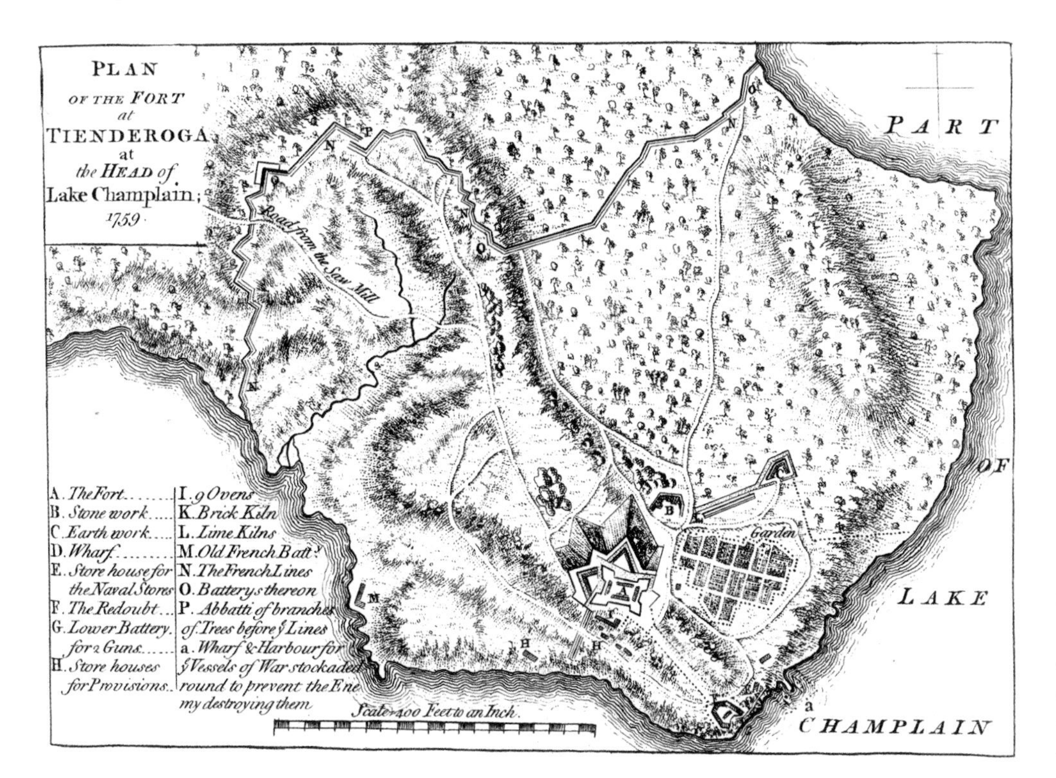

On the southwest bank *of Lake Champlain and close to the north end of Lake George, Fort Ticonderoga occupied a strategically critical point on the main route between Canada and the New England colonies.*

INSTRUMENTS OF BATTLE

Revolutionary-era firearm
A musket from Fort Ticonderoga

Powder horn
A powder horn from Fort Ticonderoga

Musket balls
Colonial musket balls with nails embedded in them

Snare drum
A drum believed to have been used at the Battle of Bunker Hill

Flintlock pistol
A 66-caliber smoothbore flintlock pistol made in Annapolis, Maryland, in the early days of the Revolution

Cartridge box and belt
A Revolutionary-era cartridge box and belt, worn at the soldier's right hip

Colonial sword
A saber from Fort Ticonderoga in New York

for peace, they prepared for war. In mid-June, they voted to form the Continental Army, whose soldiers would sign on for one-year enlistments and would join the 20,000-some troops then outside Boston. By a unanimous vote, they also appointed George Washington commander in chief of "all continental forces, raised, or to be raised, for the defense of American liberty." Washington would report directly to the Continental Congress.

With his military bearing and experience and quiet authority, Washington may have been an obvious choice for the congress—though other candidates had been considered—but Washington himself doubted that he had the experience to command an army. The French and Indian War he had fought in had been a wilderness campaign. This war would not be. Even more problematic, Washington's troops would be mostly inexperienced and untrained, a far cry from the seasoned British Regulars who had fought on his side before.

Soon after his appointment, Washington wrote his wife,

> I am now set down to write to you on a subject which fills me with inexpressable concern . . . It has been determined by Congress, that the whole Army raised for the defence of the American Cause shall be put under my care, and that it is necessary for me to proceed immediately to Boston to take upon me the Command of it. You may beleive me my dear Patcy, when I assure you, in the most solemn manner, that, so far from seeking this appointment I have used every endeavour in my power to avoid it . . . its being a trust too far great for my Capacity . . . But, as it has been a kind of destiny that has thrown me upon this Service, I shall hope that my undertaking of it, designd to answer some good purpose.

Washington now faced making an army of "a mixed multitude of people under very little discipline, order or government." That final word is telling: While the Continental Congress was available to coordinate measures, there was no real continental government, no treasury, no organization to field or ensure continued funding for an army. The current congress had voted two million dollars to finance the military, but how long would those funds last—and, indeed, how long might the war last?

Just two days after Washington's appointment, both Britain and the colonies got a taste of what lay ahead. Again, the setting was the Boston environs, where General Gage had been joined by three other seasoned major generals who would play prominent roles in the year ahead: William Howe, John Burgoyne, and Henry Clinton. With two armies now facing off, "We are every hour expecting an attack by land or water," wrote one Bostonian.

The battle lines began to form in mid-June, when the Americans learned that Gage planned to send a force to secure the heights on Charlestown Peninsula overlooking Boston. The colonial forces moved quickly to get there before the British. On the evening of June 16, a motley crew of willing men wearing homespun clothing (rather than uniforms) and carrying their own muskets and rations crossed to the peninsula and began digging fortifications

SOON AFTER *his questionable victory at the Battle of Bunker Hill, Gen. William Howe (1729–1814) was named commander in chief of the British forces in North America and remained so until 1778. His brother Richard was in charge of naval forces, but the two entertained doubts about the prospects for British victory against the Continentals.*

BELIEVED TO BE *the first portrait of George Washington, Charles Willson Peale's 1772 painting shows him in his Virginia militia colonel's uniform, a reminder of his service during the French and Indian War.*

on Breed's Hill rather than on the highest ground—the adjacent Bunker Hill. In truth, the colonists had no guns that would reach Boston no matter what hill they occupied.

As dawn broke on a clear summer day, the British stationed on ships in the Charles River spotted what the Americans were up to and began shelling. The ships' cannons could not range high enough to hit Breed's Hill, but the roar and reverberation of the cannonading unnerved the colonial forces, most of whom had no experience of battle at all. Some of the men melted away; others stood firm, as their commander, Col. William Prescott, encouraged them. The men had worked through the night to dig fortifications with the barest of hand tools. They were hungry, thirsty, and exhausted; they were also expecting to be reinforced at any time. Prescott said that wasn't going to happen because the few additional American troops on hand were needed to defend other positions.

By noon, all the might and splendor of empire was crossing the river toward the tired, hapless Americans: 28 barges aflame with redcoats, their bayonet-tipped muskets flashing in the sun. From the rooftops, steeples, and shorelines of Boston, the townsfolk watched the awesome spectacle unfold. One column of 1,100 men landed and marched to the foot of Breed's Hill, where

WASHINGTON TO HIS WIFE, MARTHA

PHILADELPHIA, JUNE 18TH, 1775.

My Dearest,

I am now set down to write to you on a subject which fills me with inexpressable concern—and this concern is greatly aggravated and Increased when I reflect on the uneasiness I know it will give you—It has been determined by Congress, that the whole Army raised for the defence of the American Cause shall be put under my care, and that it is necessary for me to proceed immediately to Boston to take upon me the Command of it. You may beleive me my dear Patcy, when I assure you, in the most solemn manner, that, so far from seeking this appointment I have used every endeavour in my power to avoid it, not only from my unwillingness to part with you and the Family, but from a consciousness of its being a trust too far great for my Capacity and that I should enjoy more real happiness and felicity in one month with you, at home, than I have the most distant prospect of reaping abroad, if my stay was to be Seven times Seven years. But, as it has been a kind of destiny that has thrown me upon this Service, I shall hope that my undertaking of it, designd to answer some good purpose . . . I shall rely therefore, confidently, on that Providence which has heretofore preservd, & been bountiful to me, not doubting but that I shall return safe to you in the fall . . .

IN THIS IDEALIZED EVOCATION, *George Washington takes command of spit-and-polish American troops at Cambridge in the summer of 1775. In truth, the forces he found when he arrived in Massachusetts were a largely untrained, ragtag local militia.*

they promptly halted, pulled hearty meals from their backpacks, and happily ate as the hungry American militiamen looked down on them. For many redcoats, it would be their last meal.

By 3:30, ships' cannon were pounding the peninsula. Soon, small, vulnerable Charlestown was flaming, and smoke rimmed the landscape. Dual British columns of about a thousand men each began a two-pronged attack, crossing the jumbled fields of the peninsula below Breed's Hill. The dug-in Americans held their fire under orders; Colonel Prescott may or may not have said, "Don't fire until you see the whites of their eyes," but that is what history has reported. The men were also told to target officers and to aim low. With little powder and lead, every shot had to count.

"As the enemy approached, our men was not only exposed to the attack of a very numerous musketry, but to the heavy fire of the battery on Corps-Hill, 4 or 5 men of war, several armed boats . . . and a number of field pieces," one militiaman later recorded in his diary. "Notwithstanding we within the intrenchment . . . sustained the enemy's attacks with great bravery and resolution."

When the British were just 150 feet away, the Americans opened up fire and tore through the advancing line. As it crumpled, redcoats soon "lay as thick as sheep in a fold." The British were ordered to retreat.

Neither the Americans nor the British could believe that the ragged colonists had repulsed the finest force in the world. But the battle was not yet won. With fresh reinforcements, the British advanced once again. By then the haggard Americans were down to one round of ammunition per man. Soon that was spent, and they were at the mercy of British bayonets as redcoats poured into their redoubt and hand-to-hand fighting took another bloody toll on both sides. The Americans who could escape made a haphazard withdrawal toward the neck of land that connected the peninsula to Cambridge.

Americans Send a Message

At day's end the British held Breed's Hill and Bunker Hill, but their casualties were staggering—half of the force, more than a thousand men. American casualties numbered over 400, almost a third of the force. The patriots may have lost the coveted high ground and ultimately the battle, but they had won a tremendous victory in prestige and morale.

The previous month, 74 British officers had marched to unexpected battle in Lexington and Concord, and some had been lost. After the Battle of Bunker Hill, less than half of the original 74 were fit enough to continue serving. "From an absurd and destructive confidence, carelessness or ignorance, we have lost a thousand of our best men and officers and have given the rebels great matter of triumph by showing them what mischief they can do us," one British officer wrote in a lamenting letter. As for the king, George was determined to teach the Americans a lesson. In July, he wrote to the first lord of the admiralty, "I am of the opinion that when once these rebels have felt a smart blow, they will submit; and no situation can ever change my fixed resolution, either to bring the colonies to due obedience to the legislature of the mother country or to cast them off!" That same month, the king's cabinet backed him up with an additional 2,000 troops to be dispatched to Boston at once: By the following spring, a British army of at least 20,000 men should be on American soil.

> *I am of the opinion that when once these rebels have felt a smart blow, they will submit.*
>
> King George III

Even as the British government leaped to war, an undercover French agent operating in London reported, "All sensible people in England are convinced that the English colonies are lost to the mother country, and that is my opinion too." The Americans themselves neither knew nor shared that opinion. They were up against an enemy that outweighed them in every way—experience, matériel, empire, sheer numbers, naval might . . . the list was endless, and the fear among the colonists real and ever present.

For the next months, while the British licked their wounds and prepared to move against the colonial rebels, George Washington worked to create a disciplined, professional army. He had arrived in Cambridge on July 2, when both sides were still recovering from the

A DETAIL FROM *a painting by famous Revolutionary artist John Trumbull (preceding pages) shows the death of Gen. Joseph Warren at the Battle of Bunker Hill. A Boston physician and leader of the patriots, Warren dispatched Paul Revere on his midnight ride and harassed the British line as it marched from Concord to Boston. His death became a rallying point for the colonial cause.*

battle two weeks earlier. The 43-year-old Virginian was one of the few experienced officers in America's arsenal, and he was a man committed to duty and honor. Those qualities, more than confidence, had led him to take up the daunting job before him.

Washington was accustomed to the stately and rarefied society of Virginia's tobacco planters—virtually an American aristocracy—and he was unimpressed with the New Englanders in the militia he found encamped around Boston. For that matter, neither were the British. New England, far more than any other region of America, did not make the kinds of class distinctions Washington was used to, and he complained of "an unaccountable kind of stupidity in the lower class of these people" but also "too generally among the officers of the Massachusetts *part* of the Army who are nearly all the same kidney with the Privates." Like it or not, this was the army he had, if not the one he wanted. Washington ordered a count and was told he had some 16,600 enlisted volunteers and noncommissioned officers under his command, and barely a true officer among them; almost all of the men were from Massachusetts.

The militia camps encircling Boston were dirty, undisciplined, and, to Washington's eye, wholly unmilitary. Setting to work to change that, he improved general camp conditions and imposed a military order on the behavior—and, more important, the minds—of the men. In late July he could report to a friend that "we mend every day."

THIS DRAWING SHOWS *the view from a British redoubt on Beacon Hill, with cannon and soldiers in the foreground. The caption identifies prominent features, such as the Mystic River, North Boston, and H.M.S.* Somerset *at anchor in Boston Harbor.*

Washington was only too aware that the British were just a stone's throw away, though the redcoats were suffering the ravages of a siege: boredom, lack of food, uncertainty. But the 7,000 Bostonians trapped in the city suffered as well. "It's hard to stay cooped up here

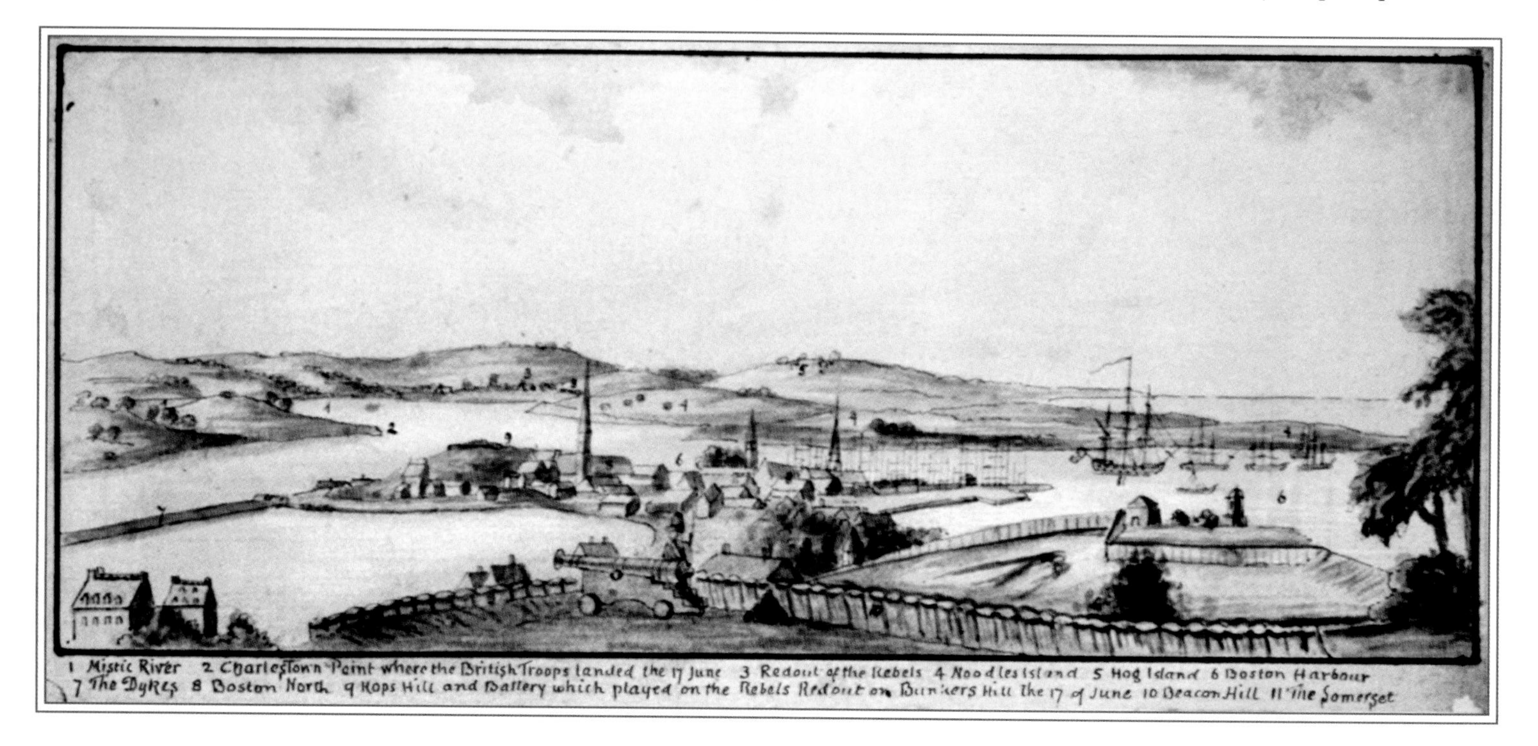

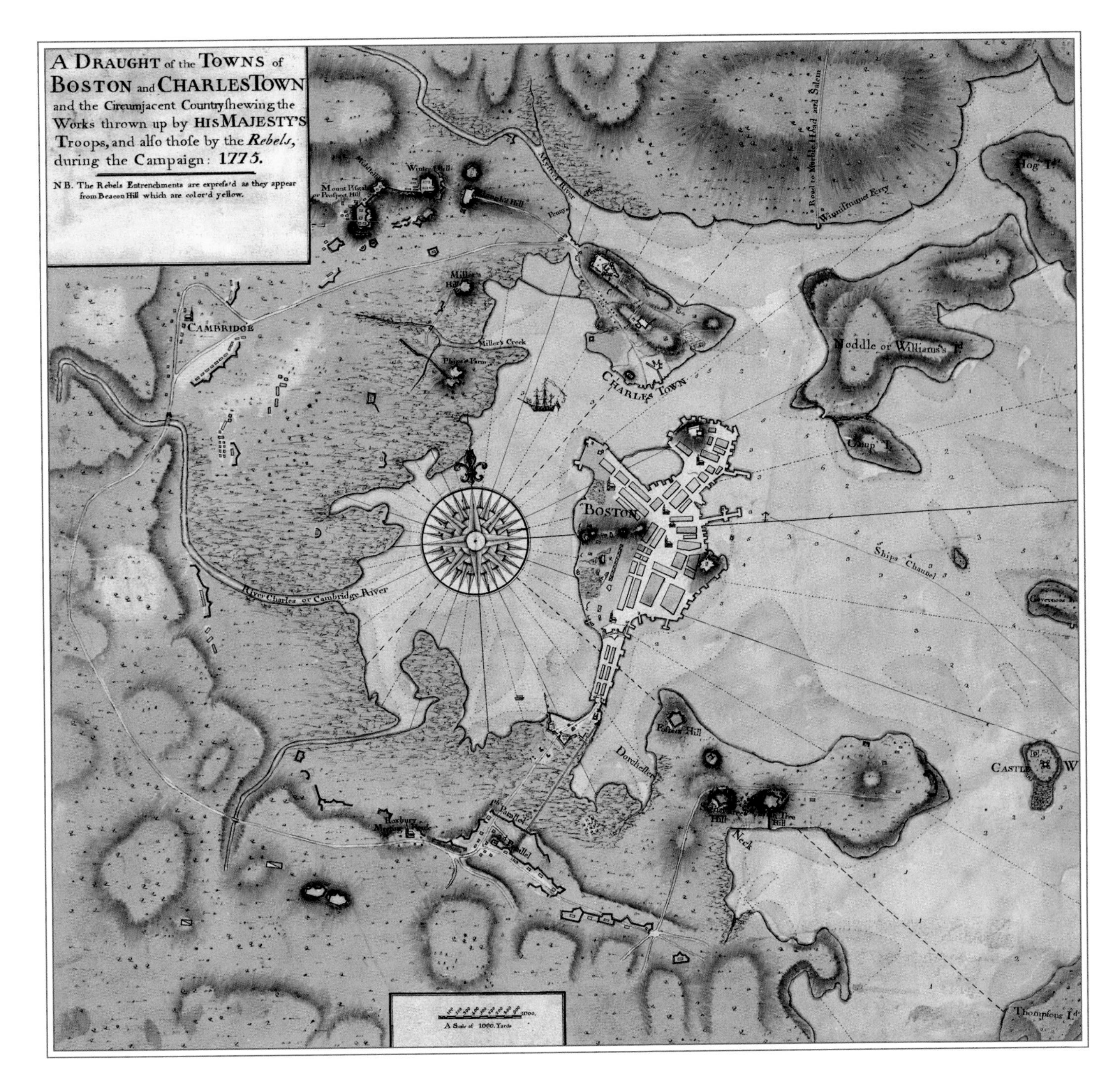
A DRAUGHT of the TOWNS of
BOSTON and CHARLESTOWN
and the Circumjacent Country ſhewing the
Works thrown up by HIS MAJESTY'S
Troops, and alſo thoſe by the *Rebels*,
during the Campaign: 1775.
N B. The Rebels Entrenchments are expreſs'd as they appear
from Beacon Hill which are color'd yellow.
CAMBRIDGE
Winter Hill
Miller's Hill
Miller's Creek
CHARLES TOWN
Noddle or Williams's I.
BOSTON
Ships Channel
River Charles or Cambridge River
Roxbury
Dorchester
Neck
Thompsons I.
A Scale of 1000 Yards

and feed upon salt provisions . . . pork and beans one day, and beans and pork another, and fish when we can catch it," one resident reported. Another man recorded repeated clashes, bombardments, and "very trying scenes" between the British and the Bostonians.

In other colonies the tensions between British authority and the polity had also reached a breaking point. Royal governors had fled their posts and left colonies without government of any kind. In Virginia, a third convention was convened to begin the process

CREATED BY *a loyal subject in 1775, this is described as "a draught of the towns of Boston and Charles Town and the circumjacent country shewing the works thrown up by His Majesty's troops, and also those by the rebels, during the campaign."*

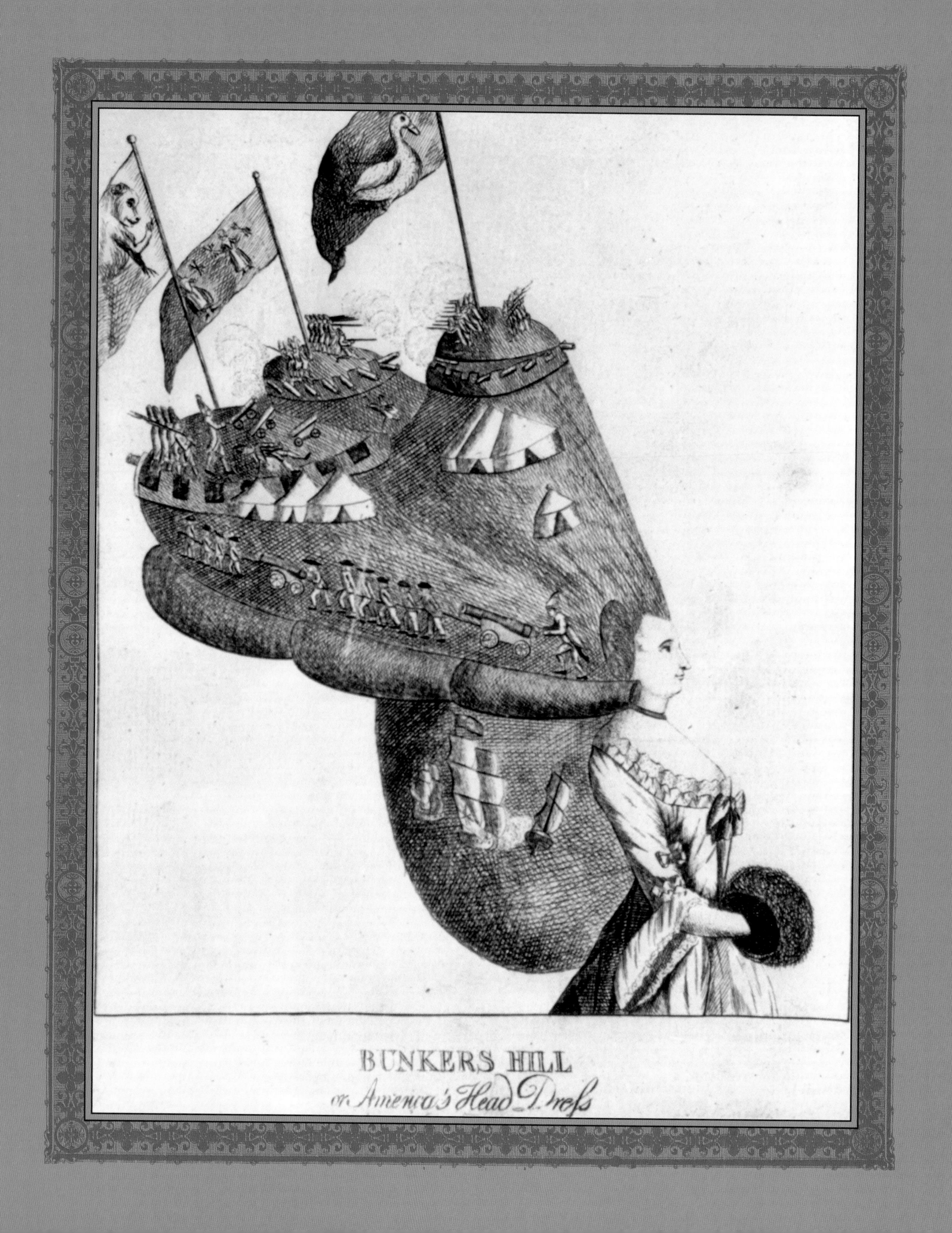
BUNKERS HILL
or America's Head-Dress

of establishing a new self-government. It was no easy task. "We are of as many different opinions as we are men, undoing one day, what we did the day before," one delegate lamented. George Mason, a northern Virginia planter, was the driving force behind many of the convention's final decisions, including preparing militarily by creating an army of defenders—some to remain as local militias, others to be sent to Washington for defense of the common cause.

Throughout the former colonies, these concerns of governance and defense loomed large, as they surely did in Philadelphia. In July Benjamin Franklin had presented the Continental Congress with a handwritten draft of what he called "articles of confederation," unifying the colonies enough to provide for a "common defense against their enemies" and the "security of their liberties and properties, the safety of their persons and families, and their mutual and general welfare." As Franklin had expected, his ideas for confederation were rejected, but they at least planted the seed of union. He did manage to convince his colleagues at the Continental Congress of the need for an intercolonial form of communication—a postal system. And to that end, he himself was given the newly created position of postmaster general. At least when it came to mail delivery, the former colonies were willing to unite.

Virginian George Mason *(above) exercised a profound influence on America's political philosophy both during and after the Revolution. A mentor to Thomas Jefferson, who called him "the wisest man of his generation," and a friend and neighbor of George Washington, Mason drafted the 1776 Virginia Declaration of Rights, which years later served as a template for the U.S. Bill of Rights. Opposite: Published in London after the Battle of Bunker Hill, this political cartoon shows a woman whose enormous headdress symbolizes the field of battle itself, with infantry and artillery firing at close range and a sea battle involving two or three ships.*

The 13 colonies had just come unglued from the mother country, and while they worked hard to maintain consensus for the common cause, they weren't ready to do more than that. After all, for a century or more they had been competitors, vying for economic and territorial advantage. Why should they now, suddenly, hitch their stars and fate together into this strange new thing called a confederation, especially while some of them were still hoping for rapprochement with Britain and a return to the grander, safer, more prosperous arms of empire?

That conflict between the old ways of security and tradition and the new, untested waters of independence must have been a constant source of personal tension for most 18th-century Americans. They could not conceive then of what the United States eventually would represent: freedom, hope, prosperity. In those troublesome days, Americans had two choices: look forward to war with the indomitable forces of Great Britain if they pushed their claims to the broader natural rights that Enlightenment thinkers preached, or have peace again if they bowed to the mother country's ultimate authority. And was not loyalty to king as important as these so-called natural rights of man? Some colonists chose one path, some the other. Among those loyal to the king, some gave up their American world and sailed for Britain. Among the almost half million who stayed, many became the eyes and ears of British forces—Tories, or Loyalists, working covertly and constantly to derail the patriots' cause.

THE KING STANDS FIRM

AS THE COLONISTS CONSIDERED THEIR WEIGHTY CHOICES DURING THE LONG SUMMER OF 1775, the king turned against the rebellious Americans once and for all. The Olive Branch Petition had reached London in late August and had been officially presented to the British secretary of state. The king refused even to consider the document and quickly proclaimed that the colonies had "proceeded to open and avowed rebellion, by arraying themselves in a hostile manner, to withstand the execution of the law, and traitorously preparing, ordering and levying war against us . . ."

Two months later, on October 26, George III paraded through the streets of the world's largest city in full monarchical splendor on his way to address the opening of Parliament. Some 60,000 people thronged his path, wishing His Majesty well. Standing before Parliament, the king succinctly focused on the American problem:

> The rebellious war now levied is become more general, and is manifestly carried on for the purpose of establishing an independent empire. I need not dwell upon the fatal effects of the success of such a plan. The object is too important, the spirit of the British nation too high, the resources with which God hath blessed her too numerous, to give up so many colonies which she has planted with great industry, nursed with great tenderness, encouraged with many commercial advantages, and protected and defended at much expence of blood and treasure.
>
> It is now become the part of wisdom, and (in its effects) of clemency, to put a speedy end to these disorders by the most decisive exertions. For this purpose, I have increased my naval establishment.

The might of empire was collecting against the puny resources of a few small, disparate colonies, and George Washington, still headquartered in Cambridge, knew it only too well. A New England winter lay ahead for his poorly equipped troops, and his pleas for more men and support had not been answered. With many of the current enlistments due to expire on December 31, it looked as if his ragged protoarmy might collapse before it took form. He desperately needed more recruits, but even if they appeared by the end of the year, Washington knew that he was attempting the impossible. "It is not in the pages of History . . . ," he wrote the Continental Congress, "to maintain a post within musket shot of the Enemy . . . and at the same time to disband one Army and recruit another . . ." Despite the odds, he kept at the task he had set himself:

To the Kings most excellent Majesty

Most gracious Sovereign,

We your Majesty's faithful subjects of the colonies of New-Hampshire, Massachusetts-bay, Rhode-island and Providence plantations, Connecticut, New-York, New-Jersey, Pennsylvania, the counties of New Castle Kent & Sussex on Delaware, Maryland, Virginia, North-Carolina and South Carolina in behalf of ourselves and the inhabitants of these colonies, who have deputed us to represent them in general Congress, entreat your Majesty's gracious attention to this our humble petition.

The union between our Mother country and these colonies, and the energy of mild and just government, produced benefits so remarkably important, and afforded such an assurance of their permanency and increase, that the wonder and envy of other nations were excited, while they beheld Great Britain rising to a power the most extraordinary the world had ever known.

Her rivals observing, that there was no probability of this happy connection being broken by civil dissentions, and apprehending its future effects if left any longer undisturbed, resolved to prevent her receiving such continual and formidable accessions of wealth and strength, by checking the growth

THE SO-CALLED *Olive Branch Petition, adopted by the Continental Congress in July 1775, was addressed to the "King's Most Excellent Majesty" and assured George III that the colonies were his "most faithful subjects" but asked him for "releif from our afflicting fears and jealousies" caused by "a new system of Statutes and regulations." George refused even to accept the petition.*

JOHN LOCKE
(1632-1704)

There could hardly be a greater contrast between people than between John Locke and Thomas Paine, and yet both left an indelible stamp on Western thinking and America's early ideas of itself. Locke preceded Paine by a century, and his writings must have had an influence on Paine. But while Paine was a dilettante and a flame thrower, Locke led a well-heeled, careful life as a medical doctor and political adviser, deeply involved in the mechanics of governing an empire and the machinations of political life in 17th-century Great Britain. In the midst of that, he managed to contemplate the overarching, timeless topics he's now remembered for: the nature of human understanding, the meaning of the self, and of natural rights versus the role of government.

Born to a Puritan father in 1632, John Locke entered a world in flux. Unassailable institutions were being assailed, and the unrest only grew as the Age of Enlightenment moved thinking beyond the centuries-old trust in faith and into a new era driven by science and rationality over spirituality. At the same time, the industrial revolution had begun to displace the rural agrarian life, and more and more people found themselves working in factories rather than on farms and living in cities instead of in the countryside.

As a young man, Locke spent 15

years in scholarship at Oxford, where he was exposed to the new experimental philosophy that extolled nature and experience over books as the keys to living. Locke finally settled on medicine as his field and eventually went to London as the family physician for Lord Anthony Ashley Cooper, the English chancellor of the exchequer. Once in Ashley Cooper's household, Locke moved beyond medicine and into governmental affairs, as he helped Cooper in the empire's colonial adventure. By the 1680s, as British politics began to boil again, Ashley, an outspoken opponent of absolute monarchy, was imprisoned twice in the Tower of London and released. In 1682 he fled to Holland, and Locke soon followed.

Amid all the turmoil and demands of those earlier years, Locke had been steadily, if sporadically, writing his great four-volume opus, *An Essay Concerning Human Understanding,* yet he never published a word of it until 1686, when he was in his mid-50s and in exile. The essay first appeared in an abridged form in a French magazine.

Locke had also written *Two Treatises of Government,* refuting the divine right of kings, which King James II vehemently asserted. His claim led to his demise in England's Glorious Revolution. James was deposed, William of Orange took the throne, and Locke, who may have worked surreptitiously in the campaign against James, returned to England on the royal yacht that bore William's queen, Mary.

Back in England, Locke continued to write and to expand his views on the nature of human thought and human rights. Today, he is heralded as the "father of classical liberalism," and his ideas echo through American ideals of freedom and morality: "I will faithfully pursue that happiness I propose to Myself . . . ," Locke wrote, "all innocent diversion and delights, as far as they will contribute to my health, and consist with my improvement, condition, and my other more solid pleasures of knowledge and reputation . . ." These were radical words for the 18th century but simple truths on the American horizon. ■

COLONEL ARNOLD.
Who Commanded the Provincial Troops sent against QUEBEC, through the Wilderness of Canada,
and was Wounded in Storming that City, under General Montgomery.

to create a professional "national" army that would be far more unified than an aggregation of colonial militias. And to add to his burden, he dutifully supported the invasion of British-held Quebec, as the Continental Congress had instructed.

In late August, American forces began their move north, setting out from Fort Ticonderoga and sailing up Lake Champlain. Both Ethan Allen and Benedict Arnold, heroes in the battle for the fort the previous spring, had lobbied for the invasion with the argument that the province of Quebec was poorly fortified and could easily be taken. If Quebec fell, the Americans hoped, they could bring the large French-Canadian population into the war on their side, or at least neutralize their sympathies. They also wanted to get rid of a British stronghold on their northern border.

The first leg of the American expedition laid siege to Montreal's critical Fort St. Johns in mid-September. By mid-November, the Continental forces were in control of Montreal. As enlistments expired, the Americans returned home, but the small contingent that was left behind began to move up the St. Lawrence River toward Quebec City and was joined by another regiment.

Notwithstanding all . . . obstacles, the officers and men, inspired and fired with the love of liberty and their country, pushed on.

BENEDICT ARNOLD

Meanwhile, in Massachusetts, the ever ambitious Benedict Arnold had successfully lobbied George Washington to send him out with a second invasion force that would approach Canada through the wilds of Maine via the Kennebec River. The going was tough, the river so shallow that the men often had to portage heavy bateaux and equipment across the swampy morass of central Maine. They lost food and powder to the river and suffered mightily from the cold and wet. "Every prospect of distress now came thundering on with a twofold rapidity," one man reported. Arnold himself, writing to the commander of the American force already in Canada, recounted the hardships his men had faced but proclaimed, "Notwithstanding all these obstacles, the officers and men, inspired and fired with the love of liberty and their country, pushed on."

By the time Arnold reached Canada, he had lost some 400 men in his force of over a thousand to desertion and the wilderness. Still, he was determined to continue with the mission. When he reached the Plains of Abraham on Quebec City's eastern edge, he called for the British to surrender. He also waited for reinforcements to arrive from the other American expeditionary force. When they did, the general leading them, Richard Montgomery, was more realistic than Arnold. Montgomery reported that, "The works of Quebeck are extremely extensive, and very capable of being defended." A siege was out of the question, though, because the poorly equipped Americans could never sustain it. Having come so far and battled the elements to get to Quebec, the Americans refused to give up, despite the city's defenses. As a blizzard pelted the dark early hours of December 31, the Americans attacked.

BENEDICT ARNOLD PROVED *himself a young officer of great valor and skill during the early years of the war, earning him the trust and respect of George Washington.*

"The Death *of General Montgomery at Quebec, December 31, 1775," is one of eight paintings in a famous series by John Trumbull, who served in the early years of the Revolution as aide-de-camp to George Washington and adjutant to Horatio Gates. After the war he consulted with John Adams and Thomas Jefferson about creating a series of images capturing great moments in the war.*

Montgomery fell quickly with a shot through his head, and Arnold took a bullet in the leg. After only a few short hours, it was over, with some 400 Americans held captive and the rest in retreat from the city. The Canadian campaign had been a valiant but ill-conceived failure.

In Virginia, though, the Continentals could claim a small but symbolic victory. After abandoning the capital of Williamsburg, Lord Dunmore had positioned himself in the port of Norfolk and encircled it with fortifications. In early December he had ordered a regiment to take out a strategic patriot stronghold at nearby Great Bridge. As at Breed's Hill, the Continentals held their fire until the British Regulars were within point-blank range. "I then saw the horrers of war in perfection; worse than can be imagin'd . . . ," one Virginian reported. "Limbs broke in 2 or 3 places; brains turned out. Good God, what a sight!" The successful Virginia commander was more sanguine; he reported to the Virginia Convention that "the victory was complete" and compared the Battle of Great Bridge to "a second Bunker's Hill affair, in miniature, with this difference, that we kept our post and had only one man wounded in the hand."

War With Words

As men across the colonies took up arms to fight the British, a new immigrant in Philadelphia took up his pen to wage war. Thomas Paine was 40 years old and had been in America only 14 months. An Englishman by birth, he had been, among other things, a maker of stays for corsets and a tax assessor. He had failed at all of his occupations, but he had great native intelligence and curiosity, a profound interest in Enlightenment ideas, and a key friend and supporter in Benjamin Franklin. Once in America, Paine was taken on as the editor of the *Pennsylvania Magazine,* an entertaining, all-purpose magazine like others of the day. But such fluff didn't satisfy Paine's intellect, and in the fall of 1775 he began drafting a history of the relationship between the colonies and the mother country.

Paine's ideas were treasonous, heretical, inspiring, and expressed in a prose that dispensed with the ornateness of the day. Anyone could understand his proposition that every man had rights, while monarchies did not: "Government by kings was first introduced into the world by the Heathens . . . It was the most prosperous invention the Devil ever set on foot for the promotion of idolatry." Paine's rant against kings, aristocrats, and government in general urged his readers to action:

"The cause of America is, in a great measure, the cause of all mankind . . .

"O ye that love mankind! Ye that dare oppose, not only the tyranny, but the tyrant, stand forth!"

This was treason, and it was a new approach to the old conflict. It attacked the king and the very idea of Britain, and even in America, it pushed the limits of public sentiment. Some printers refused to produce Paine's lengthy pamphlet, but finally, as the troubles of 1775 gave way to 1776, his *Common Sense* "burst from the press with an effect which has rarely been produced by types and papers in any age or country," Paine's friend and publishing agent, Dr. Benjamin Rush, exclaimed. The thousand copies that initially appeared were soon gone, and thousands more were printed in America and abroad. John Adams reported that *Common Sense* was received in France and in all of Europe with rapture. Thomas Paine, the new immigrant, had given voice to America. He had explained what its struggle meant—and what the success of that struggle could mean—to mankind.

A British cartoon *shows Thomas Paine holding a scroll of his writings, with his ideas on the rights of man arcing above his head. Such ideas and Paine's ability to convey them to the common man helped spark Revolutionary zeal in Americans.*

By the end of 1776, between 150,000 and 200,000 copies of *Common Sense* had been sold, and the former colonies had followed Paine's clarion call, daring "to oppose tyranny and the tyrant." Their opposition had almost crushed them, body and soul. If Paine had been the man who fired that year of foment, George Washington was the man who saw it through to its bitter but hopeful end.

of Man

Thomas Paine
(1737-1809)

WHATEVER QUALITIES DEFINE A FOUNDING FATHER in the minds of many Americans, Thomas Paine probably lacked most of them. He was, according to one acquaintance, "coarse and uncouth in his manners, loathsome in his appearance, and a disgusting egotist . . ." The ever acerbic John Adams was particularly fulsome in his disgust with Paine, calling him "a mongrel between pig and puppy, begotten by a wild boar on a bitch wolf." And yet this "mongrel" gave voice to the essence of what America wanted for itself and could not yet articulate. Without the pen of Thomas Paine, would the former colonists have been roused to revolution, and would they, in the "times that try men's souls," have persevered with their cause? We'll never know, but even Adams grudgingly acknowledged that his era could be called the Age of Paine.

If Thomas Pain (as his surname was spelled at birth) was a mongrel, it was only owing to his parents' different religions—his father a Quaker, his mother an Anglican who raised her only son to be one as well. The boy was born and grew up in Thetford, Norfolk, where his father, Joseph, made a small living as a farmer and a maker of stays for women's corsets. Maybe because he was an only child, Tom was indulged with some formal schooling. That ended when he was 13 and became his father's apprentice. About three years later, he made his first attempt to run away to sea, but his father intervened and managed to keep him on land. History has Joseph Pain to thank for the pen that fueled the Revolution because the ship young Tom had planned to sail on was attacked by a French privateer and most of its crew was lost.

COMMON SENSE;
ADDRESSED TO THE
INHABITANTS
OF
AMERICA,
On the following interesting
SUBJECTS.
I. Of the Origin and Design of Government in general, with concise Remarks on the English Constitution.
II. Of Monarchy and Hereditary Succession.
III. Thoughts on the present State of American Affairs.
IV. Of the present Ability of America, with some miscellaneous Reflections.
Written by an ENGLISHMAN.
By Thomas Paine
Man knows no Master save creating HEAVEN,
Or those whom choice and common good ordain.
THOMSON.
PHILADELPHIA, Printed
And Sold by R. BELL, in Third-Street, 1776.

THOMAS PAINE *(opposite) wrote* Common Sense *at the end of 1775. It was widely read in 1776, establishing the newly arrived British immigrant as the scribe of the Revolution.*

Thomas did not return to Thetford but instead found a stay-making position in London, a city that immediately captivated him. The Enlightenment was in full bloom, nourished in part by "invisible colleges"—loose associations of intellectuals enthralled by the new age of science and natural philosophy and an appreciation for the common man and an unadorned style of expression—"a close, naked, natural way of speaking . . . preferring the language of Artisans, Countrymen, and Merchants, before that, of Wits and Scholars." Pain most likely frequented St. Paul's Coffee House and its Club of Honest Whigs, whose members included such luminaries as philosopher Joseph Priestley and inventor Benjamin Franklin. The backbone of Pain's own philosophy and writing style was probably set in those brief formative years in London.

Pain managed to eke out a living in London on stay making and on a nest egg he had received for briefly serving as a crewman on an English privateering ship. By 1758 his money was gone, and he left London behind for Dover. For the next 16 years, struggling to make a living, Pain failed in one endeavor after another. He went in and out of stay making and customs work—the latter an odd choice given what lay ahead for him. The public disliked excise men—customs assessors—for their general corruptness, and smugglers openly attacked them. Pain lasted less than a year his first time around, but he managed to get reinstated, and it was during his second stint in the job that he had a moment presaging his future. Britain's excise men, united in their troubles, planned to petition Parliament for better salaries, and in 1772 Pain wrote his first notable pamphlet, arguing their cause in prose so plain but forceful that his fellow excise men sent him to London to present his petition, *The Case of the Officers of Excise*, to Parliament. And there he waited two years, with no results.

By 1774 Pain had lost his job, he was in debt, and his second marriage (his first wife had died) had apparently disintegrated. He and his wife separated, and he booked passage to America. As Pain explained it, "I happened when a schoolboy to pick up a pleasing natural history of Virginia, and my inclination from that day of seeing the western side of the Atlantic never left me."

By the time his ship docked in Philadelphia in December 1774, Thomas Pain, another struggling aspirant hoping to reclaim his future in the New World, was near death from typhus. He was 39 and had failed at virtually everything he had ever attempted. He did have one saving grace, though: a letter of introduction from his London friend Benjamin Franklin, who extolled him as "an ingenious worthy young man." With that as collateral, a local doctor cared for Pain and nursed him back to health.

That turn in Pain's luck foreshadowed his American life. He very soon had a job as executive editor of the fledgling *Pennsylvania Magazine*, whose mission, according to Pain, was to provide its readers with "utility and entertainment." This, Pain found, he was good at, and both the magazine and its editor flourished for several months.

RIGHTS OF MAN:
BEING AN
ANSWER TO MR. BURKE'S ATTACK
ON THE
FRENCH REVOLUTION.
PART I.
BY
T. PAINE,
AUTHOR OF
COMMON SENSE,
LETTER TO THE ABBE RAYNAL, &c. &c.
LONDON:
PRINTED FOR J. PARSONS, No. 21, PATER-NOSTER ROW:
OF WHOM MAY BE HAD, THE SECOND PART OF THE SAME WORK, AND "COMMON SENSE," PRICE SIX-PENCE EACH.
1792.
[PRICE SIX-PENCE.]

THOMAS PAINE *wrote* Rights of Man *in response to a treatise on the French Revolution by his friend, Parliamentarian Edmund Burke. Opposite: A British cartoon lampoons "Tommy Paine, the little American Taylor, taking the Measure of the Crown for a new Pair of Revolution-Breeches."*

The magazine's owner, Robert Aitken, later recalled that Pain's genius was fueled by brandy: "He would never write without that." According to Aitken, Pain had three glasses when he set down to write. "When he had swallowed the third glass," continued Aitken, "he wrote with great rapidity, intelligence and precision; and his ideas appeared to flow faster than he could commit to paper."

But Pain was not content to write easily digestible entertainment for long, and his natural inclination to champion a cause soon overcame him. He added his own diatribe against slavery to the magazine mix. It was an indictment of both the practice and its practitioners: "Our Traders in MEN (*an unnatural commodity!*) must know the wickedness of the SLAVE-TRADE, if they attend to reasoning, or the dictates of their own hearts: and such as shun and stiffle all these, wilfully sacrifice Conscience, and the character of integrity to that golden idol." Pain's fiery prose inspired the first abolitionist society to take form in Philadelphia in April 1775, but it also chilled his relations with Aitken. That didn't stop Pain. Throughout the ensuing months of 1775, he added his own bombshells to the magazine—essays on slavery and on the erupting tensions between the colonies and the great enemy, Britain, which had "lost sight of the limits of humanity."

Humbly dedicated to the Jacobine Clubs of France & England!!!
"These are your Gods, O, Israel!"
Pubd May 23th 1791, by H. Humphrey No. 18, Old Bond Street
"Fathom & a half! Fathom & a half! Poor Tom!"
ah! mercy upon me! that's more by half than my poor Measure will ever be able to reach! - Lord! Lord! I wish I had a bit of the Stay-tape or Buckram which I yous't to Cabbage when I was prentice, to lengthen it out; — well, well, who could ever have thought it, that I, who have served Seven Years as an Apprentice, & afterwards worked Four Years as a Journeyman to a Master Taylor, then follow'd the business of an Exciseman as much longer, should not be able to take the dimensions of this Bauble!" for what is a Crown but a Bauble? which we may see in the Tower for Six-pence a piece? - well, altho' it may be too large for a Taylor to take Measure of, there's one Comfort, he may make mouths at it & call it as many names as he pleases! - and yet, Lord, Lord, I should like to make it a Yankee doodle Night Cap & Breeches, if it was not so damn'd large, or I had stuff enough. Ah! if I could once do that, I would soon stitch up the mouth of that Barnacled Edmund from making of any more Reflections upon the Flints — & so Flints & Liberty for ever — & damn the Dungs
Vive la Liberte
"THE RIGHTS OF MAN; — or TOMMY PAINE, the little American Taylor, taking the Measure of the CROWN, for a new Pair of Revolution-Breeches.

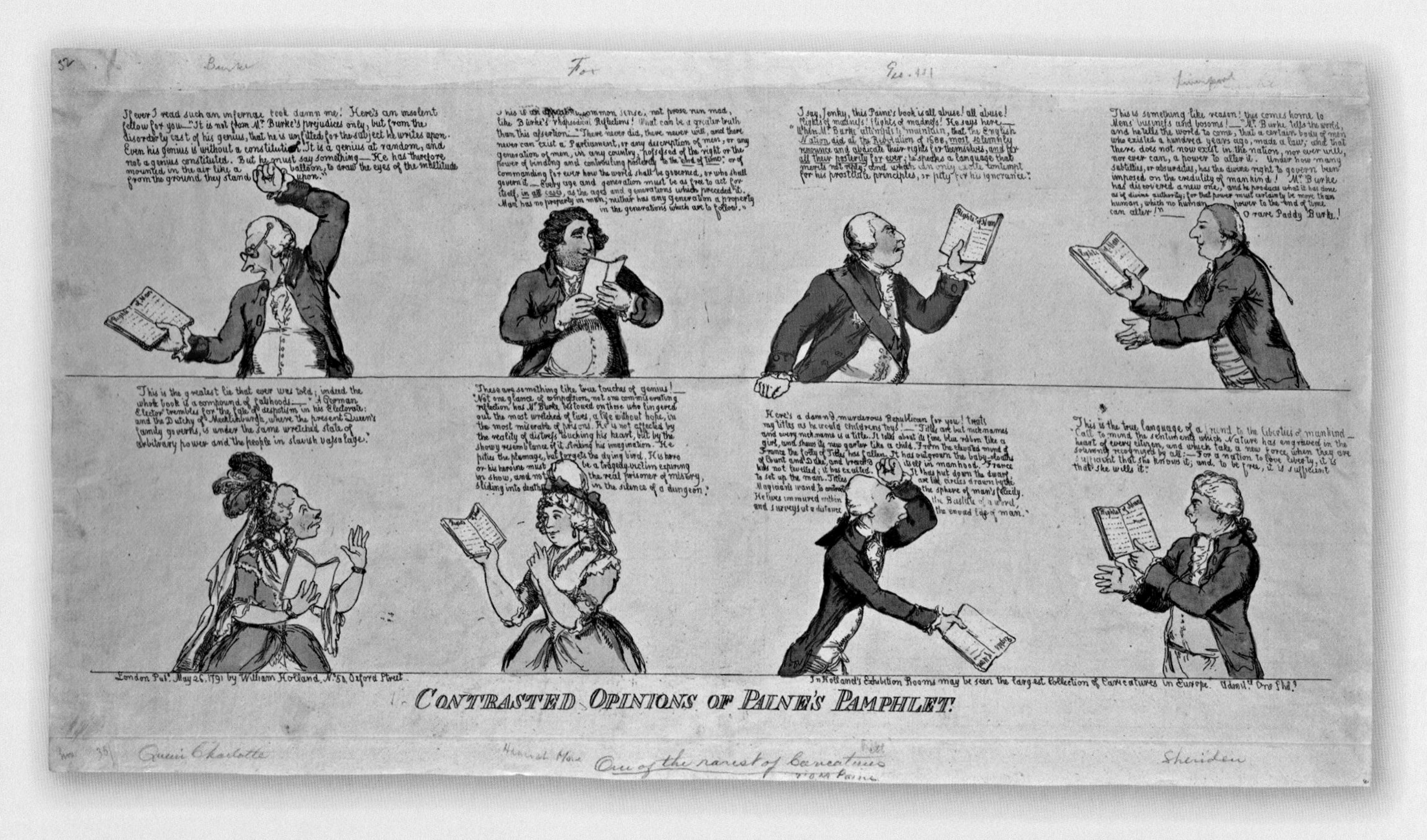

CARICATURES OF WELL-KNOWN *personalities, such as Edmund Burke (top row, left), reacting to Paine's* Rights of Man

Well positioned in Philadelphia, Pain was at the heart of political foment as the Second Continental Congress deliberated and reports of battles poured in. At some point he began work on a piece that he originally called *Plain Truth* but later, at the behest of his well-placed friend, Dr. Benjamin Rush, changed to *Common Sense*. Benjamin Franklin was also involved, and he offered Pain "such materials as were in his hands towards completing a history of the present transactions" in the conflict between Britain and the colonies. With that auspicious backing and his own need to hold forth, Pain worked away, knowing his words would infuriate the government. But the British were not his audience. The Americans of his newfound country were. Later in life, Pain would explain, "When the country into which I had just set my foot was set on fire about my ears, it was time to stir. Those who had been long settled had something to defend; those who had just come had something to pursue; and the call and the concern was equal and universal. For in a country wherein all men were once adventurers, the difference of a few years in their arrival could make none in their rights."

In *Common Sense,* Pain set out in prose an articulation of those rights, so clear that all readers could find inspiration: "The cause of America is, in a great measure, the cause of all mankind," he proclaimed, and then went on to assert that "government even in its best state is but a necessary evil in its worst state an intolerable one . . . Government, like dress, is the badge of lost innocence; the palaces of kings are built on the ruins of the bowers of paradise." Pain argued vehemently against kings and aristocracies and for republics. His long, winding arguments invoked biblical history and even laid out, in figures, America's military condition versus that of Britain.

In his lengthy tract, Pain was at times lofty, at other times lawyerly, but his prose always held conviction and authority and, not infrequently, prophecy:

> Youth is the seed-time of good habits, as well in nations as in individuals. It might be difficult, if not impossible, to form the Continent into one government half a century hence. The vast variety of interests, occasioned by an increase of trade and population, would create confusion. Colony would be against colony . . . The intimacy which is contracted in infancy, and the friendship which is formed in misfortune, are, of all others, the most lasting and unalterable. Our present union is marked with both these characters: we are young, and we have been distressed; but our concord hath withstood our troubles, and fixes a memorable area for posterity to glory in.

Pain's ideas voiced a fresh, new approach to the old conflict, and Pain and his friend Dr. Rush were determined to send it forth. Rush undertook to find a printer, and he was turned down again and again. Finally, he found a willing Scot who cut a hard deal financially but had a thousand copies ready on January 10, 1776.

Common Sense changed both Pain's life and the course of history. Americans were captivated and inspired, as was much of the Western world. "The light which that performance threw upon the subject," Pain wrote, "gave a turn to the politics of America which enabled her to stand her ground. Independence followed in six months after it, although before it was published it was a dangerous doctrine to speak of."

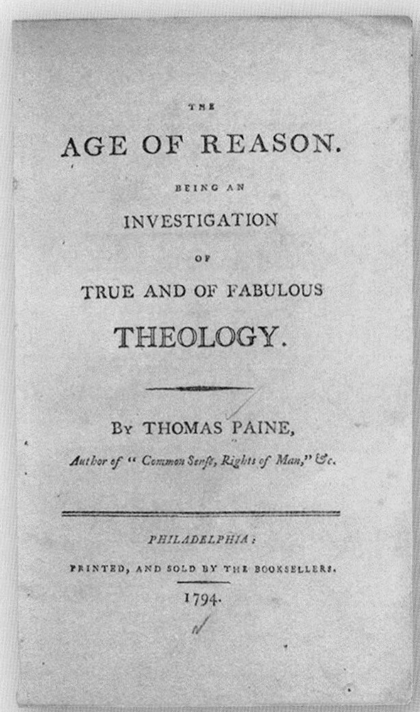

To some pious Americans, *Paine's* Age of Reason *was the "atheist's bible."*

Pain now added an *e* to his name and became an ardent patriot. He wanted his earnings from *Common Sense* donated to the Continental Army for mittens, and in the bitter, downtrodden fall of 1776 he himself joined the army as an aide to Washington. He was brave, but he lacked the discipline to be a good soldier and soon went back to his true skill—writing. He first composed an ardent essay that became part of a collection he called *The American Crisis.* "These are the times that try men's souls," Paine began. "The summer soldier and the sunshine patriot will, in this crisis, shrink from the service of their country; but he that stands by it now, deserves the love and thanks of man and woman." The pamphlet was published and quickly made its way to George Washington. As the sun sank in the winter sky on December 23, the commander ordered it read to his dwindling army. Two days later, when they attacked the enemy in Trenton, the Americans let loose with their battle cry, "*These* are the times that try men's souls."

Paine continued his *Crisis* essays through much of the war, but the high point was in the collection's earliest moments. His outspokenness at times got him in trouble, and he found himself enmeshed in colonial scandals. Near war's end he spent some time in France, where he was a great celebrity. Years later, the French Revolution inspired him to write *Rights of Man,* and that in turn inspired thousands of people. But his *Age of Reason* earned him 11 months in a Parisian prison in 1793. Even there, he continued to write, among other things, an open letter to George Washington. Paine was bitter that America and Washington, then President of the new nation, had not come to his rescue, and he excoriated his former hero as a "doing nothing" general and an elitist leader. Washington's reputation in America did not suffer, but Paine's never recovered.

Still, in 1802, Thomas Paine returned to America. Virtually penniless, he settled on a farm he had been given by the state of New York not far from Manhattan. A few years later he moved to the city itself, where he died in 1809. "I have no marked place," Paine had said in the early days of the American Revolution. "I am neither a farmer, mechanic, merchant nor shopkeeper. I believe, however, I am of the first class. I am a *farmer of thoughts,* and all the crops I raise I give away."

CHAPTER
3

All men are by nature equally free and independent and have certain inherent rights . . . the enjoyment of life and liberty.

Virginia Declaration of Rights

1776
Times That Try Men's Souls

As 1776 opened, Washington was still working to make an army out of a hodgepodge of untrained, undisciplined farmers and tradesmen. Most of them were independent-minded New Englanders who had come with their local militias to support the siege of Boston. Their lack of military training was palpable and, to Washington, appalling. But lack of experienced manpower was only part of Washington's problem. He also had precious little armament or gunpowder for his army. "The reflection upon my situation and that of this army produces many an uneasy hour when all around me are wrapped in sleep," he confided in a personal letter as the New England January dragged on. "Few people know the predicament we are in."

The one critical weapon the protoarmy had was Washington himself. When he made his appearance among the men, "Joy was visible on every countenance, and it seemed as if the spirit of conquest breathed through the whole army," Nathanael Greene reported. A Rhode Island volunteer, the 33-year-old Quaker had catapulted to brigadier general in Washington's army, though he had no military training. For that matter, he probably had no uniform. Most of the men did not, and in order to keep some

A popular legend *says that deep in the woods near the Valley Forge camp in Pennsylvania George Washington made a solemn prayer for the safety of his men and the future of his nation. Preceding pages: Emanuel Leutze's iconic image of George Washington crossing the frigid waters of the Delaware River on Christmas Day, 1776* sort of order, Washington had devised a makeshift way to distinguish at least officers from enlisted men: colored insignia. As a brigadier general, Greene's would have been a pink ribbon across his chest.

At least Greene had that insignia of rank. The British military governor and commander, Thomas Gage, had lost his when he had been recalled to Britain after the defeats at Bunker and Breed's Hills. Now the British forces were in the hands of Sir William Howe, a slow-to-act but courageous military man with a taste for the pleasures of a good table and beautiful women (whether they were other men's wives or not). While his men suffered every kind of privation during that winter under siege—from little food to bitter weather and a lack of firewood for warmth—the 44-year-old Howe apparently enjoyed himself, particularly in the company of Elizabeth Loring, who, with her husband, Joshua, were among the Loyalists ensconced in British-held Boston. Howe had fought in the French and Indian War; he generally liked Americans and seemed disinclined to prosecute a war against them, though he had valiantly and personally led the charge at the Battle of Bunker Hill. But he later called that clash "a dear bought victory" and predicted that "another such would ruin us." And so Howe bode his time during the winter of 1776 and generally ignored the dictates of the war ministry in London: to evacuate Boston and move his troops to New York. In reality, he didn't have the ships to accomplish that, but he also flatly responded with "a better policy." He wanted to "withdraw entirely from the delinquent provinces and leave the colonists to war with each other for sovereignty."

A group of *German mercenaries prepare to travel from Hesse to America to fight for the British. These soldiers, called Hessians, were recruited by King George III to bolster his army.*

Howe wasn't the only Briton with that opinion. Others in Parliament and elsewhere had argued forcibly against war with the American colonies, sure that it was a terrible mistake. "We are fighting for the subjection, the unconditional submission of a country infinitely more extended than our own . . ." the Lord Mayor of London had argued. "Should we not succeed . . . the grandeur of the British empire [will] pass away."

Cooler heads in Great Britain understood that prosecuting a war an ocean away, on wild and foreign terrain, posed immense difficulties that the might of empire did little to mitigate. First, how would they supply, feed, and maintain an army 3,000 miles from the homeland? And how would they communicate effectively with it? In the 18th century, that communication would be carried by ships that moved at the fickle mercy of wind and weather. Every directive could take weeks to arrive, and even within the American theater, communiqués among commanders could be passed only as quickly as horses or ships could carry them. And then, of course, the Americans would be fighting on home territory and would know how to maneuver in it far better than the British, with their more cumbersome, formal military style.

Despite these problems, George III was determined to subjugate the rebellious Americans and teach them their place. He had the navy to do it—the most impressive in the world—but he needed to bolster his army for an oversees war, and he did it with an additional 30,000 German mercenaries, rented on the cheap from German states that needed money and offered up their soldiers for profit. Since most of the Germans were from the principalities of Hesse-Cassel and Hesse-Hanau, they all came to be called Hessians. Some in Parliament protested the use of mercenaries. One member warned the king, "[W]hen the colonies come to understand that Great Britain is forming alliances, and hiring foreign troops for their destruction, they may think they are well justified by the example, in endeavoring to avail themselves of the like assistance; and that France, Spain, Prussia, or other powers of Europe may conceive that they have as good a right as Hesse, Brunswick, and Hanau to interfere in our domestic quarrels."

As the war progressed, other European powers were indeed drawn into the North American war, with a good deal of persuading by the Americans. But in that first year of the Revolution, Washington was essentially on his own and virtually—but not quite—without a plan. Over the course of the summer and fall, he had become friends with Henry Knox, a rotund young Boston bookseller who had led troops during the Bunker Hill battle. Since then, Knox and his wife had abandoned their business and home in British-held Boston, and the young man had devoted his energies to the Continental Army. On December 5 Washington dispatched Knox to Fort Ticonderoga, probably at Knox's own urging, to retrieve the fort's much-needed artillery and to bring it back to Boston.

Most of Washington's advisers considered the plan ill-advised, if not downright impossible, but Knox was determined. Accompanied only by his 19-year-old brother, William, and a servant named Miller, he traveled the 300 miles to Ticonderoga in four days. With the help of American forces at the fort, Knox disassembled 43 heavy brass and iron cannons, some smaller mortars, and two howitzers and prepared them for the winter trek back to Boston. He expected to make the

Henry Knox

1750–1806

Henry Knox was not a small man. It is said he weighed more than 300 pounds, but his legacy loomed even larger because of his contributions to the Revolutionary War. Born in Boston, Knox had always wanted a career in the military. He enlisted in the local company at 18 and went on to a successful career. He became a major general in the Continental Army and most notably led the successful mission to transport heavy artillery from Fort Ticonderoga to Boston. Knox took part in most of the major battles of the War for Independence and became a close friend and adviser to George Washington. After Washington became President, Knox became his secretary of war and remained in that position throughout Washington's Presidency.

return trip in two weeks—a serious underestimate, as he soon learned. At virtually every step the weather thwarted his small band. After negotiating Lake Champlain, the expedition portaged the heavy artillery overland to Lake George, where some of the men had to row the armament through a raw gale before finally reaching Fort George at the southern end of the lake. Once there, Knox wrote ahead to a local farmer for help: "I must beg that you would purchase or get made immediately 40 good strong sleds that will each be able to carry a long cannon clear from dragging on the ground and which will weigh 5400 pounds each & likewise that you would procure oxen or horses as you shall judge most proper to drag them."

OVERCOMING UNCOOPERATIVE WEATHER, *Henry Knox and his men successfully moved 43 heavy cannon, smaller mortars, and 2 howitzers 300 miles from Fort Ticonderoga to Boston. Relying on sleds to move them over the Green Mountains, the mission took more than two months to complete.*

Within the week, Knox had everything he needed, except the snow that would ease the sleds' way. On December 17 he had written to Washington, "It is not easy to conceive the difficulties we have had," but, he wrote, he hoped "in 16 or 17 days to be able to present your Excellency a noble train of artillery." Now that hope would be forestalled.

Not until Christmas Day did snow fall, and then there was so much of it that it made for hard going. Knox and his men resolutely pressed on, their noble train plowing its own roads through the fresh snow. For a week, sleds transported the mass of artillery back and forth between Fort George and the shores of the Hudson in the south. Then the weather foiled them again. Knox had counted on the Hudson being frozen to a depth that would support the heavy-laden sleds, but it was not. He set to work cutting holes in the ice, so that river water would come through the ice, spread over the already-frozen surface, and gradually thicken the mantle. When he finally risked the crossing, he lost two big cannons to the Hudson, but "were so lucky as to get the [one] Cannon out of the River, owing to the assistance the good people of the City of Albany gave."

On the far side of the Hudson, the winter-wrapped Berkshires and the entire length of Massachusetts lay ahead. Knox's expedition covered the distance in two and a half weeks. Finally, on January 24, 1776, he presented Washington with his noble train. It had taken Knox almost two months to accomplish his herculean task, but he had done it.

Word of Knox's success spread quickly through the army camps, and the men could feel things shifting, activity increasing. At last they had more than sheer determination to fight their cause; they had serious artillery. They also had impressive fortifications, dug at Washington's command. In a letter to a friend, the British general Burgoyne, still pinned down by the siege, had written, "[T]he country near Boston—it is all fortification. Driven from one hill you will see the enemy retrenched upon the next and every step we move must be the slow step of a siege." The hills that the Americans held were critical positions, but without heavy artillery, they were virtually useless. They needed something that would allow them to fire down on the British in the town and harbor below, and now they had it. "Great activity and animation are observed among our officers and soldiers who manifest an anxious desire to have a conflict with the enemy," one American reported.

Since the previous summer the enemy had grown to a force of 7,000 to 8,000, but the Continental troops had been reinforced as well, and they now outnumbered the British two to one.

By February Washington had a strategy in place, and he appealed to his motley army to follow his lead. "Our worthy commander in chief (in orders a day or two past) has in the

Drawn by *a British soldier in the early months of 1776, this map details Boston Harbor and the damage done to Charlestown, which was burned by the American colonists on January 8. The British would be forced to evacuate the city after George Washington captured Dorchester Heights in March 1776.*

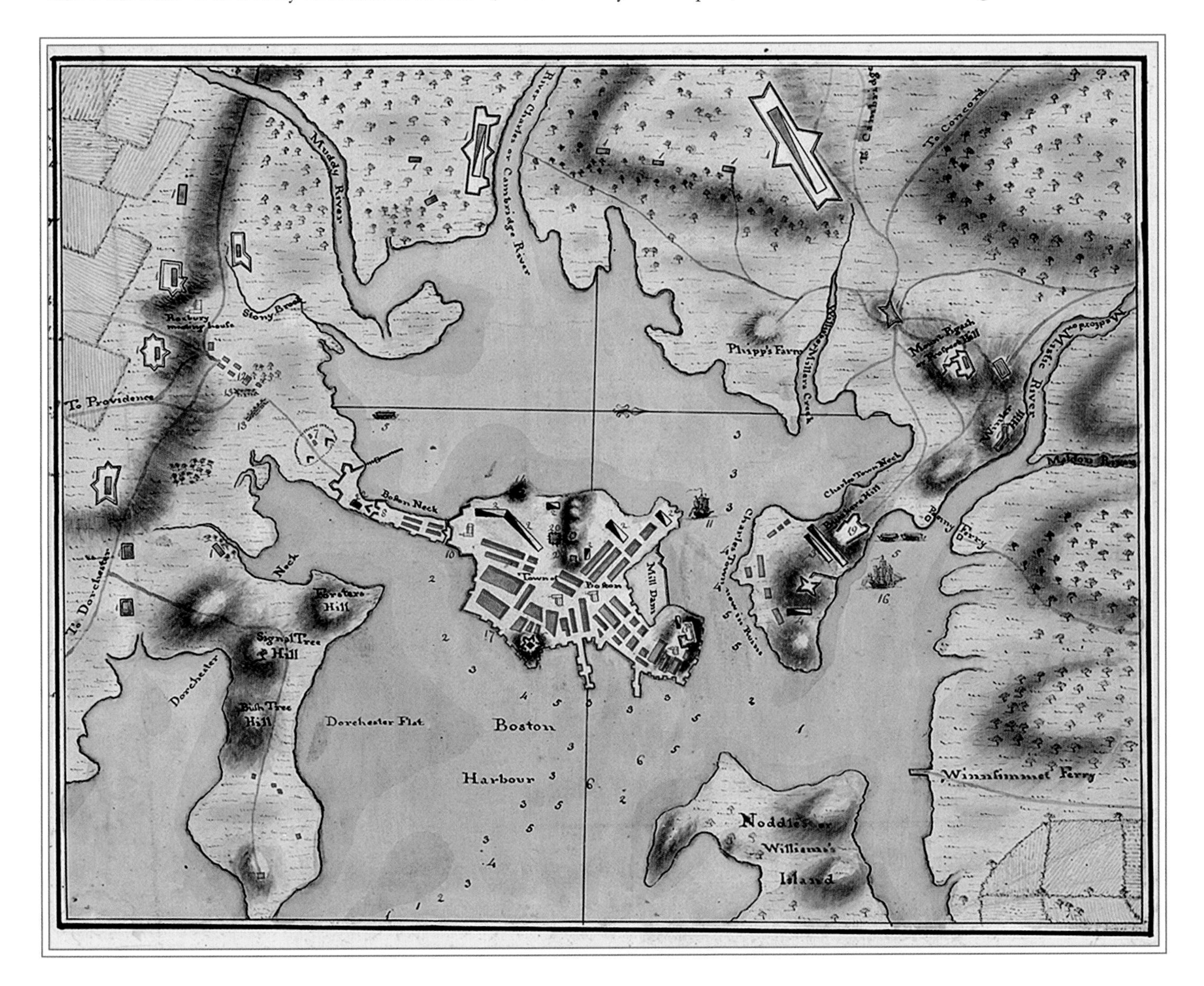

most pathetic terms told the soldiery that on our present conduct depends the salvation of America . . . ," a lieutenant wrote in his journal on March 1, and "he is confident his troops will behave as deserves the cause we are contending for." In fact, Washington may not have felt a great deal of confidence, but the time to attack had come. On March 2, Washington began a heavy bombardment of Boston, and the British replied until the sky was lit with "sheets of fire." The townspeople cowered under the heavy fire, "particularly the women, who were several times driven from their houses by shot, and crying for protection."

The American bombardment was intended not as an attack but as a diversion from what was going on south of town, where Knox's hard-won artillery was being positioned on Dorchester Heights. The wheels of the wagons transporting the artillery and the portable, prefabricated entrenchments were covered in straw to deaden their rumbling. Once on the heights, a force of some 2,000 men worked through the night to create entrenchments. By dawn on March 5, the sixth anniversary of the Boston Massacre, the American position was virtually impregnable, to the utter amazement of the British. One British engineer called it "a most astonishing nights work, and must have employed from 15 to 20,000 men." In fact, the Americans had only a few thousand men on the heights, but they were doing all they could to mislead the British into believing the patriots were stronger than they were, including painting logs black and positioning them as if they were cannons.

We were in high spirits, well prepared to receive the threatened attack.

ARTIST JOHN TRUMBULL

BRITISH EVACUATE BOSTON

GENERAL HOWE, HIS REPUTATION ON THE LINE, DECIDED TO ATTACK WHEN NIGHT FELL, a move most of his officers felt was suicidal. Howe had been ordered to abandon Boston and had planned to do so, but he would not be bested by Washington's band of rebels. From their perch on the heights, the Americans watched the bustle of redcoats along the shoreline of Boston. The sight must have been reminiscent of the previous summer, as the British, in all their finery, had rowed forward to retake the hills above Charlestown. This time, though, the Americans were operating as a professional army instead of a jumble of haphazard, ill-equipped units. "We were in high spirits, well prepared to receive the threatened attack," artist John Trumbull, watching from the heights, later recorded.

Sometime during the afternoon, as the British boats began to cross the harbor, the mild weather turned, and by night the area was in the grip of a virtual hurricane, with "so high a wind . . . that it was impossible for boats to take to sea." Howe's planned attack was called off, and instead the British prepared to evacuate, moving in a quick chaos. Afraid that Howe's men would torch the town when they left, some of the town's selectmen petitioned Howe "that the town might not be burnt; the General made the answer that if the enemy molested

MOUNTING CANNON *and the other heavy artillery procured by Henry Knox on the hills of Dorchester Heights allowed George Washington's forces to end the British siege of Boston in March 1776.*

GEN. WILLIAM HOWE, *the commander of the British forces in Boston, ordered his troops to evacuate after his plans to retake Dorchester Heights were thwarted by a snowstorm. On March 17 the British forces sailed for Halifax, Nova Scotia.*

him in his retreat he would certainly burn it; if not, he would leave the town standing."

Washington held his fire, even as the British plundered the town's shops and homes, took what they wanted, and destroyed what they thought could be useful to the Americans if left behind. To the British soldiers and sailors, the town had been a prison, and this was their revenge. They felt the same disdain for Bostonians that Bostonians felt for them, but they surely no longer felt quite the disdain for the enemy forces they had felt earlier. The spring before, a British surgeon had described the American forces around Boston as "truly nothing but a drunken, canting, lying, praying, hypocritical rabble, with no order, subjection, discipline, or cleanliness." He had predicted that the Continental Army would "fall to pieces of itself in the course of three months, notwithstanding every endeavour of their leaders . . ." Three months had long past, and now the British were in retreat before the American "rabble."

THE CONTINENTAL ARMY'S *morale was boosted by the victory in Boston, but General Washington knew that continued challenges lay ahead in creating a fighting force out of men whose sectional rivalries threatened their national unity.*

On St. Patrick's Day the redcoats finally vacated Boston, though it would take another ten days before they sailed out of sight. The Regulars headed toward Halifax, where Howe could re-provision. Boston's long ordeal was at an end. For several years, the town had borne the brunt of English ire and occupation and had given back to the British as good as it had gotten. Defiantly, the Sons of Liberty had pressed the cause of freedom, and the empire had pressed down on them at every turn. The revolution had been seeded along its New England shores, and now, after the first bruising battles, the war moved on.

Washington, untested until then, had become the hero of the hour, and through the colonies Americans cheered him on. Washington had no illusions that the triumph would last, but he took a moment to revel in what he had managed to accomplish in nine months. Writing to his cousin and confidante Lund Washington, he dispensed with his public cloak of modesty: "I believe I may, with great truth, affirm that no man perhaps since the institution of armies ever commanded one under more difficult circumstances than I have done."

Anticipating Howe's next move, the Continental forces moved toward New York in early April. Marching south and west through the New England countryside, the army paraded past enthusiastic villagers and farmers waving them on toward victory. "I am a good deal tired of marching," one young lieutenant wrote to his wife, "though we get good entertainment in general. People are very kind to us."

One of the problems in those early days of the Continental Army was the mutual dislike that the New Englanders and Southerners, though marching side by side, felt for each other. Sectionalism threatened Washington's hard efforts to create a true fighting force, and in the coming months he issued a General Order that expressed his concern in poignant

CONTINENTAL UNIFORMS

Officer's hat
An American officer's cocked hat, commonly worn in the 18th century

Mitre cap
Embroidered mitre cap, worn by the Governors Foot Guard of Connecticut, circa 1774

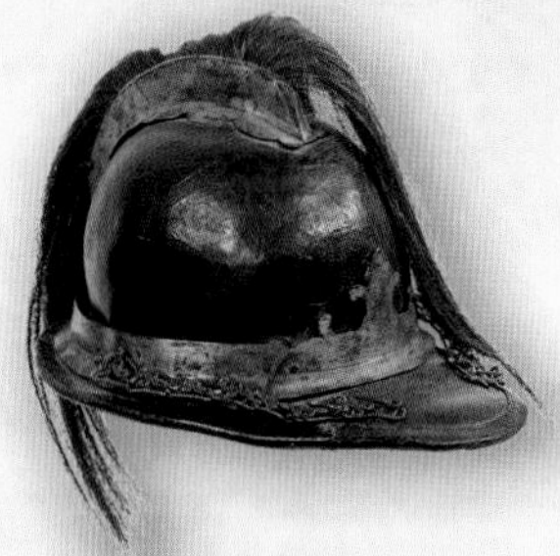

Leather helmet
American Light Dragoon helmet made of heavy leather with brass trimmings and horsehair crest

Tricorner hat
The triangular-style hat, popular during the 18th century

Minute-Men's uniform
Regimental coat, which belonged to Lt. Col. Benjamin Holden of Col. Ephraim Doolittle's Minute-Men's Regiment

Waistcoat
Striped linen waistcoat worn by Lt. Col. William Ledyard of the Connecticut Militia

Regimental coat
Continental Army uniform coat worn by Col. Peter Gansevoort, Jr., of the Third Regiment of the New York Continental Line

Drinking vessel
A wooden canteen used by a New Jersey soldier

Rifle gear
Belt with powder horn, carried by an American rifleman

language: "Jealousies &c are arisen among the troops from the different Provinces . . . which can only tend to irritate each other, and injure the noble cause in which we are engaged, and which we ought to support with one hand and one heart. The General most earnestly entreats the officers, and soldiers, to consider the consequences, that they can no way assist our cruel enemies more effectually, than making division among ourselves . . ." Whatever disdain Washington himself had initially felt for the New Englanders had passed as he had come to appreciate their stoic heroism, and as his own identity had shifted. He was no longer an aristocratic southern planter but the commander of a national army.

AMERICAN DIPLOMAT SILAS DEANE *(right) went to France to seek foreign aid for the colonists. There Baron de Kalb (center), a German-born French soldier who served as a general in the Continental Army, introduced him to the Marquis de Lafayette.*

The delegates to the Continental Congress were also gradually moving beyond sectional jealousies and suspicions and beginning to understand that they were responsible for forming the government of a new nation, with all that implied. Ben Franklin, ever the pragmatist, had been charged with assessing the army's exact needs and had gone with two other delegates to visit George Washington in Cambridge the previous fall. Together with Washington, this "secret committee" determined precisely what each member of the army would need per week in provisions, from meat and salt fish to flour, soap, and candles. Then the group made a monthly and yearly estimate of the total cost, as well as a calculation of exactly how many troops Washington needed: 20,372. With that figure in hand, Franklin contacted his pro-American friends in Britain and offered a simple calculation for the British to consider: "Britain, at the expense of three millions, has killed 150 Yankees this campaign, which is 20,000£ a head; and at Bunker's Hill she gained a mile of ground, half of which she lost again . . . During the same time 60,000 children have been born in America." Extrapolating from this, Franklin assured his friend it would be easy to "calculate the time and expense necessary to kill us all, and conquer our whole territory."

While Franklin offered his backdoor inducements to end the conflict, the Continental Congress began an official quest for allies. The search started with France. In early March a Connecticut merchant and former delegate to the congress, Silas Deane, had been dispatched to Paris to negotiate secretly for aid. Even before Deane's arrival, Louis XVI and his ministers were carefully weighing and analyzing the American situation. The Americans had a powerful ally in the French foreign minister, Count de Vergennes, who had been pressing the reluctant young king to provide the Continentals with support. What better way to bolster trade and to weaken Britain, France's old enemy, than to help the former 13 colonies break free of the empire? And it was clear that would not happen without foreign help. After some hesitation, the French decided to funnel money and munitions to the Americans, but only through a bogus trading company, so that the British would have no cause to label France an official ally of America.

When Deane at last arrived in Paris, he became a player in this financial setup, but Deane had neither the subtlety nor the organization to pull it off cleanly, and the entire enterprise became a muddle. In the years to come, Deane's questionable bookkeeping and diplomacy created hard feelings and scandal for him and others. But in the summer of 1776, the foreign funds that filtered through his hands kept the American cause afloat. The Spanish, believing that a prolonged war would weaken its enemies, matched the French monies with their own million-livres equivalent.

During the spring and summer of 1776 America gradually moved from an idea to a reality—a nation with allies and a true, united sense of itself. Just a few months earlier, in January, Thomas Paine's call for the "free and independent states of america" had seemed radical, but by spring, the colonies individually began to repudiate their allegiance to the crown. The idea of independence had infiltrated the American imagination. In late May, delegates to the Fifth Virginia Convention adopted its Declaration of Rights, which boldly asserted, "All men are by nature equally free and independent and have certain inherent rights, of which, when they enter into a state of society, they cannot, by any compact, deprive or divest their posterity; namely, the enjoyment of life and liberty, with the means of acquiring and possessing property, and pursuing and obtaining happiness and safety."

Richard Henry Lee *(1732–1794) was a delegate to the Second Continental Congress who proposed in 1776 that the colonies should be independent from Great Britain, his most famous political contribution.*

The Declaration of Independence

In Philadelphia the Continental Congress was poised to act too. On June 7 Virginia's Richard Henry Lee introduced three resolutions: "That these United Colonies are, and of right ought to be, free and independent States, that they are absolved from all allegiance to the British Crown, and that all political connection between them and the State of Great Britain is, and ought to be, totally dissolved; That it is expedient forthwith to take the most effectual measures for forming foreign Alliances; and That a plan of confederation be prepared and transmitted to the respective Colonies." In the debate that followed, it became clear that the middle states were "not yet ripe for bidding adieu to the British connection but they were fast ripening . . ." To give them time to ripen, the congress decided to delay a vote on the resolution until July 1 and in the meantime appointed three committees to prepare a tentative declaration of independence, articles of confederation, and a plan for making treaties with foreign powers.

The declaration committee represented a mix of temperaments and regions—John

Adams (Massachusetts), Roger Sherman (Connecticut), Robert Livingston (New York), Benjamin Franklin (Pennsylvania, one of the "unripe" colonies), and Thomas Jefferson (Virginia). Since some of the other members had assignments they felt were more important and Franklin was bedridden and suffering from gout, the 33-year-old Jefferson, who "had the reputation of a masterly pen," was given the task of writing the document, even though he too had hoped to spend the summer differently—in Virginia, helping to draft his own state's new constitution. Many years later, Adams contended that he had graciously passed the assignment on to Jefferson because he was a Virginian, "and a Virginian ought to appear at the head of this business." Also, Adams admitted, he, Adams, was "obnoxious, suspected, and unpopular."

Outwardly, Jefferson bore a small, superficial resemblance to his older fellow Virginian, George Washington. Both were tall redheads who towered above others, at six two or thereabouts. And both were planters used to the rarefied air of the Virginia aristocracy, an aristocracy so pronounced that one Philadelphia observer had called its members to the First Continental Congress "the haughty sultans of the South." But where Washington was a robust, athletic man—a dancer, horseman, and military man—Jefferson was willowy, reserved, and intellectual. Jefferson knew the works of Enlightenment philosophers like Locke and scientific pioneers like Newton, and he pulled their ideas into his composition. In the second-floor rooms he had rented on Market Street, working through Philadelphia's heat and humidity, Jefferson composed on a lap desk he had designed. He also drew on the Virginia Declaration of Rights, whose primary author, George Mason, he considered "the wisest man of his generation." At times Jefferson's prose soared; at others he built, in good 18th-century style, a legalistic argument against kings who become tyrants and thereby "dissolve all ties of allegiance between themselves and their people."

Yes, we must, indeed, all hang together, or most assuredly we shall all hang separately.

BENJAMIN FRANKLIN

Once he had a draft he was satisfied with, Jefferson sent it to Adams, who made a few small changes. It was passed next to Franklin, with the ornate request that he "suggest such alterations as his enlarged view of the subject will dictate." Franklin obliged with his own relatively minor changes, mostly in phrasing. The document was then ready to be considered by the congress.

BENJAMIN FRANKLIN, JOHN ADAMS, *and Thomas Jefferson worked closely together to draft the United States' Declaration of Independence. Jefferson wrote the bulk of the document, while Franklin and Adams provided crucial edits before the document was presented to the Continental Congress in July 1776.*

On July 2 the delegates first voted on Richard Henry Lee's resolution for independence, and it passed with the endorsement of 12 colonies; New York abstained and finally voted approval on July 15. Then the congress turned its attention to Jefferson's draft declaration and, to his dismay, condensed the final five paragraphs, ultimately making the document stronger but distressing its author in the process.

On July 4 the Continental Congress adopted the 1,817-word Declaration of Independence,

and a Philadelphia print shop quickly created broadsides that riders carried through the colonies. On July 8 church bells rang out in celebration of the newly declared independence, and Jefferson's words rang out in public gatherings:

> When in the Course of human events, it becomes necessary for one people to dissolve the political bands which have connected them with another, and to assume among the powers of the earth, the separate and equal station to which the Laws of Nature and of Nature's God entitle them, a decent respect to the opinions of mankind requires that they should declare the causes which impel them to the separation.
>
> We hold these truths to be self-evident, that all men are created equal, that they are endowed by their Creator with certain unalienable Rights, that among these are Life, Liberty and the pursuit of Happiness . . .

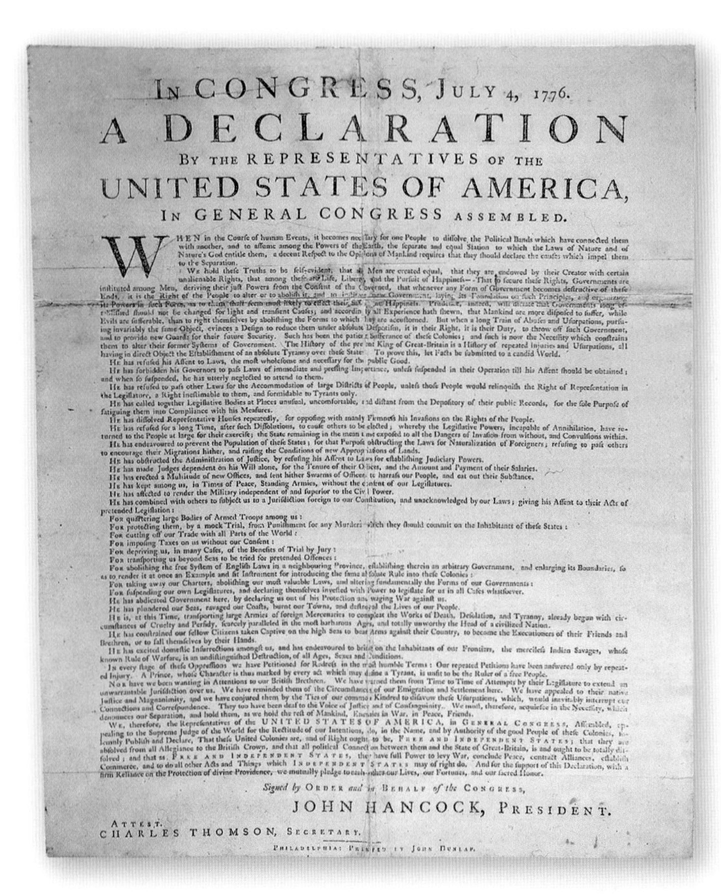

IN CONGRESS, JULY 4, 1776.
A DECLARATION
BY THE REPRESENTATIVES OF THE
UNITED STATES OF AMERICA,
IN GENERAL CONGRESS ASSEMBLED.

Signed by ORDER and in BEHALF of the CONGRESS,
JOHN HANCOCK, PRESIDENT.
ATTEST.
CHARLES THOMSON, SECRETARY.
PHILADELPHIA: PRINTED BY JOHN DUNLAP.

THOMAS JEFFERSON DRAFTED *the Declaration of Independence in June 1776. After revisions, it was officially adopted by the Continental Congress on July 4, 1776. This cherished document broke the bonds of the colonies from England and grew to be a towering symbol of individual liberty and freedom.*

The news of independence reached Washington's army in New York on July 6, and the city erupted in celebration. Three days later, following a request from John Hancock, the Continental brigades were marched onto parade grounds in the early evening, and at six o'clock the declaration was read aloud throughout the city, along with a personal statement from the commander in chief: "The general hopes this important event will serve as a fresh incentive to every officer and soldier to act with fidelity and courage, as knowing that now the peace and safety of his country depends (under God) solely on the success of our arms."

An official version of the declaration was embossed on parchment, and on August 2 those members of the Continental Congress still in Philadelphia met for the signing. Not all who had voted for it were on hand, and some who hadn't voted were present. In all, 56 members put their names to the document. Signing began with the President of the Continental Congress, whose florid "John Hancock" became legendary. "We must all hang together," Hancock advised, to which Franklin reportedly added, "Yes, we must, indeed, all hang together, or most assuredly we shall all hang separately." They were now, publicly and irreversibly, enemies of the empire they had until so recently embraced. "We are in the very midst of a revolution," John Adams proclaimed, "the most complete, unexpected and remarkable of any in the history of nations."

Word of the Declaration of Independence reached Europe in August and helped bolster French support for the revolution. "If the resistance of the Americans is successful," wrote one French minister, "this memorable epoch will reduce England to a point where she will

To celebrate the Declaration of Independence a mob pulls down an equestrian statue of King George III in New York City on July 9, 1776.

no longer cause disquietude to France, whose consideration on the Continent will increase in proportion to the enfeeblement of the British Empire." But in 1776 the empire was far from enfeebled. It could claim 11 million souls to America's 2.5 million, a fifth of whom were enslaved black people. Still, in the summer of 1776, the fragile Continental forces had successfully held off a British attack on the critical port city of Charles Town, South Carolina. Could Washington hold off Howe as well when the moment came?

At almost the same time the Continental Congress had been voting for independence, a large British force had been putting ashore on Staten Island. In the month that followed, more and more ships arrived from South Carolina and Halifax, England, and disgorged troops in wave after red wave. Two ships, their captains unperturbed by the cannons firing from American batteries, even sailed up the Hudson as far as the Tappan Zee. By mid-August His Majesty had a force of some 32,000 ready to face off against Washington's divided force, dug in on the south end of York Island (Manhattan) and across the East River on nearby Brooklyn Heights.

To the British soldiers who had endured the hostile Bostonians and the privations of siege, the New York posting was almost luxurious. The redcoats were "amongst a loyal and liberal people," who were anxious to sell the king's army fresh meat, butter, eggs, milk, and vegetables. Gen. William Howe was still at the head of that army, and his brother, Adm.

JOHN TRUMBULL'S famous painting "Declaration of Independence" (1817) (preceding pages) measures 12 by 18 feet and hangs today in the Capitol Rotunda in Washington, D.C.

Richard Howe, was at the helm of the royal fleet now parading in New York waters. Both Howes wanted decisive action that would end the hostilities once and for all, yet neither felt great enmity toward the Americans. The admiral had even sent an emissary with a conciliatory letter addressed to George Washington. Since it had no acknowledgment of his rank as general, the letter was refused, but the emissary kept trying. Finally, Washington met with him. Describing the encounter to his wife, Henry Knox said, "After a considerable deal of talk about the disposition of Lord and General Howe, he [the emissary] asked, Has your Excellency no particular commands which you would please to honour me to Lord and General Howe?" "Nothing, sir, but my particular compliments to both," was Washington's laconic reply, which Knox called "a good answer."

Neither cowed nor confused, Washington had commanded the situation. It was harder to exercise as firm a command over his troops. During the summer, reinforcements had poured into his army, but camp fever and desertions had also taken a toll. And any day now the British would attack.

BATTLE OF BROOKLYN

ON AUGUST 22, IN THE GRAY LIGHT OF PRE-MORNING, THE REDCOATS BEGAN THEIR MOVE, first landing 4,000 of their best troops at Gravesend, on the southwestern shore of Long Island. Soon 90 British ships crowded into the Narrows, and by noon General Howe had

PREPARING FOR AN attack on the American forces in New York, the British Fleet of Lord Howe sails inland on the Narrows between Long Island and Staten Island, July 12, 1776.

With the American forces *in disarray, General Howe was able to land 20,000 of his men on Long Island in August 1776 with no opposition from colonial forces.*

a force of 15,000 men and accompanying artillery on Long Island, south of Brooklyn Heights. As they proceeded north, they met virtually no resistance. "The whole guard had fled without firing a gun," Brig. Gen. Samuel Parsons later reported to John Adams. The Continental Army was in complete disarray, and the scant intelligence Washington received underestimated the number of troops the British had landed. Washington worried that the move on Brooklyn could be a bluff, and that Manhattan was the true target.

A fierce wind kept Howe's ships from sailing up the East River when the tide was right, and the attack suddenly stalled. Washington's divided forces waited, some in their positions on lower Manhattan and the rest across the river in Brooklyn.

By August 26 Howe had 20,000 men on Long Island; Washington had less than half that, and they were inexperienced, undisciplined, and poorly positioned along a six-mile line. Some were holding the ridgetop spine that runs through Brooklyn; others were scattered through the rough, thickly wooded country below. That night the British quietly moved forward, pouring through a vital pass in the ridge that had been left unguarded and, in a flanking maneuver, getting behind Washington's forces on the heights. Hoping to distract the enemy, the British in front of the line attacked, and the Americans answered, giving "fair fire" and holding their position. But at about nine in the morning of August 27, cannonading at the American rear signaled what the British had managed to accomplish. The Americans were surrounded, but they "fought with more than Roman valor," one Continental soldier later reported, even after their left flank collapsed.

At some point that morning Washington had more troops rowed over to Brooklyn and joined them himself. Men reported him exhorting the troops to "quit yourselves like men, like soldiers." Despite the odds, many of the Continental regiments battled on for hours, until retreat became their only recourse. "It is impossible for me to describe the confusion and horror," one private said of his retreat through a marsh. "Some of them [the men] were mired and crying to their fellows for God's sakes to help them out. But every man was intent on his own safety."

For six hours the fighting went on, with the Americans losing ground, hemmed in, and unable to escape Brooklyn. A northeast wind pushed into New York Harbor and drenched both sides in a chilly downpour, and the sound of cannonading combined with the pitch of the storm. Miserable and even more vulnerable, the fighting men now found their ammunition drenched and virtually unusable. The Americans had had no food and little sleep, and yet on the night of August 29, the men were told to have their packs ready and to be prepared to launch an attack. The orders were a feint. After conferring with his inner council, Washington now planned a retreat across the East River to lower Manhattan. It was almost an act of hubris, "to move so large a body of troops, with all their necessary apendages, across a river full a mile wide, with a rapid current, in face of a victorious well-disciplined army nearly three times as numerous." But in an impressive hush, boatload after boatload pushed off from the Brooklyn ferry landing and crossed the river. As if on cue, the wind had died and quieted the chop. At dawn a heavy fog rose from the river and blanketed the men still waiting to be ferried across. By the time it had lifted, the British found the Americans gone.

Washington had lost some 1,300 men—about 300 killed, the rest taken prisoner. Howe had suffered fewer than 400 losses but had failed to press his advantage. "Far from taking the rash solution of . . . crushing at once a frightened, trembling enemy, he generously gave them time to recover their panic, to through up fresh works, to make new arrangements,

and to recover the torpid state the rebellion appeared in from its late shock," the British commander of one of the warships in the harbor recorded disdainfully—though he also reported the "indignation" of the British troops at the sight of "rebel's standards" waving "insolently in the air from many different quarters of New York."

Washington felt anything but insolent after the disastrous Battle of Brooklyn. On August 31 he wrote to the Continental Congress and apologized for belatedly informing them of his "removal of the Troops from Long Island and its dependencies to this City, the night before last." He explained that "the extreme fatigue, which myself and family have undergone (as much from the Weather as any thing else) since the incampment of the 27th. rendered me entirely unfit to take a pen in hand. Since Monday, we have scarce any of us been out of the Lines, till our passage across the East River was effected yesterday Morning, and for the 48 hours preceeding that; I had hardly been off my horse and had never closed my Eyes, so that I was quite unfit to write or dictate till this Morning."

On September 2 Washington wrote again to warn, "Our situation is truly distressing. The Check our Detachment sustained on the 27th. Ulto. has dispirited too great a proportion of our Troops and filled their minds with apprehension and dispair. The Militia, instead of calling forth their utmost efforts to a brave and manly opposition, in order to repair our

AFTER BEING DEFEATED *at the Battle of Long Island, George Washington and the Continental Army retreated south through New Jersey and Pennsylvania.*

DESPITE FIGHTING BRAVELY *(opposite), American forces lost the Battle of Long Island. The British scored a major victory and secured control of New York City on August 27, 1776.*

GAZETTEER

Losses, are dismayed, Intractable and Impatient to return. Great numbers of them have gone off, in some instances almost by whole Regiments, by half ones and by Companies at a Time." He warned that he might have to abandon the city, and in that case, he asked, should he burn it (as he wanted) to keep the British from using it for winter quarters? He also argued for a longer enlistment period and suggested land, rather than more money, as an incentive for a more permanent enlistment. He ended by saying he had estimated his force at 20,000 after the battle, but since then desertions had lowered that number.

While Washington deliberated his meager options, one of his generals, John Sullivan, who had been taken prisoner, was dispatched by Admiral Howe with his own message to the Continental Congress. The admiral, Sullivan reported, was "desirous of an accommodation with America." After some debate, the congress appointed John Adams, Edward Rutledge of South Carolina, and Benjamin Franklin to visit the admiral, "ask a few Questions and take [his] Answers." Franklin and Lord Howe had been friends during Franklin's London years, but the war had chilled their friendship. Still, Franklin, far more than the other two, understood British subtleties.

Sir William Howe

1729–1814

One of three brothers with distinguished military careers, Sir William Howe was a British army officer with a career that had a series of highs and lows. Entering the British army at age 17, Howe eventually rose to command the British forces during the American Revolution. Howe arrived in North America in 1775 and led the British to victory in the Battle of Bunker Hill. After this triumph, Howe became commander of the British forces and captured both New York City and Philadelphia. But military setbacks in the following years dimmed the lights of Howe's career. He resigned his post as commander in 1778 and returned to England.

As he and Adams traveled north together to New York, they found themselves moving with a tide of mid-Atlantic refugees who expected the fighting would begin to edge south and were anxious to get out of harm's way. The inns were crowded, and en route, Franklin and Adams had to share a "chamber little larger than the bed"—as well as the bed itself, not unusual in those days. Adams, who had been ill, closed the window against the night. Franklin objected and proceeded to offer his own scientific "harangue," as Adams described it, "upon air and cold and respiration and perspiration."

At the meeting with Howe on September 11, the three American delegates presented a more united front. Howe indicated that "His Majesty was graciously disposed to a revision of such of his royal instructions as might have laid too much restraint on their [the colonists'] legislatures." Whether His Majesty was actually so disposed is unclear, but the American delegation assured Howe that "the associated colonies would not accede to any peace or alliance but as free and independent states." That too may have been an exaggeration. Had some of the colonies, particularly in the mid-Atlantic, heard Howe's offer, they may well have run happily back into the fold of empire. When Howe replied that he felt for America as for a brother, and that if it should fail, he would mourn its loss, Franklin responded, "My lord, we will do our utmost endeavours to save your Lordship that mortification."

Franklin had honed his wry diplomacy over years in London, and now he was ready to put it to whatever use necessary in support of American independence. Understanding how strong

Congress sent John Adams, *Edward Rutledge, and Benjamin Franklin to meet with Lord Howe at the Peace Conference on Staten Island in September 1776.*

an asset he was, the Continental Congress now appointed him part of a three-man commission to negotiate an alliance with the French. Jefferson had been elected to the commission as well but had declined; Adams had declined even to be nominated. But the 70-year-old Franklin took the assignment. "I am old and good for nothing," he said, "but, as the storekeepers say of their remnants of cloth, 'I am but a fag end, you may have me for what you please.'"

On York Island, Washington and his commanders waited anxiously through the final days of summer. They worried that at any time the British fleet would move upriver and open fire on them. Finally, on September 12, the Americans came to a decision: They would retreat north across the Harlem River to King's Bridge but leave a minimal contingent behind to hold the British at bay should they try to follow. The city of New York would be left intact, under orders from the Continental Congress.

Action at Harlem Heights

BY MID-SEPTEMBER MOST OF WASHINGTON'S FORCE HAD MADE IT NORTH TO HARLEM Heights or across the Harlem River to King's Bridge. As the Americans left the island, the

BENJAMIN FRANKLIN PRESENTED *the case for American independence before King Louis XVI of France. Franklin's diplomacy in France was a great success, as it helped secure a critical military alliance for the Americans.*

British poured in behind them. On September 15 British ships on the East River off Kips Bay began pounding a small American contingent still dug in near the lower end of the island. The barrage produced was "so terrible and so incessant a roar," Lord Howe's secretary Ambrose Searle recorded, that "few even in the army and navy had ever heard before." It was, he said, an "awful and grand" scene. "I might say beautiful, but for the melancholy seriousness which must attend every circumstance where the lives of men, even the basest malefactors, are at stake . . ." Following the bombardment, the "King's forces took possession of the place . . .

"Thus this town and its environs, which these blustering gentlemen had taken such wonderful pains to fortify, were given up in two or three hours without any defence or the least appearance of manly resistance."

I only regret that I have but one life to lose for my country.

NATHAN HALE

It could hardly be said that Washington himself did not attempt manly resistance. Looking down over the island from Harlem Heights that day, he had seen the smoke of battle and had gone racing toward it on horseback. When he saw his troops in disorganized retreat, he ordered his men to hold their positions, but they were beyond ordering. He lost his legendary but generally well-controlled temper. "The General was so exasperated," reported one American commander, "that he struck several officers in their flight, three times dashed his hatt on the ground, and at last exclaimed, 'Good God, have I got such troops as those!' It was with difficulty his friends could get him to quit the field, so great was his emotions. He however got of safe, and all the troops as you may think."

The next day the two sides encountered each other again on Harlem Heights in a battle that was militarily insignificant but a victory for American morale. Washington ordered an attack on an advancing British column, and this time the British were the ones in disorganized retreat, briefly. Soon enough, though, the redcoats regrouped and held their positions. By September 20 one American general could report, "We [the Americans and British] are now very near neighbours, and view each other every hour in the day. The two armies lay within two miles of each other and a general action is every hour expected."

Washington fully appreciated how precarious his position was, and in a letter to his cousin at the end of September he let loose his anguish: "[If] I were to wish the bitterest curse to an enemy on this side of the grave, I should put him in my situation." He went on to confess that he "never was in such an unhappy, divided state since I was born." Whatever doubts he had—about himself, the army, and the futility of the war—he didn't share them with his compatriots. To them, he explained a general strategy for the future, "that on our side the War should be defensive" and "that we should on all occasions avoid a general Action or put anything to the risque unless compelled by a necessity into which we ought never to be drawn."

THE BATTLE OF HARLEM HEIGHTS, *fought on September 16, 1776, was George Washington's first battlefield victory in the War for Independence.*

Washington also believed strongly in espionage and had sent a young Yale graduate, Nathan Hale, into the Loyalist city to listen and to learn. When much of New York's west side burned to the ground on September 20, Hale was arrested and accused of setting the fire. About to be hanged for his crime, Hale reportedly said the line that secured him a place in history: "I only regret that I have but one life to lose for my country."

As the last weeks of September faded into October, the two armies continued to eye each other without making a move. On the American side, conditions were tough and desertion a rampant problem. On the British side, the troops reveled in their well-fed position among the city's Loyalists, and their commanders waited for a favorable tide, literally. On the morning of October 9, a flood tide gave Admiral Howe the opening he had been waiting for, and three of his battleships moved up the Hudson past the Americans' Fort Washington and Fort Constitution. Nothing the Continentals attempted stopped them—not a pounding from American cannons and not the sunken debris with which the Americans had littered the river. Three days later, a far greater parade of ships moved up the East River into Long Island Sound and landed a force of about 4,000 men on the shoreline just across from the

American line on Harlem Heights. More followed farther north a few days later. Once again, the British were successfully maneuvering to get behind the American line and to cut off any path of retreat from the island. On October 16 Washington and his advisers made a decision: Fort Washington on Harlem Heights would be "retained as long as possible" by a meager force of 1,000. The rest of the army would leave York Island and march northeast to White Plains.

It took several days for all of Washington's ill-equipped army to reach White Plains, and there again, they dug in and awaited a move from the British. It came on October 28, and it drove the Americans back. They expected a new and even more ferocious—and permanently devastating—assault any day, but it never came. By November 5 the British were on the move away from Washington's forces and back toward the Hudson, for what strategic purpose the Americans could only guess. Washington worried that "the enemy will bend their force against Fort Washington . . ." and, even worse, that the Howe brothers had a strategy to control the Hudson, gateway to New England and Canada. Acting against classic military strategy, Washington split his army into uneven quarters. The largest contingent would remain in the White Plains area to protect the Hudson corridor; another would stay at Fort Washington on Harlem Heights; a third at Fort Lee, to the south on the western bank of the Hudson; and the smallest quarter, some 2,000 men, would follow Washington back across the Hudson.

Young Nathan Hale *receives instructions from George Washington for his intelligence mission behind the British lines in New York City.*

Washington had borne the weight of the war alone for almost a year and a half, and his exhaustion may have accounted for his questionable tactics—dividing his army and reinforcing vulnerable Fort Washington, with assurances from Gen. Nathanael Greene that he could not "conceive the garrison to be in any great danger."

This time Greene, one of Washington's most trusted commanders, was wrong. By November 15 the British had the fort surrounded on three sides, and General Howe had sent an emissary under a white flag to demand surrender. The fort's commander wrote back confidently, assuring "his excellency that actuated by the most glorious cause that mankind ever fought in, I am determined to defend the post to the very last extremity." The following morning, Washington and three other generals, including Greene, rowed over to Harlem Heights from Fort Lee in New Jersey "whence they viewed the position of our troops," one officer later wrote, "and the operations of the enemy

In October 1776, *three British battleships,* Phoenix, Roebuck, *and* Tartar, *braved heavy bombardment from American forces to navigate the Hudson River successfully and move into a strong strategic position.*

in that quarter," but apparently without undue concern. They returned to Fort Lee. Soon afterward, the British attacked.

It was hard going for the Hessian mercenaries and redcoats, struggling to climb the rock-mantled heights to the fort, but they persevered. By three o'clock the American commander, who had the previous day disdained Howe, surrendered to him. The loss was cataclysmic: a strategic position on the Hudson, critical armaments, and almost 3,000 men, an irreplaceable chunk of Washington's army. Throughout the camps and colonies, one question began to take shape: Was George Washington the man to lead the army fighting for the glorious cause? Even Washington's closest aides were beginning to doubt him. His trusted friend and aide, Joseph Reed, had begun quietly questioning Washington's indecision. "An indecisive mind," Reed had written in a complaining letter, "is one of the greatest misfortunes that can befall an army; how often I have lamented it in this campaign."

Washington was now on the run, literally and metaphorically. After the disaster at Fort Washington, a British force under Lord Cornwallis had attempted to take Washington's force at Fort Lee, but the patriots had escaped, narrowly. A young Virginia lieutenant, James Monroe, wrote admiringly of Washington as he brought up the rear of the retreating army,

SIX THOUSAND BRITISH *soldiers led by General Cornwallis landed at the foot of the Jersey Palisades near Fort Lee in November 1776. There they attempted to capture General Washington's forces, who managed to escape.*

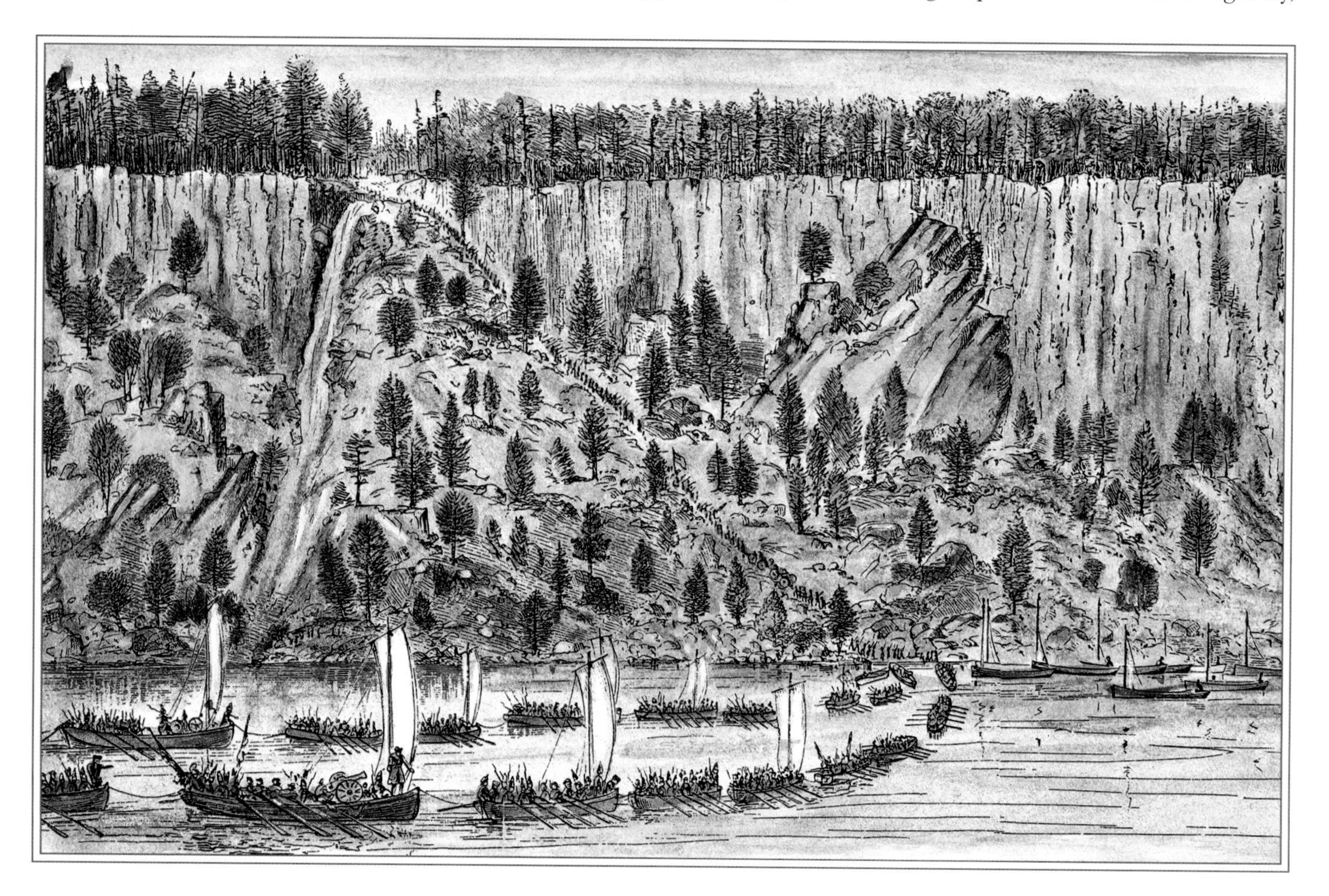

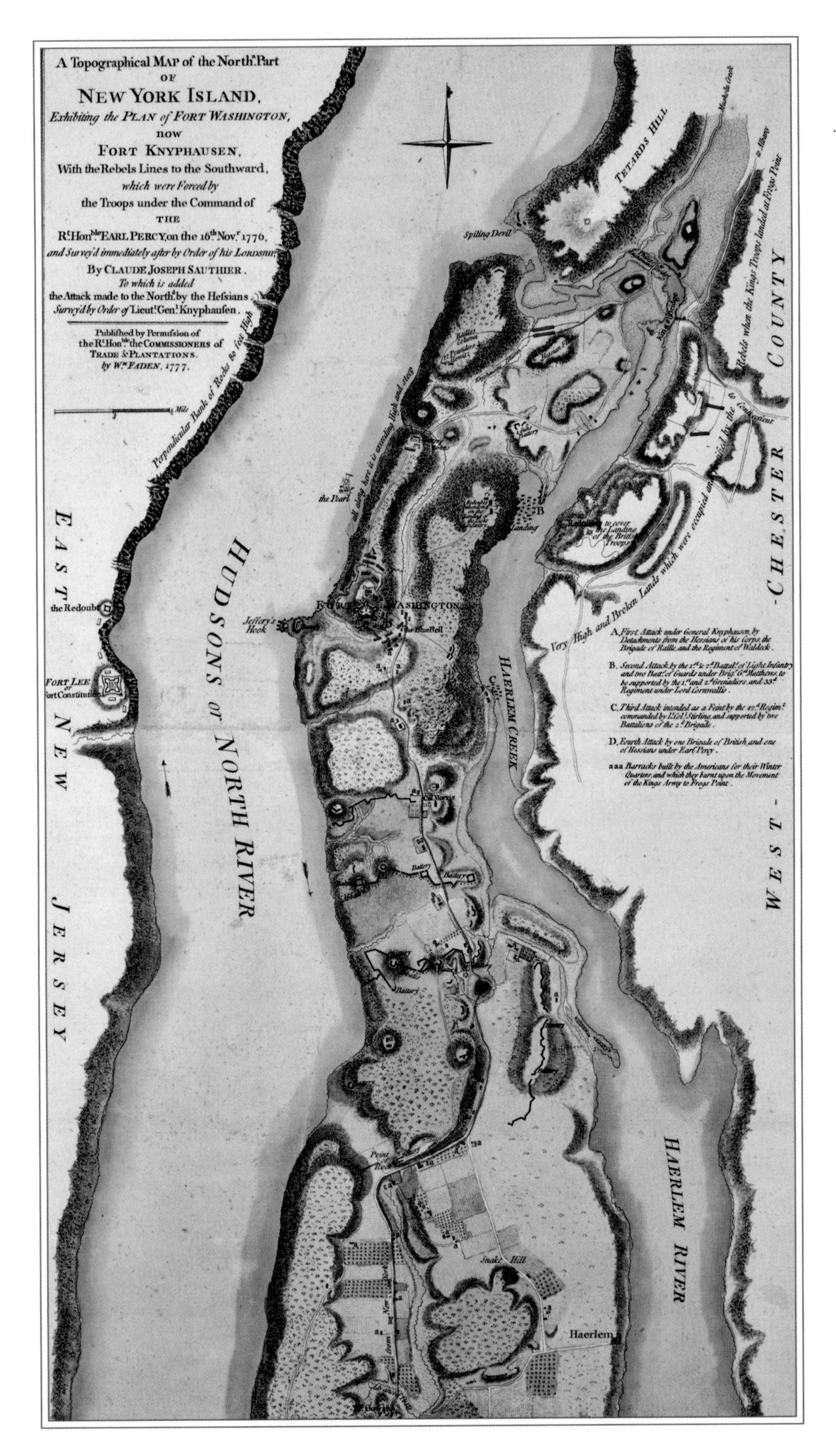

DRAWN IN 1777, *this topographical map of the northern part of New York island shows the plans for Fort Washington, a site of a major defeat for American forces in November 1776.*

The Loyalists
(1776)

The Revolution threatened to rip apart the fabric of life that had been woven over a century and a half in the British colonies, and not everyone was willing to see that happen. Thousands of Americans believed themselves to be Britons first and foremost, and they had no interest in divorcing their world from that of king and empire. They saw the call for independence as moral and political disloyalty, and they refused to break faith with their country.

In the early days of the tumult with Britain, many of these Loyalists, as they called themselves, left their native land behind and sailed back to the mother country. Others took refuge in New York City and Charleston, South Carolina, where British sympathies and sympathizers were strong. After the British managed to oust Washington's forces from the New York area in 1776, the city remained a Loyalist- and British-held bastion until the war was well over and treaties were signed in 1783.

The revolution drove between 80,000 and 100,000 Loyalists to flee to England, Canada, Bermuda, and Jamaica. Most never returned, though some tried. Other Tories, as the patriots called the Loyalists, stayed in America throughout the war, and they accounted for roughly 20 percent of the population of about 2 to 2.5 million. Some spied on the Americans for the British, some fought alongside the redcoats (in some cases, whole regiments were composed of Tories), and some simply made it difficult for the American army. During the dismal fall of 1776, as Washington's defeated army moved through New Jersey, Tories harassed the Americans in any way they could. "Not a stick of wood, a spear of grass, or a kernel of corn, could the troops in New Jersey procure without fighting for it . . ." one local Loyalist reported. "Every foraging party was attacked in some way or another."

This 1776 engraving shows American patriots as they parade a captured Loyalist into a town past onlookers.

Traveling with Washington's forces, Thomas Paine witnessed that harassment firsthand, and in his first and most famous *American Crisis* essay, he railed against the Tories: "Why is it that the enemy hath left the New-England provinces, and made these middle ones the seat of war? The answer is easy: New-England is not infested with Tories, and we are . . . And what is a Tory? Good God! what is he? . . . Every Tory is a coward, for a servile, slavish, self-interested fear is the foundation of Toryism; and a man under such influence, though he may be cruel, never can be brave."

Paine, as usual, was guilty of hyperbole. In truth, many Loyalists fought hard for the British cause, particularly in the 1780 to 1781 campaign in South Carolina, where two wars went on—one between armies, and the other between Tory and patriot civilians. "The division among the people is much greater than I imagined," American Brig. Gen. Nathanael Greene wrote. The two groups, he said, persecuted each other "with little less than savage fury. There is nothing but murders and devastation in every quarter."

The Revolution was more than a war with the mother country. It was, as writer Thomas Allen has labeled it, America's first civil war. ■

with "a deportment so firm, so dignified, but yet so modest and composed, I have never seen in any other person." Washington's haggard, war-weary force of less than 3,000 men was now moving through the flat fields of the New Jersey countryside, where they were beset by Tory spies and bereft of any hilly terrain where they could dig in or take cover.

Problems With General Lee

Thomas Paine was with the army and recording his thoughts by the light of nightly campfires. Paine was another Washington enthusiast, calling his mind a "cabinet of fortitude" and a "public blessing." Often in the general's company, Paine must have bolstered Washington's spirits some in the bleak fall of 1776. There was not much else to lift his spirits or expectations—including Gen. Charles Lee, for whom Washington had had such high hopes.

Lee, a former British officer who had fought in the French and Indian War and was an American enthusiast, had moved to Virginia in 1773. When revolution had become inevitable, he had joined the Continental cause with the expectation of being appointed commander in chief. But Lee was an odd duck—sloppy, not infrequently obscene in his language, devoted to his small platoon of dogs, and arrogant. Despite that, Washington had praised Lee as "the first officer in military knowledge and expertise we have in the whole army" and had put him in charge of the large force at White Plains. Now the general refused even to answer Washington's repeated and polite entreaties that Lee come to the aid of Washington's own vulnerable band. Again, Washington confided his fears to his cousin Lund. "I tremble for Philadelphia," he wrote on December 10. "Nothing in my opinion, but General Lee's speedy arrival, who has been long expected, though still at a distance, can save it." With the British in determined pursuit, Washington had virtually nothing left with which to turn and fight them. With his forces gone, Philadelphia would be undefended.

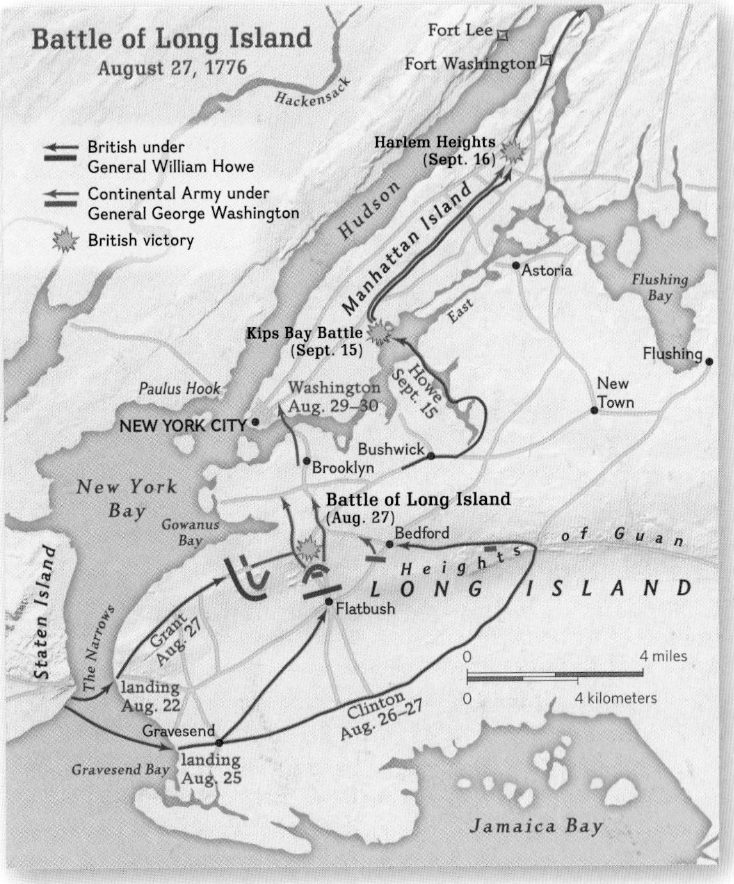

In fact, by then Lee was well on his way. In late November he had crossed the Hudson and begun to march south and west to Washington's aid. Yet again, though, the difficulties of distance and 18th-century communications had left Washington unaware of critical developments. He and his men were retreating as fast as their limited strength and equipment (wagons and horses were in scant supply) allowed them. By the night of December 7, they

The series of battles *fought in New York between August and September 1776 were a crucial victory for the British and a crushing defeat for the Americans. George Washington was ultimately forced to abandon New York and escape south to New Jersey.*

were crossing the Delaware River at Trenton, New Jersey, and making for the Pennsylvania shore on the far side. Charles Willson Peale, an artist who had painted a portrait of Washington in 1772 and had recently arrived with a Philadelphia militia unit, watched the crossing, and the next morning was stricken by the desperate shape the men were in. Many were shoeless and in tatters. One poor soul "was in an old dirty blanket jacket, his beard long, and his face so full of sores that he could not clean it." The man, Peale suddenly realized, was his own brother, James.

GEN. CHARLES LEE
1731–1782

Born and raised in England, Charles Lee served the British army in the Seven Years' War. Lee moved to North America in 1773 and became a Virginia planter. When revolution broke out in the colonies Lee volunteered to serve with the American forces. Somewhat eccentric and unreliable, Lee became a valuable asset to the colonial forces as a result of his experience with the British army. But his unreliable nature made him something of a liability. Lee was captured in a tavern by the British in 1776 but eventually released. He returned to the Continental Army and led American forces in the Battle of Monmouth in June 1778 but ordered a questionable retreat, which earned him a rebuke from George Washington. Lee was eventually court-martialed, which he contested unsuccessfully. After being released from duty in 1780, he died from a fever in 1782.

Lee, meanwhile, had moved into northern New Jersey and was marching through much the same inhospitable countryside Washington had traveled weeks before. Loyalists watched Lee's movements closely and reported back to the British, and he must have known it. Yet despite that, he chose to spend the night of December 12 at a tavern in the crossroads of Basking Ridge with only a small contingent of about 15 men. When a scouting party of British dragoons got wind of his whereabouts, they quickly moved on him. A young officer named Banastre Tarleton led the charge on the inn. "I went on at full speed," Tarleton later wrote his mother in a letter full of self-admiration. "The sentrys were struck with a panic, dropped their arms and fled. I ordered my men to fire into the house thro' every window and door and cut up as many of the guard as they could." Fifteen minutes later, the obstreperous Lee was taken away in his dressing gown and held as prisoner.

Publicly, it was seen as a great blow to the Americans, and in London, jubilation reigned at news that the traitor had been bagged. Privately, Washington probably felt more relief than regret at the loss of Lee. He had come to understand that Lee was no loyal officer; instead, he was questioning Washington's decisiveness and countermanding his authority. Whatever indecisiveness Lee and other detractors had accused Washington of seemed to melt away. Less than a week after Lee's arrest, Washington made the decision that would change the course of the war and become emblematic of his generalship. On Christmas night his army would recross the Delaware and attack Hessian mercenaries stationed in Trenton for the winter.

General Howe, ever cautious, had called a halt to campaigning until spring, and Washington expected the Hessians to spend Christmas Day celebrating, with no expectation of an attack. Still, the plan went against Washington's own belief that he should wage a defensive war. Since late summer, he had been fighting a "war of posts"—digging in, creating a strong line, and forcing the enemy to come to him. But that strategy had failed too many times, and now the Americans' ability to wage any war at all was becoming doubtful. "Necessity, dire necessity, will, nay must, justify an attempt" on

Washington to his cousin and business manager, Lund Washington

Falls of Delaware, South Side, December 10, 1776.

Dear Lund,

I wish to Heaven it was in my power to give you a more favorable account of our situation than it is. Our numbers, quite inadequate to the task of opposing that part of the army under the command of General Howe, being reduced by sickness desertion, and political deaths (on or before the first instant, and having no assistance from the militia), were obliged to retire before the enemy, who were perfectly well informed of our situation, till we came to this place, where I have no idea of being able to make a stand, as my numbers, till joined by the Philadelphia militia, did not exceed three thousand men fit for duty. Now we may be about five thousand to oppose Howe's whole army, that part of it excepted which sailed under the command of Gen. Clinton. I tremble for Philadelphia. Nothing, in my opinion, but Gen. Lee's speedy arrival, who has been long expected, though still at a distance (with about three thousand men), can save it. We have brought over and destroyed all the boats we could lay our hands on upon the Jersey shore for many miles above and below this place; but it is next to impossible to guard a shore for sixty miles, with less than half the enemy's numbers; when by force or strategem they may suddenly attempt a passage in many different places. At present they are encamped or quartered along the other shore above and below us (rather this place, for we are obliged to keep a face towards them) for fifteen miles.

[con't] December 17, ten miles above the Falls.

The unhappy policy of short enlistments and a dependence upon militia will, I fear, prove the downfall of our cause, though early pointed out with an almost prophetic spirit ! Our cause has also received a severe blow in the captivity of Gen. Lee. Unhappy man! Taken by his own imprudence . . . Our only dependence now is upon the speedy enlistment of a new army. If this fails, I think the game will be pretty well up, as, from disaffection and want of spirit and fortitude, the inhabitants, instead of resistance, are offering submission and taking protection from Gen. Howe in Jersey . . .

Gen. Charles Lee being taken prisoner by British forces in Basking Ridge, New Jersey

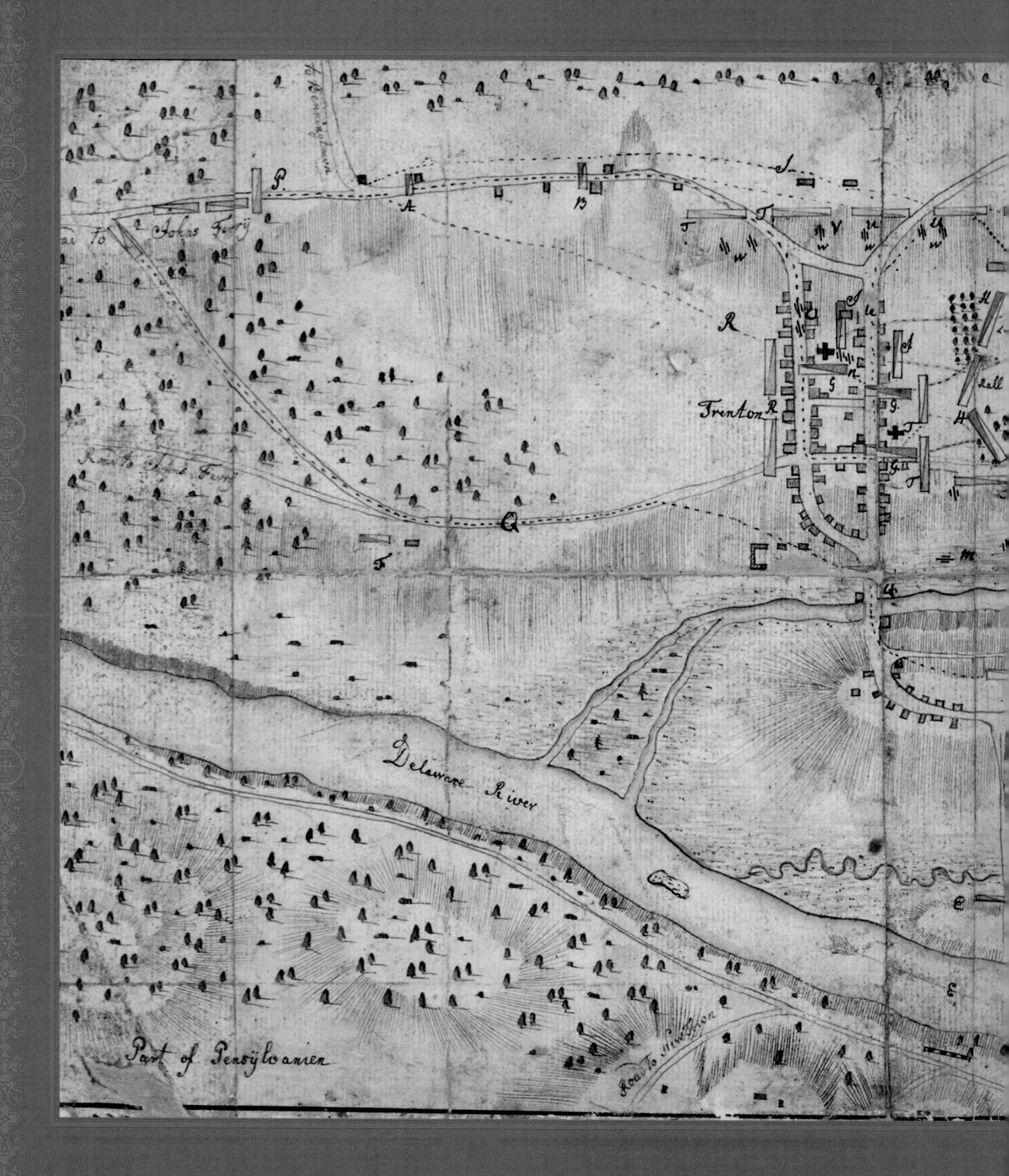

Johns Ferrÿ
Trenton
Delaware River
Part of Pensÿlvanien

Sketch

of the engagement at Trenton, given on the 26th of december 1776. betwixt the American Troops under Command of General Washington, and three Hessian Regiments under Command of Colonell Rall, in wich the latter a part surrendert themselves prisoner of War.

Explanation

A. piquet of 1 officier and 25 privet
B. Capitain de Altenbockums Compagnie of Losbergs Regmt
D. piquet of 1 Capit: 1 Off: and 75 Mann.
E. Detachement of 1 Off: and 30 privet, wich retired to Burlington.
F. detachement of 1 offic: and 50 Hounters
G. Place where the Regmt formt him self
H. Place where the Hessien formt a Line of Battle
I. Attak of the two Regmt Losberg & Rall to the Town at wich Time Knijphausen covent the left flank
K. Place at wich Losberg and Rall surrendert.
L. where Knijphausen surrendert.
M. Losbergs Cannons wich sunk in the morrass
N. Knijphaus: Cannons
O. Ralls Canons instantly dismountet
P. attake towards the piq: A and the Compagnie to B.
Q. Gen: Sulivans Brigade
R. Gen: Mercers Brigade
S. Gen: Stepha
T. Gen: Lord Ster
U. Gen: Greens
V. Place where
to look of even
W. Americanische
X. attak at the

Wiederholdt Lieut: from the Hessian Regmt of Knijphausen.

George Washington's forces captured 900 of 1,500 Hessians after surprising them during their Christmas revelry on December 26, 1776. This sketch shows the movements of the American forces during the important victory. Inset: The Battle of Trenton was a short and decisive victory for the Americans. The fighting lasted only an hour and a half.

Trenton, Washington wrote in the days before the attack. Among his many other worries, Washington knew that at the end of the month, enlistments would expire on 1,500 recruits. Victory had eluded him, and a drastic move was called for. Again, stealth would be his greatest weapon, as it had been at Dorchester Heights and on the retreat from Brooklyn. And weather would be his enemy.

On December 23 he ordered his men gathered into small squads and read Thomas Paine's newest missive, *The American Crisis:* "These are the times that try men's souls," it began. "The summer soldier and the sunshine patriot will, in this crisis shrink from the service of his country, but he that stands it now, deserves the love and thanks of man and woman."

Paine went on to acknowledge that the enemy was at the very door of the new government in Philadelphia (in fact, the Continental Congress had fled to Baltimore), but, he wrote, "I see no cause for fear." He ended his call to arms with, "Let it be told to the future world, that in the depth of winter, when nothing but hope and virtue could survive, that the city and the country, alarmed at one common danger, came forth to meet and repulse it."

These are the times that try men's souls.

THOMAS PAINE'S
THE AMERICAN CRISIS

Two days later, after sunset, Washington's forces began marching toward the ice-clogged Delaware under orders to maintain "a profound silence . . . no man is to quit his Ranks on pain of Death." Henry Knox, now renowned for his tour de force the previous winter in moving armament from Ticonderoga to Boston, headed the logistics of getting Washington's contingent of some 2,400 men and cannons loaded onto big flat-bottomed boats and across the river, churned up by a storm that had howled in out of the northeast. "It is fearfully cold and raw and a snowstorm is setting in," one of Washington's aide's wrote on that Christmas night. "The wind . . . beats into the faces of the men. It will be a terrible night for those who have no shoes. Some of them have tied only rags about their feet: others are barefoot, but I have not heard a man complain."

The crossing was finally completed at three in the morning, three hours later than planned. But Washington "determined to push on at all events."

The Americans struggled through a nighttime blizzard of snow, hail, and ice that took the lives of two soldiers. With morning, the storm continued, but Washington was within sight of Trenton. At eight o'clock the Continental forces attacked in fury with their battle cry, "*These* are the times that try men's souls!" The Hessians had had warnings that an attack might be in the offing but had ignored them. Besotted by Christmas revelries and long hours during the previous week on sentry duty, they were taken by surprise but fought valiantly, as did the Americans. One Virginia colonel told his regiment, "The *old boss* [Washington] has put us here to defend this bridge; and by God it must be done, let what will come." Most of the men fighting that day probably did it for the "old boss," as the battle became hand-to-hand, bayonet to bayonet, house to house. In 90 minutes the fight for Trenton was over. Of 1,500

After the decisive *American victory at Trenton, the surviving Hessian forces surrendered to George Washington. The victory proved to be a great boost to American morale.*

Hessians, 900 were taken captive and over a hundred killed or wounded. The rest escaped. Not a single American fell in the battle. Washington's password for the night had been "Victory or death." And without the victory in Trenton, the zeal for revolution might have died away. But with victory, hope was rekindled among the fighting troops and the American citizenry. "Never were men in higher spirits than our whole army is," wrote one soldier.

When John Hancock, President of the Continental Congress, heard about the feat at Trenton, he wrote to Washington:

> Considering the unfavorable temper of the men, broken by fatigue and ill fortune, the happy event of the expedition appears the more extraordinary. But troops properly inspired, and animated by a just confidence in their leader, will often exceed expectation, or the limits of probability. As it is entirely to your wisdom and conduct the United States are indebted for the late success of their arms, the pleasure you must naturally feel on the occasion will be pure and unmixed. May you still proceed in the same manner to acquire that glory, which, by your disinterested and magnanimous behaviour, you so highly merit.

By sheer will Washington had kept the revolution alive, and against all odds he would keep it going in the years to come.

Thomas Jefferson
(1743-1826)

Ten years before he died, Thomas Jefferson wrote to his friend, compatriot, and onetime nemesis, John Adams, "I leave others to judge of what I have done, and to give me exactly that place which they shall think I have occupied." And for the past two centuries, others have surely obliged him. Probably no Founding Father has been so closely judged, studied, probed, and dissected as Thomas Jefferson. He has been hailed as a genius and a visionary; reviled as a hypocrite and a slave master; celebrated as an architect, a gardener, and an educator; condemned as the South's inspiration for the Civil War; and extolled as one of the greatest U.S. Presidents and the author of American populism. As the distinguished Jefferson scholar Merrill Peterson put it, "In retrospect, American history has sometimes seemed little more than a protracted litigation . . . on Thomas Jefferson."

Thomas Jefferson *(shown opposite in a painting by Rembrandt Peale) wrote the Declaration of Independence at Graff's House, which stood at Seventh and Market Streets in Philadelphia.*

The facts of Jefferson's life are these: In 1743 he was born in central Virginia, where his father, Peter, was a surveyor, mapmaker, and respected landholder on the edge of the western frontier. Peter was apparently a larger-than-life figure willing to take on the New World's possibilities, and his death, when Thomas was only 14, must have been hard on his oldest son. The boy's mother, Jane, had her roots in the aristocracy of Tidewater Virginia, but little else is known of her, especially from Thomas himself, who almost never mentioned her in his writing.

At 17, Thomas entered the College of William and Mary and spent the next six years happily immersed in books and ideas. He was deeply influenced by his law professor, George Wythe, and his urbane professor of natural philosophy, William Small, who, as Jefferson later wrote, "probably fixed the destinies of my life." Jefferson's profession would be law, but as with all of Virginia's aristocracy, much of his time and attention would be consumed as a planter. In 1772 he married a young widow, Martha Skelton, and soon afterward, her father died, leaving the Jeffersons with 11,000 acres and 135 slaves. It was a troubled legacy, in part because Martha's father had left debts almost as vast as his holdings, and ultimately Jefferson became liable for them. Jefferson had also come into 2,750 acres from his own father's estate and had begun designing a house, Monticello, on a mountaintop overlooking Charlottesville in central Virginia.

Even as Jefferson settled into manhood, he found himself in an unsettled world in which the tensions with Britain increased yearly. As an elected member of the Virginia House of Burgesses, he watched the royal governor and the crown exercise greater authority over his world, and he stood firmly with those demanding more rights. In 1774 he wrote his "Summary View of the Rights of British America," intended as a set of instructions for Virginia's delegates to the First Continental Congress (he was not an elected delegate). But when his essay was published as a pamphlet without his consent, it gained him a quick reputation as a strong pen on the side of revolution.

The following spring, Jefferson was on his way to Philadelphia to replace Peyton Randolph as one of the delegates to the Second Continental Congress. He was no public speaker and contributed little to the debates on the floor, but in committee, he was "prompt, frank, explicit, and decisive." When he returned to Philadelphia for the 1776 session of the congress, a letter from a boyhood friend was waiting for him. "For God's sake," the friend exhorted, "declare the colonies independent and save us from ruin."

Jefferson had the opportunity to do just that when he was appointed to a five-person committee charged with drafting a document declaring that the "colonies are & of a right out to be free." For various reasons the actual drafting fell to Jefferson, and for 17 days in June, he worked "Not to find out new principles . . . ever before thought of . . . but to place before mankind the common sense of the subject, in terms so plain and firm as to command their ascent, and to justify ourselves in the independent stand we are compelled to take." After some revisions by the congress and a reworking of the ending that was not to Jefferson's liking, the Declaration of Independence was adopted on July 4. Although he received no strong kudos at the time for his authorship, Jefferson clearly believed that he had done what he'd set out to do: present the common sense of the subject.

A DECADE AFTER *writing the Declaration of Independence, Thomas Jefferson served as the U.S. ambassador to France in the 1780s.*

During the next three years of war, Jefferson devoted himself to his family, his estates, and his homeland, Virginia. While he was in Philadelphia in the summer of 1776, he had sent his own draft of a constitution for Virginia to a convention meeting in Williamsburg, but it had arrived late. Still, he persisted in presenting his ideas on forming a new government to his fellow Virginians. He gave advice on several topics, including how to elect members to the state senate, how the judiciary should function, and what punishments were appropriate for what crimes. The autumn after writing the Declaration of Independence, he became a member of the new Virginia House of Delegates and led a committee appointed to revise the state's laws. Among the revisions was Jefferson's Virginia Statute for Religious Freedom, which began, "Whereas Almighty God hath created the mind free."

In June 1779 Jefferson was elected Virginia's second revolutionary governor (Patrick Henry was its first), but the governorship proved to be his political low point. Near the end of his tenure, the British, led by the traitor Benedict Arnold, invaded Tidewater Virginia, took the capital of Richmond, and forced Jefferson and other legislators to flee to the Charlottesville area. Jefferson and several of the lawmakers staying with him at Monticello barely avoided capture by Banastre Tarleton, the same British officer who had taken Gen. Charles Lee by surprise early in the war. Tarleton's raid came at the very end of Jefferson's governorship. A few months later the long Revolution was over too, and America was free.

The following May Jefferson wrote to his good friend James Monroe that he would not serve again in the Virginia House of Delegates—or, for that matter, anywhere:

> Before I ventured to declare to my countrymen my determination to retire from public employment, I examined well my heart to know whether it were thoroughly cured of every

A Declaration by the Representatives of the UNITED STATES OF AMERICA, in General Congress assembled.

When in the course of human events it becomes necessary for one people to dissolve the political bands which have connected them with another, and to [illegible] assume among the powers of the earth the separate and equal station to which the laws of nature & of nature's god entitle them, a decent respect to the opinions of mankind requires that they should declare the causes which impel them to the separation.

We hold these truths to be self-evident; that all men are created equal; that they are endowed by their creator with [illegible] [inherent & inalienable], rights; that among these are life, liberty, & the pursuit of happiness; that to secure these rights, governments are instituted among men, deriving their just powers from the consent of the governed; that whenever any form of government becomes destructive of these ends, it is the right of the people to alte[r] or to abolish it, & to institute new government, laying it's foundation [on] such principles & organising it's powers in such form, as to them [shall] seem most likely to effect their safety & happiness. pruden[ce indeed] will dictate that governments long established should not be ch[anged for] light & transient causes: and accordingly all experience hath [shewn that] mankind are more disposed to suffer while evils are sufferable, than to right themselves by abolishing the forms to which they are accustomed. but when a long train of abuses & usurpations [begun at a distinguished period, &] pursuing invariably the same object, evinces a design to reduce them under absolute Despotism, it is their right, it is their duty, to throw off such [illegible] & to provide new guards for their future security. such has been the patient sufferance of these colonies; & such is now the necessity which constrains them to [expunge] alter their former systems of government. the history of the present king of Great Britain is a history of [unremitting] repeated injuries and usurpations, [among which] appears no solitary fact to contradict the uniform tenor of the rest, [all of which] but all have [have] in direct object the establishment of an absolute tyranny over these states. to prove this, let facts be submitted to a candid world, [for the truth of which we pledge a faith yet unsullied by falsehood]

The first page *of Jefferson's "original Rough draught" of the Declaration of Independence contains his handwritten notes and edits. Inset: Jefferson used this portable lap desk of his own design to write the document. The desk featured a hinged writing board and a locking drawer for papers, pens, and inkwell.*

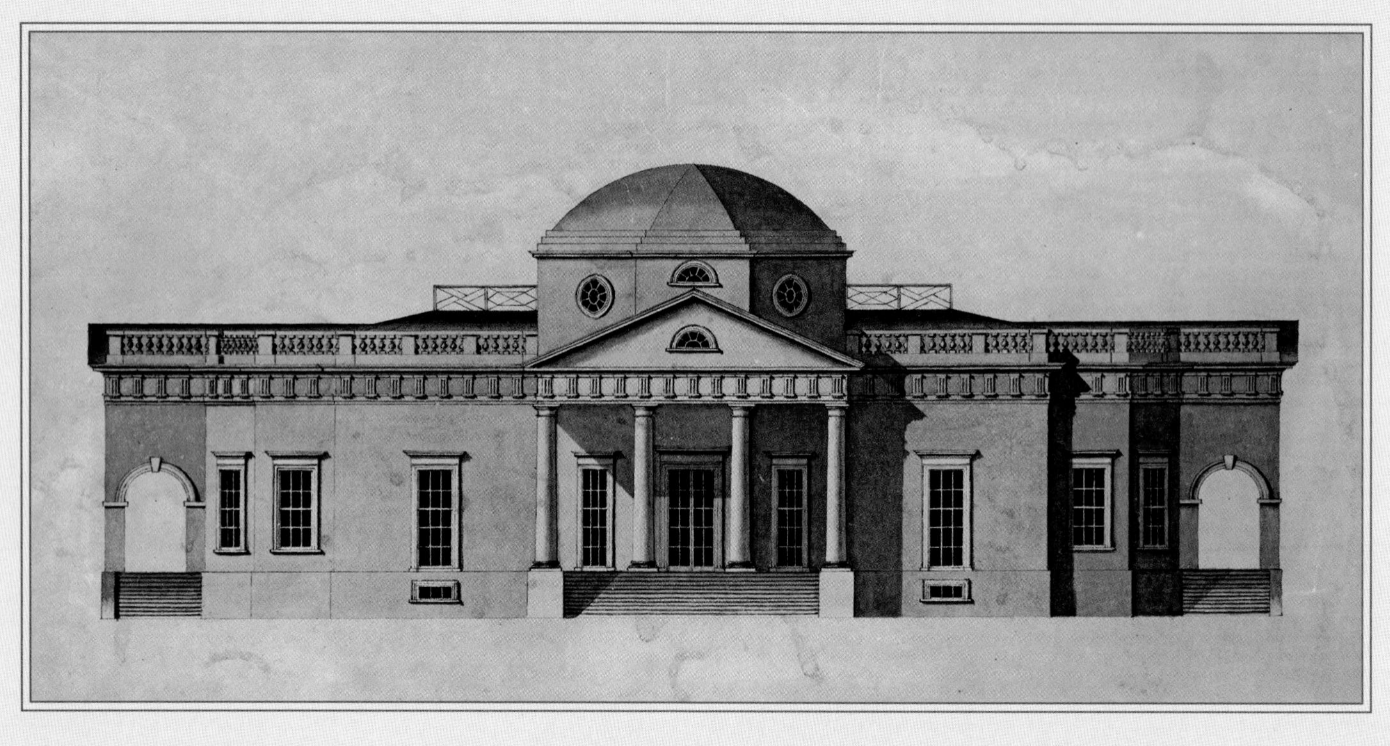

LOCATED JUST OUTSIDE *Charlottesville, Virginia, Monticello was the primary plantation of Thomas Jefferson, who began building it when he was 26 years old.*

> principle of political ambition, whether no lurking particle remained which might leave me uneasy when reduced within the limits of mere private life. I became satisfied that every fibre of that passion was thoroughly eradicated . . . I considered that I had been thirteen years engaged in public service, that during that time I had so totally abandoned all attention to my private affairs as to permit them to run into great disorder and ruin . . . that by a constant sacrifice of time, labour, loss, parental & family duties, I had been so far from gaining the affection of my countrymen . . .

A few months later, Jefferson's cherished wife, Martha, died, and his grief plunged him into further despair. That "single event wiped away all my plans and left me a blank which I had not the spirit to fill up," he wrote. Eventually, the public service he thought he had abandoned filled the void: he became a delegate to the Continental Congress and, later, succeeded Franklin as foreign minister to France. During his five years in Europe, he represented American interests and immersed himself in the rich cultural milieus, particularly of France. "Were I to proceed to tell you how much I enjoy their architecture, sculpture, painting, music, I should want words," he wrote to a friend in 1785. Jefferson was still in France as it was overtaken by its own revolution. He attempted to mediate among the king, aristocrats, and others, but his suggestions weren't taken. He also worked with the Marquis de Lafayette, America's wartime ally and his friend, to draft a declaration of rights before he left Paris on what he thought was temporary leave. He would never return.

Jefferson was abroad when the delegates to the Philadelphia convention drafted the Constitution in 1787, but during the drafting, he corresponded with James Madison, to whom he sent books and ideas about what the document should embody. When he returned to America late in 1789, a government based on the new Constitution was in place, and with some reluctance, Jefferson took the post that the newly elected President Washington pressed on him: the country's first secretary of state. As a member of Washington's cabinet, Jefferson watched the wheels of the new republic spin and was increasingly troubled by what he saw as an antirepublican rotation. Under Secretary of the Treasury Alexander Hamilton, the reach of the federal government extended far beyond what

Jefferson felt was healthy. Along with Madison, Jefferson took on Hamilton and the Federalists, and the great debate on the role of government in America that had begun even before the Articles of Confederation continued.

In 1796, when Washington refused to run for a third term as President, the new Republican Party pushed Jefferson, "the man of the people," to be their candidate, and he agreed, though he wanted nothing more than to be at Monticello with his family and his books. He lost to the Federalist candidate, John Adams, but because he ranked second in the electoral balloting, he took the Vice Presidency. In the next election he decisively defeated Adams, yet, owing to the electoral system, he tied with Aaron Burr. It took 36 votes in the House of Representatives, where lame-duck Federalists opposed him, before Jefferson was elected third President.

An 1804 satirical cartoon *entitled "A Philosophic Cock" depicts Thomas Jefferson as a rooster with his slave Sally Hemings as his Hen.*

One of the greatest achievements of Jefferson's two terms in office was the Louisiana Purchase, which almost doubled the size of the United States and extended its boundaries from ocean to ocean. Always the scientist and naturalist, Jefferson dispatched the Lewis and Clark expedition to explore the new territory. But he was forced to look east as well as west, as the Napoleonic Wars in Europe threatened to engulf America. Working mightily to keep his fledging country out of the conflict, Jefferson used commerce rather than guns as a weapon against the old enemy, Britain.

At last, in 1809, Jefferson returned to his family, friends, and home—and his endless projects. For the last 17 years of his life, he continued to improve on Monticello and its gardens by experimenting with architecture and with new plant varieties, including wine grapes. "No occupation is so delightful to me as the culture of the earth," he wrote to his friend, artist Charles Willson Peale, "and no culture comparable to that of the garden . . . though an old man, I am but a young gardener." He also sold his vast collection of books to the U.S. government to restock the Library of Congress after the British torched the original collection in the War of 1812. And he devoted himself to an educational system for the state and planned and oversaw the building and implementation of the Central College (now University) of Virginia in the valley below Monticello.

As to Monticello, it ran, as it always had, on slave labor. Despite his periodic proclamations on the evils of slavery, Jefferson did little to improve the conditions of his own enslaved people. Historians generally agree that he fathered several children by Sally Hemings, a slave who was in fact his late wife Martha's half sister; all were raised as slaves.

Jefferson's last years were hard ones, as his debts mounted and he faced the prospect of losing Monticello. He took solace in correspondence with his friends, particularly James Madison and, oddly, John Adams. The two men had healed their political differences, and both, as Adams wrote, looked "back with rapture to those golden days when Virginia and Massachusetts lived and acted together like a band of brothers." As if orchestrating a final moment of Revolutionary splendor, the two patriots died within hours of each other on July 4, 1826, exactly 50 years after the adoption of the Declaration of Independence. Adams's last words were, "Thomas Jefferson still survives." In fact, Adams was wrong, but only in the short run. For memories of Jefferson, his ideas, and his impact still run deeply through American culture.

CHAPTER 4

I've beat them, I've beat all the Americans!

KING GEORGE III

1777-1778
SUMMER SOLDIERS AND SUNSHINE PATRIOTS

"THE YEAR 1776 IS OVER," ROBERT MORRIS WROTE TO GEORGE WASHINGTON ON NEW YEAR'S DAY 1777, "AND I AM heartily glad of it and hope you nor America will ever be plagued with such another." Morris, a wealthy Philadelphian, had helped keep Washington's army alive through the last desperate months of 1776 with a loan of his own money. Morris had personal as well as patriotic reasons for wanting to see the tide of war change, but Washington knew the tide was still running against the Continentals: As commander, he faced the prospect of expired enlistments that would deplete his army in the weeks to come. And in newly captured Trenton that New Year's Day, he was waiting once again for the British. Thanks to a strong intelligence-gathering network he had put in place, he knew Cornwallis and some 8,000 redcoats would probably be on their way to him soon.

Washington and his advisers had decided that the town of Trenton, on the banks of the Delaware, was the place to fight, and they had dug in, as they had done so many times in the past year. Washington had also sent an advance force toward Princeton, another small New Jersey town 16 miles away, where Cornwallis was headquartered. The Continentals had orders to harass and delay any British force headed in the direction of Trenton.

CHARLES WILLSON PEALE *painted George Washington more times from life than any other artist, but this portrait of him, completed in 1779 after the Battle of Princeton, became Peale's most popular. Preceding pages: George Washington rallies the American forces at the Battle of Princeton, January 3, 1777.*

Cornwallis had his own orders from General Howe: to find and destroy Washington's army once and for all. So in the bleak sunrise of January 2, 1777, his men marched out of Princeton. The weather had turned warmer since Washington had crossed the ice-clogged Delaware the week before, and the redcoats slogged through the mired slush of the Post Road as they unwittingly headed for an encounter with the Continental advance team. As the marching redcoats sank to their knees and even their thighs in mud, Washington's advance force shot at them from the cover of forests. Still, the Regulars kept coming.

"At 10 a.m. we received news that the enemy was advancing, when the drums beat to arms," one American soldier in Trenton wrote. Thoroughly battle hardened by this time, Washington's troops took up their positions and waited. They held the high ground, and in front of them, Assunpink Creek, swollen from the thaw, made a swift-flowing, protective moat. Behind them and on their left flank, the Americans were wrapped by the Delaware. The position was good, but fraught. Swamps to the south could be forded, and if the enemy managed that, the Continentals would be trapped.

They waited all day for the British, but not until winter darkness threatened to close in did Cornwallis oblige them, even though only half his force had made it to the banks of the Assunpink. By then "the evening was so far advanced that I could distinguish the flame from the muzzles of our muskets," American officer James Wilkinson remembered. As Wilkinson saw Cornwallis's army arrayed across the fast-moving creek, he knew that if ever there was "a crisis in the affairs of the revolution, this was the moment." With their backs to the Delaware, clogged by "ice as large as houses," the Americans had no choice but to fight to the death, theirs or the enemy's.

As the British force swelled, the American advance unit retreated across the Assunpink bridge and into town. Waiting on the other side, "the noble horse of Gen. Washington stood with his breast pressed close against the . . . rail of the bridge, and the firm, composed, and majestic countenance of the General inspired confidence and assurance," a private reported.

Gen. Charles Cornwallis *(1738–1805) commanded the British forces during the Battle of Princeton. Cornwallis made a critical mistake in not penning George Washington in place the night after the battle, a move that allowed the American forces to gain a superior position.*

The bridge itself had become the critical chokepoint, a killing field the British and the Hessians had to cross. American fire mowed them down time and again, but they kept coming as ordered. When the fighting was finally over, "the bridge looked red as blood, with their killed and wounded and red coats." As darkness cloaked the town and its surroundings, the American troops celebrated their victory, and across the Assunpink, Cornwallis did the same. Though one of his officers warned, "If Washington is the general I take him to be, he will not be found in the morning," Cornwallis had no such misgivings. He reportedly assured his senior staff, "We've got the Old Fox safe now. We'll go over and bag him in the morning."

THE FIERCE FIGHTING *at the Battle of Princeton took a heavy toll on the British forces, who lost between 2,000 and 3,000 men. American casualties were much lower, and the victory boosted the morale of Washington's troops.*

Cornwallis would have done well to heed his officers, because Washington had no intention of being bagged. After midnight, his men moved out silently, wagon wheels again covered in cloth to muffle any rattling, campfires left blazing to signal the British they were still waiting in Trenton. By now, the Americans knew stealth; it had become one of their most powerful weapons. And almost every time they had deployed it, the weather had been on their side, as it was again that night. The cold and wind had returned, hardening roads that had been a quagmire for Cornwallis. Washington's force was headed back to Princeton, where Washington planned to attack the British garrison still in place there. The following morning the fighting began on the outskirts of town, and the outnumbered British were soon routed. Washington, deep in the fray himself, exulted, "It is a fine fox chase, my boys!"

The Battle of Princeton ended ten days of fighting, during which the British had lost some 2,000 to 3,000 men, the Americans one-tenth that. Washington contemplated pushing on to attack another British post at Brunswick, but his men were exhausted, so instead he moved toward Morristown, where the Continentals could wait out the rest of the winter in the hillier part of New Jersey and ready themselves for the spring season of war.

The past campaign year had been a volatile mix of victories and defeats. The previous winter, Knox had retrieved vital artillery from Fort Ticonderoga, and the Continentals had

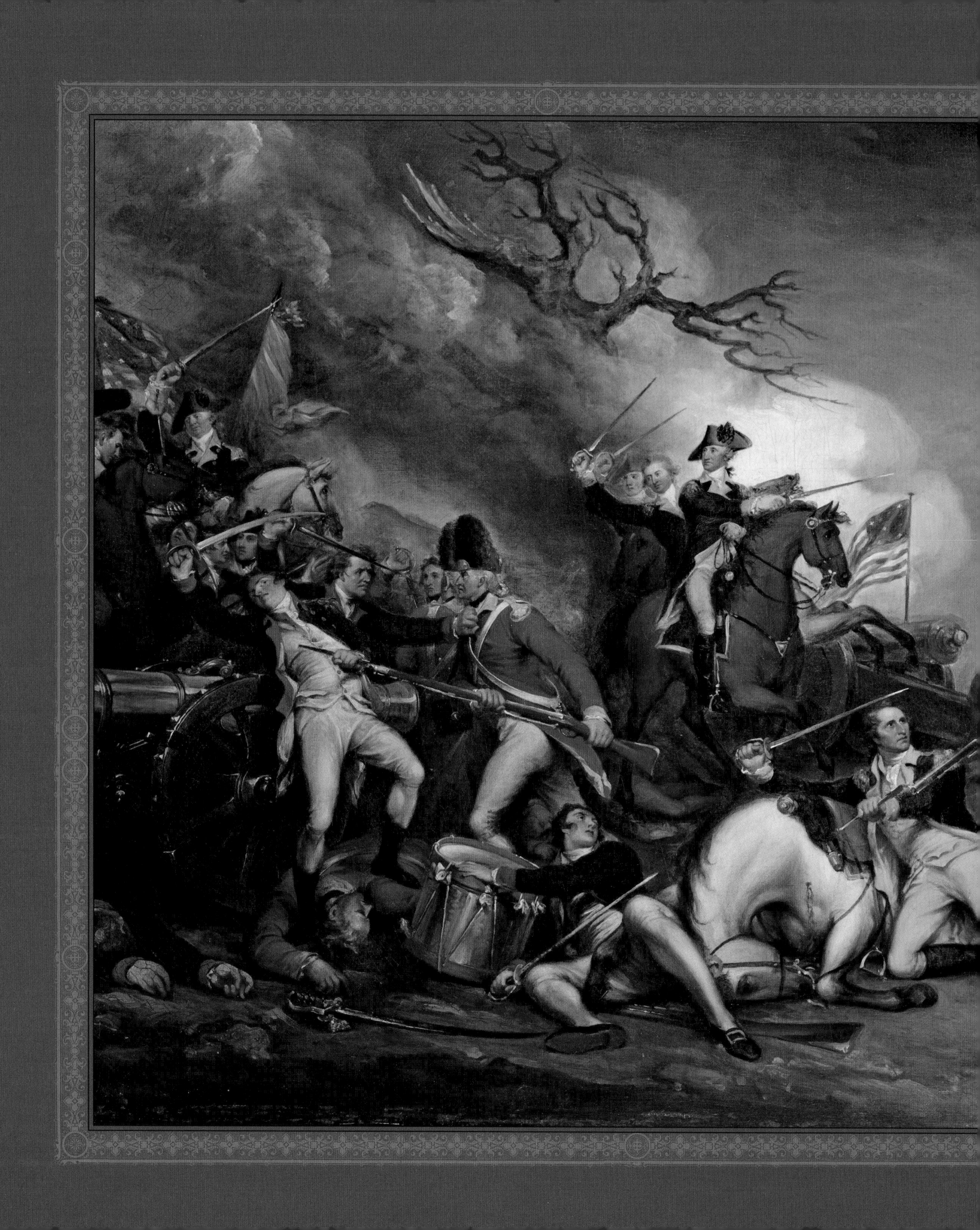

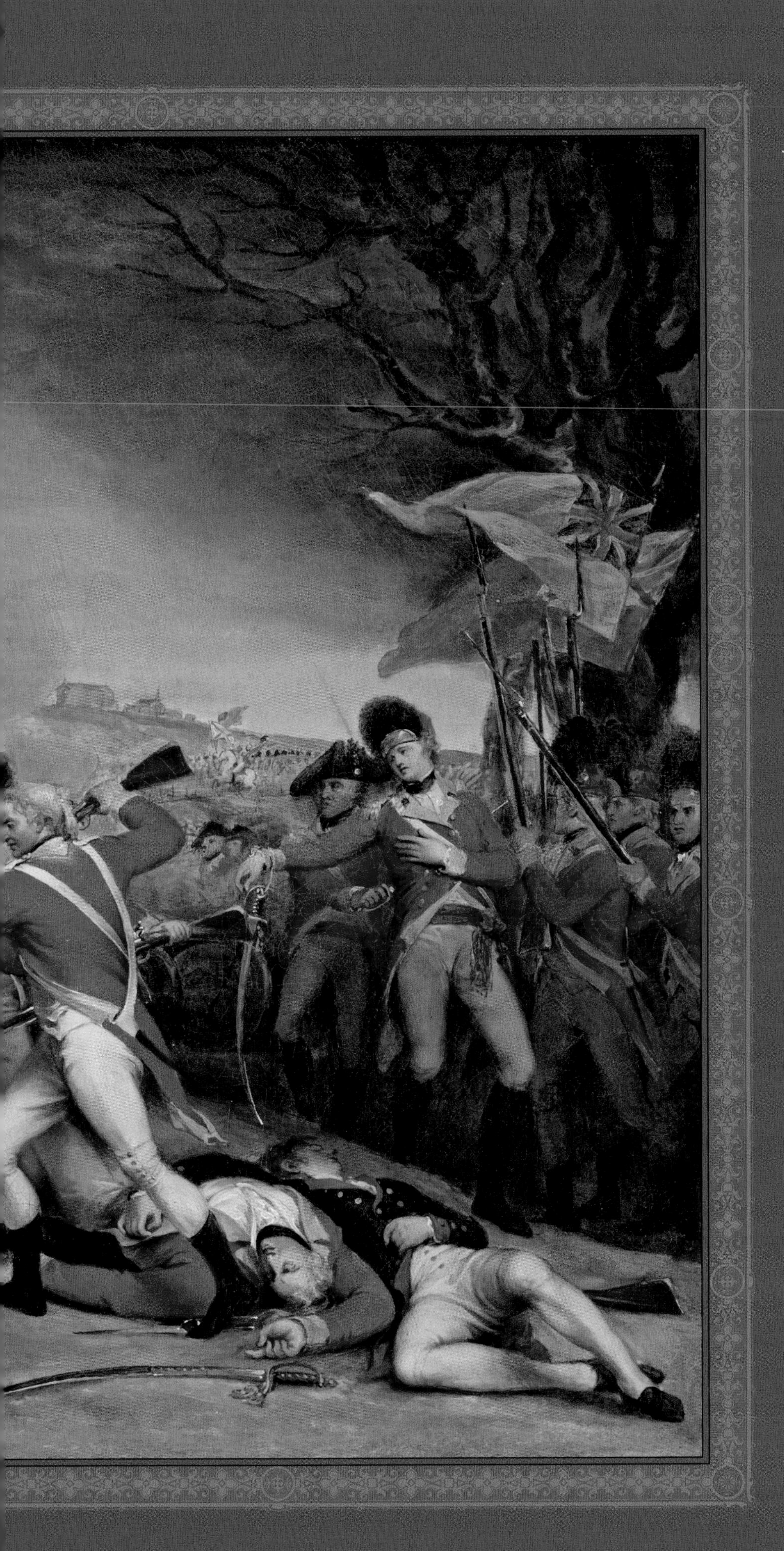

HUGH MERCER WAS *a soldier, physician, and close friend to George Washington. He rose to the rank of general and fought bravely in the Battle of Princeton. Wounded on the battlefield, Mercer died from his injuries. His death, depicted here, became a popular rallying symbol for the American forces.*

finally forced the British out of Boston. But Washington's army had also lost New York City—and an irreplaceable amount of man power in battle after battle to try to save it. Now, in New Jersey, after their initial retreat, they had bested the British badly, proving they had become a formidable fighting force. But the British had decimated the American countryside around them, despite the fact that many of New Jersey's citizens had rushed to take an oath of loyalty to the crown when it had been offered. In return, the Tories were given amnesty and their property was spared.

Washington had anticipated that the Loyalist-leaning "middle states" would be one of his greatest challenges. Earlier in the winter, he had written his cousin Lund that he did not "apprehend half so much danger from Howes Army, as from the disaffection of the three States of NY, Jersey & Pensylvania."

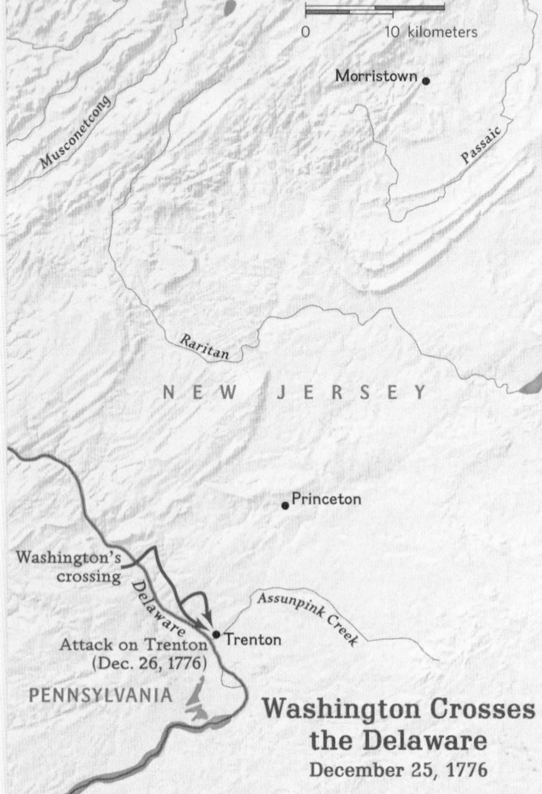

GEORGE WASHINGTON'S CAMPAIGNS *in New Jersey began with his crossing the Delaware River on Christmas Day in 1776. He and his forces would fight crucial battles at Trenton and Princeton before moving north to winter quarters at Morristown.*

The opportunistic new Loyalists in New Jersey had worked on the side of the British in any number of ways and would even, according to Nathanael Greene, "lead the relentless foreigners to the houses of their neighbors and strip poor women and children of everything that they have to eat or wear, and after plundering them in this sort, the brutes often ravish the mothers and daughters and compel the fathers and sons to behold their brutality."

The British claimed it was the Hessian mercenaries who were responsible for the barbarity and the plundering, and that was probably largely true. The Hessians were seasoned warriors who saw America as a land of almost impossible plenty and composed ballads to it—one exulted over "That red gold, that red gold / That comes rolling out from there." Though they were well paid by 18th-century standards and technically forbidden to plunder, the Hessians felt plundering was almost a right of warfare, and across New Jersey, they took their due.

Oddly, despite New Jersey's wavering loyalties, Washington seemed comfortable enough to settle into winter quarters in the hilly woodland around Morristown, where local farms could supply his troops.

As both armies rested, their commanders reviewed the victories and defeats of the past campaign year and planned for the coming season of war. Washington had spent a tragic year learning how best to fight the British, and he had come to understand that he had to lay aside conventional European notions of warfare. He had to be bold yet careful and strike audaciously but not imprudently, with an eye to maximizing gains and minimizing losses. After all, there was very little he could afford to lose—in man power or firepower or public opinion. And yet, in an ironic way, the leanness of Washington's army was a distinct advantage. Far faster moving than the encumbered British, it could seize the initiative and strike with greater surprise and precision.

THE HESSIAN MERCENARIES *developed a reputation for greed as a result of their actions in New Jersey. Many felt entitled to the spoils of war and engaged in acts of brutality.*

General Howe, meanwhile, thought and rethought his campaign strategy, and by winter's end he had submitted three different campaign plans to London, where word of the New Jersey defeats did not arrive until late February. As far back as March 1775, parliamentarian Edmund Burke had warned that delays in communication would hamper the war effort: "Seas roll, and months pass, between the order and execution . . . and the want of a speedy explanation of a single point is enough to defeat a whole system."

Anxious to shore up the forces in America, the British ministry committed six more ships of the line and 6,000 additional men to the conflict. War officials also listened to the entreaties of Gen. John Burgoyne, who was home on leave from the American front. Ambitious and disingenuous, Burgoyne made the rounds of officialdom and proposed various campaign strategies for the coming season of war. By the time he sailed for Quebec, he had convinced the government to give him several thousand troops with which to lead an invasion south from Canada into New York the coming summer.

In the meantime, the Continental Congress, back in Philadelphia to attend to the business at hand, was looking for any means it could reasonably find to strengthen Washington's dwindling army. Smallpox had taken a toll, and as enlistment periods expired, many soldiers returned home; most had had their fill of the ragged, dirty, hungry, and exhausted life of a soldier in the glorious cause. That spring, in order to bring in fresh man power, the congress issued resolves requesting that each state institute a draft from its militia to reinforce the Continental Army and assigning quotas to be filled by states based on their size. Potential recruits were enticed with money, and recruiters fanned out, selling their wares—the glories of enlistment—aggressively. But even these strategies failed to bring in enough men to meet the goal of 75,000 new recruits by year's end. In fact, only about half that number joined Washington's army in 1777.

The Continental Congress was far more successful with a less fraught undertaking. In June it resolved, "That the flag of the United States be thirteen stripes, alternate red and white; that the union be thirteen stars, white in a blue field, representing a new Constellation." The resolution did not specify exactly how the stars were to be arranged, and various handmade versions appeared, including one with the stars forming a circle—the apocryphal "Betsy Ross" flag. (The legend that Washington himself commissioned the Philadelphia widow and seamstress to make the first flag was promulgated by Mrs. Ross's grandson 94 years later, in 1870, and quickly adopted by another war-weary public, this time recovering from a civil war.)

It is said *that George Washington asked Philadelphia widow and seamstress Betsy Ross (1752–1836) to sew the first American flag. There is little proof for this story beyond the testimony of Ross's grandson, William Canby, who said his grandmother told it to him in 1836.*

In the summer of 1777 Washington had been in Philadelphia when he first met a young French marquis from an illustrious family. The Marquis de Lafayette had crossed the Atlantic to serve in the Continental Army. He was barely 20 years old, and the patriotic cause seemed to have roused all of his youthful idealism. "The happiness of America is intimately connected with the happiness of all mankind," he had proclaimed.

Washington had been inundated with such French volunteers, most of them arrogant and worthless to him. They bore letters of introduction from Ben Franklin or Silas Deane, who had no choice as America's commissioners in Paris but to accept such help. Finally, Washington wrote Franklin to say he could take no more of these gentlemen soldiers. Lafayette went anyway and made a good first impression on Washington. A week later, the young marquis was invited to review troops with the general. As they passed in review, Washington felt he had to apologize for his poorly armed, threadbare men: "We should be embarrassed to show ourselves to an officer who has just left the French army," he said. Lafayette replied, "It is not to teach but to learn that I come hither." Such deference—and unbridled admiration—won Washington over, and the young man soon became not only a trusted aide and officer, but almost a son to the childless Washington.

Through the late spring and summer of 1777, Washington waited for some move from Howe in the eastern theater, while in the west the war was churning. In western South

The Marquis de Lafayette
(1757–1834)

A French marquis, the legendary Lafayette, ranks among the great heroes of the American cause. His passion, connections, wealth, and courage proved critical weapons in the fight for independence. From childhood, he had been determined to become a military officer like his father, who had been lost to war when he was only two, and the American fight for independence increasingly captivated him. He made plans to join the Revolution under stealth; he did not even confide in his new wife, as he knew her father would object. Deeply wealthy, he bought a ship to transport himself and a handful of other French volunteers across the Atlantic. The scheme was discovered before he could set sail, and Lafayette almost gave it up. Then he reversed himself, sneaked across the Spanish border, and met his ship there. By mid-June 1777 he was anchored off Charleston, with an 800-mile overland march to Philadelphia ahead. "We traveled a great part of the way on foot, often sleeping in the woods, starving, prostrated by the heat . . ." a member of the group wrote. Lafayette himself seemed oblivious to the hardships: "The farther I advance north, the better pleased I am with the country and its people."

Despite Lafayette's efforts, the Continental Congress seemed unimpressed with the nobleman. At the behest of Washington—who felt there

were too many useless French poseurs insinuating themselves into his officer corps—the congress was no longer granting commissions to young Frenchmen. Lafayette refused to be deterred and negotiated an honorary commission. Washington soon lost his skepticism concerning this particular French officer and was further impressed with the marquis's fighting spirit at the Battle of the Brandywine. As the months and years progressed, Washington developed a father's love for Lafayette. "I do not know a nobler, finer soul, and I love him as my own," he told a visiting French diplomat. And to Martha, he wrote, "He is one of the sweetest-tempered young gentleman. He has left a young wife and a fine fortune . . . to come and engage in the cause of liberty."

In 1779 Lafayette returned to France and helped convince Louis XVI to send a large fleet and a thousand men in support of the Revolution. "I had left as a rebel and fugitive," Lafayette wrote of that trip home, "and returned in triumph as an idol." During this time his first son was born, and he named the child Georges Washington de Lafayette. He was soon back at the American front, and in the final months of fighting, he again played a critical role: harassing Cornwallis and pinning him down at Yorktown, Virginia.

The Revolution was not Lafayette's last fight. He became an ardent supporter of the French Revolution, yet his nobility made him suspect. From 1792 to 1797, he was imprisoned, as were his wife and daughters. The family survived, but their fortune did not.

In 1824 Lafayette made his final tour of America as a great hero of independence. "We shall look upon you always as belonging to us, during the whole of our life, as belonging to our children after us," President John Quincy Adams proclaimed. Lafayette left America with sacks of Bunker Hill soil to top his coffin. "The welfare of America is intimately linked with the happiness of all mankind," Lafayette once stated. "She will become the respected and safe asylum of virtue, integrity, tolerance, equality, and a peaceful liberty." ■

Carolina, whites had vanquished the Cherokee, who had allied briefly with the British, and pushed the native people from their land via the rapacious Treaty of DeWitt's Corner. Farther north, the British had enlisted Mohawk and Iroquois support as Burgoyne prepared to make his move south from Canada.

Lafayette Joins Washington

Burgoyne landed in Quebec in early May and soon found that he did not have the man power he had anticipated—fewer soldiers (only about 7,200 soldiers would march south with him), fewer sawyers to clear roads, and fewer Indians to act as scouts. In light of the shortfalls, Burgoyne was forced to fall back on his own arrogance and essential nature. In London he had been "Gentleman Johnny," a famously inveterate gambler and a dramatist. If his move into New York was a dramatic gamble, so be it. The fact that he had never held an

Created in 1777, *this map details the troop locations and fortifications around Fort Ticonderoga overlooking Lake Champlain in upstate New York.*

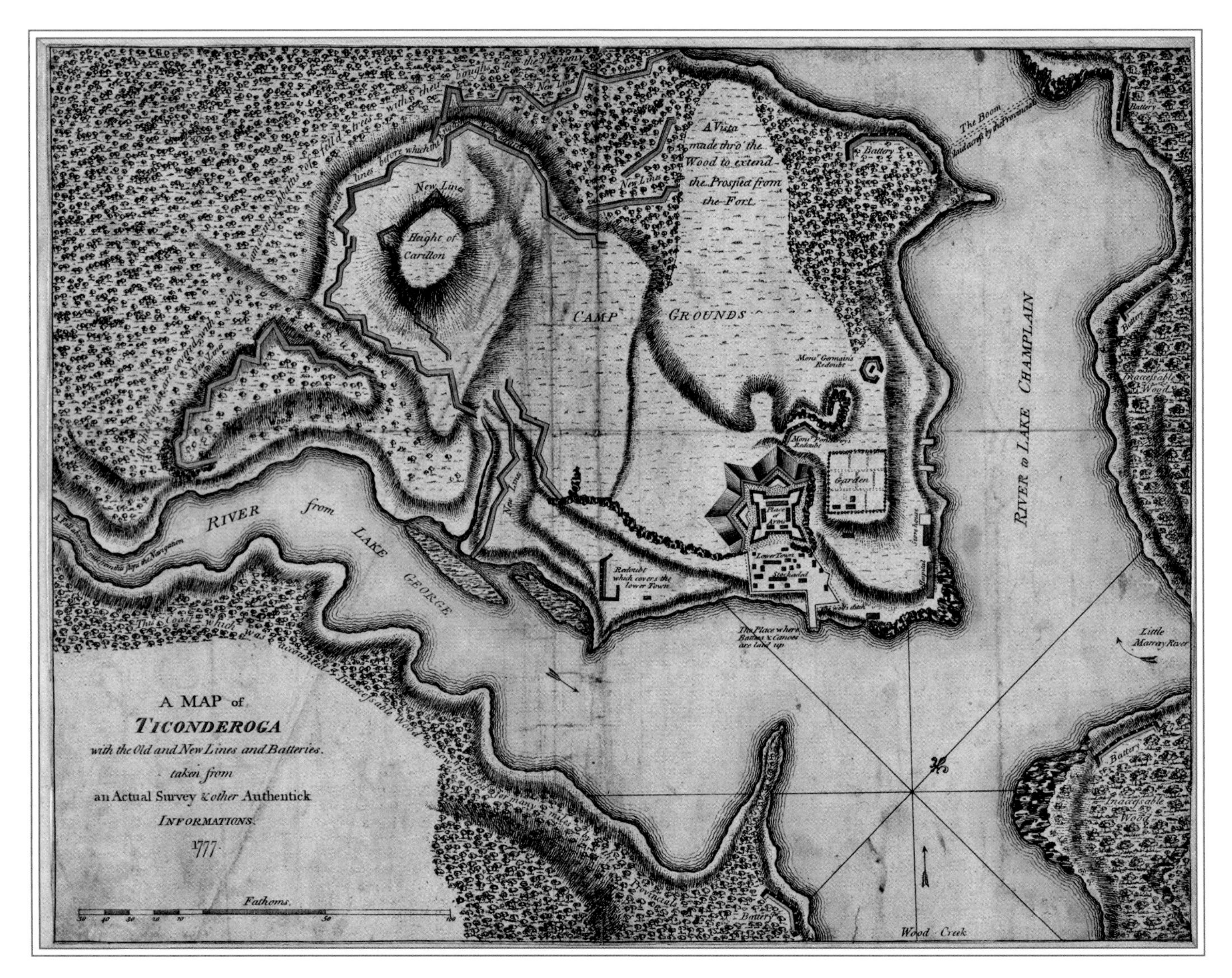

British general John Burgoyne *(1722–1792) enlisted Native American allies to help in his plans to attack and recapture Fort Ticonderoga in July 1777.*

independent command did not seem to faze him. He was sure his plan would work and that once he was in New York, the Loyalists there would flock to his side as comrades-in-arms.

Burgoyne's plan was simple enough: Take back Fort Ticonderoga and secure Lake Champlain, then roll through the Hudson River Valley to Albany. This would effectively separate New England from the other colonies—something the British had attempted almost since the war began.

As Burgoyne set his army in motion, he "shone forth in all the tensel splendour of enlightenment absurdity," a member of his expedition observed. (One British wag had dubbed him "Pomposo.") To the citizens of northern New York, he issued a proclamation stating that his intentions were most honorable—to restore the "Rights of the Constitution," and to quell the "unnatural Rebellion." He also threatened those who would not join his righteous cause with, among other things, "Devastation, Famine, and every concomitant Horror" as well as "the Indian forces under my direction."

> *It is not to teach but to learn that I come hither.*
>
> Marquis de Lafayette

If the Americans were left unimpressed with his bravado, Burgoyne's soldiers were enthralled by the panache and confidence of their commander. Initially, their enthusiasm seemed well placed. By July 5 Fort Ticonderoga was theirs, after they took the undefended high ground nearby and aimed cannons in the fort's direction. The fort's commander, Arthur St. Clair, had fewer than 3,000 able troops, far too small a force to take on Burgoyne, and so St. Clair ordered the strategic fort abandoned.

The British gave chase and caught the American rear guard as it fled. The fighting was vicious, and the Americans held their own, until enemy reinforcements proved too much and the Continentals broke and ran. The rest of St. Clair's force was doing the same: moving as fast as it could away from the pursuing British.

In England, when news of Ticonderoga's fall finally reached the king, he exclaimed, "I've beat them, I've beat all the Americans!" With Lake Champlain in his hands, Burgoyne could easily resupply himself. Oddly, he seemed in no hurry and sat splendidly still for three weeks as American reinforcements poured into Albany. New England militiamen, freed from farm work after the fall harvest, swelled troop numbers to over 6,000. The commander in Albany, Philip Schuyler, an industrious but inflexible New Yorker of Dutch extraction, took a page from Washington's book and "let the forest fight for him" by cutting down trees to block roads and waterways. Finally, in late July, Burgoyne's overburdened army began to inch forward, removing Schuyler's felled trees as it went.

GENERAL BURGOYNE BELIEVED *he could capture Bennington, Vermont, with a small force of 750 men but greatly underestimated the fighting capabilities of American general John Stark's New Hampshire militiamen, who defeated the British forces. Opposite: American general Horatio Lloyd Gates had been a retired British soldier before joining the colonial cause. He commanded the American forces during the defeat of the British at the Battle of Saratoga in 1777.*

Despite his successful forest strategy, the irascible Schuyler had long been an unpopular commander, particularly with the New Englanders, and by early August he was gone. The new commander, Horatio Gates, was not American born either. Gates was a former British officer who had settled in America and joined the Revolutionary cause.

After an arduous march, Burgoyne's army reached Fort Edward, roughly a dozen miles from Saratoga, and rested and resupplied for another ten days. Scanning for a fertile nearby area that could provide food for his army, Burgoyne dispatched a unit of 750 men under the command of German officers to Bennington, Vermont, with the expectation they would meet little or no resistance. But Gen. John Stark's New Hampshire militiamen were waiting for them and were eventually joined by Seth Warner's Green Mountain Boys. "My men, yonder are the Hessians," Stark famously, and perhaps apocryphally, declared. "They were bought for seven pounds and ten pence a man. Are you worth more? Prove it. Tonight, the American flag floats from yonder hill or Molly Stark sleeps a widow."

BATTLE OF TICONDEROGA

THE FIGHTING WAS INTENSE, BUT THE AMERICANS PREVAILED. THE BRITISH DEFEAT WAS catastrophic. Burgoyne lost between 800 and 1,000 men, and his relationship with his Indian allies crumbled. They were already angry that he had not stood by them when they had been publicly vilified for scalping an American woman, Jane McCrea, who was actually a Loyalist. Now they believed the British were too weak to fight successfully against the Americans.

General Burgoyne's forces *set up camp on the west bank of the Hudson River, New York, in September 1777, just before the first skirmish at Saratoga.*

On some level, Burgoyne himself feared the same thing as he anticipated the "gathering storm." Still, he was determined to move on Albany, and to do that he needed to cross the Hudson to the west bank. He chose a spot above Saratoga as the crossing point, and on September 13 his army began crossing on a bridge of bateaux. While the British crossed, the Americans fortified, digging in on Bemis Heights, bluffs along the river about ten miles south. The morning of September 19, the two armies—or parts of them—finally engaged.

BURGOYNE'S CAMPAIGN *to divide New England from the southern colonies began when he landed in Quebec and moved to take Fort Ticonderoga. Miscommunications among the British commanders hampered his campaign, resulting in his ultimate defeat at Saratoga.*

On the American side, the hero of the day was young Benedict Arnold, whom Washington had dispatched earlier in the summer to help save the day against Burgoyne. Arnold was an audacious fighter, far more so than the cautious "Granny" Gates. On that September morning, the younger man convinced Gates to take the initiative against a British advance guard of Tories and Indians. Arnold had turned to his fellow officer Daniel Morgan and proclaimed, "Colonel Morgan, you and I have seen too many Redskins to be deceived by that garb of paint and feathers; they are asses in lions' skins, Canadians and Tories; let your riflemen cure them of their borrowed plumes."

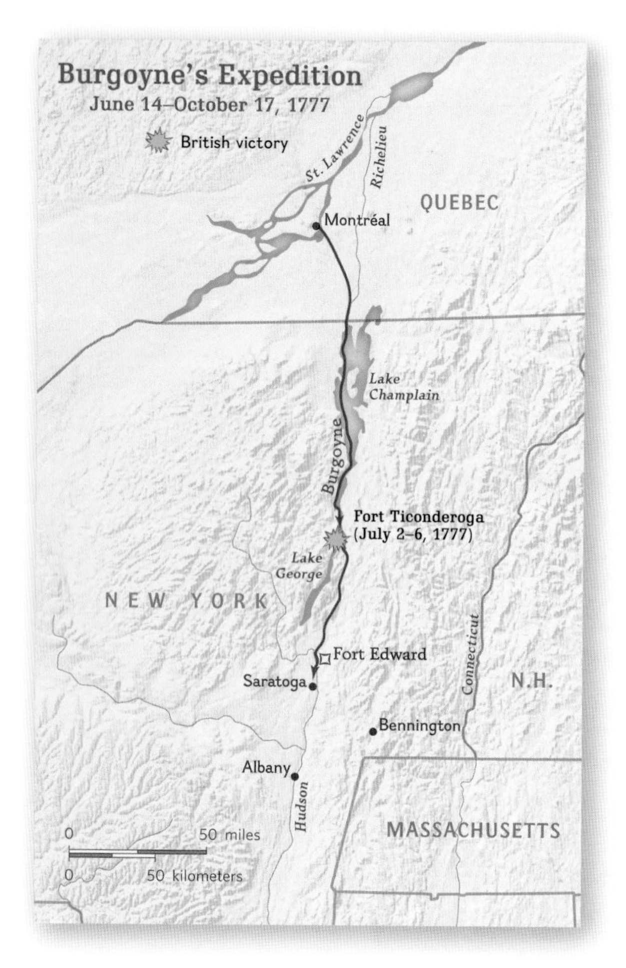

Later in the day, Arnold led a fearless charge against the enemy, and a furious battle ensued, with "fire . . . much heavier then ever I saw it any where," one seasoned British officer claimed. Arnold pushed his superior, Gates, for reinforcements to finish off the enemy, but Gates hesitated. After three hours of thunderous conflict, the fighting ended. And again, the two armies waited, Burgoyne for reinforcements from Sir Henry Clinton, commanding the British troops around New York City and presumably on the way to Burgoyne's rescue.

As the days passed, British supplies dwindled. By October 3, the redcoats were down to half rations—and they were outnumbered two to one, with no sign of Clinton.

On October 7 Burgoyne could wait no longer. He moved on Bemis Heights and attacked. When word reached Gates, his subordinate, Benedict Arnold, asked to lead a counterattack. Gates refused, but Arnold then refused to accept Gates's orders. Instead, Arnold mounted up and rode toward the sound of fighting. Entering the battlefield, he rallied the Continentals already in the fray with "Come on, brave boys, come on!" He took a bullet to the thigh—the same leg wounded in the attack on Quebec—and was carried off the field on a litter. But his heroics had vastly benefited the American cause.

The British had lost a strong commander, Brigadier Fraser, at Saratoga, and sustained some 1,200 casualties. Critical armament and some 6,000 prisoners of war were now in the hands of the Americans. On October 8, what was left of Burgoyne's tattered army

In this painting, *General Burgoyne confronts American forces during the heat of battle at Saratoga. The Americans scored a major victory when Burgoyne was forced to surrender his entire fighting force.*

began to retreat toward Ticonderoga in a heavy rain that mired their supply-filled wagons in mud, forcing them to abandon the supply train to the Americans. Gates's army, now swelled by local militias to some 12,000, soon blocked the British escape route. Burgoyne had no choice but to petition Gates for terms, and on October 17, the once resplendent army of Gentleman Johnny ceremoniously stacked their arms in surrender. Later, Gates and Burgoyne, bedecked in his formal uniform, dined together. "General, the caprice of war has made me your prisoner," Burgoyne conceded. Gates replied reassuringly, "I shall always be ready to testify that it was not through any fault of your excellency."

Again, the British had failed in their efforts to cut New England off from the rest of the states, just as they had failed in 1776, when the Howe brothers had attempted to control the Hudson. This time, though, the British losses were dire—so dire that most historians see Saratoga as a turning point in the war. But it had significance beyond the battlefield. It highlighted the political battles being waged among officers in high command on both sides, but particularly among the British. Burgoyne's great hope that he would be reinforced by Clinton, positioned in New York, had been ill placed. While Clinton did sail up the Hudson as far as Kingston, he had no intention of risking his forces in the strategic morass that Burgoyne had created. Besides, he stood to gain by Gentleman Johnny's

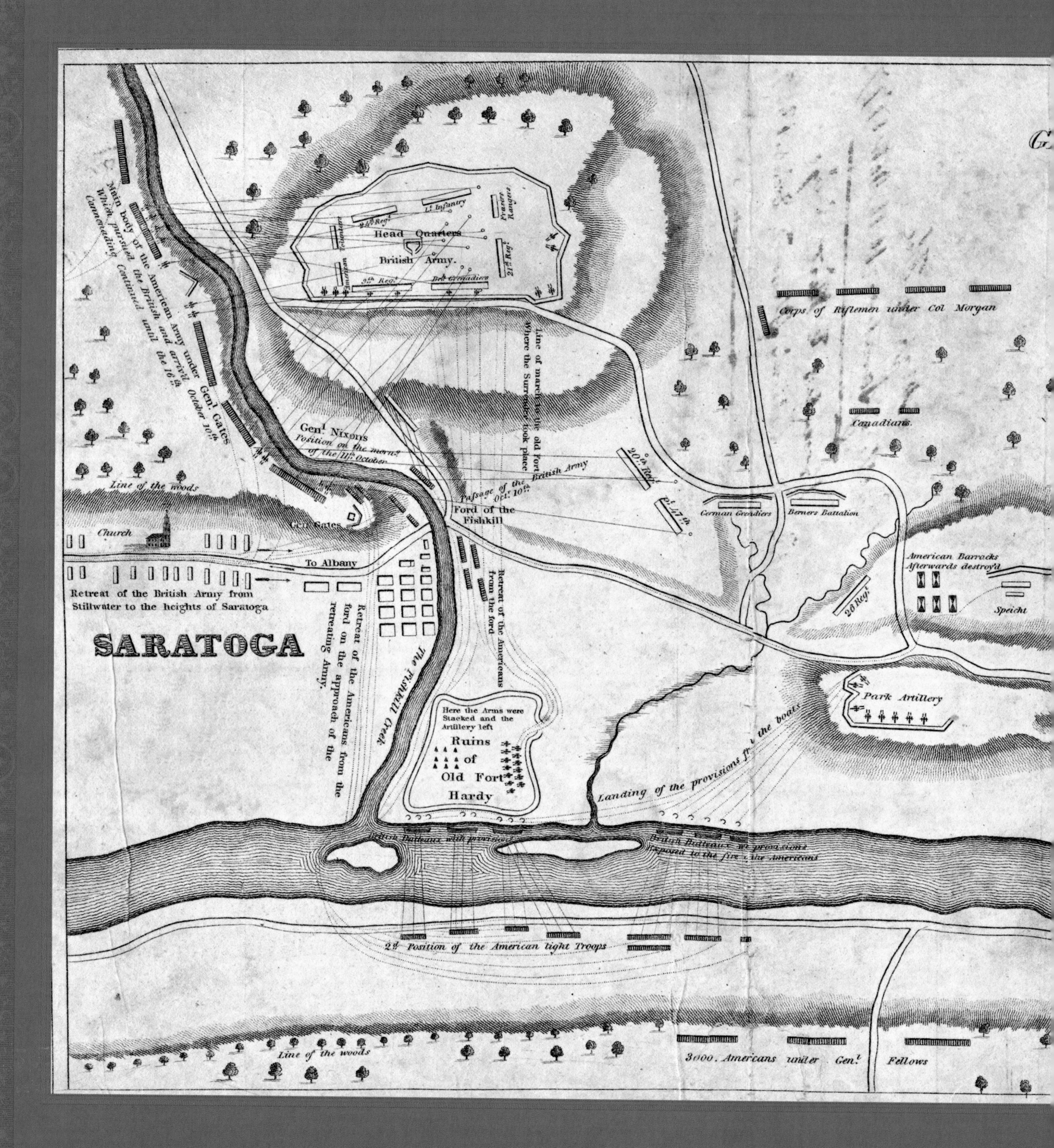
SARATOGA
Head Quarters
British Army.
Lt. Infantry
24th Regt.
Frasers Rangers
21st Regt.
9th Regt.
Brit. Grenadiers
Main body of the American Army under Genl. Gates
Which pursued the British and arrived October 10th
Cannonading Continued until the 16th
Line of march to the old Fort
Where the Surrender took place
Corps of Riflemen under Col Morgan
Canadians.
Genl. Nixons
Position on the morng of the 11th October
20th Regt.
Passage of the British Army Oct. 10th
Ford of the Fishkill
Line of the woods
Church
To Albany
German Grenadiers
Berners Battalion
American Barracks Afterwards destroyd
Speicht
26 Regt.
Retreat of the British Army from Stillwater to the heights of Saratoga
Retreat of the Americans from the ford
Retreat of the Americans from the ford on the approach of the retreating Army.
The Fishkill Creek
Park Artillery
Here the Arms were Stacked and the Artillery left
Ruins of Old Fort Hardy
Landing of the provisions from the boats
2d Position of the American light Troops
Line of the woods
3000. Americans under Genl. Fellows

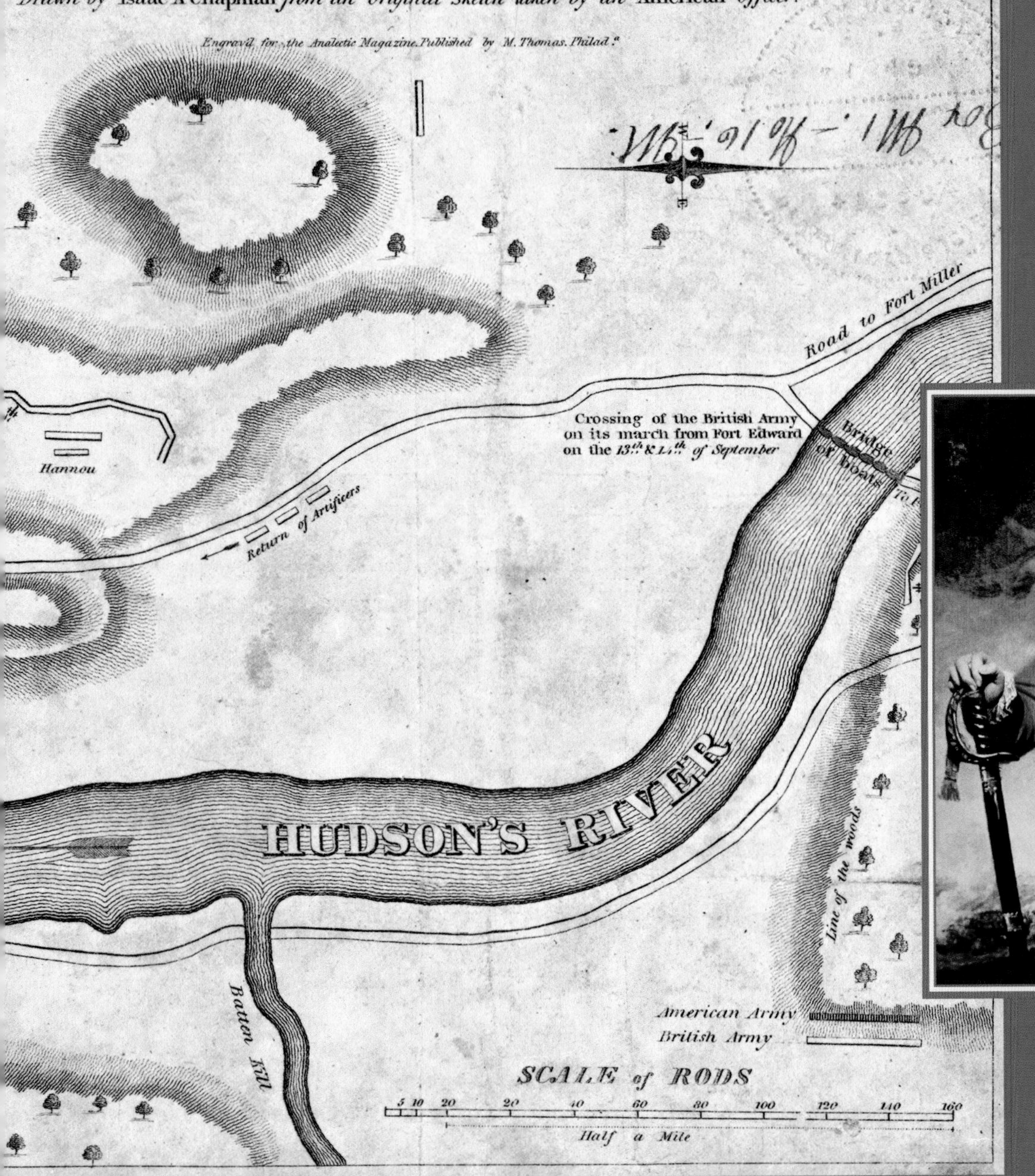

THE AMERICAN VICTORY at the Battle of Saratoga was a major turning point in the war, showing that the colonists were capable of mounting a serious military threat to the British. This map shows the positioning of artillery and the positioning of troops on the battlefield. The defeat of John Burgoyne (inset) at Saratoga was his undoing. After his return to England, he was never given another command.

defeat. In the ways of the military, it would reflect badly on Burgoyne's own commander, Gen. William Howe, thus paving the way for Clinton to succeed Howe as commander of the British forces in America. On the American side, General Gates assumed his victory would put him in a position to replace Washington (though his success against Burgoyne was really the result more of Arnold's heroism than of any tactics Gates brought to bear). Washington was well aware of what Burgoyne had called "the caprice of war." It could affect generals both on the battlefield and off it.

I confess the conduct of the enemy is distressing beyond measure and past our comprehension.

GEN. GEORGE WASHINGTON

While Burgoyne and Gates had circled each other in that summer of 1777, Washington and Howe had done the same. Washington kept a wary eye out for any sign of movement from Howe's army in New York and by mid-July had moved his own army north to the Clove, a gorge in the highlands on the Hudson's west shore. From there, he could have moved quickly to reinforce Gates in northern New York, had the need arisen. It had not, so instead Washington watched as Howe began assembling an impressive flotilla. Washington suspected that Howe was planning a move south on Philadelphia, roughly a hundred miles away. Then, in late July, the flotilla set sail, and disappeared over the Atlantic horizon. "The most general suspicion now," John Adams wrote to Abigail, "is that Howe has gone to Charleston S.C. But it a wild Supposition. I may be right however: for Howe is a wild General."

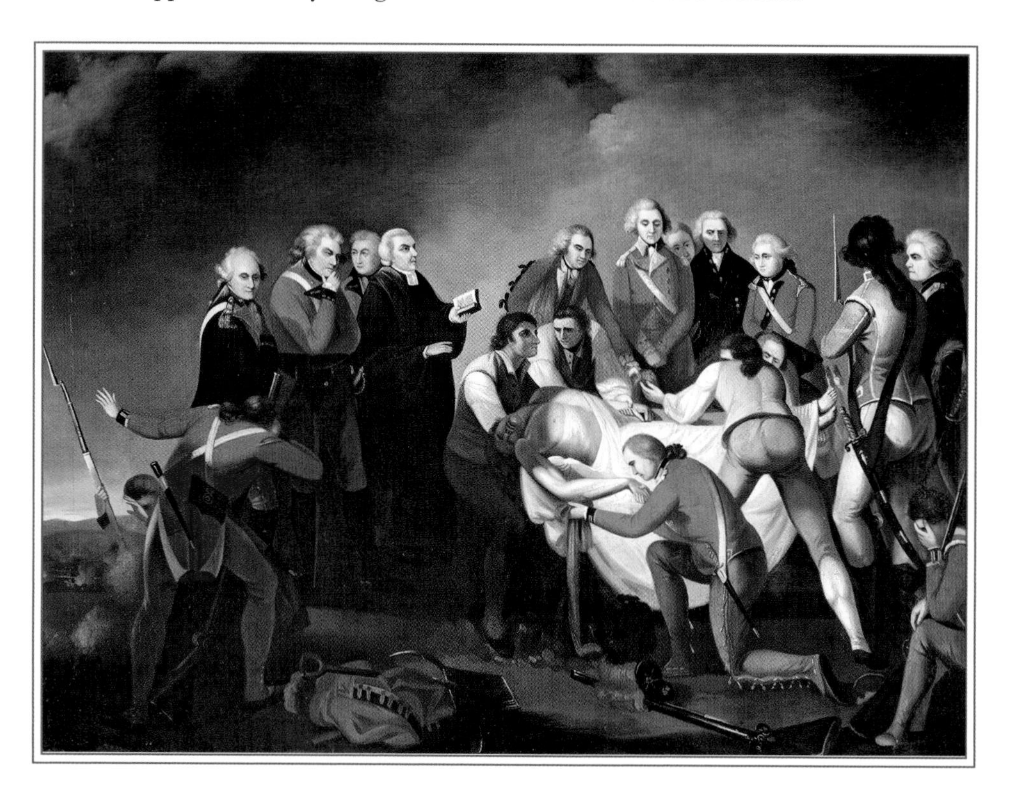

DURING THE BATTLE *of Bemis Heights, British general Simon Fraser (1729–1777) was mortally wounded by an American sniper, Timothy Murphy, who targeted the Englishman on direct orders from Benedict Arnold.*

AMERICAN ARTIST JOHN TRUMBULL *painted the historic moment when, after the Battle of Saratoga, British general John Burgoyne surrendered to the American general, Horatio Gates.*

With so few major cities and ports in America, Charleston was as good a guess as any, but Howe's real target had always been the same: Philadelphia, the patriots' de facto capital. He had strongly considered coming at it from Delaware Bay, but the banks there were well fortified. So he decided to move farther south, into the broad Chesapeake, and then double back overland to Philadelphia.

In late July, as Howe's flotilla of almost 230 ships set sail, they were thwarted by summer winds as capricious as the winds of war. The trip down the coast to the mouth of the bay in Virginia, then up the Chesapeake to Maryland should have taken about a week. Instead, it took the British masters of the sea 32 days. From hour to windless hour, men and horses baked under a relentless sun that rotted food and spoiled water. Finally, at the end of August, Howe's force landed near Head of Elk, Maryland. A 57-mile march to Philadelphia still lay ahead, and many of the British horses either had died or been incapacitated from the voyage. Once ashore, the slow-moving Howe paused again for three weeks to rest his force.

Washington's consternation had grown as Howe had remained beyond sight during the prolonged voyage. "I confess the conduct of the enemy is distressing beyond measure and past our comprehension," he wrote. But by the time Howe reached Head of Elk, Washington

understood that Howe's objective was Philadelphia. Both generals were eager and primed for a decisive confrontation.

Washington now had between 12,000 and 14,000 men under his command, and as he headed south to meet Howe, he marched his men down the streets of Philadelphia—a victorious, if ragtag, army of survivors who had bested the finest military in the world. They would soon have to do it again, and they knew it—as did the citizens who cheered them on, despite their haphazard parading and roughness. John Adams watched too, then repaired to a nearby church to seek divine reassurance.

Finally, Howe began the march north, and Washington moved to intercept him southwest of Philadelphia along a jumble of ravines and woodlands bordering Brandywine Creek. Washington had little time to deploy his troops, and his haste hampered him. He was back in Loyalist territory, and he had every right to expect the British would benefit from that. In fact, Joseph Galloway, who had a few years earlier served honorably in the First Continental Congress—though he had argued against rebellion—was now a confirmed Tory and had paid locals to reconnoiter for Howe. Through locals, Howe learned of two unguarded fjords across Brandywine Creek. As he had in his march on Brooklyn, he divided his army. Sending half of it against Washington's concentrated force, he took the other half on a flanking maneuver. Howe led the way on a horse barely fit to ride after the month-long sea voyage it had just endured.

After serving bravely *on the battlefield, young Alexander Hamilton became George Washington's chief of staff and close confidante. Opposite: The Marquis de Lafayette became a popular wartime hero, famously depicted here standing on a hill and preparing to lead his troops in a charge against the British.*

With Lafayette at his side, Washington watched the anticipated charge against his main line. Oblivious to his own safety, he commanded his troops from horseback and watched as they quickly—too quickly—beat back the British. The enemy strength in the charge, Washington realized, was far less than it should have been. He began receiving conflicting reports from his outlying officers about British troop movements elsewhere. Initially, he seemed to disbelieve the news that the greater force of Howe's army was moving into position to flank him.

Thick, sticky fog dimmed visibility through the early hours and became a boon to the British as they marched forward. By four o'clock that hot, late summer afternoon, they were in place to squeeze the American line in a classic pincer movement. When the roar of artillery suddenly erupted, it echoed through the countryside as far away as Philadelphia. Neither side gave way as shot after shot rang out, taking down men and the limbs of the forest canopy. One soldier described "trees crackling overhead" and "leaves falling as in autumn." Washington was in the thick of it all day, as was Lafayette. The young French officer fought bravely and took a bullet to the left calf. According to Lafayette's account, Washington told the army doctor tending him to "Take care of him as if he were my son, for I love him the same."

It took sundown to end the fighting, with the Americans in retreat toward Chester, Pennsylvania. Their defeat had been unequivocal—some 1,100 casualties to half that for the British. Yet Washington seemed unwilling to acknowledge the debacle. In his official letter to John Hancock, he claimed, "Our loss of men is not . . . very considerable; I believe much less than the enemy's."

The following day, both generals hoped to engage again, but heavy rain made marching—much less fighting—almost impossible. The men sank in mud up to their calves, and their ammunition was soaked. Washington understood that he could no longer defend Philadelphia, and he sent word to the Continental Congress by one of his trusted aides, Alexander Hamilton, that Howe was on his way and could arrive by the following morning.

BATTLES AND MILITARY OPERATIONS *engulfed the upper mid-Atlantic, as detailed in this map of Pennsylvania, New Jersey, Maryland, and Delaware.*

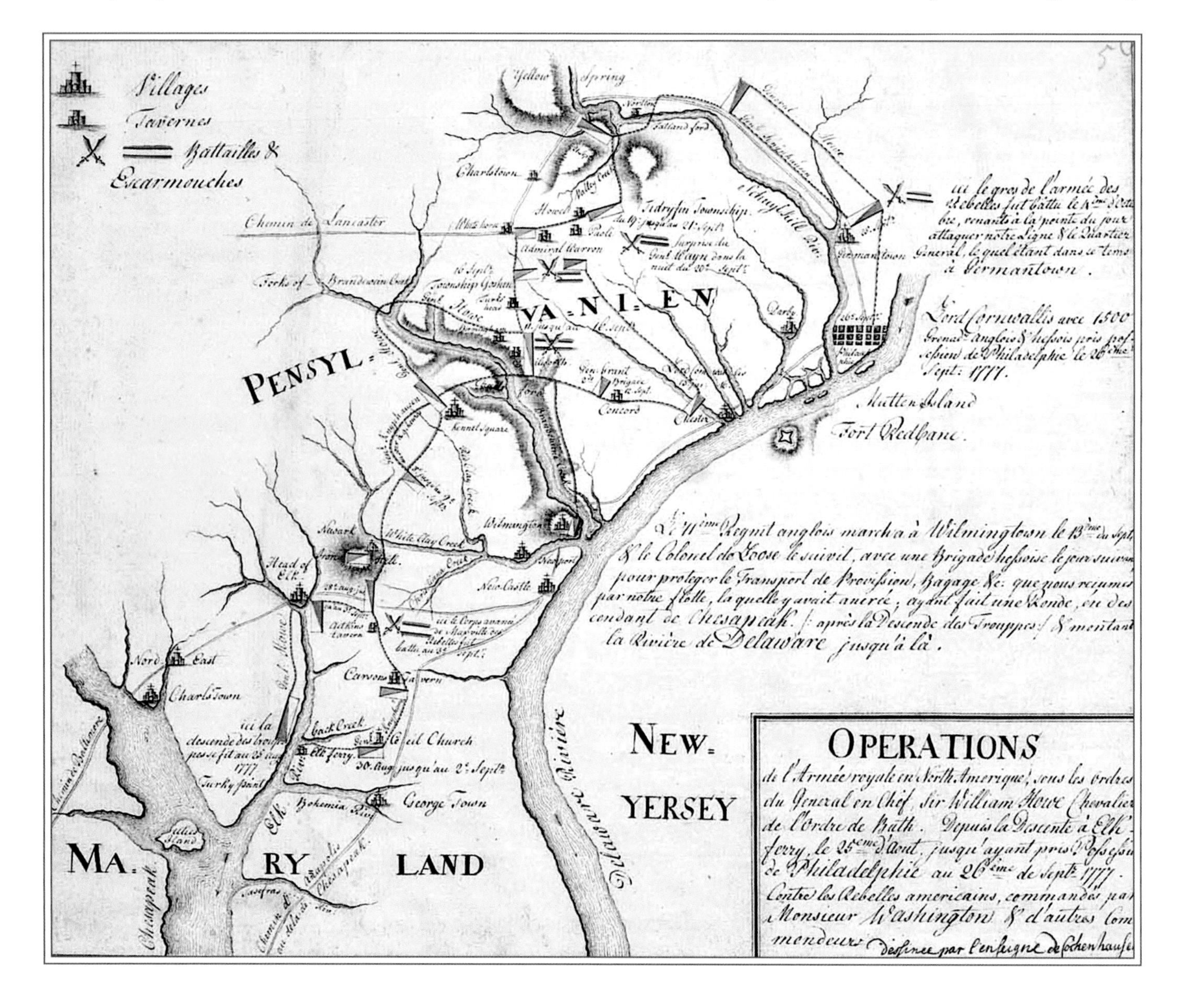

Members of the Continental Congress and local citizens filled the night streets in their rush to evacuate.

Thomas Paine, newly appointed as Secretary of the Committee of Foreign Affairs, was in Philadelphia and did not join the evacuees that night. He was ready with his next cri de coeur, *Crisis IV:* "Howe has been once on the banks of the Delaware, and from thence driven back with loss and disgrace: and why not be again driven from the Schuylkill?" he wrote encouragingly. He went on to exhort and reassure: "Men who are sincere in defending their freedom, will always feel concern at every circumstance which seems to make against them; . . . But the dejection lasts only for a moment; they soon rise out of it with additional vigor; the glow of hope, courage and fortitude, will, in a little time, supply the place of every inferior passion, and kindle the whole heart into heroism."

It was another week before the British, under Lord Cornwallis, marched in to claim the city. By then the Continental Congress was safely ensconced in York, Pennsylvania, where John Adams wrote to Abigail a letter that seemed to embody the patriotic sentiment: "I shall avoid every Thing like History, and make no Reflections. However, General Washington is in a Condition tolerably respectable, and the Militia are now turning out, from Virginia, Maryland and Pennsylvania in small Numbers." He went on to credit Howe's triumph in part to the passive obedience of the Quakers, who were the prime inhabitants of "the whole country through which he passed."

IN COUNCIL OF SAFETY,

PHILADELPHIA, *December* 8, 1776.

SIR,

THERE is certain intelligence of General Howe's army being yefterday on its march from Brunfwick to Princetown, which puts it beyond a doubt that he intends for this city.—This glorious opportunity of fignalizing himfelf in defence of our country, and fecuring the Rights of America forever, will be feized by every man who has a fpark of patriotic fire in his bofom. We entreat you to march the Militia under your command with all poffible expedition to this city, and bring with you as many waggons as you can poffibly procure, which you are hereby authorized to imprefs, if they cannot be had otherwife—Delay not a moment, it may be fatal and fubject you and all you hold moft dear to the ruffian hands of the enemy, whofe cruelties are without diftinction and unequalled.

By Order of the Council,

DAVID RITTENHOUSE, Vice-Prefident.

To the COLONELS *or* COMMANDING OFFICERS *of the refpective* Battalions *of this* STATE.

TWO O'CLOCK, P. M.

THE Enemy are at Trenton, and all the City Militia are marched to meet them.

THIS HANDBILL *from the "Council of Safety" warned residents of British general William Howe's impending approach to Philadelphia, Pennsylvania.*

Battle of Germantown

THE LOSS OF PHILADELPHIA WAS UNQUESTIONABLY A BLOW TO CONTINENTAL morale, but Washington had come to understand that cities were not the objective of this war and would avail the enemy little. "It is our arms, not defenseless towns, they have to subdue," he wrote. Howe seemed to understand that as well and had the better part of his army bivouacked in Germantown, across the Schuylkill River a few miles northwest of Philadelphia.

By early October Washington had become convinced that the only way to raise flagging morale and to move the Continental cause forward was an attack on Howe's force in Germantown. He planned a Trenton-style lunge for the evening of October 3. The plan was complicated, and serious, even ruinous, blunders were made in the brief three hours of fighting. One critical problem, which Washington had foreseen, was the lack of a consistent Continental uniform. In evening fog and the smoke of battle, the Americans tragically mistook each other for the enemy as it was "impossible to Distinguish our men from the Enemy at a greater Distance than Sixty yards, and many favourable Advantages were lost," one Virginia general later reported.

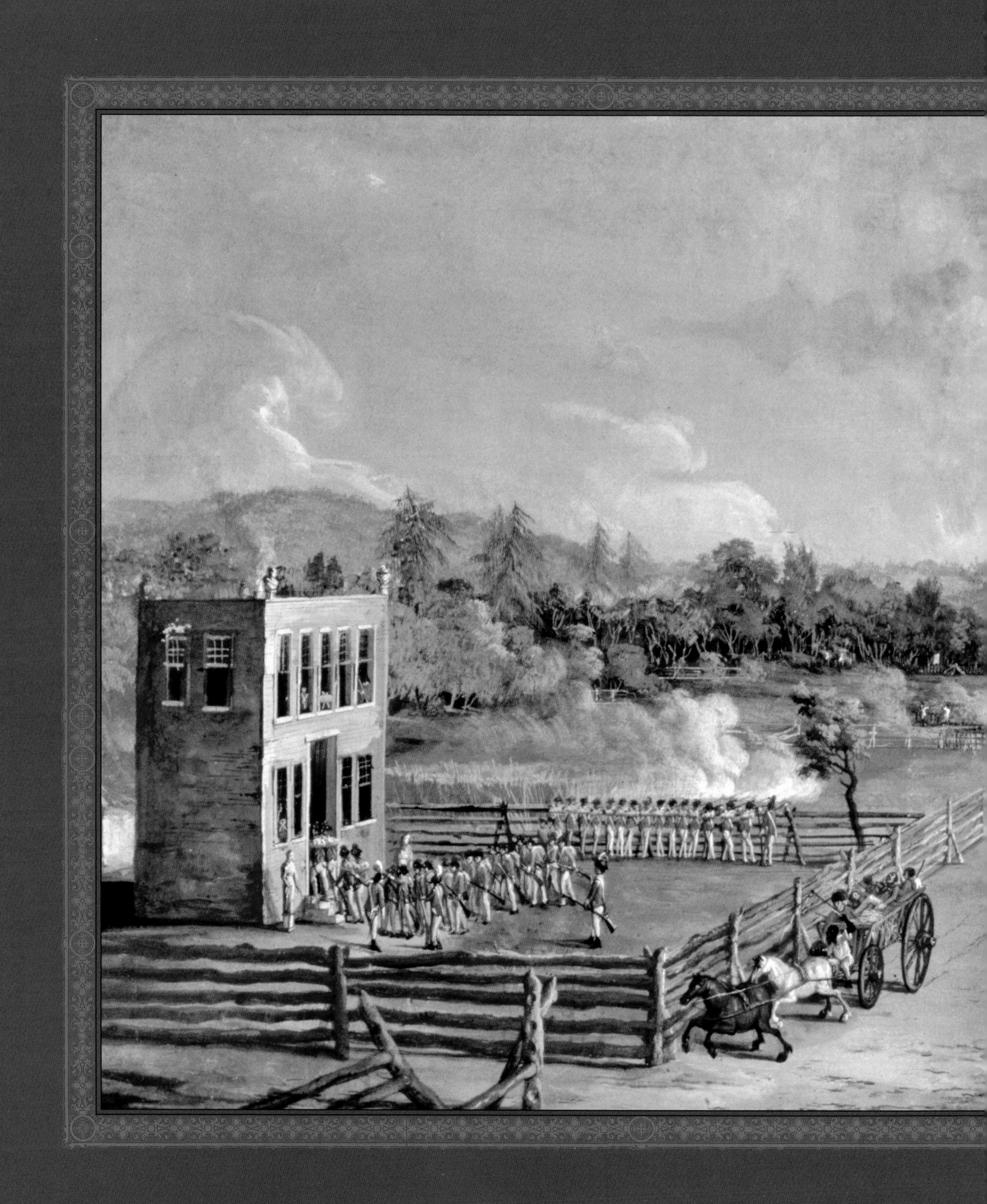

FOUGHT ON OCTOBER 4, 1777, *the Battle of Germantown, Pennsylvania, was an important victory for the British, for it ensured that they would control Philadelphia for the winter of 1777–1778.*

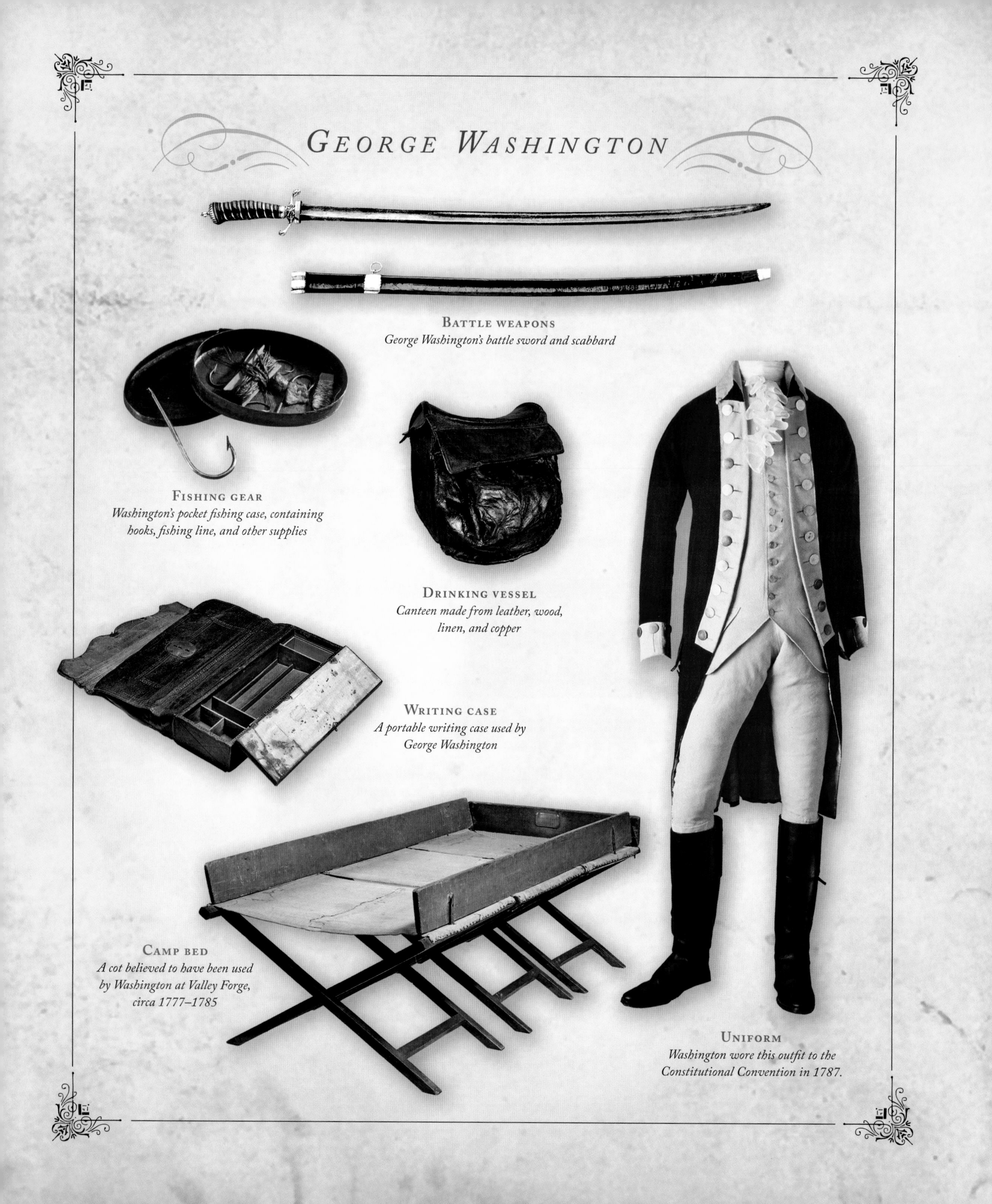

George Washington

Battle weapons
George Washington's battle sword and scabbard

Fishing gear
Washington's pocket fishing case, containing hooks, fishing line, and other supplies

Drinking vessel
Canteen made from leather, wood, linen, and copper

Writing case
A portable writing case used by George Washington

Camp bed
A cot believed to have been used by Washington at Valley Forge, circa 1777–1785

Uniform
Washington wore this outfit to the Constitutional Convention in 1787.

Again, the Americans found themselves in retreat. The campaign season was ending, and Howe had few options but to move his army into Philadelphia for the winter. He knew that Philadelphia could prove another Boston for the British: a prison from which they could not extricate themselves.

From across the Atlantic in Paris, Franklin saw it that way. When told the news of his hometown's fall, Franklin assured the messenger, "You mistake the matter. Instead of *Howe* taking *Philadelphia, Philadelphia* has taken *Howe.*"

As Washington considered his options, he also enjoyed a moment of levity. He sent Howe a note (actually penned by Alexander Hamilton): "General Washington's compliments to General Howe. He does himself the pleasure to return him a dog, which accidentally fell into his hands, and by the inscription on the Collar appears to belong to General Howe."

You mistake the matter. Instead of Howe taking Philadelphia, Philadelphia has taken Howe.

BENJAMIN FRANKLIN

Washington could do with a little levity. He had lost two battles in a row, while Gates would soon emerge the hero of Saratoga and celebrated in a new ballad that proclaimed, "Brave Gates will clear America before another year." At the same time, Washington's audacity at Germantown was not overlooked. The Continental Congress forged a medal in his honor, and across the Atlantic in France, ministers watched admiringly as the Americans took on the British giant bravely and repeatedly. The Americans may have lost Germantown, but the strike had been audacious, and then there was news of Saratoga. It was an enormous feather in the American cap, and Franklin, negotiating delicately and adroitly with the French, used it to good advantage.

Since he had arrived in France the previous winter, Doctor Franklin had become the toast of the French public, which regaled him as a philosopher in league with Plato or Socrates. Though engravings of Franklin were placed reverentially above mantelpieces, he was not quite as cherished by the French ministers, who were biding time until they better understood which way the winds of war were blowing. Franklin assured them, in writing, that an American victory would be entirely in their favor, as it would fatally weaken their great enemy Britain. Yet the ministers hesitated to declare a true alliance, and instead they offered quiet assistance by opening their ports to American goods and funneling some monies through back channels.

A COMMEMORATIVE MEDAL *issued by Congress after the war depicts the great hero of the day, Washington.*

The British, only too aware that an American-French alliance could sweep the former colonies to victory, had been making their own quiet overtures to Franklin, who engaged in diplomatic repartee with the British envoy. "Terms that come voluntarily, and shew generosity, will do honour to Great Britain and may engage the confidence of America," he encouraged them. But he also said that he would "consult" the French on any terms the

Benjamin Franklin *was beloved at the French court, where he served as a diplomat for almost a decade. Early in his tenure, he negotiated the crucial treaty between France and the United States.*

British offered. At the same time, he made the French aware of the British entreaties, skillfully playing one imperial power against the other. The generals in America furthered his cause by impressing the French with their fighting spirit. By early winter the battle news from America, coupled with Franklin's diplomacy (far more than that of his fellow commissioners, Silas Deane and Arthur Lee), persuaded the French to take up the American cause officially. In February 1778, two treaties were signed—one regarding open commerce between the countries, the other "A Treaty of Alliance Between the United States of America and His Most Christian Majesty," the newly enthroned young king, Louis XVI.

Months before the treaty signing, in November, the Continental Congress had adopted the Articles of Confederation and Perpetual Union, the first of which declared, "The style of the confederacy shall be the 'United States of America.' " But the second article seemed to negate that: "Each state retains its sovereignty, freedom, and independence, and every power, jurisdiction and right . . ." The only uniting element would be the common defense. Almost every great player in the Revolution understood from the beginning that the articles were flawed, but no one could anticipate that it would take three and a half years for all of the states to ratify them.

While news of the adoption of the Articles of Confederation easily reached George Washington, conclusive word of Franklin's great victory did not arrive until spring. By then, Washington and his army had survived, but barely, a harrowing winter of discontent, starvation, and disease at Valley Forge. More a plateau than a valley, its cluster of low, thickly forested hills lay about 18 miles from Philadelphia, close enough to keep an eye on Howe but remote enough not to overburden a civilian population already suffering from an influx of new refugees.

Winter in Valley Forge

THE 11,000 MEN WHO SET UP CAMP IN VALLEY FORGE IN DECEMBER 1777 WERE ALREADY exhausted, hungry, battered, and sometimes bleeding—red streaks of their passing stained the already winter-white ground. They made themselves log huts measuring just 14 by 16 feet to ward off the cold. A dozen men might cram into one hut—a blessing because body warmth, not blankets, was all they had to warm them. They must have dreamed of food as they worked, because they had had precious little during the previous weeks. Now they subsisted on fire cake (a thin water-and-flour bread baked on a hot stone). But even that loathed provision ran out as the winter wore on.

The week before Christmas, Washington had issued general orders assuring his men, "Altho' in some instances we unfortunately failed, yet upon the whole Heaven hath smiled

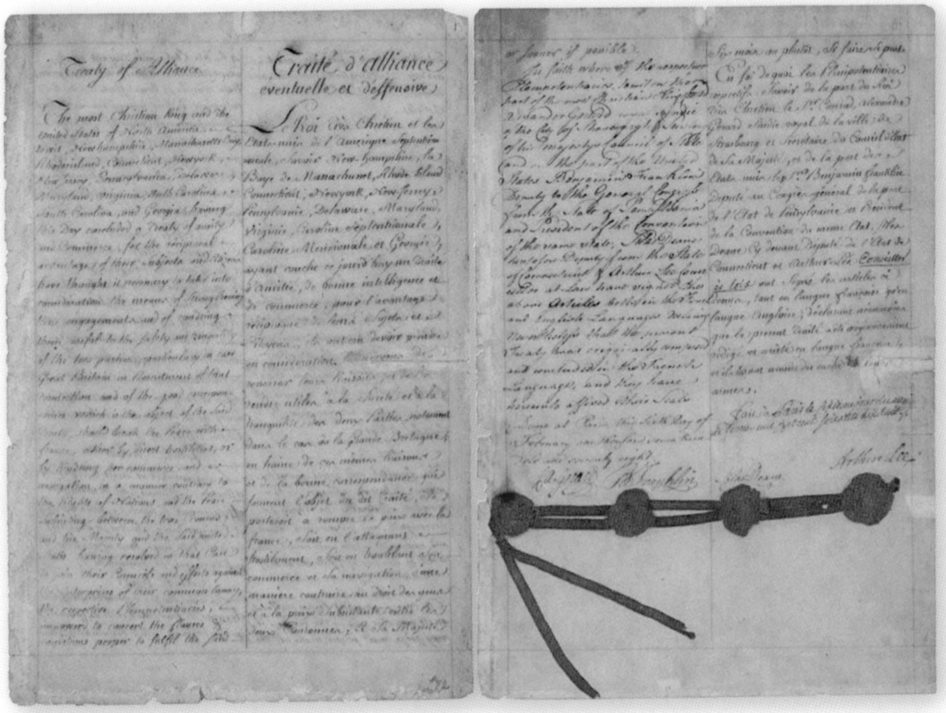
Treaty of Alliance

Traité d'alliance eventuelle et deffensive

THE TREATY OF ALLIANCE between France and the United States, signed in 1778, gave the new nation a strong ally in its fight against the British.

GEORGE AND MARTHA WASHINGTON *(preceding pages) often visited with the troops at Valley Forge, where the Continental Army encamped during the brutal winter of 1777–1778.*

on our Arms and crowned them with signal success; and we may upon the best grounds conclude, that by a spirited continuance of the measures necessary for our defence we shall finally obtain the end of our Warfare, Independence, Liberty and Peace." But Washington also knew that the winter ahead would be hard, and he told them that he himself "would take post in the neighbourhood of this camp . . . share in the hardship, and partake of every inconvenience."

The hardship was worse than he predicted. Shoeless men, their clothes in tatters, stared into bleak, unrelenting cold. Horses toppled over from starvation. Men lost limbs to frostbite and lives to typhus, typhoid, pneumonia, and dysentery. But always Washington, calm if privately distraught, moved among them encouragingly. "Naked and starving as they are," he wrote in a letter, "we cannot enough admire the incomparable patience and fidelity of the soldiery." It may have been Washington more than anything else—the men's loyalty, admiration, and confidence in him—that kept the men from deserting in droves during the hopeless winter of Valley Forge.

Adding to the misery, on February 7 a blizzard buried the camp in several feet of snow, making it virtually impossible to move. Days later, rain fell and then froze into sheets of ice. By then mutiny had begun to fill the air, among both soldiers and politicians. Washington was dealing with his fellow general, Horatio Gates, who wrote him dismissive letters. Other detractors, Washington knew, wanted to replace him; his army was facing "little less than a famine"; and he lived in the constant fear that Howe would attack his starving army (an attack that somehow never came). If the early winter of 1776 had seemed desperate, 1777–1778 seemed desolate. But he did enjoy one consolation in those horrific months. Martha came to stay with him.

The cramped second floor of the old mill house she and Washington occupied was a far cry from the comforts of Mount Vernon, yet she came as she had in previous winters and would in the war winters to come. "Mrs. Washington is extremely fond of the general and he of her," one officer's wife observed. "[T]hey are very happy in each other." Martha did more than merely console and cheer her husband—despite the fact that she was mourning the loss of her younger sister and best friend. She also worked tirelessly for the troops by tending the sick, knitting, and sewing: "Every fair day she might be seen, with basket in hand and with a single attendant, going among the keenest and most needy sufferers and giving all the comforts to them in her power."

Her ministrations could do little more than provide comfort. The winter at Valley Forge took the lives of 2,000 men. But it also transformed the army. The sloppily formed men

MARTHA WASHINGTON
1731–1802

On June 2, 1731, Martha Washington was the first child born to John and Frances Dandridge near Williamsburg, Virginia. At age 18 she married Daniel Parke Custis, a wealthy planter, with whom she had four children, only two of whom survived to adulthood. Custis died in 1757, and Martha married again two years later, this time to George Washington. The pair never had children, but Martha's two children were raised as their own. The Mount Vernon estate, on the Potomac River in northern Virginia, became the family home. When war came to the colonies, Martha traveled hundreds of miles on difficult roads to be with her husband at his winter encampments. Her time at Valley Forge, Pennsylvania, is perhaps the most famous, given the brutality of the winter. Her presence as hostess boosted morale among the officers, their wives, and other soldiers as they braved the hardships of snow and deprivation.

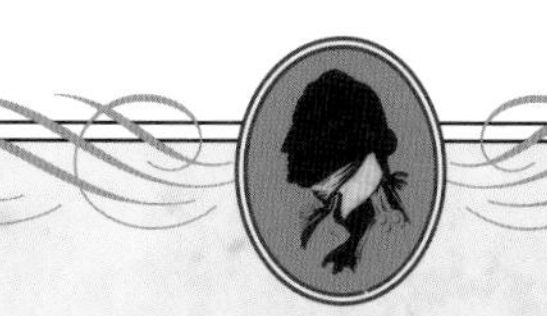

Washington to Henry Laurens, President of Congress

Valley Forge, December 23, 1777.

Sir . . .

I am now convinced, beyond a doubt that unless some great and capital change suddenly takes place in that line, this Army must inevitably be reduced to one or other of these three things. Starve, dissolve, or disperse, in order to obtain subsistence in the best manner they can; rest assured Sir this is not an exaggerated picture, but [and] that I have abundant reason to support what I say.

George Washington's army marching to Valley Forge, Pennsylvania, 1777

Yesterday afternoon receiving information that the Enemy, in force, had left the City, and were advancing towards Derby with apparent design to forage, and draw Subsistance from that part of the Country, I order'd the Troops to be in readiness, that I might give every opposition in my power; when, behold! to my great mortification, I was not only informed, but convinced, that the Men were unable to stir on Acct. of Provision, and that a dangerous Mutiny [had] begun the Night before . . .

This brought forth the only Corny. in the purchasing Line, in this Camp; and, with him, this Melancholy and alarming truth; that he had not a single hoof of any kind to Slaughter, and not more than 25. Barls. of Flour! From hence form an opinion of our Situation when I add, that, he could not tell when to expect any . . .

What then is to become of the Army this Winter? and if we are as often without Provisions now, as with it [them], what is to become of us in the Spring, when our force will be collected, with the aid perhaps of Militia, to take advantage of an early Campaign before the Enemy can be reinforced? These are considerations of great magnitude, meriting the closest attention, and will, when my own reputation is so intimately connected, and to be affected by the event, justifie my saying that the present Commissaries are by no means equal to the execution [of the Office] or that the disaffection of the People is past all belief . . . [F]inding that the inactivity of the Army, whether for want of provisions, Cloaths, or other essentials, is charged to my Acct., not only by the common vulgar, but those in power, it is time to speak plain in exculpation of myself; with truth then I can declare that, no Man, in my opinion, ever had his measures more impeded than I have, by every department of the Army . . .

Credited with instilling discipline *and order in the Continental Army, Baron Friedrich von Steuben of Prussia was an influential officer in the American Army. Shown here, he drills American troops at Valley Forge, 1778.*

who had marched through Pennsylvania gradually took on the aspect of a disciplined fighting force. This transformation was what Washington had planned for that winter—"Establishing one uniform Sett of Manoeuvres and Manual Exercise" and drilling the men on the "Tricks of Parade." He was greatly helped by the appearance of yet another European volunteer recommended by Franklin. The man who appeared at Valley Forge in late February called himself Friedrich William Augustus, Baron von Steuben, and claimed to be Prussian aristocracy and Frederick the Great's quartermaster general. Whether there was a kernel of truth in any of his claims is unknown, but Washington quickly came to admire his skills in drilling the unwieldy American troops.

Armed with no more English than "Goddamn," which he used liberally, Steuben began teaching a carefully selected Virginia guard close-order drill. Once schooled, that guard fanned out and taught other units the art of military drill, and those in turn taught more units. The men developed a fondness for the barking, volatile Steuben, and he, in his own way, became fond of the troops. In a telling letter, Steuben explained Americans to a European comrade: "In the first place, the genius of this nation is not in the least to be compared with that of the Prussians, Austrians, or French. You say to your soldier, 'Do this,' and he doeth it, but I am obliged to say, 'This is the reason why you ought to do that,' and he does it."

> *You say to [a European] soldier, "Do this," and he doeth it, but I am obliged to say, "This is the reason why you ought to do that," and he does it.*
>
> Baron Friedrich Wilhelm von Steuben

By the time spring finally broke the anxious winter, the Continental Army had achieved the kind of military discipline Steuben had always longed for it to have. And Washington, despite loud voices against him, still had command of it. General Howe was not so lucky. He had spent a winter of inaction in Philadelphia. Then, in early May, as the world was learning of the French-American alliance, the British government replaced Howe with Sir Henry Clinton, who had intentionally failed to reinforce Burgoyne in his debacle at Saratoga. Clinton, Howe, and Burgoyne had arrived in America together in 1775; they had been dispatched to Boston as a "triumvirate of reputation." But the American war had a way of dissolving reputations, and now Clinton was the only one of the triumvirate remaining.

Clinton had orders to evacuate Philadelphia after eight months of occupation. So, in late June, his 10,000 men and 1,500 wagons, followed by perhaps 3,000 Loyalists, left William Penn's City of Brotherly Love behind and began inching their way back across New Jersey to New York. Clinton's long, straggling train was an irresistible target, and Washington moved quickly toward it with his own army of over 13,000 disciplined troops. He was eager to test his newly polished men, but his war council advised against it, and Washington hesitated. At the same time, Lafayette boldly advised Washington against his practice of consulting with a war council, as it would "never be a mean of doing what is consistent with the good of the service."

Gen. Sir Henry Clinton *(1730–1795) replaced General Howe as the commander in chief of the British forces after the failed 1777 campaigns.*

Surely the fact that the recalcitrant Charles Lee was again part of the council was not good for the service. It was Lee who had so ill served Washington in the fall of 1776, when he had dragged his heels in reinforcing Washington's desperate flight across New Jersey and gotten himself arrested by the British. Freed in the spring of 1777, thanks to the negotiations of the Continental Congress, Lee had again insinuated himself into the higher echelons of the Continental officers. Washington had welcomed him back with open arms and a celebratory dinner. Now Lee was second in command and as uncooperative, obnoxious, and self-aggrandizing as ever.

As June 28 dawned, Washington ordered Lee "to move on and attack" the British, who were outside Monmouth Court House and moving across New Jersey's sandy pine barrens, sliced by streams and ravines. Washington's order to Lee ended with an equivocation: "unless

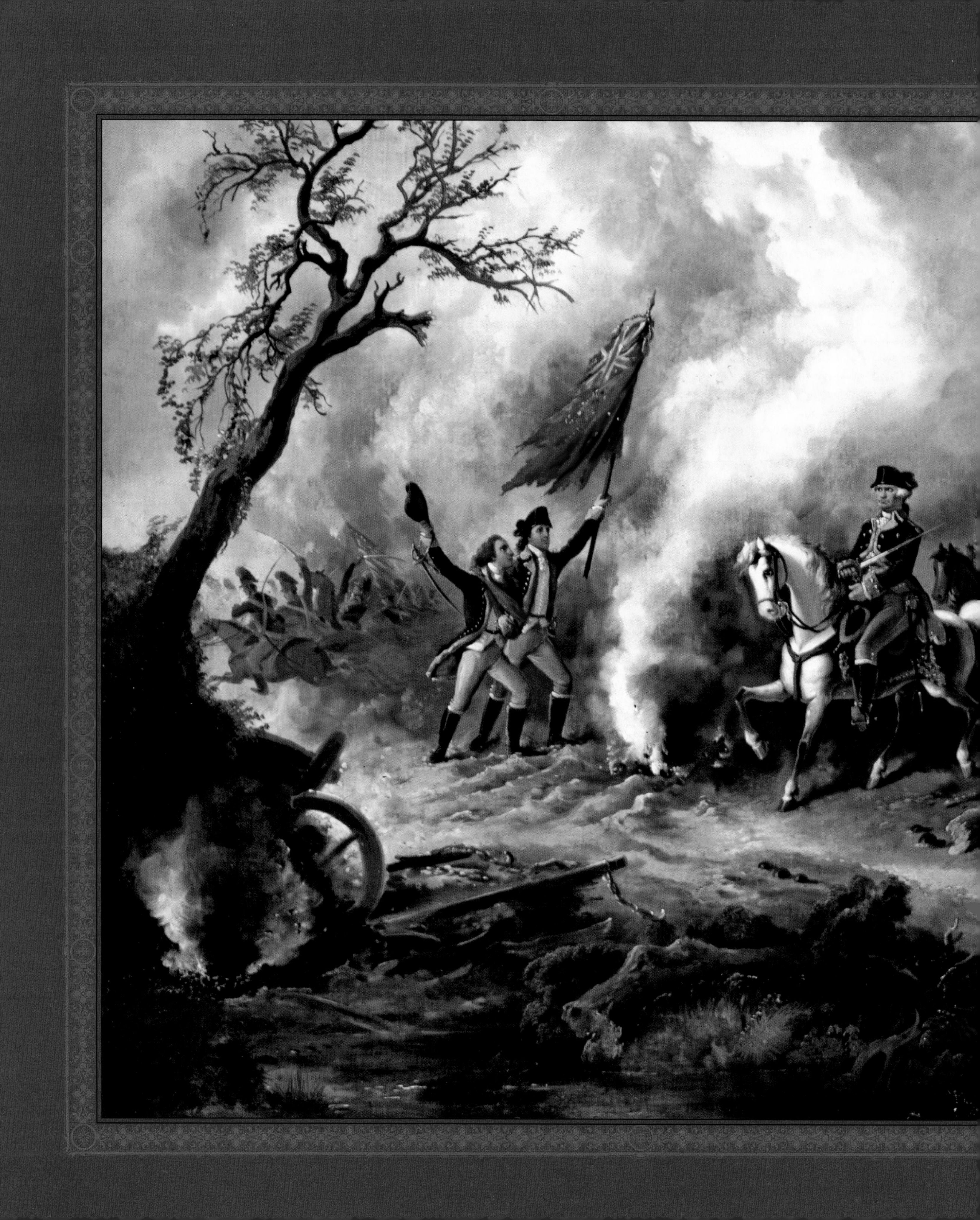

George Washington led *the American forces against Gen. Henry Clinton's troops as they left Monmouth Courthouse in New Jersey. The battle, fought on June 28, 1778, had no clear winner, as both armies still held the field at the end of the day. Clinton was able to withdraw his forces safely to New York with no interference from the Americans, but Washington's ability to hold the field indicated the growing strength and effectiveness of the American military.*

A MAP *of the Saratoga and Philadelphia campaigns (opposite), the major series of battles from 1777–1778*

there should be very powerful reasons to the contrary." At some point that hot morning, Lee made a lackluster push at the British rear guard, under the command of Cornwallis, and by noon, Lee's and Cornwallis's men were engaged.

As Washington and the main force drew near, retreating Continentals from Lee's advance force met them. And then Lee rode nonchalantly forward to Washington, who demanded, "What is the meaning of this, sir? I desire to know the meaning of this disorder and confusion?"

Lee was nonplussed by Washington's fury, and some reports claim he explained that "the American troops would not stand the British bayonets."

Washington would have none of it. "You damned poltroon," he reportedly said. "You never tried them."

"No one had ever before seen Washington so terribly excited," Lafayette reported. "His whole appearance was fearful." Fueled by rage and conviction, Washington rallied the remaining brigades, and they fought on in "heat so intense that soldiers fell dead without

Campagne du Vice-amiral Cte d'Estaing-
-en amérique, commandant une Escadre de 12-
-Vaisseaux et de 4 Frégates, sortie de Toulon-
- le 13 avril 1778
n.X
a
b
l'Escadre partie de Rhode-Island le 21 aout, double le Cap Codd, et fait voile pour Boston ou elle arrive le 28.
a le Vaisseau le Languedoc rematé avec des mats d'hune-
-liés aux tronçons restans de sa précédente mature
b. son Gouvernail remplacé par une vergue garnie de-
-flasques d'affûts et de boulets, selon le Sistême d'olivier.

COUNT D'ESTAING'S FLEET OF SHIPS, *which were supposed to take part in a siege of Newport, Rhode Island. Inset: Charles Henri (1729–1794), Count d'Estaing, was generally unimpressed with America's prowess in war, and refused to risk his own fleet when he felt blunders had been made.*

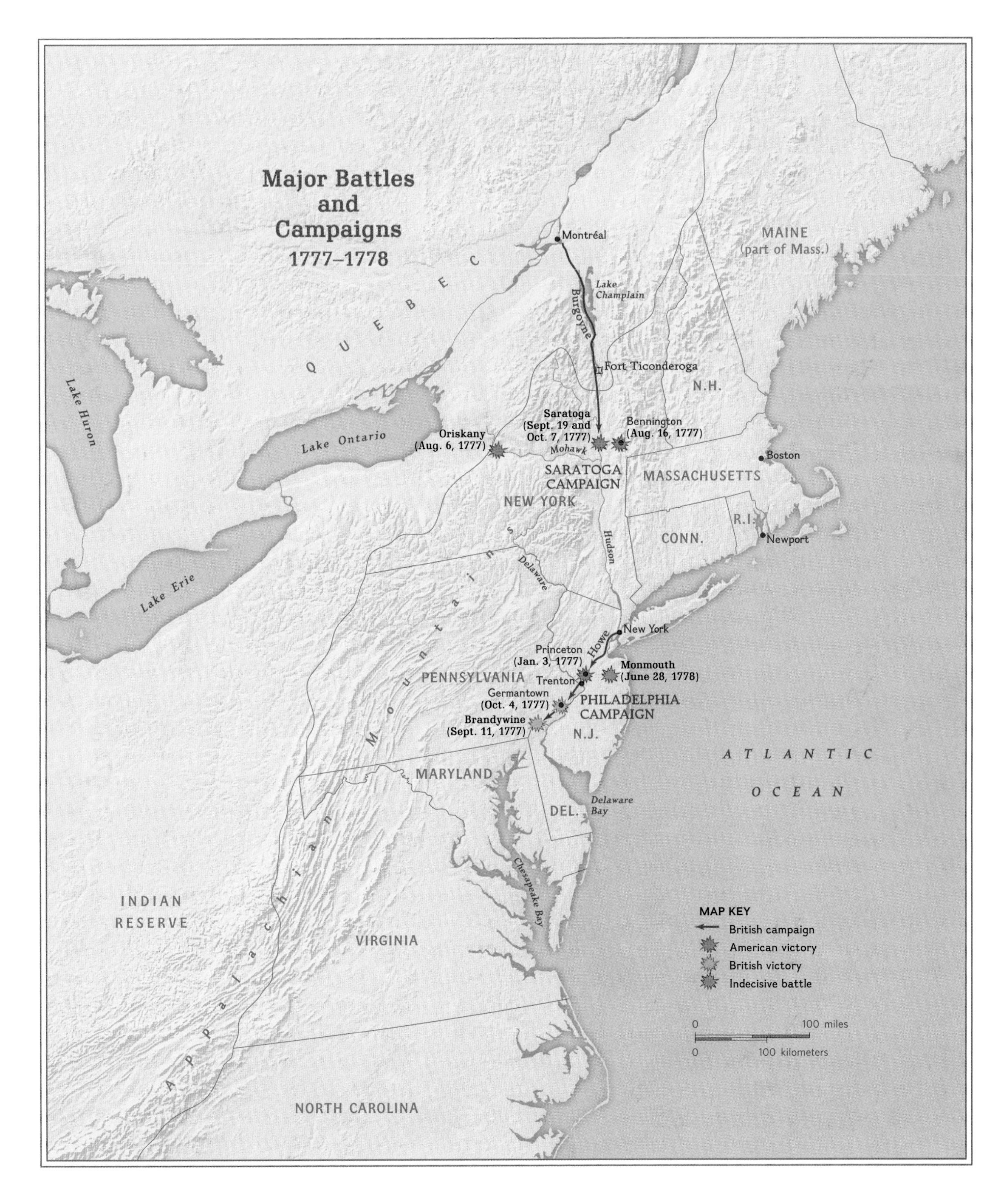
Major Battles and Campaigns 1777–1778
QUEBEC
Montréal
Lake Champlain
Burgoyne
Fort Ticonderoga
MAINE (part of Mass.)
N.H.
Lake Huron
Lake Ontario
Oriskany (Aug. 6, 1777)
Saratoga (Sept. 19 and Oct. 7, 1777)
Bennington (Aug. 16, 1777)
Mohawk
SARATOGA CAMPAIGN
Boston
MASSACHUSETTS
NEW YORK
R.I.
CONN.
Newport
Hudson
Delaware
Lake Erie
New York
Howe
Princeton (Jan. 3, 1777)
Monmouth (June 28, 1778)
PENNSYLVANIA
Trenton
Germantown (Oct. 4, 1777)
PHILADELPHIA CAMPAIGN
Brandywine (Sept. 11, 1777)
N.J.
ATLANTIC OCEAN
MARYLAND
DEL.
Delaware Bay
Chesapeake Bay
Appalachian Mountains
INDIAN RESERVE
VIRGINIA
NORTH CAROLINA
MAP KEY
British campaign
American victory
British victory
Indecisive battle
0 100 miles
0 100 kilometers

Created in 1780, *this hand-drawn French map shows the battle plan and locations of French forces for the Franco-American siege of Newport, Rhode Island.*

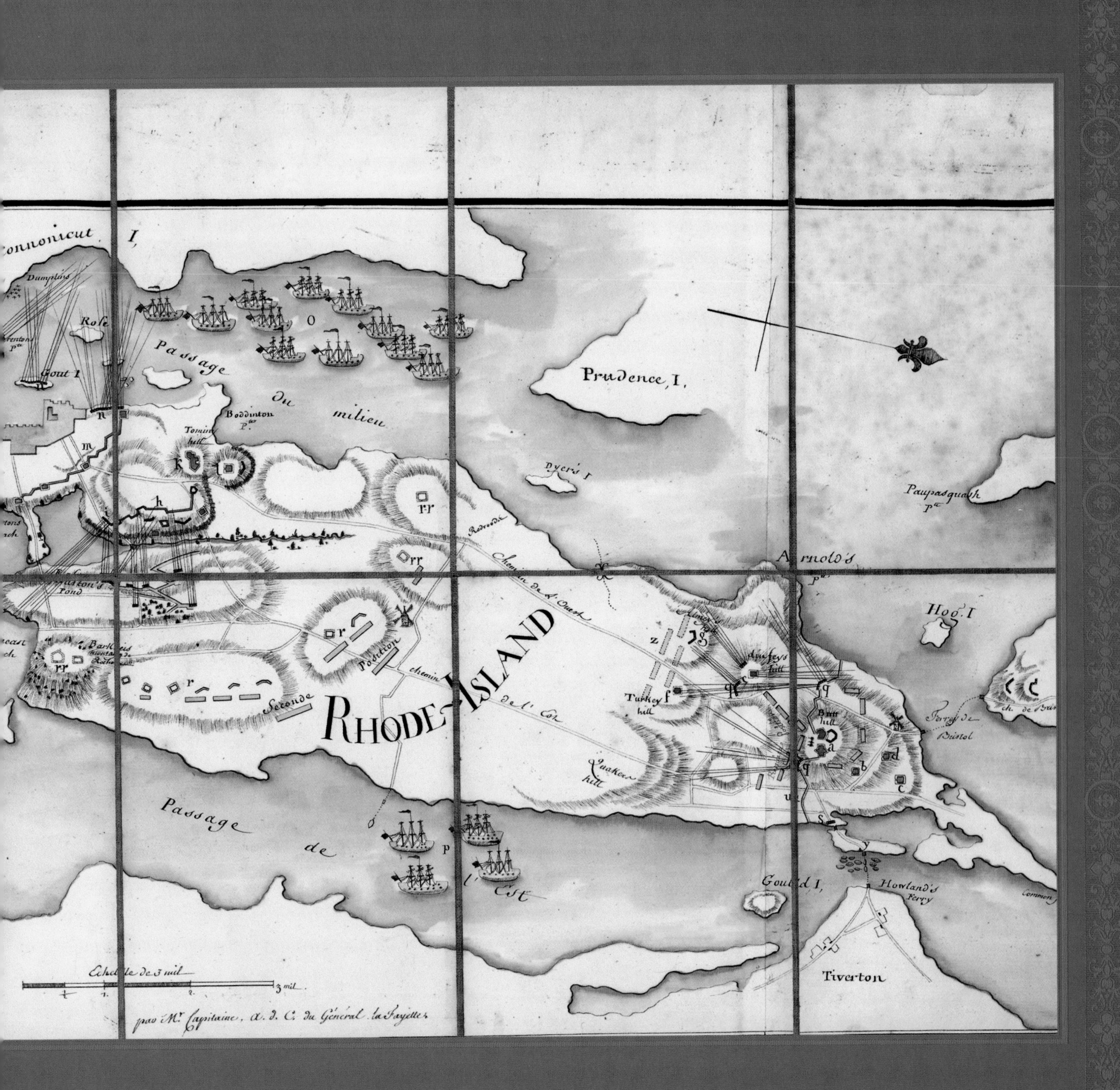

Connonicut I,
Dumplins
Rose
Gout I
Passage du milieu
Boddinton Pte
Prudence, I.
Dyers I
Paupasquash Pte
Arnold's
Hog I
Chemin de l'Ouest
RHODE-ISLAND
Position
Seconde
chemin de l'Est
Turkey hill
Quaker hill
Butt hill
Ferry de Bristol
Passage de l'Est
Gould I,
Howland's Ferry
Tiverton
Echelle de 3 mil
par Mr. Capitaine, A. D. C. du Général la Fayette

having been touched," Lafayette declared. Again sunset brought an end to the bloodshed, but Washington planned to resume the attack at daybreak. By then, Clinton had slipped away.

SULLIVAN AND D'ESTAING CLASH

NEITHER COMMANDER COULD HAVE KNOWN IT AT THE TIME, BUT MONMOUTH COURT House was the last true Revolutionary battle fought on northern soil. With the loss at Saratoga the previous summer, the British had effectively lost the war in the North. And to complicate the redcoats' situation, France had now fully joined the American cause. In early July a French fleet of 12 ships of the line and four frigates sailed into view and dropped anchor off Sandy Hook. The fleet's commander, Count d'Estaing, sent Washington more than official regards, proclaiming, "The talents and great actions of George Washington have insured him in the eyes of all Europe the title, truly sublime, of deliverer of America."

MAJ. GEN. JOHN SULLIVAN
1740–1795

John Sullivan was an American general during the Revolution and a delegate to the Continental Congress. The son of Irish immigrants who had come to the colonies as indentured servants, Sullivan grew up in New Hampshire and studied law. He supported the rebellious colonists after the Boston Tea Party and joined up with the military in 1775 as a brigadier general. Sullivan bravely led troops in several battles, most notably in the Battle of Rhode Island in 1778. There, his forces were to coordinate an attack with the French Navy on British-held Newport. The French admiral, Charles Henri, Count d'Estaing, called off the attack because of a storm and withdrew his ships to Boston. Sullivan made repeated entreaties to d'Estaing to reengage, but to no avail. He then wrote an angry letter to d'Estaing, which soured relations for a time between the Americans and the French.

The compliment was bittersweet. Had the fleet arrived only a few days earlier, it might have fatally crippled the British by catching their ships bound for New York in open waters. But that opportunity had been missed, and now Lord Howe—brother of the recently deposed General Howe—had his ships safely tucked into New York Harbor, where the French, whose ships drew several feet more water, could not follow.

With New York an impossibility and d'Estaing in need of a safe port to land and a replenished water supply, d'Estaing and Washington turned their eyes on Newport, Rhode Island. War had greatly diminished the once thriving port and put it in the hands of a British garrison, but its harbor was still intact. So, as General Howe had done the previous summer, d'Estaing disappeared into the Atlantic later in July, leaving the British to wonder and worry at his destination. He reappeared off Newport at the end of the month and entered Narragansett Bay.

The plan to take Newport involved an attack from land and water. The French would handle the naval end of things, and the Americans would launch the overland thrust from nearby Providence, Rhode Island. Yet there was one large flaw in the plan. The person in command in Providence was Gen. John Sullivan, an officer of renowned weakness and repeated failures, notably at Saratoga and Brandywine. He would be reinforced, certainly, but the command would fall to him. In several letters to Sullivan, Washington warned him not to be deliberate rather than brash and to take the "good advice of those about you."

But Sullivan, the son of Irish immigrants who had come to America as indentured servants, disliked d'Estaing's noble cast and made that clear to him. The two forces were to attack simultaneously from land and sea, but reinforcements to Sullivan were still pouring in as d'Estaing, increasingly impatient, waited offshore. Then, suddenly, on August 8, Sullivan moved precipitously and put his men into action a day early without informing the French admiral. Another disaster followed: the appearance of a formidable British fleet, larger than d'Estaing's by several ships. Howe had cobbled his fleet together from ships patrolling the American coast, and now the two naval powers faced off, circling each other for advantage, particularly with the winds. They got more than they had wished for when a violent gale heaved in, dismasted ships, and generally blew the coming battle into oblivion.

A FRENCH POLITICAL CARTOON *celebrates Count d'Estaing. He is shown presenting a palm frond to a Native American, who is holding a staff with a liberty cap perched on top and seated upon boxes and barrels of produce for France.*

As Sullivan pleaded that the attack on Newport resume, d'Estaing sailed away to Boston for repairs. Even there, Sullivan hounded him with a letter that he and nine other generals had signed. In their letter, the generals accused the count of dishonoring France. By early November, d'Estaing had determined to take his war efforts to the Caribbean and fight the British there. The great hope that the alliance would quickly turn the war in the Americans' direction was fading, despite Washington's attempts to heal d'Estaing's wounds with flattering letters. Washington's words may have assuaged the admiral, but the French were coming to understand how undermanned and unskilled in the art of war the Americans truly were.

And the British understood that it was time to focus their energies on the South. In late November 3,500 redcoats were dispatched from New York, and by December 23 they were just off the Georgia coast. With little resistance, they easily took poorly defended Savannah, a small river town that was also the capital of the new state. They were helped immensely by an enslaved black man who led them through swamps and behind the light American defenses. If Savannah itself was no great prize, Georgia was. The state was a well-stocked storehouse of cattle, grain, and potential man power in its many Loyalist sympathizers and slaves, who were offered freedom to join the British cause—and did, in droves.

From his position in the beleaguered North, Washington seemed unconcerned. But his compatriot, "Lighthorse" Harry Lee, would say of the fall of Savannah that, for the British, "never was a victory of such magnitude so completely gained, with so little loss." As 1778 ended, the Southern Strategy became Britain's new hope and focus. The Revolution had entered new territory.

George Washington
(1732–1799)

"First in war, first in peace, and first in the hearts of his countrymen." That famous description of George Washington by his friend and fellow patriot Lighthorse Harry Lee is probably still the best summation of the man who, over a hard but resolute lifetime, became the savior of a war and the father of a country.

Washington's earliest ambitions, though, aimed more at the prosaic than at the glorious. He probably imagined nothing better than following in the footsteps of his father, Augustine, who had been an ambitious Virginia planter and merchant. Augustine was hardly a major player in the hierarchical world of the Virginia aristocracy, but he was nonetheless a bona fide member of the lesser gentry. George was the eldest son of Augustine's second wife, Mary, who was not a member of the upper class gentry and did not aspire to be.

When George was just eleven, Augustine died, leaving his younger children in the hands of Mary, a domineering, pious, possibly pipe-smoking woman who ran her farm with a firm hand and read daily to her children from *Contemplations Moral and Divine.* Though George's two older stepbrothers, then grown, had been sent to the fine colleges attended by the Virginia gentry, George had no resources for that, and Mary, in any case, had no interest in investing in her eldest son's education. The two clashed their entire lives, and some biographers speculate that George modeled himself after everything that his mother was not.

Perhaps the most *famous image of George Washington, painted by Gilbert Stuart (opposite). Mary Ball Washington, mother of George Washington (above)*

Apparently determined to better himself from a young age, George found mentors among the gentry and emulated their ways. He also copied by hand something called *Rules of Civility & Decent Behavior in Company and Conversation.* The 110 rules, conceived by French Jesuits as teaching tools almost a century and a half before George's time, dealt with everything from table manners to posture to facial expressions to gossip. Despite their stuffy formality, it seems that George internalized them, because they echoed through his behavior for the rest of his life.

As a young man, George impressed the colonial power brokers of British Virginia, who made him a surveyor of western lands and an officer serving with the British during the French and Indian War. He first saw battle in his very early 20s, and he learned that he liked war. As far away as Britain, the young Virginia colonel's calm and courage under fire made an impression, and a London gazette ran a line from one of his letters: "I have heard the bullets whistle; and believe me, there is something charming in the sound."

But Washington had also experienced other aspects of war: the meddling of politicians and the disdain of the British for the American officers. By 1758 he was tired of it all. He resigned his commission and enthusiastically took up the life of a Virginia planter.

Almost serendipitously, Washington had become lord

of the considerable farm of his beloved older stepbrother, Lawrence, who had died of tuberculosis. Situated on the broad, bountiful Potomac, Mount Vernon could be called, without hyperbole, one of the great loves of Washington's life.

At about the same time that he began ambitious improvements on Mount Vernon, Washington became involved with an extremely wealthy young widow, Martha Dandridge Custis. After a brief few months, the two were married. Washington had been infatuated with other women in his young life, but Martha proved a perfect life partner and comfort to the reserved, driven, often overburdened Washington.

GEORGE WASHINGTON *(opposite) became a Freemason at age 20 in 1752. Joining the Masons was an important rite of passage for young men of his stature, and Washington would continue to embrace the tenets of Freemasonry for the rest of his life. George Washington, shown at home with his family at the Mount Vernon estate (above)*

Along with the wealth and social standing that Martha brought to the marriage, she also brought two young children, and Washington cherished them as his own. He settled easily into the life of a respected planter and reveled in days filled with his family. He improved the farm (heavily dependent on slave labor), fished, hunted (for fox in particular), rode, feasted, danced, and generally reveled in the style of the Virginia aristocracy. He no doubt assumed he would end his days growing Mount Vernon and paying homage to the king.

That, of course, was not to be. Like his fellow delegates to the Virginia House of Burgesses, Washington became increasingly disillusioned with the king and his colonial minions. Yet through the 1760s, as Washington supported various protests against British taxes, he also dined with the royal governor and assumed, as did most of his landed countrymen, that the British would be reasonable. By 1774 he had changed his mind. "The measures which [the British] administration hath for sometime been, and now are, most violently pursuing are repugnant to every principle of natural justice," he wrote to a friend. In the course of a decade, Washington had become a full-throated patriot and one of Virginia's seven elected delegates to the First Continental Congress. At the end of August 1774, he left Mount Vernon for Philadelphia with fellow delegates Patrick Henry and Edmund Pendleton. Martha saw them off spiritedly. "I hope you will stand firm," she told Henry and Pendleton, adding, "I know George will."

The six-foot-two Washington had a way of impressing other men simply by his bearing, and the other delegates to the Continental Congress were duly impressed; they saw in him the reassuring promise of a true military commander and natural leader. And that was clearly what Washington wanted them to see. He was not a fiery or inspired speaker, nor was he an intellect, but he was confident that he could command men.

Washington got his chance a year later, when the Second Continental Congress appointed him commander in chief of the Continental Army. John Adams championed him for the position, and Abigail Adams described him as "Dignity with ease and complacency—the gentleman and soldier look agreeably blended in him. Modesty marks every line and feature of his face."

Certainly, Washington exuded modesty when he addressed the congress with what sounded like a protestation at his appointment: "I beg it may be remembered by every gentleman in the room, that I this day declare with the utmost sincerity, I do not think myself equal to the command I am honored with." He may have been overwhelmed by the command, but he had also wanted it. And now, for better or worse, he had it.

Arriving in Cambridge, Massachusetts, in early July to meet his "army," he found an obstreperous, disorganized band of New England militiamen, most of them hardscrabble farmers

WASHINGTON AS A FREEMASON.
G
BORN FEB. 22
DIED DEC. 14

and small-time merchants, holding the British army at bay in Boston. Washington was determined to impose the discipline of a true army on these "exceedingly dirty and nasty people" and to protect them, to some extent, from themselves by putting in place hygiene practices to ward against the diseases that plagued military camps. Despite his private initial disdain for them, he moved tirelessly and confidently among them. He understood, even if they did not, how precarious the American military was.

If that summer tested Washington, it was only a taste of what was to come. By 1776 he and his men were in a struggle for survival, yielding battle after battle to the British in New York. By year's end, Washington had lost more than half of what had been, at best, a hobbled army. The Continental Congress had essentially turned its back on him, and his closest confidants and officers had intrigued against him, complaining of his indecisiveness and inability to lead.

In fact, Washington *had* been indecisive and overly deferential, and now his army was in danger of collapse, as enlistment periods ended and desertion grew. "No man, I believe, ever had a greater choice of difficulties and less means to extricate himself from them," he wrote to his brother Jack in late November. Yet, despite his own despondency, Washington rallied. He knew that if he did not turn the tide somehow, the Revolution would be a short-lived disaster. And so on a bitter cold Christmas night, Washington led his broken, barefoot army across the Delaware and into Trenton, New Jersey. The American victory there was small but profound. It reinvigorated Washington, his forces, and the patriotic cause.

THE FAMOUS LANSDOWNE *portrait by American artist Gilbert Stuart is one of several made of the great Washington in his lifetime. This one portrays the 64-year-old as he renounces a third term as President.*

For the next four years, Washington battled on, carping at the congress to feed and supply his men, fending off attacks on his own leadership, and all the while keeping an eye firmly on the enemy. Gradually, he learned to fight the British more strategically, using local militia to harass them and avoiding "a general action" that would "put anything at Risque." His men came to revere him for his courage, calm, determination, and, above all, his presence at their side battle after battle, march after march, and year after grueling year. The Philadelphia patriot Benjamin Rush once declared that Washington had "so much martial dignity in his deportment that you would distinguish him to be a general and a soldier from among 10,000 people. There is not a king in Europe that would not look like a *valet de chambre* by his side."

By 1781 Washington's resolve had triumphed over the British, and two years later America could officially claim her hard-won independence. By then Washington was more icon than man to most of the world. One Dutch merchant, who caught sight of Washington as he rode through Philadelphia with a contingent of light cavalry, wrote to his wife, "I saw the greatest man who has ever appeared on the surface of this earth . . . I don't know if, in our delight at seeing the Hero, we were more surprised by his simple but grand air or by the kindness of the greatest and best of heroes."

The war had taken a toll on the health of the best of heroes. At 51 Washington was no longer the vigorous, athletic man he had been. He wore crude, ill-fitting dentures of human teeth and ivory that hooked on to his one remaining tooth and made his gums ache. His great consolation was that he could return to Mount Vernon and his family and live out his days with his "mind . . . unbent," gliding "down the stream of life till I come to that abyss from whence no traveler is permitted to return."

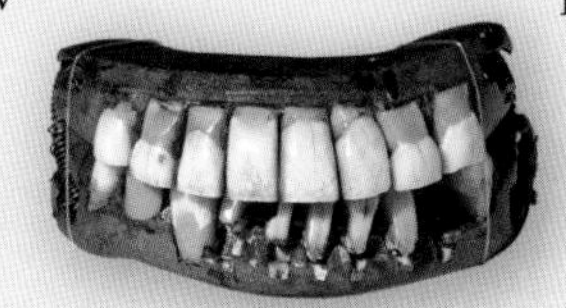

GEORGE WASHINGTON'S DENTURES *with ivory and human teeth*

For a few years Washington was allowed the life of an unbent mind, reveling in his daily routine as a planter and coming up with strategies to improve the operations and production of Mount Vernon and other nearby farms that had been neglected over the nine years of his absence. He and Martha also entertained an endless stream of visitors.

As such, Washington's destiny was too completely entwined with the new nation's to allow him escape. He watched its growing pains with the cautious eye of a concerned parent, and at the same time, he unobtrusively tended his own image, guarding it for posterity and holding himself in abeyance in case he should be needed again. By 1787 he was again on his way to Philadelphia, as he had been a dozen years earlier, this time as a delegate to the Constitutional Convention. He was elected its president and, within two years, President of the new nation. He expected "that at a convenient and an early period my services might be dispensed with and that I might be permitted once more to retire." But the "early period" dragged into eight years, as the former patriots argued and debated over America's character and future.

Finally, in 1796, at the age of 64, Washington refused to continue into a third term. He was granted three years of his own happiness at Mount Vernon. Then, in mid-December 1799, he spent a cold, wet day touring his farms on horseback. He kept to his routine, though he complained of a sore throat. A day later he was gone. In his farewell address to the nation, he had assured his fellow citizens, "I shall carry . . . with me to my grave . . . unceasing vows that heaven may continue to you the choicest tokens of its beneficence; that your union and brotherly affection may be perpetual; that the free Constitution, which is the work of your hands, may be sacredly maintained; that its administration in every department may be stamped with wisdom and virtue; that, in fine, the happiness of the people of these States, under the auspices of liberty, may be made complete."

SLAVES WORKED AND LIVED *on Washington's Mount Vernon estate. At the time of his death, there were several hundred people enslaved there. Washington's own feeling on slavery changed throughout his life, and he mandated in his will that the slaves be freed upon his wife's death.*

CHAPTER
5
Richard Willis

J. PAUL JONES
COMMODORE

Our affairs must soon become desperate, beyond the possibility of recovery . . . Indeed, I have almost ceased to hope.

GEN. GEORGE WASHINGTON

1779-1780
IN THE VERY MIDST OF A REVOLUTION

THREE YEARS OF WAR HAD SPREAD DESPAIR IN AMERICA AND BRITAIN. VICTORY WAS IN NEITHER SIDE'S grasp, while defeat seemed always around the corner. Washington had hopes that the French alliance would soon turn the tide in favor of the Continentals, but in the meantime, it had only increased the disaffection among the general population. America needed money quickly if it was going to play its part in the military alliance with France, and so more paper currency was printed, backed not by gold or silver but by the promise of future tax revenues. Persistent depreciation led to the saying "not worth a Continental," and wartime inflation became hyperinflation. Prices climbed to eight times what they had been at the beginning of the conflict, and the barely formed nation faced bankruptcy. Many people suffered, but others got richer. Samuel Adams worried, "I am afraid the cry of too many is, Get Money, Money still. And then let Virtue follow it if she will! . . . He is the best Patriot who stems the Torrent of Vice, because that is the most destructive enemy of his country."

Washington shared Adams's sentiments. "Speculation, peculation, and an insatiable thirst for riches seems to have got the better of every other consideration," he railed in the winter of 1779 during a six-week

CAPT. JOHN PAUL JONES *(1747–1792), American naval hero, is said to have uttered the famous words "Sir, I have not yet begun to fight!" during the heat of battle. Preceding pages: The Battle of Flamborough Head took place on September 23, 1779, between the American ship* Bonhomme Richard *and H.M.S.* Serapis *off the coast of England. The terrible battle lasted more than four hours. The British captain ultimately surrendered, but not before almost half of the British and American crews had been lost.*

stay in Philadelphia. While his men endured the spare comforts of winter cantonments, the wealthy of the city lived lavishly, seemingly oblivious to any privations of war. And the Continental Congress seemed unable to handle the affairs of the nation. Washington met with congressional members over the crisis, but he found them far less impressive than his former colleagues from the first days of the Revolution. "Where are our Men of abilities?" he lamented. "Why do they not come forth to save their Country?" He mentioned specifically Jefferson, who had returned to Virginia and was now governor. Adams had joined Franklin in Paris. John Hancock too was gone, back to Massachusetts, and the previous fall he had participated in the military debacle to take Newport, Rhode Island. Washington had respect for the new president of the congress, John Jay, but that did little to reassure him. "Our affairs are in a more distressed, ruinous, and deplorable condition than they have been in since the commencement of the war," Washington worried in a letter to one friend. To another he confessed, "Our affairs must soon become desperate, beyond the possibility of recovery . . . Indeed, I have almost ceased to hope."

The Ladies of Philadelphia *organization zealously worked to raise money for the Continental Army by sewing shirts for the soldiers.*

Washington might have vented his doubts in personal correspondence, but he did not display them in public. He returned to the field with a campaign plan for 1779—a modest one that involved minimal risk to his army. Focusing his military strength against the nations of the Iroquois Confederation in the west, he planned to punish them for aiding the British and scatter them from their lands. He hoped that the enemy would mistake the maneuver for the overtures of an invasion of Canada, and indeed there had been loud support for such an invasion in Philadelphia and among some of his own officers, including Lafayette. But Washington was convinced it would fail. And should it succeed with French help, he worried that France would claim back its lost Canadian territory. With France to the north and Spain holding everything west of the Mississippi, the United States, still in its infancy, would be in a precarious position.

Washington's orders for the Iroquois campaign were simple, and brutal: "lay waste all the settlements . . . that the country may not be merely *overrun* but *destroyed.*" General Sullivan, who had so botched the Newport assault the previous summer, was nonetheless put in charge of the campaign along the border of western Pennsylvania and New York. This time, with little resistance to speak of and much of the area already deserted by the time he arrived, he succeeded, turning native villages to ash and torching winter food supplies. It was an

ignominious display of terror, and it sent some 4,000 men, women, and children fleeing to western New York or Canada as refugees. The Continentals did not follow them there, and by mid-September the campaign was over.

On the coast Clinton had waged his own miniature terror campaign earlier that summer as he impatiently waited for reinforcements. Unwilling to make any major move until help arrived, Clinton instead harassed the small coastal towns of nearby Connecticut. In July he

GEN. JOHN SULLIVAN *led the campaign against the Iroquois. This map shows his route from Easton to Seneca and Cayuga country. Facing little resistance, Sullivan's forces devastated the natives' homes and villages. Inset: Ki-on-twog-ky, chief of the Seneca tribes, eventually established peace with the United States in 1786.*

General Wayne commanded *American forces during the Battle of Stony Point, a daring and effective attack on the British outpost at Stony Point, New York.*

burned much of New Haven, Fairfield, and Norwalk. He also pushed up the Hudson and claimed two forts on the river, one at Stony Point and another at Verplanck's Point, a dozen miles from West Point. Washington considered the seized forts "key to the continent," and he wanted at least Stony Point back. In July he sent Gen. Anthony Wayne to take it with a force of 1,350 men.

Wayne had proved himself in the Pennsylvania campaigns of the previous year, fighting with such reckless abandon that he had earned the sobriquet "Mad Anthony." On hearing Washington's plans for recapturing Stony Point, Wayne reportedly said, "I'll storm hell, sir, if you'll make the plans!" The plan promised some kind of hell, as the fort stood on a promontory 150 feet above the Hudson and was reachable only at low tide, when the marshland wrapping it was passable. To complicate matters, Wayne's force was to take the fort with bayonets, not muskets. "The attack was made about midnight and conducted with great spirit and enterprise," Nathanael Greene reported after the fact, "the troops marching up in the face of an exceeding heavy fire with cannon and musketry, without discharging a gun." The brazen assault would, Greene predicted, "for ever immortalize Gen. Wayne." Wayne's own letter to Washington assured him, "Our officers and men behaved like men who are determined to be free." Indeed, their fierceness apparently brought the British to their knees, with shouts of "Mercy! Mercy! Dear Americans, mercy! Quarter! Brave American, quarter! Quarter!" Wayne's force sustained about a hundred casualties, while the British lost close to 700, as well as the fort and 15 cannon, vital to the Americans. Mad Anthony, as predicted, was immortalized. The British advance up the Hudson was at an end, at least for the time being, and throughout the Northeast they were floundering.

The War at Sea

Long before the bloody Sullivan campaign, an Iroquois leader had observed, "The King of England is like a fish. When he is in the water, he can wag his tail; when he comes on land, he lays down on his side." In three years of war, the British had had little success against the Americans on land. But with France in the fight, the war at sea was heating up.

The previous January, the *Alliance,* a proud new frigate in America's meager navy, had sailed out of Boston Harbor on its first mission: ferrying Lafayette back to France to petition Louis XVI and his ministers for more support. A month out of port, the frigate's officers discovered that the English sailors among the mixed crew had planned a mutiny in order to take the *Alliance* and Lafayette hostage. Lafayette himself took on the mutineers, and they were soon in chains. The *Alliance* put into port at Brest as planned.

Anthony Wayne earned *the nickname "Mad Anthony" through his daring exploits and fiery personality.*

But Lafayette's visit did not go exactly as he had anticipated. Although he was received with high acclaim at court, he could find no enthusiasm among the ministers for the invasion of Canada he was promoting. It was Britain, not Canada, that France had in its sights, and in a reversal of roles, America's help was enlisted.

Rather than sailing for America, both the *Alliance* and Lafayette became part of a French thrust against Britain. Lafayette himself had proposed a plan to take hostage British towns—Liverpool, Bristol, Bath—and hold them for ransom. The ministers were intrigued. A captain in the American navy, John Paul Jones, already had gained fame for his raids on towns along the British coast. The raids had signified little militarily, but they had spread terror of the "pirate Paul Jones," who reported to Benjamin Franklin in Paris. "The cry of Versailles and the clamor of Paris became as loud in favor of Monsieur Jones as of Monsieur Franklin," John Adams observed. Jones, the son of a Scottish gardener, was as anxious for *la gloire* as the young marquis, and he reveled in the clamor. Jones and Lafayette were assigned to partner in the audacious British operation. Franklin had told the pair, "In war, attempts thought to be impossible do often for that very reason become possible and practicable, because nobody expects them and no precautions are taken to guard against them."

But before an anchor was weighed, the operation was scuttled and Jones was reassigned. He was to become part of a much larger plan: a joint Franco-Spanish invasion of Britain, the first time such a thing would be attempted in hundreds of years. Through the summer of 1779, a combined fleet of some 60 ships of the line assembled. The plan was to claim the English Channel from the Royal Navy in preparation for a land invasion of Britain. Captain Jones was not part of this fleet. Instead, he was to take a small squadron of only five ships to the coast of Great Britain and harass towns there to create a diversion from the main invasion force.

Jones's ship was "an old Indiaman, clumsy and crank, smelling strongly of the savor of tea, cloves and arrack, the cargoes of her former voyages." The description, though supplied a century later by novelist Herman Melville, was probably reasonably accurate. Despite the Indiaman's age and sluggishness, Jones was devoted to it, and rechristened it the *Bonhomme Richard,* in homage to his champion at court, Ben Franklin, and Franklin's own alter ego, Poor Richard.

I have not yet begun to fight.

CAPT. JOHN PAUL JONES

Jones Captures the Serapis

ON AUGUST 14, 1779, JONES'S SQUADRON OF FIVE SHIPS SAILED OUT of Brest, and by mid-September they were at the mouth of the Firth of Forth leading to Edinburgh. With the wind in his favor, Jones suddenly decided upon an impetuous plan to take Leith, Edinburgh's port, and hold it ransom. He was only a "cannon shot" away from his target when the winds turned against him and scuttled any hope of the raid. Instead he pushed south, looking for prizes—British ships.

On September 22, off the Yorkshire coast, two sails were spotted in the distance. The two sails soon grew to almost 50 as Jones drew nearer. His small squadron had happened upon the Baltic fleet—"the very fleet which I have been so long cruising for," Jones exulted. Its 44 merchant ships were carrying critical Scandinavian rope, canvas, and timber to the British navy. The fleet was guarded by two naval warships, the formidable *Serapis* and a smaller sloop, the *Countess of Scarborough.* Jones understood immediately that the *Serapis* had to be taken out—a daunting task for the lumbering old Indiaman, *Bonhomme Richard.* But Jones had begun to use a new approach to naval warfare. Rather than relying only on cannon, he sent marksmen aloft into his ship's rigging to fire down on the enemy ship.

As night fell and a harvest moon spangled the sea, Jones hoisted British colors, an acceptable ruse under naval combat of that period. But on *Serapis,* Captain Pearson was only briefly fooled. "What ship is that?" came the hail from the British. "Answer immediately, or I shall be under the necessity of firing into you." No answer came.

"The battle thus begun was continued with unremitting fury," Jones later recorded. "Men were falling in all parts of the ship by the *scores,*" one officer wrote. The *Bonhomme Richard* was reduced to little more than a dying carcass. But Jones would not quit the fight. The wind died away as the two ships tangled together, with the *Serapis*'s bowsprit driving into the *Bonhomme Richard*'s rigging. Seeing an advantage, Jones lashed the two ships more firmly together, catching *Serapis* up in his own ship's death throes as the fighting raged on,

COMMODORE JOHN PAUL JONES *bravely led the American forces during a heated battle between his ship, the* Bonhomme Richard, *and the H.M.S.* Serapis. *His persistence and bravery led to the American victory and capture of the British ship.*

THE BRITISH USED *decommissioned warships as floating prisons in the waters of New York Harbor. During the course of the war about 11,000 prisoners died aboard them. One ship, the H.M.S.* Jersey *(shown here), was so notorious for cruelty and harsh conditions that it earned the nickname Hell.*

both ships now on fire. At some point, Jones's officers, believing themselves to be the senior surviving officers, attempted surrender, and the British called back to confirm. But Jones, busy elsewhere, suddenly reappeared in a fury to call off any surrender, though not with the apocryphal words with which he is remembered—"I have not yet begun to fight." Finally, the British captain asked for quarter—effectively surrender. It was a remarkable reversal in the fortunes of battle.

The *Bonhomme Richard* was lost, but the *Serapis* had been acquired—a great prize of war taken at great human cost. Jones's impossible feat was the only victory of the planned invasion. The Franco-Spanish fleet had been defeated, not by the British but by disease. Smallpox and typhus swept through the crews on the cramped ships that summer and took hundreds of lives.

Smallpox was the scourge of the Continental Army as well, and Washington believed its destruction was greater than "the Sword of the Enemy." The redcoats, who had grown up in areas where the disease was endemic, did not suffer from it as the American troops did, and General Howe had used that to his advantage during the siege of Boston in 1776.

Howe had sent refugees infected with smallpox back to the Americans, "with a design to spread the Small-Pox among the Troops." His germ warfare worked, at least on the populace. "Boston is become a hospital with the small-pox," one resident wrote.

The Pilgrims had originally brought the disease to America, and prior to the Revolution it had been confined mostly to the large port cities. But the war spread it far beyond that. Washington himself had had a mild case when he was 19, on a trip to Barbados with his stepbrother Lawrence (it would be his only trip abroad). He understood how it could sweep through a population, and from his first days as commander, he had taken pains to ward it off, quarantining any of his troops with potential symptoms. In 1777 he ordered the primitive inoculations of the day, which brought on the disease—albeit a generally mild case—and went a long way to quell an outbreak of epidemic.

All medicine was primitive at that time, and being treated was often more dangerous than not being treated. Hospitals that treated Washington's troops were filthy, and the doctors were unskilled, with no real notion of germs and how they spread or of anesthesia. One doctor described how "four to five patients die on the same straw before it is changed." Wounded or ill men learned to avoid medical care and tend to their own health, when they were able.

By 1779 the composition of the Continental Army had changed significantly. At the height of Revolutionary fervor in 1776, farmers and merchants had joined the cause, but they were largely gone, and the current army was composed of young men of no property or family. Many were immigrants to America—German or Irish enlisted men and officers from France, Prussia, Poland. And more and more African Americans had joined up, despite early opposition to their enlistment.

The number of men actually serving varied from month to month, depending on where an active campaign, shored up by militia, was under way. The peak number—almost 24,000 troops—was reached in September 1778. Thereafter, it dwindled significantly year by year to less than 10,000 men. It was no wonder, then, that Washington initially felt he could not spare men from his northern army. He remained convinced that "New York is the first and capital object, upon which every other is dependant." He continued to believe that British activity in the South was only a feint, and, despite his own Virginia roots, he had some anxiety about sending forces into the miasmic climate of the South. Oddly, it took Washington longer than others to realize that from his stronghold in Georgia, Clinton could easily move into South Carolina. Finally, though, the help of d'Estaing's fleet, still operating in the Caribbean, was enlisted. Ignoring orders to return to France before the hurricane season, d'Estaing sailed north to Savannah's aid with a force of 3,500 men.

Arriving in early September, d'Estaing found a situation similar to what had dismayed him in Rhode Island: an undermanned and disorganized Continental effort. A force from

An Historical
ACCOUNT
OF THE
SMALL-POX
INOCULATED
IN
NEW ENGLAND,
Upon all Sorts of Perfons, *Whites*, *Blacks*, and of all Ages and Conftitutions.
With fome Account of the Nature of the Infection in the NATURAL and INOCULATED Way, and their different Effects on HUMAN BODIES.
With fome fhort DIRECTIONS to the UNEXPERIENCED in this Method of Practice.
Humbly dedicated to her Royal Highnefs the Princefs of WALES, by *Zabdiel Boylfton*, Phyfician.
LONDON:
Printed for S. CHANDLER, *at the* Crofs-Keys *in the* Poultry.
M.DCC.XXVI.

AN ENGLISH PAMPHLET *published in London in the 1720s details the early efforts to inoculate settlers against the dreaded disease smallpox.*

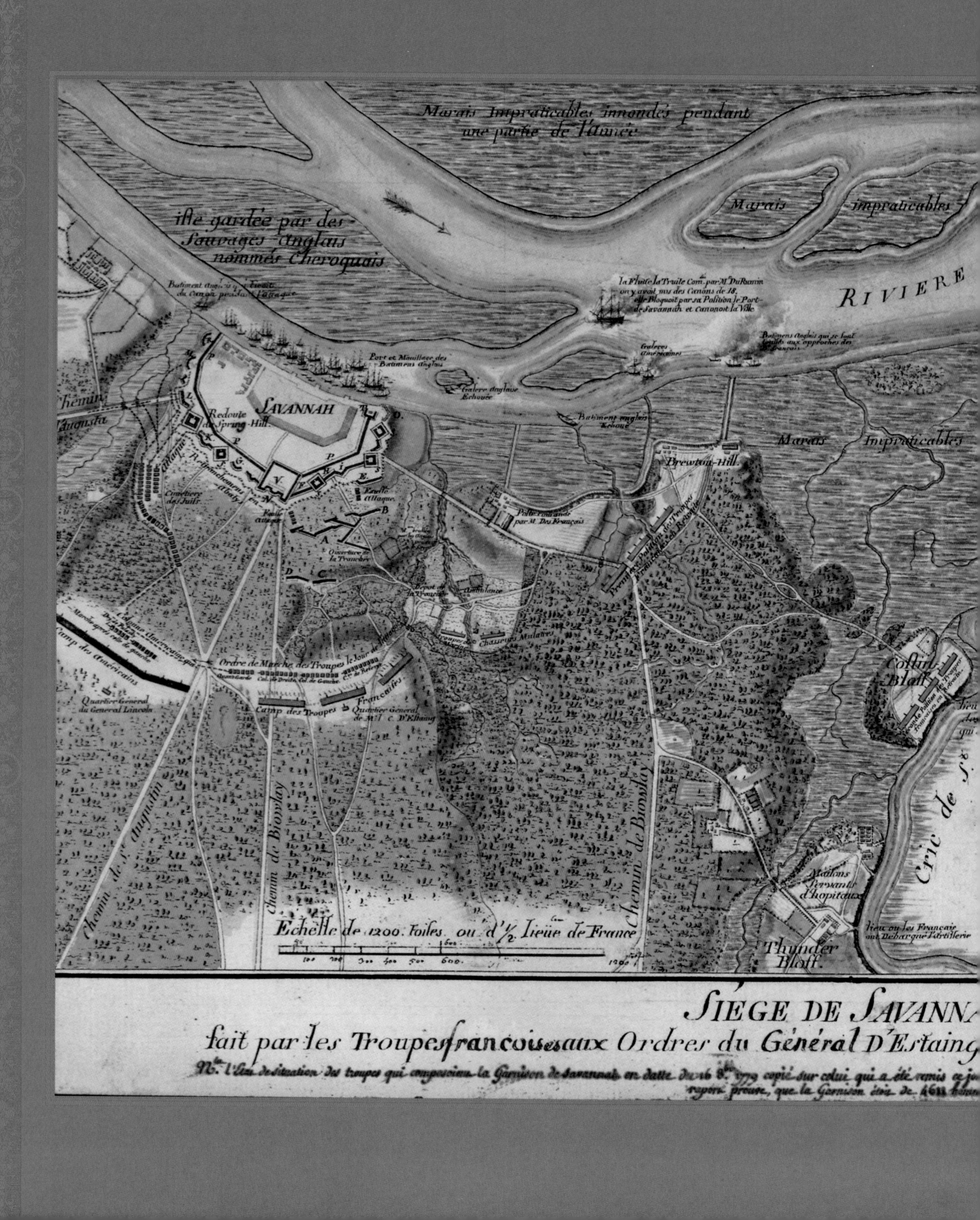

Marais Impraticables innondés pendant une partie de l'année
Marais
impraticables
isle gardée par des Sauvages Anglais nommés Cheroquais
RIVIERE
La Flute la Truite Com. par M. Du Rumain
Port et Mouillage des Batimens Anglais
Galere Anglaise Echouée
Batiment Anglais Echoué
Galeres Américaines
SAVANNAH
Redoute de Spring-Hill
Augusta
Cimetiere des Juifs
Ouverture de la Tranchée
Poste commandé par M. Des Français
Ambulance
Brewton-Hill
Marais
Impraticables
Camp des Americains
Quartier Général du Général Lincoln
Ordre de Marche des Troupes le Jour de
Camp des Troupes Françaises
Quartier Général de M. le C. D'Estaing
Chemin de St. Augustin
Chemin de Biowlay
Chemin de Biowlay
Coffin Bluff
Maisons Servants d'hopitaux
Thunder Bluff
Lieu ou les Français ont Debarqué l'Artillerie
Echelle de 1200. Toises ou d'½ Lieüe de France
SIÉGE DE SAVANNA
fait par les Troupes françoises aux Ordres du Général D'Estaing

SAVANNAH

la Chimere, Frégatte françoise, que son Tirant d'Eau a empêché de Remonter plus haut

Marais Impraticables.

la Bricole Flutte portant du Canon de 18. elle n'a pû Remonter plus haut

Augustin

EXPLICATION DES LETTRES DU PLAN

A. Batterie de Gauche des Français de 6. Pièces de 18. et de 6. pièces de 12.
B. Batterie de Droite de 5. pièces de 18. et de 6. pièces de 12. a laquelle on a fait un retour pour 5. autres pieces de 12. pour Opposer a la Batterie des Ennemis
C. Batterie des françois de 9. Mortiers du Calibre de 6. pouces jusqua celui de 9. p.
D. Batterie des Américains de quatre pièces de 4. placées sur la Face gauche du Redent.
E. Batterie des Ennemis d'Onze pièces de canon quils ont Démasquée pendant le Siege.
F. Batterie des Ennemis de 9. pieces de canon (G.) Batterie des ennemis de 5. pieces de Canon.
H. Batterie des Ennemis de 7 Mortiers. (I.) Batt. des ennemis de 5 pieces de Canon.
K. Batterie ennemie a Gauche de la Redoute de Spring Hill de 5 pieces de Canon.
L. Batterie ennemie de 5 pieces de canon dont deux flanquent la Redoute de Spring-Hill.
M. Batterie des ennemis de 5. pièces de Canon.
N. Batterie de 5. pièces de canon que les ennemis ont élevés pendant le Siege
O. Batt. ennemie sur la Riviere, de 2. pièces de 22. qui tiroit sur la Flutte du Roy la Truitte et sur les Galeres Améri
P. Retranchement en Sable en Seconde ligne, avec un Fossé large et Profond dans lequel la Garnison de Savannah se tenoit a couvert du Feu des Assiégeans
R. Batterie ennemie de 5 pieces au Bord de la Riviere a Gauche de la Ville
S. Place d'Arme en forme de Redoute (T.) Magasin a Poudre
V. Carps de Caserne Démolis pendant le Siége

...barquement Françaises le 20. 8bre.

NOTA

...ponctuées en Rouge en avant de la Redoute de Spring Hill Désignent la Marche que les Colonnes ont eu Ordre de Suivre.
...ponctuées en Noir Désignent la Marche qu'elles ont Suivies lors de l'Attaque.
Débarquement des Français s'est fait de nuit dans un endroit nommé Biowlay a deux lieues dans la Riviere d'Hosaba qui a Son...re a six lieües au Sud de Savannah. il y a 5. lieües ½ de Biowlay a la Ville de Savannah Située elle même a 5. lieües ½ de l'isle Thyb...ure de la R. de Savannah. l'Escadre Française etoit Mouillée a 3. lieües au large de la Côte.
...es violens coups de Vent; en occasionant des avaries considérables a l'Escadre, en rompant plusieurs fois sa Communication avec les ...ille avoit mis a terre, et en faisant craindre enfin qu'elle ne se trouvat forcée de partir sans avoir pû rembarquer ses troupes, Sont les Motifs qui ont empêché la Prise de Savannah, et qui ont mis dans les Opérations une lenteur qui a laissé a l'Ennemi le tems de raßembler des Forces considérables qu'elles des assiégeans obligés par la circonstance, a un Siège qu'on n'eut jamais dessein de Faire.

...e-Amiral de France. en 7.bre, et 8.bre 1779.

...a Major Général Prevost par Mr. Miller son aide de camp; est détaillé au revers de ce plan: ce

THE DISASTROUS SIEGE *of Savannah lasted for a week. Despite objections from Americans, French ally Admiral d'Estaing believed he could take the city by force. This French map, drawn in 1779, details the assault. Inset: After British forces shifted their focus to the southern colonies, they seized Charleston, South Carolina, to be their center of operations. The siege lasted roughly six weeks and resulted in the surrender of the city and more than 5,000 American soldiers.*

Charleston under the newly appointed commander Benjamin Lincoln did not arrive until September 16, bringing the total allied force to some 7,700 men. The British had been busy fortifying the city, and d'Estaing began to prepare for a siege operation. Throughout the Georgia heat of late September his men dug parallels, as the British waited anxiously for reinforcements and continued to strengthen the city's defenses.

Savannah and Charleston

ON OCTOBER 4 THE ALLIED BOMBARDMENT BEGAN AND CONTINUED FOR A WEEK. ONE Loyalist in town lamented Savannah's "deplorable" situation: "A small garrison in an extensive country was surrounded on the land by a powerful enemy, and its seacoast blocked up by one of the strongest fleets that ever visited America. There was not a single spot where the women and children could be put to safety." Despite objections from the Americans, d'Estaing was determined to take the town by assault. Leading the charge himself, he suffered wounds to an arm and leg during the ill-conceived attempt. The allies suffered 1,100 casualties, while the British lost only 55 men. A ballad summing up the Savannah failure quickly made the rounds:

BRITISH GENERAL HENRY CLINTON *fought in the American Revolution in 1775, serving in many battles including Bunker Hill and Long Island. He was dispatched to the southern colonies to lead military efforts there.*

> To Charleston with fear
> The rebels repair;
> D'Estaing scampers back to his boats, sir,
> Each blaming the other,
> Each cursing his brother,
> And—may they cut each other's throats, sir!

In the North, Washington made light of the loss. The 1779 campaign season was at an end, and he struggled to get his always ill-provisioned army through yet another winter. Again, he chose a spread-out area around Morristown, New Jersey, and put the men to work building small cabins for shelter. Hyperinflation and profiteering made the prospect for the coming months bleak. "A rat, in the shape of a horse, is not to be bought at this time for less than £200," he complained. And as always he worried, "What will be our situation this winter? Our army by the 1st of January diminished to little more than a sufficient garrison for West point . . . The army is . . . dwindling into nothing."

Clinton was not planning to hunker down for the winter. He had gotten approval from the war ministry to make a concerted strike on the richest city in America, Charleston, and he and his army were heading south. In the cold of late December 26, 1779, small boats skirted the ice in New York Harbor as they transported 8,500 soldiers and their provisions to a virtual armada waiting just offshore—90-some transports and 14 warships under Adm. Marriot Arbuthnot. Rough seas, something Clinton hated, made the loading tough, and

CURRENCY OF THE TIME

Virginia currency
A paper note from 1775, worth 15 pence

A $50 note
American currency dated 1778

New Jersey currency
A three-pound note dated 1776

South Carolina currency
A colonial note worth $70

Halfpenny
The front and back of a British coin dated 1775

North Carolina bills
Two 1779 certificates using "secret" marks to help distinguish genuine bills from counterfeit ones

Low tides and bad weather *made it difficult for the colonists to defend Charleston, South Carolina, from a British attack in 1780. British lieutenant general Sir Henry Clinton and his army of 10,000 soldiers captured the southern city, handing the patriots one of their worst defeats of the war.*

once at sea, the ships faced "Always the same weather—heaving surf" and "Storm, rain, hail, snow . . ." Some ships went down, and one was pushed all the way across the Atlantic before finally making landfall in England.

The distance the fleet had to cover was many times what General Howe had faced two summers earlier, when he had sailed south for his attack on Philadelphia. But the summer doldrums proved more decelerating than winter storms did. By the end of January, wind and weather had pushed Clinton's fleet far south of Charleston and into Florida waters. Clinton worried that it was "almost beyond hope of being able to regain the American coast." Yet it did regroup on February 1, at the mouth of the Savannah River. On Tybee Island, men and ships rested and made repairs to the damaged and dismasted ships. By February 11, the force had sailed closer to the target, landing without incident on Simmons (now Seabrook) Island, 30 miles south of Charleston.

This was not Clinton's first attempt on Charleston. Very early in the war, in the summer of 1776, he had led a star-crossed expedition to take the South's only significant city. But the patriots had come to Charleston's defense, and the British had been driven off decisively in a humiliating defeat. One surgeon on the expedition had moaned, "This will not be believed when it is first reported in England. I can scarcely believe what I myself saw that day—a day to me one of the most distressing of my life."

Part of that early defeat could have been blamed on nature, which had provided Charleston a superb defense: a sandbar following the contours of its harbor. "There are five channels through the Bar," one Hessian captain explained. "The deepest, the Ship Channel has twelve feet of water at low tide and twenty-one and one-half at high tide and does not permit the passage of ships heavier than an English 40-gun ship without their being lightened. At some places the Bar is covered with only three to four feet of water." Fully aware of that advantage, the Americans had been busy fortifying the harbor, with floating guns and emplacements on Sullivan's Island, but they too had to deal with the bar. Because of low water, they could not get their own flotilla beyond the bar and anchored securely in front of the town, in a position to defend Charleston.

On April 8, the British caught the flood tide and sailed past Fort Moultrie, which guarded the harbor, and through the narrow channel. They met with little resistance and suffered only 27 casualties. Clinton's plan was to lay siege to the city, and soon his men were digging approach trenches across the peninsula, where the Ashley and Cooper Rivers came together. By the first week of April, the British soldiers were taking fire from American ships and troops behind the city wall. They kept digging, inching their trenches and cannon closer. Americans sent reinforcements overland and by water along the Cooper River, which flowed from the northern interior into the harbor. Their city would not fall—unless the supply routes into it were shut off.

British admiral Marriot Arbuthnot *fought alongside Henry Clinton to capture Charleston, South Carolina.*

One way to shut off supply routes was to take Moncks Corner, about 30 miles north of Charleston, and the man to do it was Banastre Tarleton. The young officer had first proved his audacity in the fall of 1776, when he had taken Gen. Charles Lee captive in the New Jersey countryside. Since then, he had only grown more audacious and skilled, and his British Legion had become an elite corps. Now, on the night of April 12, his men moved through the dark toward the American force of 500 stationed at Moncks Corner. "Profound silence was observed on the march . . . The Americans were completely surprised," Tarleton later recounted, and "fled on foot to the swamps." The British quickly took control of the crossroads, then a critical bridge and the surrounding countryside, effectively blocking access to Charleston via the Cooper River as well.

That accomplished, Admiral Arbuthnot, along with a prominent captain on the expedition, sent word to another commander to "burn the Town [Charleston] as soon as possible and send 24 pound shot into the stomacks of the women to see how they will deliver them." But Clinton, at loggerheads with Arbuthnot almost from the beginning of the expedition, countermanded the order. "Absurd, impolitic, and inhuman to burn a town you mean to occupy," he railed.

Inside the city, civilians and soldiers suffered all the privations of siege: hunger, lack of sleep, the stress of endless enemy bombardment. The American commander there, Benjamin Lincoln, was inexperienced and indecisive. He was pushed and pulled by the town's powerful barons, who wanted not victory but protection of their city and wealth from the British.

This view *(preceding pages) shows Charleston as seen from the British lines during the siege, which lasted for six weeks before the Americans were forced to surrender.*

Lincoln considered retreat, but that had become a poor alternative, with the enemy holding all the ground beyond the city. Finally, on May 11, he signaled surrender.

The fall of Charleston gave Clinton the South's great port and some 5,700 American soldiers and 1,000 sailors, as well as hundreds of artillery pieces, powder, rice, rum, and indigo. The loss of men and materiel was a tremendous blow to America's dwindling army. "This victory will within a short time make the Crown of England dominant again from Pensacola to the James River," one Hessian crowed. Even Washington now understood that the South had become the primary battleground, and it would become a brutal one, in part because of the enemy's "Bloody Ban," Banastre Tarleton.

Tarleton's quick-moving legion of dragoons and light cavalry, swelled by southern Loyalists, was soon terrorizing the countryside and the Continental forces it engaged. Cornwallis, Tarleton's commanding officer and Clinton's second in command, described the young lieutenant as "indefatigably laborious and active, cool and intrepid in action, discerns as by intuition, seizes with rapidity, and improves . . . the short, but favorable and decisive moments of victory."

Maj. Gen. Benjamin Lincoln *fought in most of the major battles of the Revolution before being assigned to Charleston, South Carolina. Unable to repel the British attack in March 1780, Lincoln was forced to surrender the city.*

After the fall of Charleston, Cornwallis learned that a large Virginia force, which had been marching to the city's defense, was still at large and moving north again. He dispatched Tarleton to intercept the Virginians, even though they already had a ten-day lead. Tarleton pushed his men with characteristic relentlessness, and they covered 105 miles in 54 hours, resulting in "the loss of a number of horses, in consequence of the rapidity of the march, and the heat of the climate." Near the border between North and South Carolina, he realized he was within 20 miles of his prey. Resorting to subterfuge, he sent a messenger forward under a white flag with a letter to the American commander, John Buford. Tarleton told Buford in the letter that he was "almost encompassed by a corps of seven hundred light troops on horseback" and that "Earl Cornwallis is likewise within a short march with nine British battalions . . . If you are rash enough to reject the terms, the blood shall be upon your head." Buford fired back, "Sir, I reject your proposals and shall defend myself to the last extremity."

Waxhaws Massacre

On May 29 the two forces met in an "open wood" near Waxhaws Creek. Buford's infantrymen, deployed in a single line, were ordered to hold their fire until the British were "within ten yards." But Tarleton and his cavalry roared toward the Continentals with such ferocity that they were upon the Americans before Buford's men could deliver a second volley. The American force "was totally broken," and "a slaughter was commenced before

BANASTRE TARLETON (1754–1833)

One of Britain's greatest weapons during the conflict in America was a young dragoon whose terrors remain legendary. Banastre Tarleton fought hard and ruthlessly for his country, and for his efforts the British considered him a hero. But to Americans, he was—and remains—Bloody Ban, Butcher Ban. In Thomas Jefferson's words, Banastre was "the most active, enterprising and vindictive Officer who has ever appeared in Arms against us."

The son of a prosperous Liverpool sugar trader, Tarleton had little interest in commerce himself and signed on to the British army. He joined a day after the fighting at Lexington and Concord, though he could have known nothing of those events at the time. One of hundreds of ambitious young officers in Cornwallis's contingent, he sailed for the colonies in December 1775.

Tarleton might have remained an unknown had not serendipity shined on him, putting the American general Charles Lee squarely in Tarleton's path a year later. In describing his raid on the inn where Lee was staying, Tarleton exulted, "I went on at full speed. The sentrys were struck with a panic, dropped their arms and fled. I ordered my men to fire into the house thro' every window and door and cut up as many of the guard as they could." The success of the attack sealed Tarleton's fate. He understood that audacity and

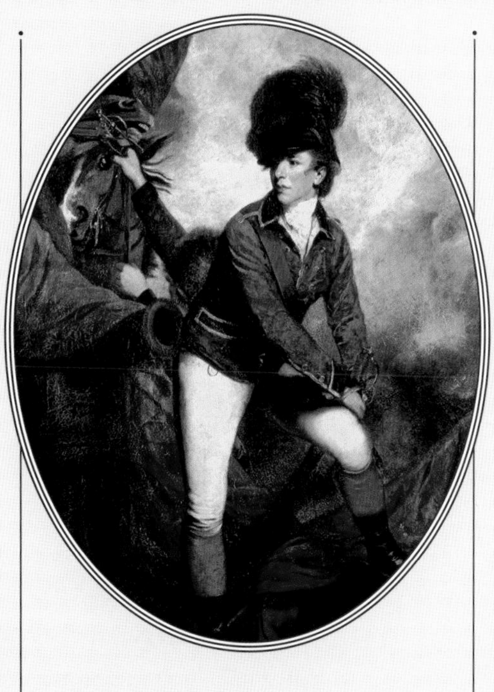

ruthlessness were his great talents, and others in the British military understood that about him as well.

Tarleton was soon given command of the British Legion—an agile, disciplined cavalry and light-infantry force comprised mostly of Loyalists. They raided throughout the middle states until 1780, when they moved south with Cornwallis and began what patriots saw as a reign of shock and awe in the Carolina backcountry. The sheer speed of the legion's movements made it formidable, and Tarleton well understood this, driving his men relentlessly. In 1781, when Tarleton arrived in Virginia, his reputation had become its own weapon, and his legion's very presence in the state spread "an universal terror." Cornwallis relied on the legion's reputation and speed late in the war, when he dispatched it on a covert raid to take Thomas Jefferson, Benjamin Harrison, and several other prominent patriots who were then in Charlottesville, Virginia. The raid almost succeeded, with Jefferson narrowly escaping his home, Monticello, before the legion arrived.

As the war suddenly coalesced around Yorktown, Tarleton was assigned the role of guarding Gloucester Point, a critical supply depot across the York River from the main fighting. When the battle was over and the de rigueur civilities of that time—rounds of dinner parties attended by officers on both sides of the conflict—began, Bloody Ban was excluded. He alone among the major British commanders received no invitations from the American victors.

But once back in Britain, Tarleton was hailed as a great hero of the war. The luster wore off as the years wore on, and when Tarleton began to face criticism for defeats he had suffered in America, he characteristically fought back, exonerating himself in his lengthy *History of the Campaigns of 1780 and 1781 in the Southern Provinces of North America,* a classic that, if not fully believable, is nonetheless more highly respected than most of the other exploits of the infamous, or famous (depending on your allegiance), Banastre Tarleton. ■

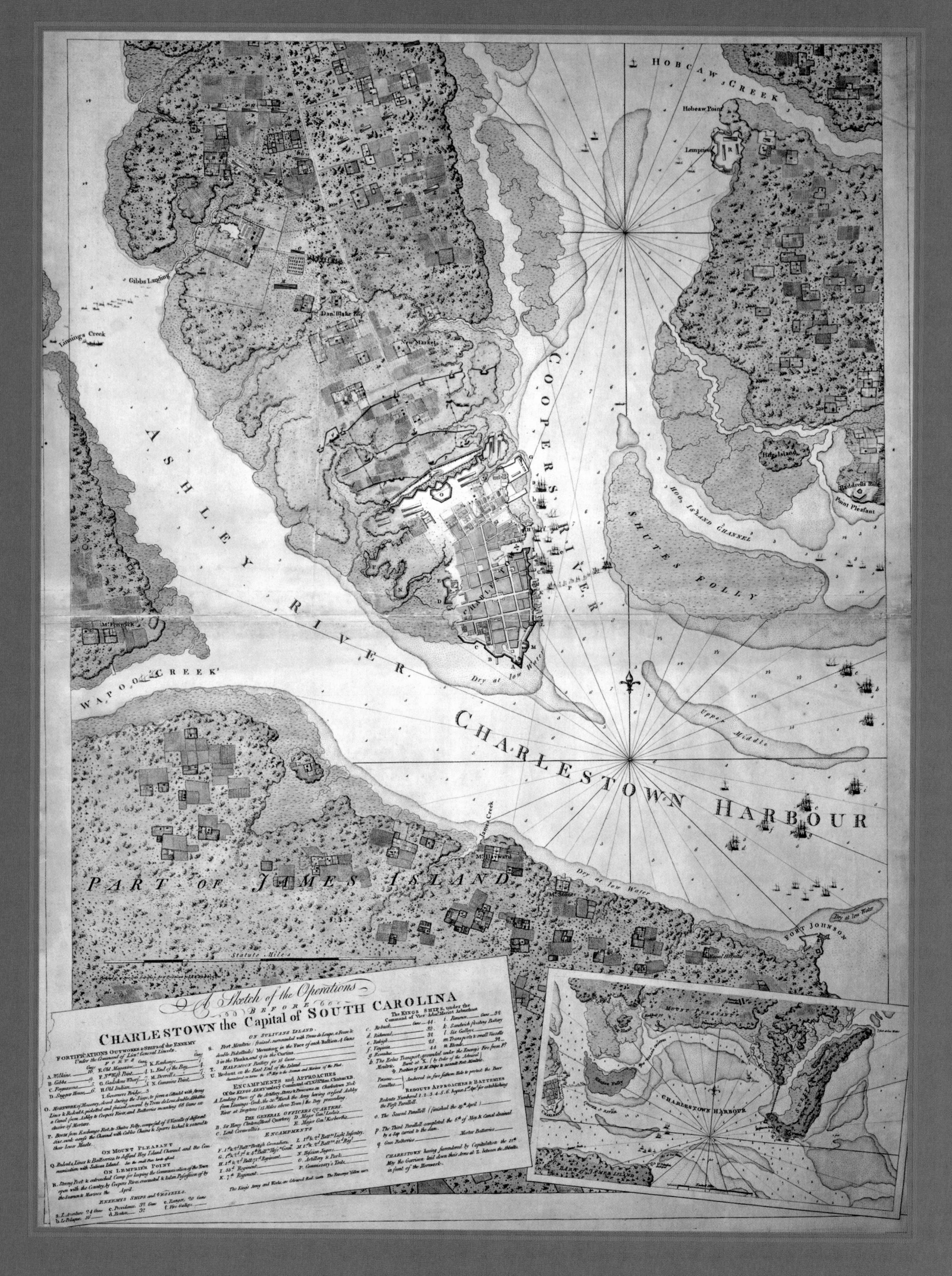

A Sketch of the Operations
before
CHARLESTOWN the Capital of SOUTH CAROLINA
HOBCAW CREEK
Hobcaw Point
Gibbs Landing
Danl. Blake Esq.
New Markets
COOPERS RIVER
ASHLEY RIVER
Hog Island
HOG ISLAND CHANNEL
SHUTES FOLLY
Point Pleasant
WAPOO CREEK
Dry at low Water
Upper Middle
CHARLESTOWN HARBOUR
James Creek
PART OF JAMES ISLAND
Mr. Stone
FORT JOHNSON
Statute Miles
MOUNT PLEASANT
CHARLESTOWN HARBOUR

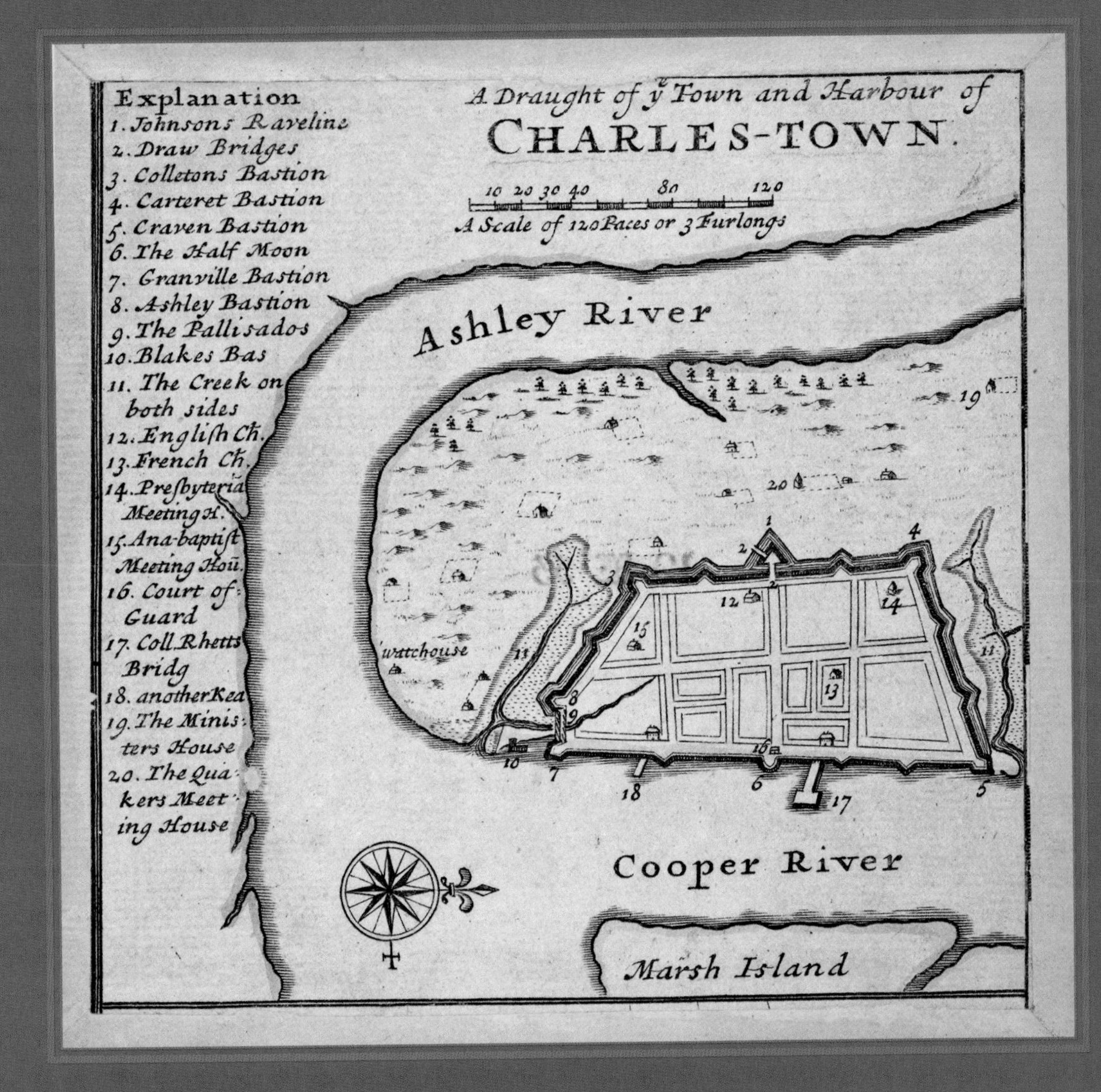

A HAND-DRAWN MAP *shows a detailed look at the position of the Charleston settlement and its position along the Ashley and Cooper Rivers. Opposite: A large engraved map shows military operations, fortifications, and outlying plantations, together with shallows and swamps surrounding Charleston, South Carolina.*

Lieutenant-Colonel Tarleton [whose horse was shot out from under him in the first volley] could remount another horse." This was Tarleton's later account of the battle in his epic *History of the Campaigns of 1780 and 1781.*

Dr. Robert Brownfield, a Continental surgeon who survived the attack, told a different version. He said that Buford quickly "ordered a flag to be hoisted and the arms to be grounded, expecting the usual treatment sanctioned by civilized warfare." But the American surrender went unheeded, and as Tarleton himself reported, a "slaughter was commenced."

"The ostensible pretext for the relentless barbarity that ensued was that his [Tarleton's] Horse was killed under him just as the flag was raised," Brownfield said, and then went on to describe how even after the Continentals were prostrate on the ground, Tarleton's men "went over the ground plunging their bayonets into every one that exhibited any signs of life."

THE LEGACY *of the Battle of the Waxhaws, fought on May 29, 1780, remains hotly debated to this day. Americans maintain that the British forces slaughtered them even after they laid down their arms in surrender.*

Tarleton's own account admitted that his soldiers unleashed "a vindictive asperity not easily restrained." He also called the attack a "complete success." Historians call it the Waxhaws Massacre. It lasted for all of 15 minutes, but its repercussions echoed through the rest of the war and beyond. "This bloody day only wanted the war dance and the roasting fire to have placed it first in the records of torture and death in the West," Capt. Lighthorse Harry Lee declared. The new Continental battle cry soon became "Tarleton's Quarter."

The fact that so many of Tarleton's Legion were American Loyalists was symptomatic of the South, which was as divided in its loyalties as the northern "middle states" had been. Loyalists flocked to the British cause, as Cornwallis had hoped. He had set up garrisons in the backcountry, particularly along the North-South Carolina border, to make it easy for Tories to step forward and join the British. He also had used the powerful tool of economics by buying his supplies from Loyalists while having the property of patriots confiscated. The dissension this caused throughout the countryside was palpable.

One Tory colonel, John Moore, who had served with Cornwallis outside Charleston, managed to enlist the help of 1,300 fellow sympathizers when he returned home to North Carolina—with considerable help from a bedecked British major who assured all who would listen of "the success of the British army in all operations of the South and the total inability of the Whigs [Patriots] to make further opposition." Despite such reassurances, on June 20 a "Whig" contingent of 400 men routed Moore's force of 1,000 at Ramsour's Mill. It was a humiliating defeat, and it was followed on August 6 by another one at Hanging Rock, South Carolina. Back and forth, back and forth through the summer, the two sides—the British and the Loyalists versus the Continentals and the patriot militias—traded victories and defeats. And then in October came the denouement, when an American contingent of some 900 horsemen learned that a British force of 1,100—virtually all Tories, except for a few officers and the Scot commander, Patrick Ferguson—was encamped on Kings Mountain, again in the volatile border region between North and South Carolina. The American force split into two columns and, on October 7, moved quietly "up a branch and ravine between two rocky knobs, beyond which the top of the mountain and the enemy's camp upon it were in full view," one man remembered. Another recalled, "The sky was overcast with clouds, and at times a light mist of rain was falling; our provisions were scanty, and hungry men are apt to be fractious . . . everything was at stake—life, liberty, property, and even the fate of wife, children and friends seemed to depend on the issue: death or victory was the only way to escape the suffering."

MAJ. PATRICK FERGUSON, *a Scottish soldier for the British, led a force of Loyalists in the Battle of Kings Mountain. During the fighting, Ferguson was shot from his horse and died from multiple gunshot wounds.*

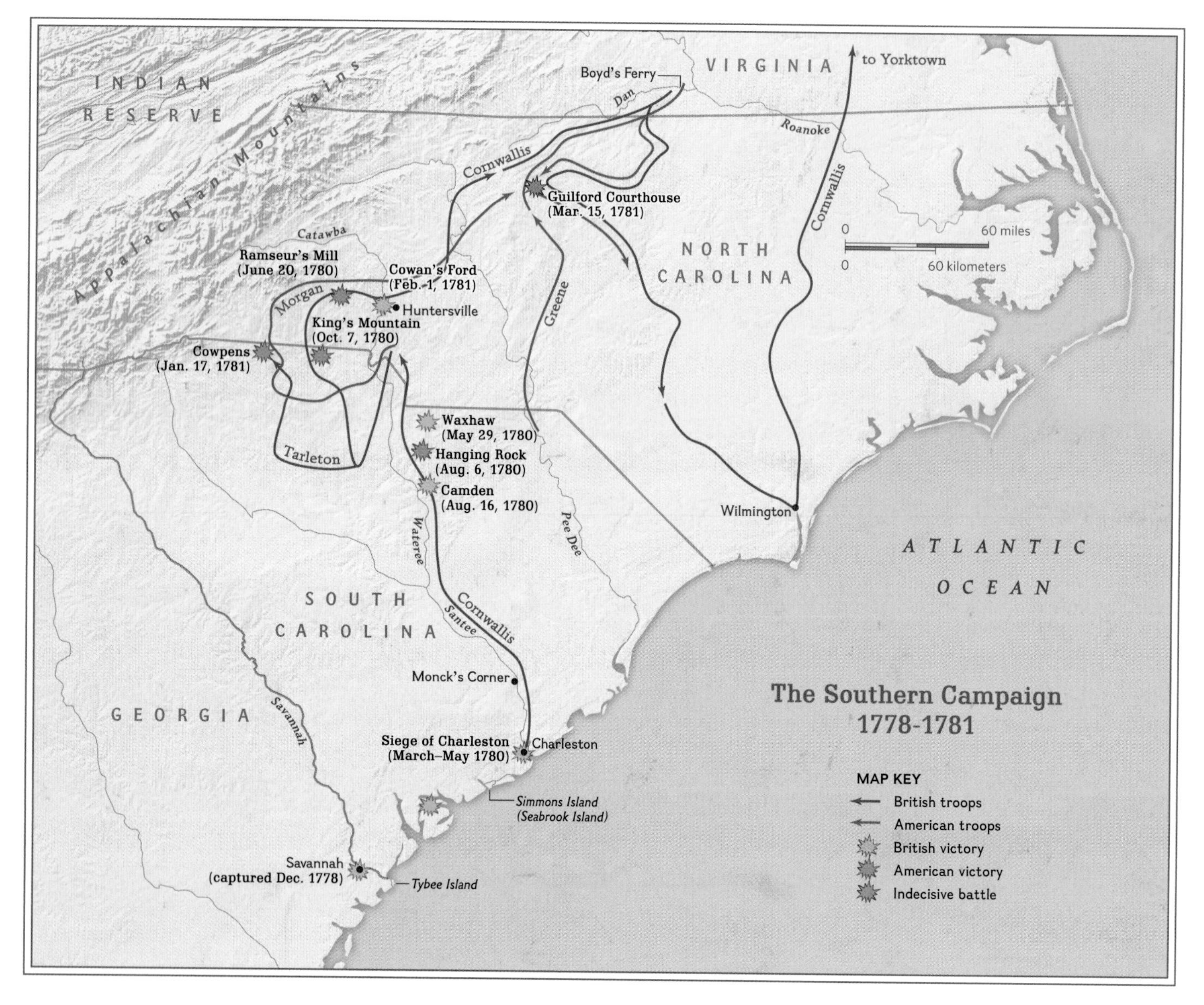

THE BRITISH REFOCUSED *their strategy on the southern colonies and waged several important battles there, beginning with the capture of Savannah in 1778 and the siege of Charleston in 1780.*

It was victory for the Americans. They had taken the British completely by surprise by fighting "in their favorite manner . . . from behind trees and other cover." Fighting valiantly through the hour-long conflagration, Ferguson took bullet after bullet even when it was clear his cause was lost. When finally the white flag was raised, the Americans kept fighting, shouting "Buford! Buford! Tarleton's quarter!"—a taunting, bloody revenge for Waxhaws. At last the Americans ceased fighting, but rumors of their brutality spread, as did word of the decisive Tory defeat. Jefferson called the victory "the turn of the tide of success." One-third of Cornwallis's army was now gone. Over the summer he had moved north into North Carolina, claiming Charlotte, but that fall he retreated to South Carolina to assess his next move.

Early in the campaign season, Cornwallis had delivered a resounding defeat to the American general Horatio Gates at Camden, South Carolina. The hero of Saratoga and

Washington's rival, Gates had been warned by the irascible Gen. Charles Lee to "Take care lest your Northern laurels turn to Southern Willows." But Gates seemed incapable of heeding good advice. By October he had been suspended, and a commander Washington trusted, Nathanael Greene, was put in charge of the army's newly created Southern Department. Greene was appalled at what he found in the South: "The Whigs [Patriots] and Tories pursue one another with the most relent[less] Fury filling and destroying each other wherever they meet. Indeed a great deal of this Country is already laid waste & in the utmost danger of becoming a Desert." The war had "so corrupted the Principles of the People that they think of nothing but plundering one another."

Still, Greene understood that he could put to good use the partisans who had been harassing and spying on the British since they began their backcountry campaign. The most legendary leader among them was Francis Marion, the "Swamp Fox," one of the so-called Rice Kings of South Carolina. Marion was a small man of French Huguenot descent, and neither he nor his ragtag force had received much respect from Gates or Gates's soldiers, who made sport of the small band. One officer described Marion's force as "twenty men and boys, some white, some black . . . their appearance . . . burlesque." The same officer, though, corrected that initial impression, saying that, "The history of the war in South Carolina will recognize Marion as a brave partisan . . ." Even Tarleton, who had inadvertently given Marion his nickname, recognized his wiliness. At one point Tarleton had chased after the partisan for seven hours, until Marion disappeared into a swamp. Tarleton admitted defeat, saying, "As for this damned old fox, the Devil himself could not catch him." Nor could Cornwallis. As Cornwallis retreated south during the last weeks of October, Marion interrupted his communications with Charleston and disrupted his supply chains.

FRANCIS MARION

CIRCA 1732–1795

Francis Marion grew up on a plantation in South Carolina. As a young man, he joined the military and fought in the French and Indian War. He is best known for his service during the American Revolution, when he fought for the Continental Army. After the loss of Charleston to the British, Marion organized a small unit of soldiers numbering between 20 and 70. This group became extremely loyal to Marion and helped him to antagonize the British forces during 1780 and 1781. Marion's men were a consistent thorn in the side of the British Army, staging raids and quick surprise attacks. Nicknamed the Swamp Fox by Col. Banastre Tarleton, Marion was known for being able to elude the British because he was so familiar with the South Carolina terrain. Today he is considered one of the fathers of modern guerrilla warfare.

Benedict Arnold Turns Traitor

While the war in the South ground on, in the North, Washington and the Continental Congress were dealing with a malevolent new development: the news of Benedict Arnold's treachery. In the summer of 1778, Arnold had become military governor of Philadelphia, a city still rife with Loyalists. Among them was a local Tory merchant, Joseph Stansbury, who had become a favorite of General Howe during the British occupation of the city. Stansbury was in league with Joseph Galloway and his spy network. But it did not take a great deal of espionage to see that Arnold was sympathetic to the Tories in the city and had a highly antagonistic relationship with the patriots in the Pennsylvania Council, who were officially

After Horatio Gates's *defeat at the Battle of Camden, South Carolina, George Washington appointed Gen. Nathanael Greene as the new American commander of the Southern Army. This painting depicts the meeting of the two men as Greene arrives to take over.*

The Pedee River, *or Great Pee Dee River, runs through North and South Carolina. Here Francis Marion scored one of his last great victories when he put down a Loyalist uprising in June 1782.*

running the state. In fact, the patriots had accused Arnold of certain crimes, and when these were dismissed, the council threatened to withhold its support of the Continental Army. The congress threatened to move out of Philadelphia over the Arnold affair. Washington, who knew Arnold as a battlefield fighter, remained supportive of him and tried to mollify the various factions, but the vainglorious Arnold had a way of provoking controversy. He had been at the center of dissension from Ticonderoga to Quebec to Saratoga. Arnold had nursed one humiliation after another at the hands of the patriots, whom he felt he had served heroically. He had done enough. He wanted gold, and he wanted glory, and the Americans were delivering neither.

In 1778 Arnold had begun courting Peggy Shippen, the daughter of an extremely wealthy and outspoken Philadelphia Loyalist, and the two married the following year. A small beauty who was "bright and quick and capable of conversing at length about politics and business to anyone," she had been much admired by the British officers in the city. "We were all in love with her," one naval captain confessed. Before her marriage, one of her escorts had been Maj. John André, an aide to Henry Clinton, who rose to head Clinton's secret service in the spring of 1779. Shortly thereafter, André received word through Stansbury that Arnold abhorred the idea of war and separation between Great Britain and America. André understood immediately what this could mean for the British cause. Arnold was still a trusted part of Washington's coterie and the military governor of Philadelphia, so he was

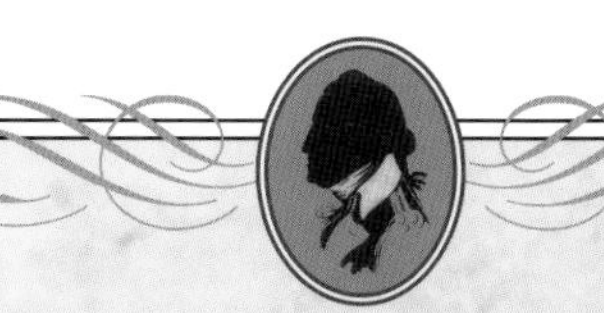

Washington's Circular to the States

Head Quarters, Near Passaic Falls, October 18, 1780.

Sir:

In obedience to the orders of Congress, I have the honor to transmit you the present state of the troops of your line, by which you will perceive how few Men you will have left after the 1st of Jany. Next . . .

I am religiously persuaded that the duration of the War and the greatest part of the misfortunes and perplexities we have hitherto experienced, are chiefly to be attributed to the System of temporary enlistments. Had we in the commencement raised an Army for the War . . . we should not have suffered those military Checks which have so frequently shaken our cause, nor should we have incurred such enormous expenditures as have destroyed our paper Currency and with it all public credit. A moderate compact force on a permanent establishment capable of acquiring the discipline essential to military operations would have been able to make head against the enemy without comparison better than the throngs of Militia which at certain periods have been, not in the field, but in their way to and from the Field . . . [W]e have had a great proportion of the time two sets of Men to feed and pay, one coming to the Army and the other going from it. From this circumstance and from the extraordinary waste and consumption of provisions . . . it is easy to conceive what an immense increase of public expence has been produced from the source of which I am speaking. I might add the diminution of our Agriculture by calling off at critical Seasons the labourers employed in it, as has happened in instances without number . . .

But there are evils still more striking that have befallen us. The intervals between the dismission of one Army and the collection of another have more than once threatened us with ruin, which humanly speaking nothing but the supineness or folly of the enemy could have saved us from. How did our cause totter at the close of 76, when with a little more than two thousand Men we were driven before the enemy thro' Jersey and obliged to take post on the other side of the Delaware to make a shew of covering Philadelphia while in reallity nothing was more easy to them with a little enterprise . . . than to make their passage good to that City and dissipate the remaining force which still kept alive our expiring opposition! . . .

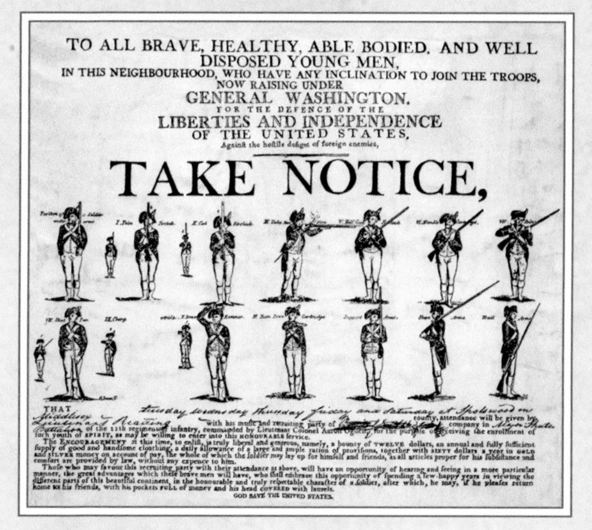

A recruitment flyer for the Continental Army

privy to troop movements and military strategy. After negotiating a financial arrangement with the British, Arnold began corresponding with André, sometimes writing in invisible ink and sometimes passing his letters through his wife, Peggy.

Even with his spymaster André, Arnold's demeanor was demanding and arrogant, and relations between them were uneasy. Meanwhile, Arnold's situation as military governor of Philadelphia had become more and more strained, and that gave him a valid reason to request a new post. He began lobbying for command of West Point, the strategic key to the upper Hudson. But Washington had even greater plans for him. In late July 1780, he saw the young man in person and offered him a great plum: a field assignment as divisional commander of half of Washington's infantry. To Washington's utter surprise, Arnold's "countenance changed and he appeared to be quite fallen, and instead of thanking me or expressing any pleasure at the appointment, never opened his mouth." Later, Arnold explained to Washington that the wound to his leg from the fighting in Saratoga had not healed enough for such an assignment, and again he petitioned for command of West Point. In hindsight, Washington recalled, "it appeared somewhat strange to me that a man of Arnold's known activity and enterprise would be desirous of taking so inactive a part." But Washington had endless issues far more pressing to deal with, and he "thought no more of the matter." By August Arnold had the real plum he had desired—command of West

Head Quarters Robinsons
House Sept. 20th. 1780

Permission is granted to Joshua Smith Esqr. to go to Dobbs's Ferry with three Men and a Boy in a Boat with a Flag to carry some Letters of a Private Nature for Gentlemen in New York and to Return immediately

B Arnold M Genl.

N.B. He has permission

AFTER TURNING TRAITOR, *Benedict Arnold persuaded British major John André to conceal the plans of West Point in his boot at their meeting on September 21, 1780. Inset: Pass carried by John André, signed by Benedict Arnold*

Point—and he made plans to turn it over to the British in exchange for the modern equivalent of one million dollars.

The garrison there, Arnold discovered, was small, only some 1,500 men—not surprising given the generally poor shape of the Continental Army—and the defenses in poor shape. But as he and André plotted the exchange of the fort, an even greater opportunity presented itself. On Friday, September 15, 1780, Washington wrote to Arnold, "I shall be at Peekskill on Sunday evening on my way to Hartford . . . You will be pleased to send down a guard . . . at that time . . . You will keep this to yourself, as I want to make my journey a secret." Immediately, Arnold informed André that the great general could easily be taken, but his letter was waylaid, and Washington, oblivious to what could have been his catastrophic capture, made it safely across the Hudson, almost within sight of the British ship *Vulture.*

Margaret "Peggy" Shippen Arnold *(1760–1804), Benedict Arnold's wife, was the daughter of Philadelphia Loyalists. Peggy played a part in the treasonous attempt to cede West Point to the British.*

Meanwhile, André stuck to an earlier plan to disguise himself and sneak behind American lines for a meeting with Arnold about 15 miles below West Point, where, Arnold had assured him, "you will be perfectly safe." When the two met, Arnold handed off documents detailing the strength of the troops and artillery at West Point, along with Washington's September 6 war council minutes, sent to Arnold by the commander himself. André carefully rolled the treasonous documents and stuffed them into his boot. Arnold also gave André a pass that identified him as Mr. John Anderson and instructed anyone who might stop him to permit him to pass, "he being on public business by my direction." The pass bore Arnold's signature.

The next day André was stopped by three "skinners," rebel militiamen who operated as little more than brigands. When they discovered André's British uniform under his cape, even Arnold's pass could not save him. They took their prisoner to the militia commander, who ordered that Anderson (André) be taken to Arnold at West Point. That plan was scuttled by a more senior officer, who harbored suspicions about Arnold. Still, Arnold was informed of the arrest, and the documents were sent on to Washington, with a note that said they had come from "a certain John Anderson, who has a pass signed by General Arnold."

The documents had not yet reached Washington two days later, when he set out with Alexander Hamilton, Lafayette, and other aides to visit Arnold in the mansion he occupied two miles below West Point. All of the men looked forward to the visit, since the entrancing Mrs. Arnold would be entertaining them. When they arrived at the mansion, though, they were told that Arnold had been called to West Point and that Mrs. Arnold was in bed upstairs. Later in the morning, Washington was ferried to West Point, but instead of finding Arnold, he found the fort's defenses in deplorable condition. Why wasn't Arnold there to

greet him? Washington later confessed that he still "had not the least idea of the real cause."

When Washington returned to the mansion, the documents seized from André were waiting for him. Lafayette recalled entering Washington's room, to be greeted with "Arnold has betrayed us! Whom can we trust now?" Despite the shock of the betrayal, or maybe because if it, none of Washington's group seems to have entertained suspicions of Peggy Arnold, still in her chambers and reportedly delirious. Instead, Washington, Hamilton, and Lafayette were roused to utter sympathy by the comely Peggy's delirium. Clutching her infant to her breast, she wailed, "General Arnold will never return. He is gone forever, there, there, there." She pointed at the ceiling. "The spirits have carried him up there. They have put hot irons in his head."

"It was the most affecting scene I ever was witness to," Hamilton wrote.

It was surely quite a performance, and it worked. The poor Mrs. Arnold was spared any pain, while Washington's agents hunted her husband in the streets of Loyalist New York, where he had taken refuge.

Arnold has betrayed us! Whom can we trust now?

Gen. George Washington

On the very day he fled West Point, Arnold had written Washington a typically self-serving letter: "I have ever acted from a principle of love to my country, since the commencement of the present unhappy contest between Great Britain and the colonies. The same principle of love . . . actuates my present conduct, however it may appear inconsistent to the world." He also sent Washington pleas to spare André's life—or else, he added boldly, "I call heaven and earth to witness that your Excellency will be justly answerable for the torrent of blood that may be spilt in consequence."

Arnold's pleas and threats were ignored. On October 2 André was hanged publicly in Tappan, New York, to set an example to any other enemy spies. He grabbed the noose himself from the hangman's hand, tightened it around his own neck, saying, "Nothing but to request you will witness to the world that I die a brave man."

Arnold's deception had overwhelmed Washington, but he soon recovered himself, issuing general orders that put a positive face on the defection: "Great honor is due to the American Army that this is the first instance of Treason of the kind where many were to be expected from the nature of the dispute, and nothing is so bright an ornament in the Character of the American soldiers as their having been proof against all the arts and seductions of an insidious enemy."

While Washington worked hourly to keep the spirit of '76 alive in America, John Adams, in France for a second time at the behest of the Continental Congress, promoted American interests but managed to offend the French with his pugnacious style. But then, the French in turn offended Adams's puritanical sensibilities. Benjamin Franklin, his fellow minister and beloved idol of the French, was just as bad; Adams found him "too old, too infirm,

After being caught *in an intrigue with Benedict Arnold to engineer the surrender of West Point to the British, British officer John André was hanged as a spy by the Continental Army.*

too indolent and dissipated" to be an effective diplomat. Yet Adams was hardly cut out for the subtleties of French diplomacy and was on particularly bad footing with the Count de Vergennes, the French minister who was still America's greatest champion. Adams complained of Vergennes, "He means . . . to keep his hand under our chin to prevent us from drowning, but not to lift our heads out of the water."

That may have been true, but it was the way of geopolitics, and Adams knew this too. From his uncomfortable perch in Paris, he wrote and wrote—some 95 unanswered letters to the Continental Congress by late July 1780. He also wrote impolitic letters to Vergennes and pressed repeatedly for more French involvement. Vergennes would not be pushed by an unskilled American minister, and he finally refused any more communication with Adams, announcing he would deal only with Franklin. "Mr. Adams has given extreme offense to the court here," Franklin wrote to inform the congress and endorsed Vergennes's request that Adams be recalled. But by then Adams was in Holland to see "whether something might be done to render us less dependent on France."

Dependent America may have been, but by 1780 the French were certainly backing the Revolution. In mid-July 6,500 men under General Rochambeau had disembarked at Newport, Rhode Island, and another 2,500 men were on the way. To Rochambeau, Washington pushed his constant refrain—that New York should be the goal of a major engagement. "This is the time for America by one great exertion to put an end to the war," Washington assured the French. But they were not assured and seriously doubted Washington's claim that he could field 35,000 men, which in truth was a huge exaggeration. Rochambeau waited, considering his options, while Washington despaired as he faced the same old problems: getting his men through the winter and dealing with a shrinking army and a public with little taste left for war. Despite how uplifting his general orders about the glorious cause might have been, Washington feared that unless a grand move was made soon, the cause would be lost.

Nathanael Greene had said, "We fight, get beat, rise, and fight again." But how long could that go on, particularly among an army so much neglected by the very people it was fighting for? As he had done so often, Washington wrote to the Continental Congress, pleading for more supplies for his men: "It would be well for the troops if, like chameleons, they could live upon air, or like the bear, suck their paws for sustenance during the rigor of the approaching season." But his men were neither bears nor chameleons. Sooner or later, they would break.

While Washington worried that his army might not survive another winter, Arnold, who

Abigail Smith Adams

1744–1818

Born on November 11, 1744, Abigail Smith grew up in Weymouth, Massachusetts. Her father was the pastor of the local church, and young Abigail took advantage of her father's well-stocked library, studying the Bible, history, philosophy, and poetry. Her future husband, lawyer John Adams, found her erudition attractive, and the two were married in 1764. Their marriage was a strong one, enduring the long absences that resulted from her husband's career. Abigail wrote often to her husband, and her political legacy can be found in many of these letters. An advocate for women's rights and education, Adams believed that women should be recognized for their intellectual capabilities and as much more than mere companions to their husbands. While John Adams was at the Continental Congress in 1776, she famously wrote to them to "remember the ladies, and be more generous and favorable to them than your ancestors . . . Remember all Men would be tyrants if they could."

had escaped to the British and was now a brigadier general in the king's army, complained to Clinton, "A life of inaction will be prejudicial to my health." He had presented a bold plan to take back Philadelphia, but it had been denied. By late December, he was sailing for Virginia instead, with orders to destroy military supplies and keep any troops or militias in the state engaged, so they couldn't reinforce the American efforts farther south in the Carolinas. Like Clinton's fleet the previous winter, Arnold's was scattered by weather, and three transports were lost. But by December 30, what remained of it was in Hampton Roads. The war had come to Virginia.

The French Army *occupied Rhode Island on the orders of Jean-Baptiste-Donatien de Vimeur, Count of Rochambeau. This map reflects the French occupation and allocation of military resources.*

John Adams
(1735–1826)

If Ben Franklin was the elder sage of the Revolution, Thomas Paine its somewhat intemperate voice, Washington its heroic warrior, and Jefferson its rarefied intellect, John Adams was its messy, tenacious, disputatious, verbose conscience.

Adams's Puritan ancestors had come in the Great Migration of the 1630s, and he was proud of their long "line of virtuous, independent New England farmers." He grew up surrounded by the mores of Massachusetts village life and in a world full of kin—his own family of 11 children, of which he ranked as oldest, as well as cousins, aunts, and uncles in nearby villages and in Boston. "What has preserved this race of Adamses in all their ramifications . . . ?" he asked. Then he answered the question himself: "I believe it is religion."

After his studies at Harvard, Adams eventually followed his father into the life of a small farmer, but he also hung out a shingle announcing his other occupation: the law. Both pursuits suited his temperament, and his life seemed settled, particularly as it included his new bride and the dear companion of his soul, Abigail. The daughter of a Congregationalist minister in nearby Weymouth, Abigail was hardworking and cheerful but also bookish, with an incisive and curious intellect. She was both a grounding solace to the impetuous John and the love of his life. The two began their lives together on the Braintree farm where John had grown up, with breezes from the ocean, only a mile away, salting the air. Despite his contentedness, Adams felt a gnawing ambition for more recognition, a bigger stage. Yet he understood that "I never shall shine 'til some animating occasion calls forth all my powers."

Young Abigail Adams, *portrayed around the time of her marriage. Opposite: John Adams, patriot and second President of the United States.*

One such occasion occurred in 1770 with the so-called Boston Massacre. By then a respected lawyer, Adams took the stage in the defense of the British soldiers. Adams had been told no one else would take the case, and his conscience would not let him decline it. "Facts are stubborn things," he reminded the jury, "and whatever may be our wishes, our inclinations, or the dictums of our passions, they cannot alter the state of facts and evidence." His arguments resulted in acquittals for most of the accused and in some public opprobrium for him. It also sealed his standing as a man of principle, in the public's mind and in his own. In his old age, he called the case "one of the best pieces of service I ever rendered my country."

Four years later he was off to Philadelphia as a member of the First Continental Congress. It was a heady time for Adams, to be surrounded by the great port of Philadelphia and by men of such "fortunes, abilities, learning, eloquence." Six months later he was back for the Second Continental Congress, and he quickly distinguished himself as an ardent patriot. He was put on the Committee of Five to draft a declaration of independence, and he was appointed head of the Board of War to supply the needs of Washington's army. Adams always "saw the whole of a subject at a glance," Dr. Benjamin Rush, a fellow signer of the Declaration of Independence, wrote. "He was equally fearless of men and of the consequences of a bold assertion of his opinion." Through the long years of war, Adams's bold assertions sometimes served him and his fledgling country well, and sometimes served them ill.

In 1778 he sailed for France to replace the discredited American commissioner Silas Deane, recalled on charges of financial misdeeds. Adams's eldest son, ten-year-old John Quincy, went with him, but Abigail did not. Adams had spent endless months away from her in Philadelphia, and now an ocean would separate them. She considered going, but she could not "prevail upon him to consent." He worried for her safety on a hazardous Atlantic crossing, but she was also needed at home. Since the Revolution had begun, she had run the farm and cared for their growing family through deprivation and outbreaks of disease; she had dealt with passing troops, who had camped on her farm; and through it all she had written John letters of love and affection, politics and patriotism. "Frugality, industry, and economy are the lessons of the day," she had proclaimed in the first days of the conflict. "At least they must be for me or my small boat will suffer shipwreck." At that time she probably had no notion of how long and lonely her small boat's voyage would be.

JOHN ADAMS *was one of the "Committee of Five" to draft the Declaration of Independence in 1776. Opposite: John Singleton Copley painted this portrait of John Adams as a diplomat.*

After his own long voyage across the Atlantic, Adams arrived in France only to learn that the Treaty of Alliance had already been signed. Still, he was to be one of the three peace commissioners, along with Franklin and Arthur Lee. At first, Adams was overwhelmed with enthusiasm for Paris and the French and the "good doctor" Franklin, who, Adams wrote, the French seemed to think would "restore the golden age." But Adams's enthusiasm soon turned to disillusionment, and his typical bold assertions too soon offended government ministers and Franklin. Yet the great sights of the city still excited him, and he and John Quincy took their fill until, in mid-February 1779, Adams received word that Congress had appointed Franklin the minister plenipotentiary to the French court, and Adams's position was no more.

When Adams returned to Massachusetts, he was disheartened but glad to be home. It was during this period, as a member of the state constitutional convention, that he did some of his most significant work. He essentially authored the Constitution of the Commonwealth of Massachusetts, which, aside from establishing a tripartite form of government that included an independent judiciary, included a commitment to "The Encouragement of Literature, Etc."

By the following winter of 1780-81, Adams was back in France, charged by Congress to begin negotiating peace with Great Britain and a treaty of commerce. This time he had his sons John Quincy and Charles with him, and in a letter to Abigail he wrote one of his most insightful observations on parenthood and time and what America could become: "I must study politics and war that my sons may have liberty to study mathematics and philosophy. My sons ought to study mathematics and philosophy, geography, natural history and naval architecture, navigation,

commerce and agriculture, in order to give their children a right to study painting, poetry, music, architecture, statuary, tapestry, and porcelain."

As the war played out to its end, Adams stayed on in Europe. He left Paris for Amsterdam to become American minister to the Netherlands. There, he persuaded the Dutch to make loans to America at a dire moment. But even in Holland, his poor relations with the French plagued him. The powerful minister, the Count de Vergennes, was fomenting trouble for Adams through his own emissary in Philadelphia. Vergennes wanted Congress to know that John Adams "has a rigidity, and arrogance, and an obstinancy that will cause him to foment a thousand unfortunate incidents." Adams's obstinacy would strike Vergennes again in 1782, as peace was being negotiated. But it was Adams's very tenacity that won valuable concessions for America.

JOHN ADAMS SERVED *as the first American ambassador to the English court. He is shown here presenting his credentials to King George III.*

Adams had now grown into the role of diplomat, so much so that even with peace accomplished, his time in Europe did not end. He was soon back in Paris, and Abigail sailed to join him, despite the fear of an ocean voyage and her feeling that she was too provincial for the role she would be required to play. After all, her experience had been that of a lawyer's wife who, in her 39 years, had only rarely left the vicinity of her birth. Still, whatever lay ahead, she would at last "be in the arms of my dearest, best of friends."

In Paris both John and Abigail became dear friends with Thomas Jefferson, the new American minister to the French Court, before they moved on to Adams's next assignment: minister to the Court of St. James's. They were in London in 1787, when they received a copy of the recently adopted U.S. Constitution. Jefferson too had read the document and wrote Adams that he worried about the powers it gave the President. In his prescient reply, Adams told Jefferson that the two of them differed on this: "You are afraid of the one, I, the few . . . You are apprehensive of monarchy; I, of aristocracy."

The following year, John and Abigail at last sailed for home. Adams was 52 and had been away from America for ten years, broken only by a short visit in 1779. Now, at last, he could return to his loves—"my farm, my family and goose quill" pen. But it was not to be. In 1789 he was elected the country's first Vice President, serving under Washington.

During his first weeks in that role, Adams made blunders that would haunt his reputation through history. In heated discussions on the Senate floor regarding the use of titles, Adams championed them. Washington, he said, should be addressed as "His Majesty the President." Adams was castigated, anointed "His Rotundity," and accused of favoring a hereditary monarchy. Yet despite the inauspicious start, he served as Vice President for the eight years of Washington's two terms. It was not an office he relished. "My country in its wisdom contrived for me the most insignificant office that ever the invention of man contrived or his imagination conceived," he complained to Abigail.

Still, those years put Adams in place as a contender to replace Washington, and to his own surprise he prevailed against his closest opponent, Jefferson. (In those days, more than two candidates were often in contention, and there was no popular vote for President; the winner was determined solely by the vote of electors appointed by state legislatures.) The most pressing issue throughout the four years of Adams's Presidency was a looming war with France and Napoleon. Adams was determined to keep America out of the European struggle and, at the same time, to build up the country's naval defenses. He succeeded, but in doing so, he was battered by both pro-war Federalists and antiwar Republicans.

When the election of 1800 heated up, the race again revolved around Jefferson and Adams, and it quickly became ugly. The Federalists accused Jefferson of cowardice and atheism and "cohabiting" with his slave women. Jefferson's operatives called Adams "a hideous hermaphroditical character which has neither the force and firmness of a man, nor the gentleness of a woman." They also accused Adams of being meek in the face of a French threat. Adams lost his bid for a second term, but then there was no clear winner in the 1800 battle, as Jefferson and Aaron Burr had tied. Adams's loss bothered him, but he also assured one of his sons, "I feel my shoulders relieved from the burden." At last, he could reclaim his private life with Abigail.

The final years of John Adams's life were relatively peaceful. They were marred only by the death of a beloved daughter and a grown son, who died of alcoholism. In the last days of 1811, friends of Jefferson visited the Adamses, and Adams told them, "I always loved Jefferson, and still love him." A week or so later, on New Year's Day, he wrote to Jefferson, who replied warmly. In the ensuing years the former revolutionaries and Presidents exchanged 50 letters. "My friend!" Adams wrote in one. "You and I have passed our lives in serious times."

In the fall of 1817, 74-year-old Abigail contracted typhoid and died. "I wish I could lie down beside her and die, too," John had said, and had called her "the dear partner of my life for fifty-four years as a wife, and for many years more as a lover . . ." In the summer of 1826, he finally prepared to join her. As he lay dying on July 4, he was told it was Independence Day and replied, "It is a great day. It is a *good* day." That evening he died, and a sharp clap of thunder sounded the death knell. "Popularity was never my mistress, nor was I ever, or shall I ever be a popular man," he once had said. No, but he had been a great and good one.

THE BIRTHPLACE OF *John Adams in Braintree, now Quincy, Massachusetts*

CHAPTER 6

If you cannot relieve me very soon,
you must be prepared to hear the worst.

British Gen. Lord Cornwallis

1781-1783
The Tide of Success

In the final days of 1780, Anthony Wayne, hero of Stony Point, had written to complain about the suffering of his men in the Pennsylvania line: "Old worn out coats and tattered linen overalls, and what was once a poor substitute for a blanket (now divided among three soldiers), is but very wretched living and shelter against the winter's piercing cold, drifting snows and chilling sleet. Our soldiery . . . have now served their country with fidelity for near five years, poorly clothed, badly fed and worse paid; of the last article, trifling as it is, they have not seen a paper dollar in the way of pay for near *twelve months.*" Wayne's words echoed those Washington had written time and again. Both men knew that the soldiers were being asked for too much and being given too little in return.

On January 1 in the deep cold of winter, some 1,300 men of the Pennsylvania line had had enough. Staging a mutiny outside Morristown, they took possession of cannons and muskets and killed several officers—but not Wayne, who had arrived on the scene to reason with them. While they refused to hear Wayne's pleas, they also refused to kill him, though he dramatically opened his coat at one point and announced, "If you mean to kill me—shoot me at once—here's my breast." Having rejected Wayne's offers, and intent on taking their case to the Continental Congress, they marched off in the direction of Philadelphia.

The Count of Rochambeau *and George Washington give the final orders for the last assault on Yorktown, Virginia.*
Preceding pages: British general Charles Cornwallis surrenders to the Continental Army at Yorktown, Virginia, October 19, 1781.

GEN. "MAD" ANTHONY WAYNE *successfully put down a mutiny among Pennsylvania troops on New Year's Day, 1781. The disaffected troops took their grievances to Congress after Wayne's intervention.*

The soldiers' grievances were simple and reasonable: They had enlisted for three years and served that, and now the congress was saying that the terms of their enlistment were *either* three years or the duration of the war, and the end of the war was nowhere in sight. And, as Wayne had said, the men had not been paid in a year, though new recruits were getting $25 in silver just for enlisting. The Pennsylvania men had not joined the rebellion against an unjust England with the intention of suffering even more under an unjust and apparently uncaring congress.

Washington, then at West Point, received reports of the mutiny with anxiety but without surprise. He had often worried that something similar would happen; now he had to quell it before discontent roared through the meager ranks of his army and left it in irreparable tatters. Yet, he felt he couldn't go to Pennsylvania to quell the rebellion himself because without his presence at West Point, the soldiers there might stage their own mutiny. He summoned militiamen to halt the mutineers' progress, and the Pennsylvania men got no farther than Princeton and Trenton, scenes of the famous victories at the turn of 1777. But Washington also wrote directly to the states on behalf of his men and upbraided each government for neglecting its own soldiery: "It is in vain to think an army can be kept together much longer under such a variety of sufferings as ours has experienced."

As the army brooded in the North that January, the tide of war shifted in the South, where the mild climate ensured a continuous campaign season. Earlier in the winter, Gen. Nathanael Greene had dispatched Daniel Morgan, who had fought hard and well at Saratoga, into the Carolina backcountry. Morgan's force was to base itself at the fork between the Broad and Pacolet Rivers and from there "to give protection to that part of the country and spirit up the people, to annoy the enemy in that quarter." Through Tory spies, Cornwallis, then in Winnsboro, South Carolina, was informed of the "rebels'" presence in the backcountry, and he became convinced that they were moving on Ninety Six, a trading post about 175 miles west of Charleston that had become a critical British stronghold. Tarleton was called on to deal with Morgan and to "push him to the utmost." Meanwhile, Cornwallis would move up with his force, and together, the two British units would trap Morgan's between them.

American general Daniel Morgan *(1736–1802) is considered to be one of the finest tacticians of his time. His brilliant military strategies were put to good use in the Southern Campaign toward the end of the war.*

As the soldiers on both sides marched through the backcountry, they were pelted by a ceaseless rain that soaked the land, overflowed the rivers, and turned the roads into a muddy morass. On January 16 Tarleton wrote to Cornwallis to say that he had located Morgan, but that his own force had "been most cruelly retarded by the waters." The high waters also slowed communication and coordination between Tarleton and Cornwallis. Neither knew that the other was only 50 miles away. Yet Morgan was fully aware of the location of both enemy forces, and he knew how precarious his position was. He wrote to Greene of the "enemy's great superiority in numbers" and of the "scarcity of forage," which kept his own men spread out as they searched for food. He warned, "No attempt to surprise me will be left untried" by the British. On the night of January 16, the first attempt came, but Morgan's scouts had spotted the British movement and thundered into camp to warn that Tarleton was approaching. The Americans quickly moved out, but the fast-moving rivers impeded their retreat. They had to find a ford where a safe crossing could be made before the enemy caught up to them.

Morgan knew that Tarleton was dogging his heels, and rather than continuing to try to outpace him, Morgan stopped running and prepared to fight. He chose a meadow called Cowpens, which drovers used every spring to graze cattle on the way to market. Morgan had conceived a new strategy, probably based on desperation. He had militiamen serving under him as well as his regulars, but militiamen were notoriously unreliable in a fight; they tended to cut and run when the battle was barely under way. So Morgan put them in the

Brig. Gen. Daniel Morgan *led the American forces in the Battle of Cowpens, a decisive victory over the British forces led by Col. Banastre Tarleton. Col. William Washington, shown here, led his men bravely in this victory, which helped the Continental Army retake South Carolina from the British.*

front lines but did not order them to hold their ground as the enemy came forward. "Just hold up your heads, boys, three fires, and you are free," he told them as he went among them that night. "And when you return to your homes, how the old folks will bless you, and the girls kiss you for your gallant conduct."

The morning of January 17 dawned "bitterly cold . . . the men were slapping their hands together to keep warm." Then, "about sunrise the British advanced at a sort of trot, with a loud halloo! It was the most beautiful line I ever saw." Morgan yelled for his men to answer with "the Indian halloo, by God!" In the ensuing hour of battle, the Americans performed courageously and precisely, while, astonishingly, the British line fell into chaos. Tarleton attempted to rally his men, but his horse was shot out from under him. "All attempts to restore order, recollection, or courage proved fruitless," he admitted in his war memoir. At one point, as the Americans overwhelmed the British with bayonets, the shout of "Tarleton's Quarter" went up, but Morgan would have none of it. "Not a man was killed wounded or even insulted after he surrendered," Morgan reported. However brutally Tarleton's forces had behaved at the Waxhaws Massacre the previous spring, Morgan insisted that the vanquished enemy be treated with honor.

NATHANAEL GREENE
1742–1786

Born in Rhode Island in 1742, Nathanael Greene had a military career with humble origins and historic results. He did not start out as an officer, but at the lowest possible rank, a militia private, in 1774. One year later, he received his first promotion to major general as a result of his brave actions at the Siege of Boston. Later that same year he was promoted to brigadier and put in charge of military operations around Boston by George Washington himself, who saw Greene's true talents and reliability. In 1776 he became a major general and commanded the Continental forces on Long Island. Perhaps Greene's most famous contribution to the Revolution came during the Southern Campaign, when he forced British general Charles Cornwallis and his men to abandon the Carolinas for Virginia.

In the fighting at Cowpens, Tarleton lost almost 90 percent of his force, along with vital wagons, horses, and weaponry—an unmitigated disaster for the British. Many of his surviving officers later recorded their accounts of the day, and they had nothing but contempt for "that boy" Tarleton. As for Morgan, he was able to report back exultantly to Greene, "I have Given him [Tarleton] a devil of a whipping, a more compleat victory never was obtained."

Cornwallis confessed in a letter, "The late affair has almost broken my heart." He had lost a quarter of his army, and the reputation of his daring cavalry commander Tarleton was badly tarnished, so much so that Tarleton attempted to retire and face court-martial. But Cornwallis remained convinced that Bloody Ban was a weapon he could not spare. The two would continue their winter campaign and head north with a combined force of 2,500 men. Cornwallis would catch Nathanael Greene's army in North Carolina and avenge Cowpens.

Along the way, Cornwallis decided to strip down his army into a light, fast-moving force. The soldiers were charged with carrying their own provisions. He even had the ubiquitous rum casks destroyed, to his men's great chagrin. As one officer reported, "Without Baggage, necessaries, or Provisions of any sort . . . in this most barren inhospitable unhealthy part of North America, opposed to the most savage, inveterate perfidious cruel Enemy . . . it was resolved to follow Green's Army to the end of the World."

NATHANAEL GREENE *(opposite) and his army successfully evaded the British army by crossing the Dan River from North Carolina into Virginia in February 1781.*

LOSSING-BARRITT.

Greene, outnumbered three to one, knew the British were in pursuit, and he was moving away from them as fast as possible. He crossed river after river, "through country offering every obstacle, affording scarcely any resources; with troops destitute of every thing, who a great part of the way left the vestiges of their march in their own blood." This was the way Washington's aide-de-camp Alexander Hamilton would later describe Greene's march: he called it "a masterpiece of military skill and exertion." It was enough of a masterpiece to thwart Cornwallis, whose army had run out of supplies and had to reverse course to reprovision.

Meanwhile, on February 3, Greene and Daniel Morgan joined forces, even as rain continued to fall in torrents. They moved on toward the Virginia-North Carolina border. More militia joined them, but Morgan, wracked with rheumatism, had to leave the field for his home in Virginia. Greene knew it was a loss: "Great generals are scarce—there are few Morgans to be found."

Greene took up a position at the edge of Guilford Courthouse, where forests and thickets made the going tough. He had received a letter from Morgan that advised him to use the

DESPITE BEING *a technical victory for the redcoats, the Battle of Guilford Courthouse, fought in March 1781, in Greensboro, North Carolina, proved a strategic victory for the Americans, because British casualties ran so high.*

militia he now commanded wisely: "If they fight, you will beat Cornwallis; if not, he will beat you." Greene took Morgan's advice to heart and deployed his 4,400 troops much as Morgan had in his great victory at Cowpens, with the militiamen in the front lines. Early on the afternoon of March 15, the opposing forces at last engaged. "The battle was long, obstinate and bloody," Greene reported, and the advantage seesawed back and forth as the fighting grew fiercer. At one point, Greene might have overwhelmed Cornwallis by throwing all of his forces into the melee, but the risk of losing his army was too great for Greene. He did not gain the kind of success with his militia at Guilford that Morgan enjoyed at Cowpens, so he had been "obliged to give up ground and lost . . . artillery." Still, the British had "been so soundly beaten that they dare no move towards us."

The aftermath of the battle was almost worse than the fighting had been. One soldier later wrote, "I never did, and hope I never shall, experience two such days and Nights . . . , the very ground . . . cover'd with Dead, with Dying and with hundreds of wounded . . . a violent and constant Rain that lasted above Forty hours made it equally impracticable to remove or administer the smallest comfort to many of the Wounded." Cornwallis had lost a quarter of his army, while Greene's was depleted by a mere 6 percent. Despite that, Cornwallis claimed victory, prompting one droll observer to comment, "[A]nother such Victory would destroy the British army."

The American cavalry *under the command of "Lighthorse" Henry Lee engaged British troops at the Battle of Guilford Courthouse in 1781.*

As Cornwallis headed for the coast, Greene trailed after him for a couple of weeks. Then, in early April, Greene left off his pursuit and wheeled south to reclaim South Carolina. By late April 1780, Cornwallis had had enough of the Carolinas. The Loyalist support he had anticipated had never been organized enough to pacify the countryside and to allow him to pursue any real strategic goals. Now he turned to a new, grander scheme that he communicated to his commander, Henry Clinton: As he moved north, Clinton should move south from New York and "bring our whole force into Virginia; we then have a stake to fight for, and a successful battle may give us America."

Ratifying the Articles of Confederation

A political battle for America had been going on among the former colonies themselves. The Articles of Confederation, weak as they were, had never been ratified. The congress was ineffectual, and Washington's military objectives continued to suffer from "the fatal policy too prevalent in most states, of employing their ablest men at home." Without these men of large ideas, state politics prevailed—and the great, overarching course of revolution suffered. The congress had no ability to raise funds to support the army, and many of the states were themselves in dire financial straits after years of war. "There is no money

THIS "NEW MAP *of North America" shows the continent in transition, both as discoveries are made and as the colonies wage their fight for independence from Britain. Jonathan Carver, a Massachusetts-born explorer, created the map, which documented his explorations in the northern regions. He included it in his popular* Travels Through the Interior Parts of North America, *published in 1778.*

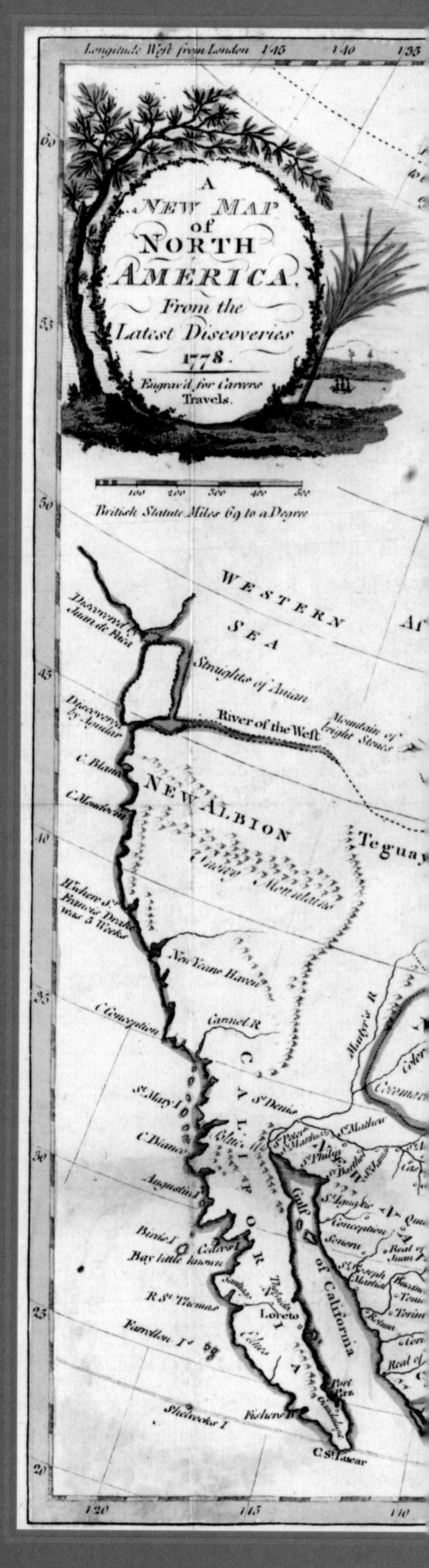

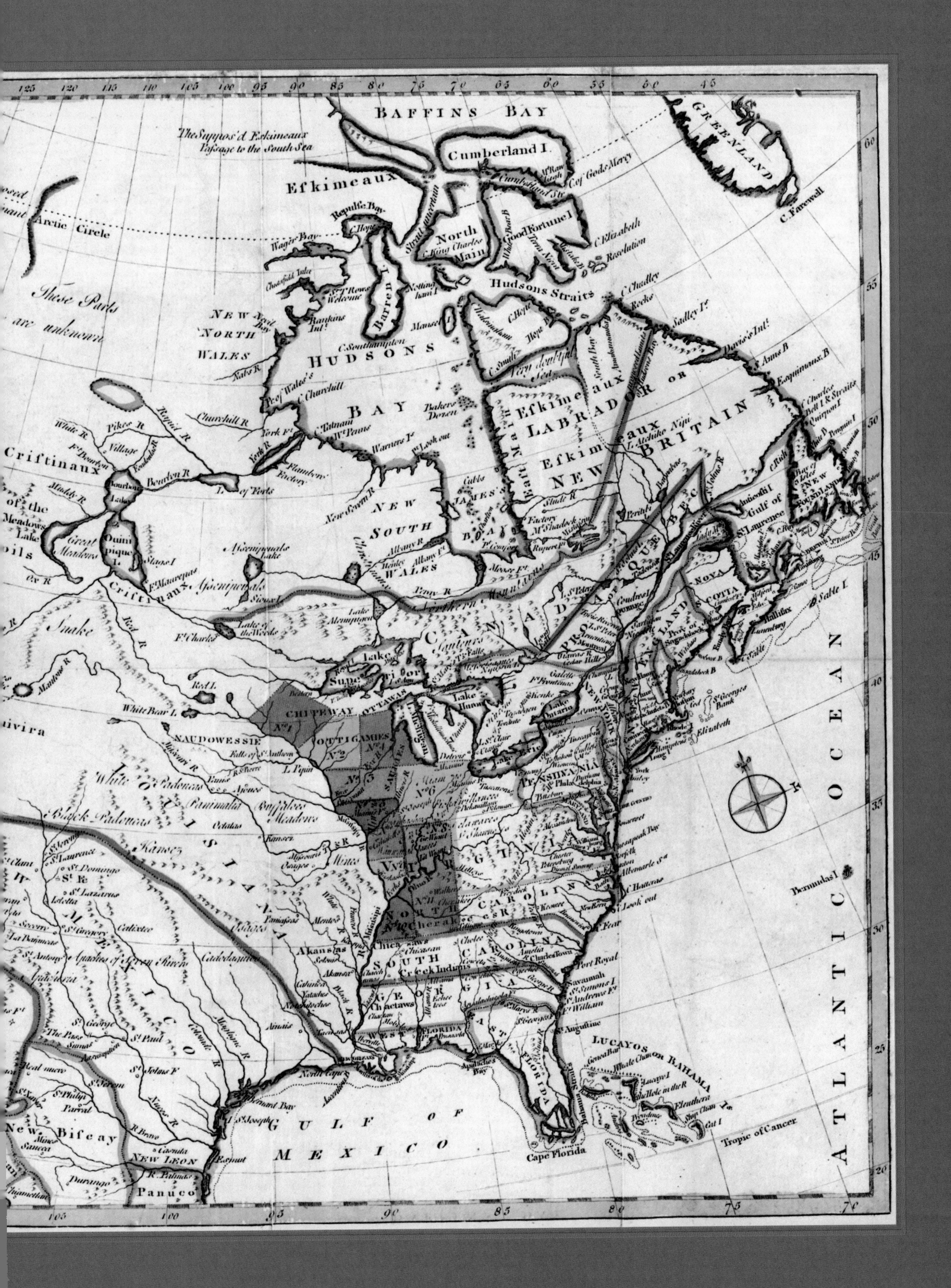

BAFFINS BAY
GREENLAND
C. Farewell
Cumberland I.
The Suppos'd Eskimeaux Passage to the South Sea
Eskimeaux
Arctic Circle
Repulse Bay
Wager Bay
North Main
Good Fortune I
C. Elizabeth
Resolution
Hudsons Straits
C. Chudley
These Parts are unknown
NEW NORTH WALES
HUDSONS BAY
Barren I.
C. Churchill
Churchill R.
York Fort
Cristinaux
Bakers Dozen
Eskimeaux
LABRADOR OR
NEW BRITAIN
Eskimeaux
NEW
JAMES'S BAY
NEW SOUTH WALES
Albany R.
Moose Ft.
Rupert Ft.
Gulf of St. Laurence
NEW FOUNDLAND
NOVA SCOTIA
Halifax
Sable I.
Lake of the Woods
Lake Alemipigon
CANADA
QUEBEC
Lake Superior
CHIPPEWAY
OTTAWAS
NAUDOWESSIE
OTTIGAMIES
Lake Huron
Lake Michigan
Lake Ontario
Lake Erie
NEW ENGLAND
NEW YORK
Elizabeth
St. Georges Bank
PENSYLVANIA
Philadelphia
Falls of St. Anthony
LOUISIANA
Buffaloe Meadows
White Padoucas
Black Padoucas
Kansez
VIRGINIA
Chesapeak Bay
Albemarle Sd.
C. Hatteras
C. Look out
NORTH CAROLINA
SOUTH CAROLINA
Charles Town
Port Royal
Creek Indians
Akansas
GEORGIA
Chactaws
Savannah
St. Augustine
FLORIDA
EAST FLORIDA
Apalachee Bay
LUCAYOS OR BAHAMA
Eleuthera
Cat I.
Tropic of Cancer
Bermudas I.
ATLANTIC OCEAN
GULF OF MEXICO
Cape Florida
NEW MEXICO
Biscay
NEW LEON
Panuco
Durango
Mississipi

in the treasury, and scarce any provision in the public magazines," a congressional committee reported.

Since the congress had proposed the Articles of Confederation in 1777, the document had been debated within the states. New England communities read the articles aloud in town halls and debated each and every clause. In other states, committees and citizens suspiciously examined the articles for any hint of overreach by a central government.

By 1780 every state but Maryland had ratified the document. Maryland held out over one large issue: territory. Of the thirteen states, six had defined boundaries in their original colonial charters, while seven had broad claims to western territories. Virginia, Maryland's behemoth neighbor, claimed all the lands to the Mississippi River and then north to the Great Lakes. That clearly left Maryland confined to a very small space and left its powerful land speculators, one of whom was the governor, particularly dissatisfied. The speculators did not share Patrick Henry's optimistic view that "There was more land than can be settled in ages," and in any case speculation and settlement were two different things. The congress had pressed Maryland and Virginia to settle their dispute and reminded them "how indispensably necessary it is to establish the federal union on a fixed and permanent basis, and on principles acceptable to all its respective members; how essential to public credit and confidence, to the support of our army, to the vigor of our councils and success of our measures, to our tranquility at home, and our reputation abroad, to our present safety and our future prosperity, to our very existence as a free, sovereign and independent people." Recognizing this, Virginia had offered various concessions, but Maryland remained immovable.

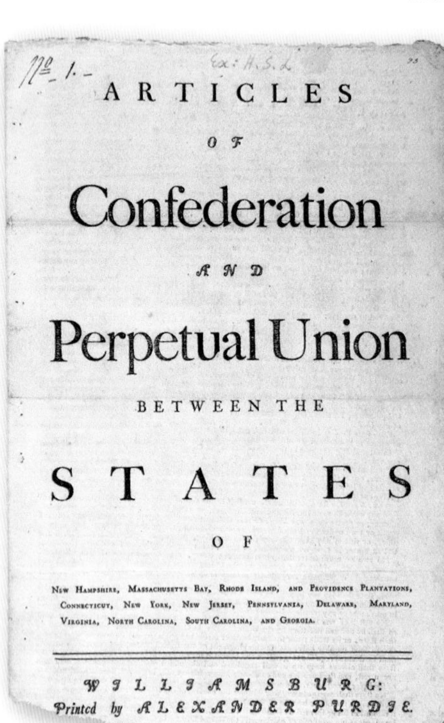
ARTICLES
OF
Confederation
AND
Perpetual Union
BETWEEN THE
STATES
OF
NEW HAMPSHIRE, MASSACHUSETTS BAY, RHODE ISLAND, AND PROVIDENCE PLANTATIONS, CONNECTICUT, NEW YORK, NEW JERSEY, PENNSYLVANIA, DELAWARE, MARYLAND, VIRGINIA, NORTH CAROLINA, SOUTH CAROLINA, AND GEORGIA.

WILLIAMSBURG:
Printed by ALEXANDER PURDIE.

THE FIRST DOCUMENT *to unite the colonies under some form of mutual government, the Articles of Confederation established the nation as a loose alliance of sovereign states.*

Finally, as 1781 opened, the Old Dominion agreed to cede its western territories above the Ohio River to the federal government under certain conditions, among them that the former Virginia lands be held by the federal government and eventually divided into new states, with the same "rights of sovereignty, freedom, and independence as the other States." The concession made it difficult for Maryland and her land speculators to continue to oppose the Articles of Confederation. And there was a new incentive to ratify: With the British suddenly moving on the Chesapeake region, Maryland needed protection. Initially, the state appealed to the French for military help, but the French minister warned Maryland that no naval support would be given until the articles were ratified. At last, on March 1, 1781, the long wait ended and the Articles of Confederation bound the nation into a tenuous whole. The *Pennsylvania Gazette* heralded the date as "a day memorable in the annals of America," a day in which "the United States of America, having, amidst the calamities of a destructive war, established a solid foundation of greatness."

The British were far from ready to give up on the destructive war, and their presence

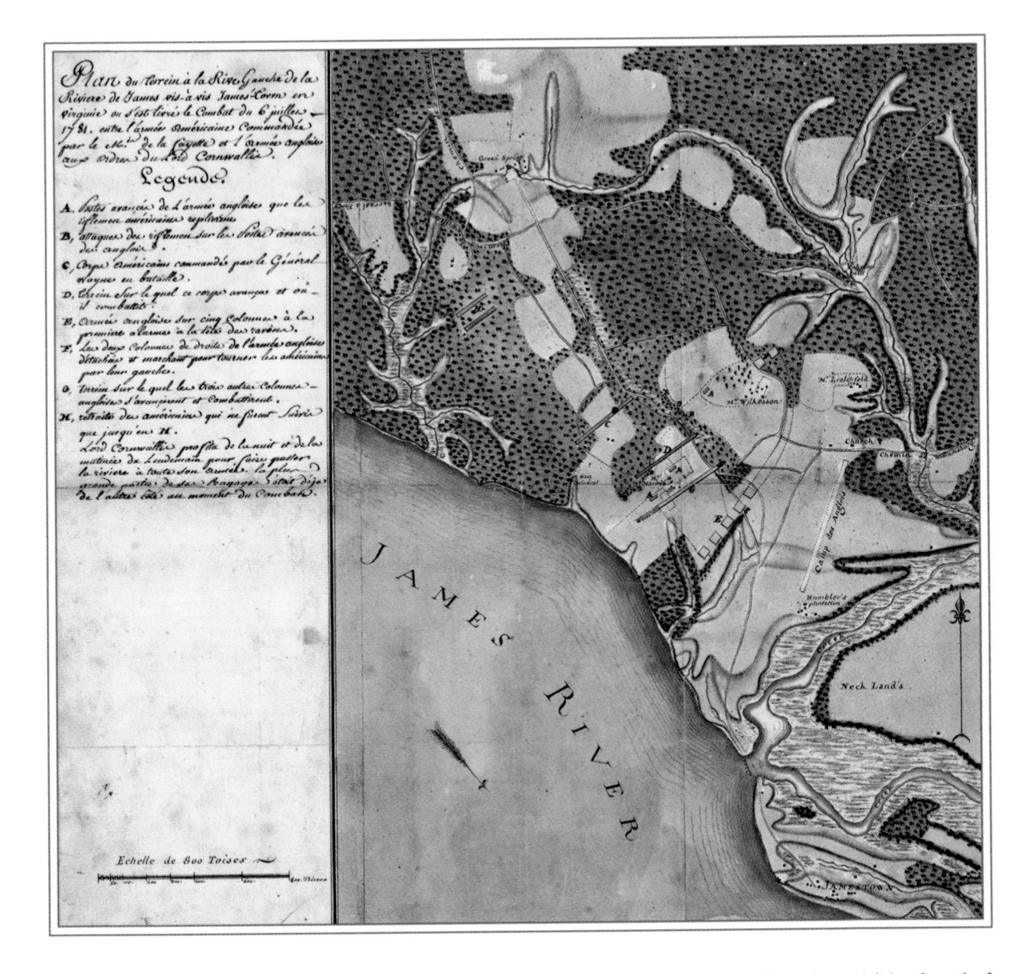

A 1781 MAP *highlights the James River, a major tributary of the Chesapeake Bay and an artery of travel for central Virginia. The traitor Benedict Arnold sailed up the James to raid Richmond, the capital of Virginia, in the opening days of 1781.*

in the Chesapeake was growing stronger. The previous winter, Benedict Arnold had sailed up the James River to Virginia's capital, Richmond, and had set much of it on fire. Still in coastal Virginia, he was creating a British stronghold in the Chesapeake. Thomas Jefferson, then governor, had written to Washington to urge him to march into the state and "restore full confidence of salvation." Washington had no intention of doing that, though he knew American forces had to take the offensive—somehow—before the army disintegrated. "Instead of having the prospective of a glorious campaign before us we have a bewildered and gloomy offensive one," Washington wrote. He still believed that the offensive should happen in the North and that the actions in Virginia were no more than a diversion. Still, in late winter he did make a concession to Jefferson and dispatched Lafayette and 1,200 troops to Virginia.

Cornwallis had written Clinton in the spring to say, "I cannot help expressing my wishes that the Chesapeake may become the seat of war . . . Until Virginia is in a manner subdued, our hold of the Carolinas must be difficult, if not precarious. The rivers in Virginia are advantageous to an invading army; but North Carolina is of all provinces in America the most difficult to attack." Relations between Clinton and Cornwallis had become increasingly strained. The fact that Cornwallis, an earl, far outranked Clinton in social standing did not help, nor did distance, which made communication between them so slow that it became almost a moot point whether they wrote to one another or not. In any case, Cornwallis had little faith in Clinton's military judgment, and the excuse of distance allowed him to act without orders, as he did that spring. Marching north into Virginia with his remaining 1,500 troops, he entered Petersburg, not far from Richmond, in late May, and joined a sizable British force of 4,000. Writing to Clinton from his new position, he ended the letter, "I shall take the liberty of repeating that if offensive war is intended, Virginia appears to me to be the only Province in which it can be carried on, and in which there is a stake." But, he warned, "a considerable army would be necessary," and added deferentially that he himself "neither wish nor expect to have command of it . . . few things could give me greater pleasure than being relieved by your presence from a situation of so much anxiety and responsibility."

Clinton was not about to abandon New York for Virginia, and he and Washington continued to eye one another across the Hudson. But Washington did send Lafayette reinforcements under the command of Baron von Steuben, whose bombastic character did not sit well with Virginians and their notions of gentility. "His Conduct gives universal disgust," one well-placed Virginian observed. Steuben was well aware of his critics, and he reciprocated their dislike: "I shall always regret that circumstances induced me to undertake the defense of a country where every farmer is a general." The American force in Virginia now numbered 4,000, thanks to reinforcements from Anthony Wayne's reconstituted Pennsylvania Line, and throughout June, Lafayette shadowed Cornwallis as the British moved closer to the coast. Lafayette was sure that he was witnessing "the retreat of the enemy."

THE COMTE DE ROCHAMBEAU

1725–1807

Jean-Baptiste-Donatien de Vimeur, the Comte de Rochambeau, was a French nobleman and soldier who played a major role in the Franco-American alliance. He joined the French army as a young man and fought in the War of Austrian Succession and the Seven Years' War. When France allied itself with the rebelling colonies, Rochambeau served as the commander in chief of the French ground troops that embarked to America to fight the British. Originally landing in Rhode Island, Rochambeau's forces moved through Connecticut and New York, and then ultimately south to Virginia where he teamed up with Washington and the Marquis de Lafayette's troops to deliver a decisive blow to the British forces at Yorktown.

In New York Clinton had learned that Cornwallis was in Virginia, and he couldn't believe it. "My wonder at this move of Lord Cornwallis will never cease," Clinton declared. That spring Clinton had learned that the French were sending an additional fleet to America's aid, and he expected Washington and Rochambeau to attack New York once the fleet arrived. Clinton needed man power, and he would get it—from Cornwallis.

Clinton called 3,000 troops from Virginia to the North—a ridiculous amount given how few Cornwallis had. By June 25, Cornwallis's depleted army was in Williamsburg, the old colonial capital that had witnessed so much Revolutionary zeal in the early years. Moving on, Cornwallis situated himself in Portsmouth, near the mouth of the James. Having been ordered to give up so much of his force, he wrote to Clinton in disgust and advised that the British pull out of the Chesapeake altogether rather than "to hold a sickly, defensive post in this bay, which will always be exposed to a sudden French attack." Cornwallis could not have known how prophetic his words were.

Lafayette and Washington's Strategies

Lafayette had learned through a spy that Cornwallis planned to pull out of Portsmouth, but he was wary of the general's next move. "Lord Cornwallis's abilities are to me more alarming than his superiority of forces," Lafayette confessed. "I ever had a great opinion of him . . . To speak plain English I am devilish afraid of him." Later in the summer, Cornwallis bedeviled the young marquis further when he loaded his troops at Portsmouth onto ships but, instead of sailing out of the Chesapeake for the Atlantic, he sailed up the bay. Lafayette concluded that Cornwallis was planning an attack on Baltimore, far up the bay—but he was wrong. Clinton had ordered Cornwallis to secure a deepwater harbor for the British in the lower Chesapeake, and now Cornwallis repositioned himself in Yorktown, a busy tobacco port on the York River almost due west of the bay's opening into the Atlantic.

Though the Marquis de Lafayette *was granted American citizenship by several individual states, it was not until 2002 that he was given honorary citizenship by the U.S. government. Owing to his fight for liberty in both America and France, he is known as The Hero of Two Worlds.*

At about the same time, Lafayette received an intriguingly encouraging communication from Washington: "I shall shortly have occasion to communicate matters of great importance to you, so much so, that I shall send a confidential Officer on purpose to you" rather than communicate in writing. "You will in the mean time endeavour to draw together as respectable a Body of Continental troops as you possibly can and take every measure to augment your Cavalry." Earlier in the summer, Lafayette had written to Washington to say, "Should a French fleet now come in Hampton road, the British army would, I think, be ours." Now on its way to the Chesapeake from the Caribbean was a French fleet—a veritable armada of almost 30 ships of the line and some 3,000 troops under the command of Admiral de Grasse. It was expected to arrive by September 3 but could stay only three weeks, due the upcoming hurricane season.

With Clinton busy reinforcing New York, Washington suddenly had a change of heart: Clearly, Virginia was the place to make a decisive move. Yorktown was its own trap—"a narrow neck of land" that could easily be "cut off." And with the French fleet making for it, the British would find it difficult to escape by sea. Cornwallis himself understood this only too well and had warned Clinton that defending Yorktown was an exercise in futility, which "cannot have the smallest influence on the War" and would only give the British "some Acres of an unhealthy swamp."

Washington moved quickly. On August 19 his army of some 7,000 men left in place the tent city they had occupied on the west bank of the Hudson and stealthily marched south. Sure the British would be watching, Washington ordered that supply wagons continue to move in and out of the post. Even his own troops were not told where they were headed; most believed they were on their way to Staten Island.

Washington and his French commander, Rochambeau, had hoped to transport the army by water most of the way, but when they could not find enough craft, they had no choice but to march some 450 miles overland through the summer heat. At three o'clock every morning reveille sounded; by four the French and the Continentals were on the move south. As the weary march plodded on into early September, Admiral de Grasse arrived at the Chesapeake. He had brought his entire fleet from the Caribbean, and it was an impressive sight anchored in the lower bay. From there supplies and troops were off-loaded and moved upriver to Lafayette in Williamsburg.

On September 5, as de Grasse's shuttle continued back and forth, a new fleet sailed into view. The French had been expecting another small fleet to sail down from Newport to join them, and they initially assumed it had arrived. But as it moved closer, it was soon obvious that a large British flotilla was storming into the bay. With many of his officers ashore, de Grasse nonetheless quickly weighed anchor and moved into the open waters off the Virginia Capes—Henry and Charles—where he formed his fleet into a line of battle as the British drew nearer. Shortly after four in the afternoon, the battle began with a fierce cannon exchange. It boomed on for two and a half hours before the admirals, de Grasse and Graves, disengaged to take stock. Six of the 19 British ships had suffered damage, and casualties numbered some 350. The French were in far better shape, with about 200 casualties and only two ships needing repair.

I shall always regret that circumstances induced me to undertake the defense of a country where . . . every farmer is a general.

BARON FRIEDRICH WILHELM VON STEUBEN

For the next several days, the enemy armadas drifted south together, always within sight of each other. Then, on September 9, de Grasse's fleet slipped from Graves's view and sailed north, back to the Chesapeake and Yorktown. Graves, fearing the damage his ships had sustained would hamper him, did not hazard pursuit. Instead, he headed back to New York for repairs. The Battle of the Capes, perhaps the most significant naval engagement of the 18th century, was over.

The anticipated small French fleet from Newport joined de Grasse and gave the allied force an impressive 36 ships, plus control of the Chesapeake and the entrance to the York River. The trap was closing slowly and deliberately around Cornwallis, who knew how vulnerable his position was. He had expected that Graves would open up the Chesapeake, allowing reinforcements to move in and save the day. Who would save it now?

When Clinton heard news of the defeat, his "faith in our naval superiority began to

The Comte François–Joseph-Paul de Grasse *was a French admiral who successfully commanded the French fleet at the Battle of the Chesapeake. His defeat of the British naval force led to the British surrender at Yorktown.*

IN THE SHORT *but decisive Battle of the Capes on September 5, 1781, the French (left), commanded by the Comte de Grasse, successfully kept the British Fleet from entering the Chesapeake Bay and supporting Cornwallis's troops at Yorktown.*

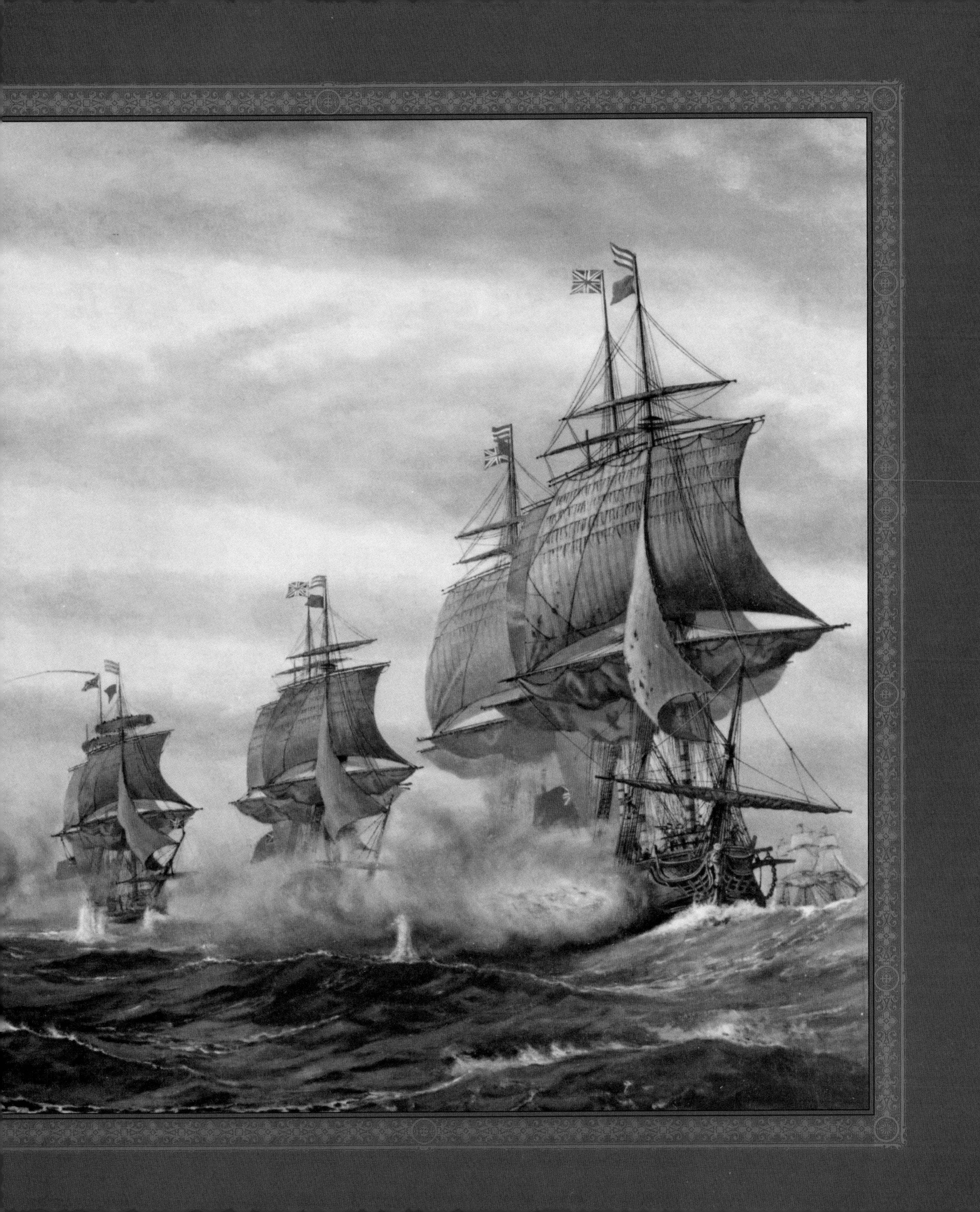

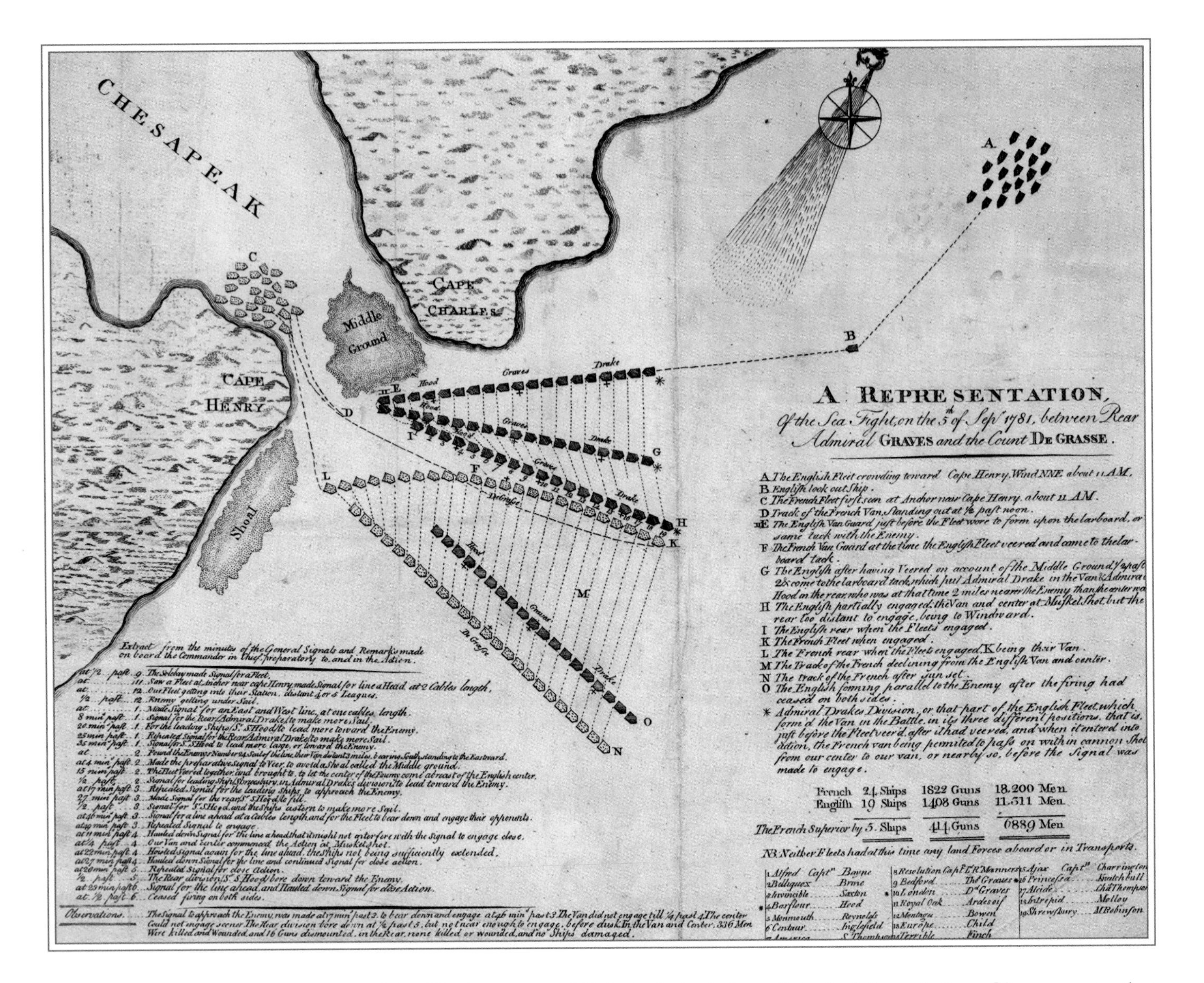

CHESAPEAK
CAPE CHARLES
Middle Ground
CAPE HENRY
Shoal
A REPRESENTATION,
Of the Sea Fight, on the 5th of Sepr 1781, between Rear Admiral GRAVES and the Count DE GRASSE.
A The English Fleet crowding toward Cape Henry, Wind NNE about 11 AM.
B English look out Ship.
C The French Fleet first seen at Anchor near Cape Henry, about 11 AM.
D Track of the French Van, standing out at ½ past noon.
E The English Van Guard just before the Fleet wore to form upon the larboard, or same tack with the Enemy.
F The French Van Guard at the time the English Fleet veered and came to the larboard tack.
G The English after having Veered on account of the Middle Ground ½ past 2 & come to the larboard tack, which put Admiral Drake in the Van & Admiral Hood in the rear, who was at that time 2 miles nearer the Enemy than the center was
H The English partially engaged: the Van and center at Musket Shot, but the rear too distant to engage, being to Windward.
I The English rear when the Fleets engaged.
K The French Fleet when engaged.
L The French rear when the Fleets engaged, K being their Van.
M The Track of the French declining from the English Van and center.
N The track of the French after sun set.
O The English forming parallel to the Enemy after the firing had ceased on both sides.
* Admiral Drakes Division, or that part of the English Fleet, which form'd the Van in the Battle, in its three different positions, that is, just before the Fleet veer'd, after it had veered, and when it entered into action, the French van being permited to pass on within cannon Shot from our center to our van, or nearly so, before the Signal was made to engage.
French 24 Ships 1822 Guns 18.200 Men
English 19 Ships 1408 Guns 11.311 Men
The French Superior by 5. Ships 414 Guns 6889 Men
NB: Neither Fleets had at this time any land Forces aboard or in Transports.
1 Alfred Captn Bayne
2 Belliquex ... Brine
3 Invincible ... Saxton
4 Barfleur ... Hood
5 Monmouth ... Reynolds
6 Centaur ... Inglefield
8 Resolution Capt. Ld R. Manners
9 Bedford ... Thos Graves
10 London ... Dd Graves
11 Royal Oak ... Ardesoif
12 Montagu ... Bowen
13 Europe ... Child
Terrible ... Finch
15 Ajax Captn Charrington
16 Princessa ... Knatchbull
17 Alcide ... Chas Thompson
18 Intrepid ... Molloy
19 Shrewsbury ... M Robinson
Extract from the minutes of the General Signals and Remarks made on board the Commander in Chief preparatory to, and in the Action.
Observations.

THIS TACTICAL MAP *shows positioning of both the French and British ships during the naval battle between the French Comte de Grasse's ships and those of British rear admiral Thomas Graves. The battle occurred off Virginia's Capes Henry and Charles, giving it the designation Battle of the Capes.*

falter," he later wrote. With the "crippled condition" of Graves's fleet, Clinton wrote that he "should not have been greatly displeased to have heard that Lord Cornwallis had made his escape to Carolina with everything he could take with him." Clinton anticipated that "his Lordship" would return to "his first idea of forcing his way through the enemy before Mr. Washington's junction with Lafayette."

But by September 14—the same day that Graves's fleet sailed for New York—it was too late for that. That afternoon, Washington, Rochambeau, and another French general, Chastellux, rode into Williamsburg, where Lafayette greeted Washington "with an ardor not easily described," one resident recorded. The young marquis grabbed "the General round his body, hugged him as close as it was possible, and absolutely kissed him from ear to ear." That evening the allies celebrated in grand style, while Washington personally celebrated the news of de Grasse's victory. For perhaps the first time in the endless war, the possibility of a conclusive victory hovered on the horizon.

Though the allied command had arrived in Williamsburg, the army coming from the North had not. It took another four days before the 17,500 troops—French, Continentals, and militias—began flooding into Williamsburg and its environs. As they did so, Washington requested a council of war with the French admiral. On September 17, de Grasse sent a cutter up the James to collect Washington and his entourage and to sail them back down to Hampton Roads, where the fleet was anchored.

The meeting on the French flagship went well, and de Grasse, agreeing to Washington's request to extend his stay, promised that his "Vessels will not depart before the first of November" and that the Americans could "count upon those [de Grasse's] troops to that period." The meeting ended at sunset, but as the Americans pushed off, a cold wind blew against them. For four days, the weather held them in Hampton Roads. Finally, on September 22, Washington, who was out of patience, insisted on being rowed 30 miles upriver to a landing near Williamsburg. But his aggravations were not over: Once there, he received word from de Grasse that a new British fleet had been spotted in the area, and so, despite de Grasse's promise, the French might soon be leaving the bay for New York. Washington wrote back almost pleadingly, "[I am] unable to describe the painful anxiety under which I have labored since the reception of your letter . . . your leaving the Bay ruins the case to all intents and purposes." His admonitions worked, and de Grasse wrote back quickly to say he would stay.

> *Lord Cornwallis's abilities are to me more alarming than his superiority of forces.*
>
> Marquis de Lafayette

Washington's Great Offensive: Yorktown

With de Grasse in place and Washington back on land, Washington could begin the great offensive he had planned. Despite the high-stakes game that lay ahead, he seemed intent on his troops' appearance, probably because the French allies made "a very fine soldierly appearance" in their white uniforms "turned up with blue, and even their underclothes white." The Americans could not match that, but Washington's orders declared that "every officer will be anxious to have his men look as neat and respectable as possible," including being "well shaven"—a lot to ask from weary men camped out in the warmth of an early southern autumn.

At dawn on September 28, everything was ready, and the allied army began the short, 13-mile march east past tidal marshes and meandering creeks to Yorktown.

Cornwallis knew they were coming and had been preparing for them. His soldiers had dug earthwork defenses around the small port town on high bluffs about the river. But he also knew that his force of some 8,300 men could not hold out long without reinforcements.

In mid-September he had warned Clinton, "If you cannot relieve me very soon, you must be prepared to hear the worst." No relief was in sight when in the late afternoon of that day, the American army arrived at Cornwallis's doorstep.

That night, Washington slept like his men—"in the field," as one soldier explained, "without any covering than the canopy of the heavens and the small spreading branches of a tree, which will probably be rendered venerable for this circumstance for a long time to come."

On September 29, "at noon the enemy appeared in front of our works, in force about 26,000," an alarmed British officer reported, wildly overestimating Washington's force. But this impression apparently worked to the allies' advantage, because the next morning they woke to find that the British "had evacuated all their exterior works, and retired to their interior defence near the town." From there, the British began a continual shelling of the allied line. It went on day and night.

Gen. George Washington, *the Marquis de Lafayette, and Washington's trusted aide, Lt. Col. Tench Tilghman, at Yorktown in 1781. Opposite: A combined allied force of mostly Continental and French troops fought the British at Yorktown. Beginning on October 6, 1781, the Franco-American forces fired their artillery relentlessly at the redcoats, smashing their defenses and weakening them for a direct assault.*

Cornwallis now had hope. He had received word from Clinton that a British fleet of 23 ships was on its way from New York with 5,000 men. The trap he was in could now be sprung, even reversed, and he wrote back saying that "there was but one wish throughout the whole army, which was, that the enemy would advance."

The Americans were busy doing that. They had immediately moved forward into the deserted British earthworks, and soon they began digging more. Thomas Nelson, Governor of Virginia, who also happened to be one of Yorktown's wealthiest residents, had known that earthworks would be critical to this battle and had ordered militiamen and locals to report with pickaxes, spades, and any other digging instruments they could lay hands on. On the night of October 6, in a rain that made enemy visibility poor, the allies began an ambitious scheme: a two-mile-long trench arcing east to the bluffs above the York River. The soft, sandy soil gave way easily to the spade, and at dawn, the British were confronted with the completed American line. Washington and his men had managed something like this in the first maneuver in the war, when overnight they had fortified Dorchester Heights above Boston. It had been an impressive feat then, and it was equally impressive in Yorktown. At some point the following morning, Col. Alexander Hamilton ordered his men "to mount the bank, front the enemy, and there by word of command go through all the ceremony of soldiery." The enemy, he reported, "did not give us a single shot."

By this time, the British were showing signs of stress. One American described them as "embarrassed, confused, and indeterminate; their fire seems feeble." They had had to drown hundreds of their horses in the York River or drive them out of town to fend for themselves, as there was nothing left in town to feed them. As the animal carcasses floated with the

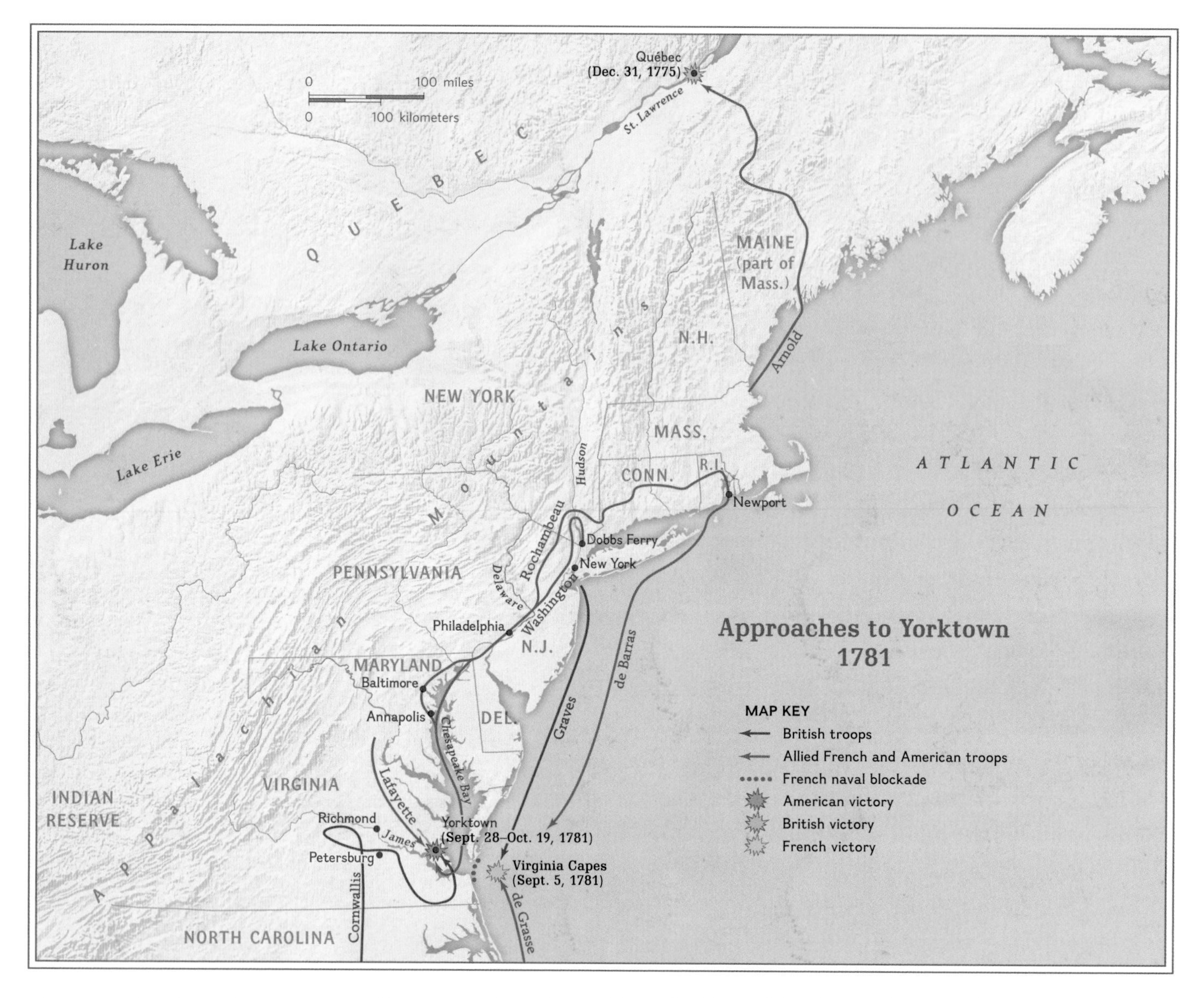

CONVERGING *from the north, south, east, and west, the French, American, and British forces ultimately met for the final battle at Yorktown, Virginia. A busy tobacco port, the town occupied the bluffs above the York River, an estuary of the Chesapeake. Bottled up there by the Americans, Cornwallis soon understood that he had inadvertently become trapped.*

tide onto salt flats, the putrid smell of decay filled the air. Deserters from the British ranks reported that 2,000 redcoats were suffering from disease in the hospital. But for the siege to be effective, all supply lines needed to be cut, and Cornwallis still had one. On the other side of the York, at Gloucester Point, Banastre Tarleton operated from a base that allowed him to forage in the countryside and send food from local farms by boat to Cornwallis. Over and over, Washington pleaded with de Grasse to sail into the York and break the enemy's connection, but the French admiral refused to take the chance. He explained to Washington that "the Wind will not permit Vessels . . . to ascend the York River. The Sea is not like the Land . . . and we have not yet found a method of sailing against the Wind."

As the allies dug and Cornwallis waited, Washington toured the growing earthworks. He was on familiar footing. Yorktown was situated on land once owned by his first American ancestor, Nicolas Martiau, and he knew it from his childhood, when it had been a prosperous tobacco port. One English visitor in 1736 had described the "great Air of Opulence amongst the Inhabitants, who have some of them built themselves Houses, equal in Magnificence to many of our superb ones at St. James's." Now, it seemed the once elegant little town was to become the fulcrum for independence. It only needed one push more to fall and deliver America her hard-fought freedom.

The heat of Indian summer days dissolved into chill autumn nights, and still the work went on. In the surrounding woodlands, soldiers cut saplings and branches to provide twigs that were bundled into fascines and used to fortify the earthworks, along with gabions—simple bottomless baskets filled with soil. As earthworks were completed, heavy artillery was moved into position.

By October 9 the great exhaustive work was nearly done. Huge guns were in place, and the fortifications were complete. Around three that afternoon, "General Washington put the match to the first gun" on the French line, and the ball struck true, ricocheting "from house to house" and apparently entering one house "where many officers were at dinner . . . and either killed or wounded the one at the head of the table." Two hours later, the American guns joined the barrage. "The shot and shells flew incessantly through the night, dismounted guns of the enemy and destroyed many of their embrasures."

Looking out *over land and sea, Gen. George Washington surveys the battle at Yorktown.*

The bombardment quickly took a toll in terror, dismemberment, and death. Townsfolk huddled against the pounding or fled to the banks of the river and "dug in among the sand cliffs . . . many were badly injured and mortally wounded by the fragments of bombs which exploded partly in the air and partly on the ground, their arms and legs severed or themselves struck dead." Each day, the allies threw some 3,600 rounds at the small village. Cornwallis had headquartered in the home of Governor Nelson, and Nelson himself directed that it be bombed. After that, the British commander took refuge in "a kind of grotto . . . where he lives underground." The very sky filled with armament, with "bombshells from the besiegers and the besieged . . . incessantly crossing each others' path in the air. They are clearly visible in the form of a black ball in the day, but in the night they appear like a fiery meteor with a blazing tail, most beautifully brilliant."

And amid the blasting the digging went on—and on. Another trench was snaking closer and closer to the enemy lines. Washington watched in elation and apprehension: "Lord Cornwallis' conduct has heretofore been passive beyond conception; he either has not the means of defence or he intends to reserve his strength until we approach very near him." By October 14 American and French guns were only 150 yards away from the British in most

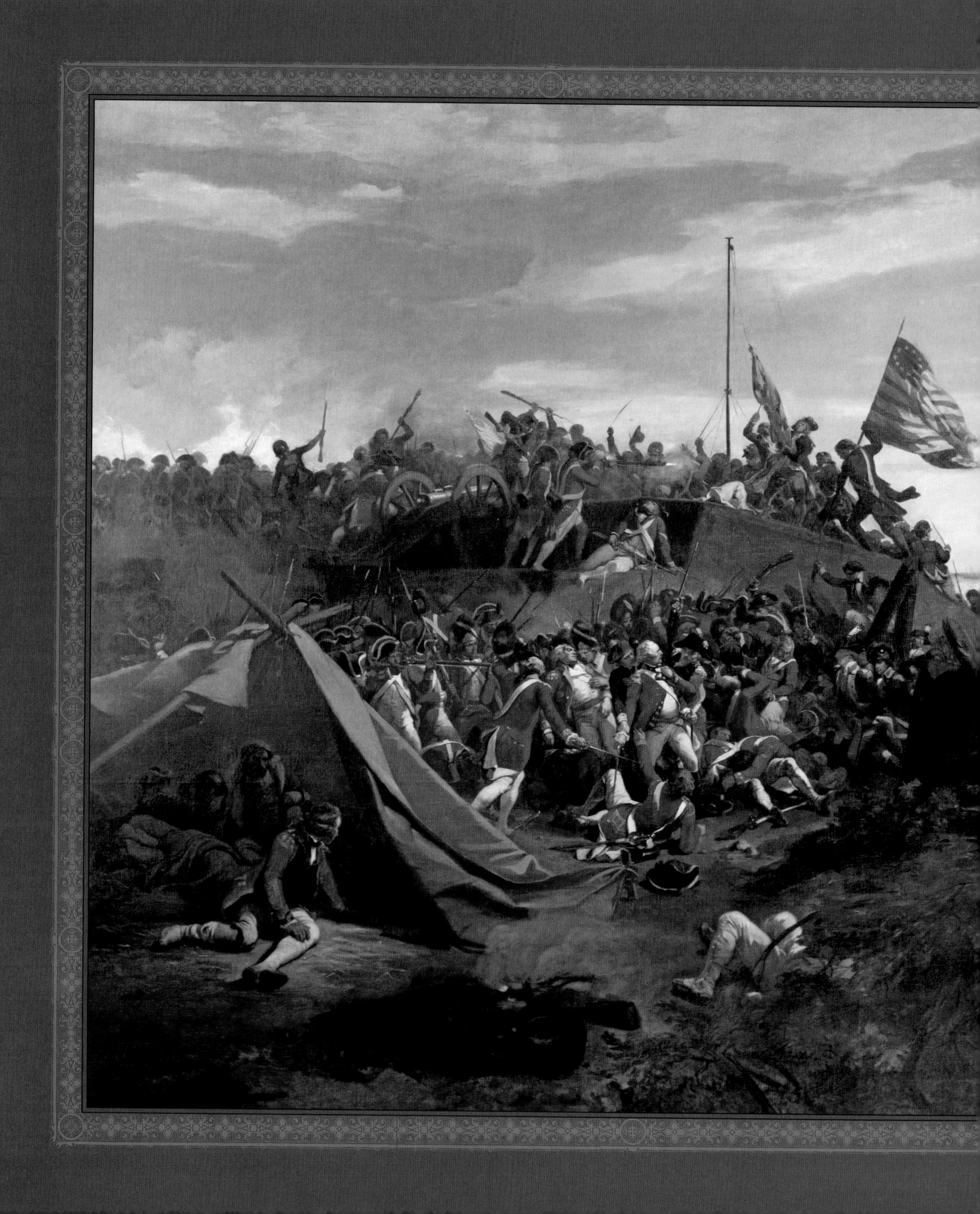

PAINTED IN 1840 *by Eugène Louis Lami, "Storming a Redoubt at Yorktown," takes up an entire wall in the Old Senate Chamber of the Virginia State Capitol. The work depicts French and American forces capturing a critical redoubt that helped assure their victory over the British.*

places. But two obstacles stood in the way of completing the second parallel all the way to the riverbank: two large enemy redoubts, or outposts, had been dug forward of their main line. The only way to take them was by hand-to-hand combat. At seven or eight o'clock the night of October 14, as darkness blurred the battlefield, two allied groups moved out with bayonets fixed. The French group attacked the redoubt on the left, held by about 120 redcoats and Hessians, while an American force under Colonel Hamilton charged the one on the right, defended by a smaller force of 45. After a savage ten minutes of fighting, the British fell.

The way forward was now open to the allies, and Cornwallis understood what lay ahead. The following night, he moved out of his passivity long enough to strike at the allied center. It was no more than a gesture—a *baroud d'honneur*—the final doomed thrust by a commander who knew the end was in sight. The next day he wrote to Clinton to say that it was too late for the reinforcements he believed were en route, as his position in Yorktown was too precarious: "I cannot recommend that the Fleet and Army should run great Risque in endeavoring to save us."

But Cornwallis himself made one last attempt to save his army. That night he began a retreat across the river to Gloucester Point, still held by Tarleton. From there, the army could escape overland. "Earl Cornwallis sent off the first embarkation before eleven o'clock . . . and purposed himself to pass with the second, when he had finished a letter to General Washington, calculated to excite the humanity of that officer towards the sick, the wounded and the detachment that would be left to capitulate," Tarleton recorded. "The whole of the first division arrived before midnight, and part of the second had embarked when a squall, attended with rain, scattered the boats and impeded their return to Gloucester . . . they returned under the fire of the enemy's batteries to Earl Cornwallis, at York town. Thus expired the last hope of the British army."

York, Virginia 17th Octr. 1781

Sir

I propose a Cessation of Hostilities for Twenty four hours, and that two Officers may be appointed by each side to meet at Mr. Moore's house to settle terms for the surrender of the Posts of York & Gloucester. I have the honour to be

Sir

Your most obedient & most humble Servant

Cornwallis

His Excellency
General Washington
&c. &c. &c.

BEFORE BEING LED *to Washington's headquarters to deliver a handwritten note (above) from Cornwallis proposing a truce to George Washington, the British officer delivering it had to be blindfolded. Opposite: Maj. Sebastian Bauman of the New York (Second Regiment) Artillery prepared a detailed map showing locations of artillery and fortifications at Yorktown and across the river in Gloucester Point for General Washington. The Americans dug elaborate earthworks around Yorktown, which allowed them to lay siege to it and creep ever closer.*

The allies had now dug a trench and moved a battery of guns so close to the British line that "one could nearly throw stones into it." And in the chill of the early morning on October 17—the anniversary of the British defeat at Saratoga—the allied pounding resumed with such relentless ferocity that it shook "the whole peninsula." Cornwallis surveyed the line and then conferred with a few of his officers. The British had almost nothing left to fight with—no batteries, no guns. If the allied shelling went on, the army itself faced destruction. Feeling that it would be "wanton and inhuman to the last degree to sacrifice the lives of this small body of gallant soldiers," he chose surrender.

BRITISH SURRENDER

LATER THAT SAME MORNING, A YOUNG DRUMMER FROM THE BRITISH LINE CLIMBED ONTO the parapet and began to beat the *en chamade*—a signal for negotiations. Amid the thunder of the allied guns, it went unheard, but in his red coat he could be seen by the Americans

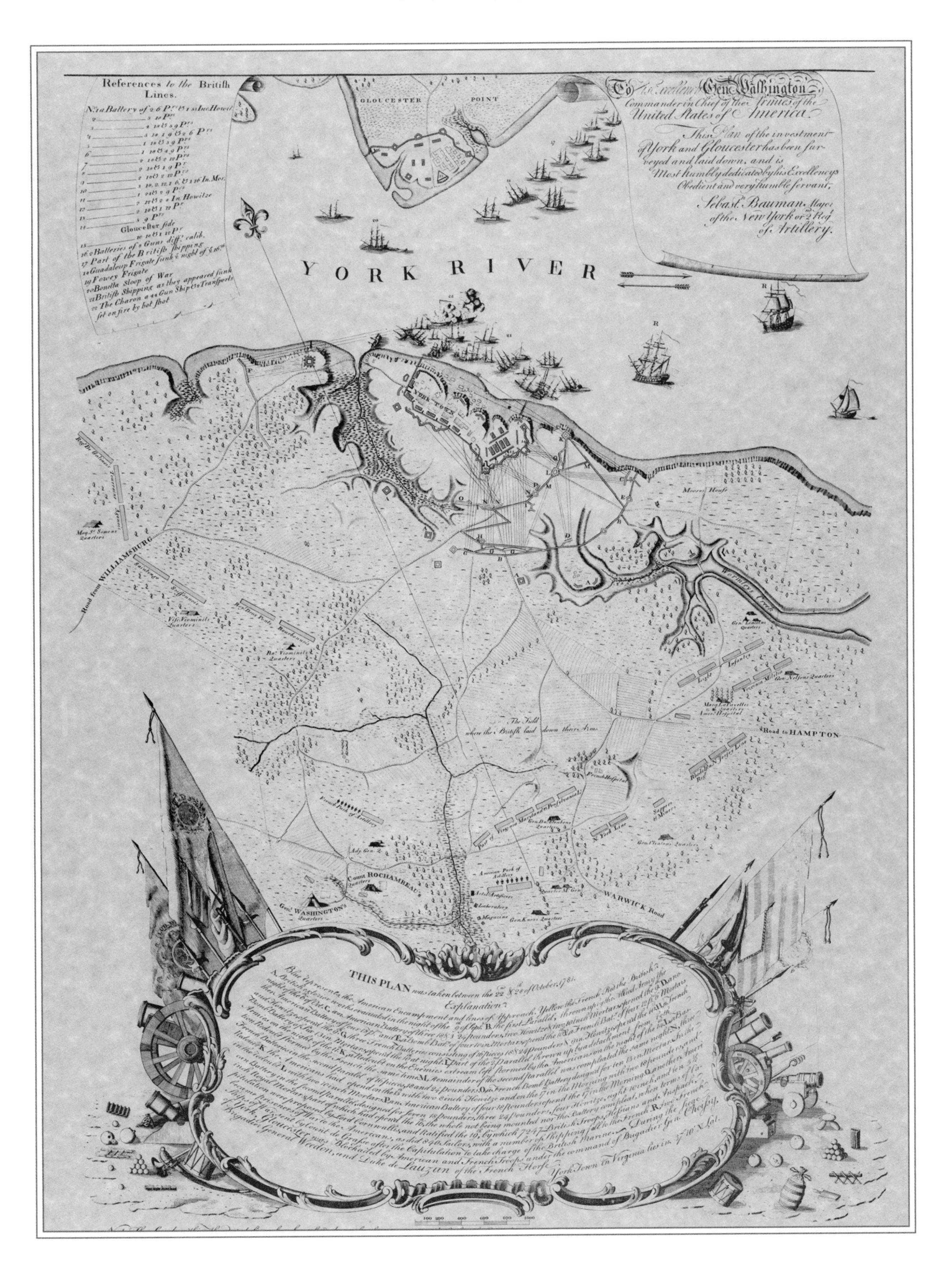

References to the British Lines.
GLOUCESTER POINT
To His Excellency Genl. Washington
Commander in Chief of the Armies of the
United States of America.
This Plan of the investment
of York and Gloucester has been sur-
veyed and laid down, and is
Most humbly dedicated by his Excellency's
Obedient and very humble servant,
Sebast. Bauman Major
of the New York or 2nd Regt.
of Artillery.
YORK RIVER
Gloucester side
Road from WILLIAMSBURG
Road to HAMPTON
Count ROCHAMBEAU's Quarters
Genl. WASHINGTON's Quarters
WARWICK Road
THIS PLAN was taken between the 22d & 28th of October 1781.
Explanation

BRITISH BRIGADIER GENERAL *Charles O'Hara presents the sword to Rochambeau and Washington as a gesture of surrender to the Continental Army.*

in the front lines, and gradually the batteries silenced and the sound of defeat quivered in the autumn air. "I thought I had never heard a drum equal to it—the most delightful music to us all," one Pennsylvania soldier said.

A British officer holding a white flag emerged from the line and was met by an American officer, who listened briefly, blindfolded the negotiator with a handkerchief, and led him away. The British officer was taken to Washington's headquarters, almost a mile away, where his blindfold was removed, and he presented Washington with a note from Cornwallis: "Sir, I propose a cessation of hostilities for twenty-four hours, and that two officers be appointed by each side, to meet at Mr. Moore's house, to settle terms for the surrender of the posts at York and Gloucester. I have the honour to be, &c, Cornwallis."

Washington was quietly amazed that the British capitulation had come so soon, but he wanted to move on it quickly before conditions changed and Cornwallis reneged. His reply was longer but without flourishes. In it, he expressed his "ardent desire to spare the further effusion of blood" but promised only "a suspension of hostilities during two hours from the delivery of this letter," during which time Cornwallis could draft and return his proposal for terms. Cornwallis replied with terms that were reasonable enough to begin negotiations. Washington agreed to suspend hostilities and meet for negotiations the following morning at Moore House, about a mile southeast of the village, as Cornwallis had suggested. That night, the redcoats scuttled two ships in the river and destroyed what remained of property in the town to keep it out of allied hands.

A pair of American colonels and a British colonel and major had been appointed to work out the terms of surrender, and for 12 hours they jockeyed back and forth. Cornwallis had initially wanted his army sent home, but that was not granted, though the redcoats were allowed to keep their personal property. Around midnight, the two Americans returned to headquarters with a draft of a potential surrender document. Washington accepted most of the terms, rejected a few, and then sent the articles to Cornwallis with the comments that he expected them signed by 11 the following morning and that the British would then march out and surrender by two o'clock in the afternoon. Cornwallis did as instructed, and Washington, Rochambeau, and a representative for de Grasse received the signed surrender in a captured redoubt that had been bloodied by fighting. Before signing himself, Washington had one line added: "Done in the trenches before Yorktown in Virginia, October 19, 1781."

> *Cornwallis held himself back from the humiliating scene; obeying sensations which great character ought to have stifled.*
>
> Lighthorse Harry Lee

At noon, as the British lines were abandoned, allied forces moved in to occupy them. One enemy corporal reported that his defeated forces "were not harmed in the least . . . were treated with justice and . . . had no complaints to make." As the redcoats marched out of Yorktown, a bright sun fired the reds and golds of the autumn foliage. The route to the designated surrender field, no more than a clearing south of town, was flanked the entire way by a mile-long line of French in their splendid dress uniforms on one side and a line of Americans, some shoeless, on the other. One European ally remarked on how "dirty and ragged" Washington's men were but exclaimed, "What does it matter! an intelligent man would say. These people are much more praise-worthy to fight as they do, when they are so poorly supplied with everything."

The redcoats did not share this man's enthusiasm, and even in this final encounter, they expressed their disdain for the "Yankees" by refusing even to look at the American line. They kept their eyes fixed on the French, but the French reversed the game, and Lafayette ordered the American band to play "Yankee Doodle." Cornwallis was not on hand to hear it. He had refused to lead the surrender column, under "the pretext of an indisposition," one allied officer said. It was a sullen show of pride. Lighthorse Harry Lee said simply, "Cornwallis held himself back from the humiliating scene; obeying sensations which great

A COLORED ENGRAVING *(preceding pages) depicts Yorktown as a medieval town rather than a Virginia port. The British finally surrendered the town on October 19, 1781.*

character ought to have stifled." In his stead, Gen. Charles O'Hara, who had fought hard in the Southern Campaign and Saratoga, led the line.

As the British line progressed toward the surrender grounds, O'Hara, ignoring Washington, rode toward Rochambeau and attempted to offer his sword in surrender. Deferring to Washington, Rochambeau refused it. When O'Hara swung toward Washington, the American general also rebuffed the proffered sword. Ever aware of protocol, Washington, as commander, would accept the sword of surrender only from the enemy commander—Cornwallis. If Cornwallis could not bestir himself to attend the ceremony, then deputies would have to make the exchange. Washington pointed O'Hara to his own deputy, Benjamin Lincoln, who had suffered a humiliating surrender to the British at Charleston. General Lincoln accepted the sword, and the British column continued on to the surrender field.

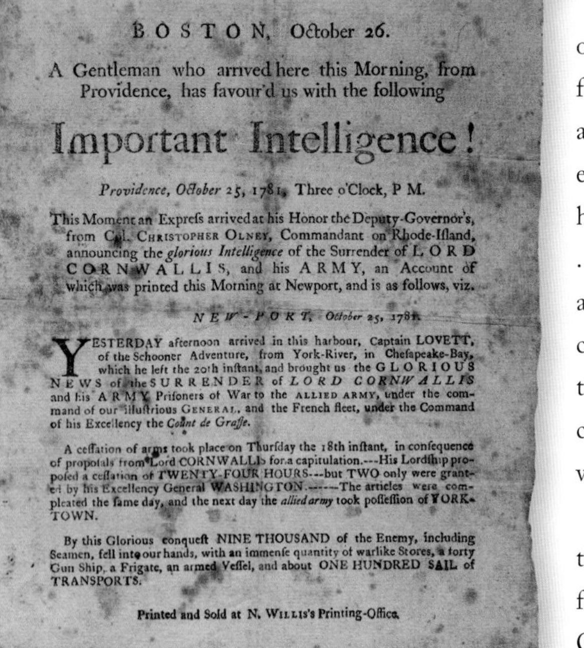

BOSTON, October 26.

A Gentleman who arrived here this Morning, from Providence, has favour'd us with the following

Important Intelligence!

Providence, October 25, 1781, Three o'Clock, P M.

This Moment an Express arrived at his Honor the Deputy-Governor's, from Col. CHRISTOPHER OLNEY, Commandant on Rhode-Island, announcing the *glorious Intelligence* of the Surrender of LORD CORNWALLIS, and his ARMY, an Account of which was printed this Morning at Newport, and is as follows, viz.

NEW-PORT, October 25, 1781.

YESTERDAY afternoon arrived in this harbour, Captain LOVETT, of the Schooner Adventure, from York-River, in Chesapeake-Bay, which he left the 20th instant, and brought us the GLORIOUS NEWS of the SURRENDER of *LORD CORNWALLIS* and his ARMY Prisoners of War to the ALLIED ARMY, under the command of our illustrious GENERAL, and the French fleet, under the Command of his Excellency the *Count de Grasse.*

A cessation of arms took place on Thursday the 18th instant, in consequence of proposals from Lord CORNWALLIS for a capitulation.---His Lordship proposed a cessation of TWENTY-FOUR HOURS---but TWO only were granted by his Excellency General WASHINGTON.------The articles were compleated the same day, and the next day the *allied army* took possession of YORK-TOWN.

By this Glorious conquest NINE THOUSAND of the Enemy, including Seamen, fell into our hands, with an immense quantity of warlike Stores, a forty Gun Ship, a Frigate, an armed Vessel, and about ONE HUNDRED SAIL of TRANSPORTS.

Printed and Sold at N. WILLIS's Printing-Office.

AS NEWS OF *the American success at Yorktown spread, handbills like this one printed in Boston celebrated the victory.*

Rather than stacking their arms, many of the redcoats threw their weapons on the ground, either in disdain or in an attempt to destroy them for further use. They seemed amazed, and even frightened, by the number of allied troops who had opposed them, and some actually trembled at the enemy's strength. "The British officers," though, "behaved like boys who had been whipped at school. Some bit their lips, some pouted, others cried . . ." one New Jersey officer reported, and added that the Hessians "made a more military appearance and the conduct of their officers was far more coming men of fortitude." Among the French and Americans, though, there was a "universal silence." Lighthorse Harry Lee believed they were contemplating the "awful sense of the vicissitudes of human life, mingled with commiseration for the unhappy."

That night the British pettinesses of the day gave way to gallantry, as the officers of the enemy camps gathered at Washington's headquarters for the dinner that military custom dictated. Again, O'Hara represented Cornwallis, and the evening "was very social and easy." Washington excused himself early to write to Congress. In his usual understated style, he said that he had "the Honor" to inform them "that a Reduction of the British Army under the Command of Lord Cornwallis is most happily effected. The unremitting Ardor which actuated every Officer and Soldier in the combined Army of this Occasion, has principally led to this Important Event, at an earlier period than my most sanguine Hope had induced me to expect."

Throughout Washington's army and the countryside, news of the victory spread like wildfire, and its meaning was clear: the war might not be over, but the Yorktown battle was decisive. America had fought its way to independence. Only Clinton seemed to have missed the news. Around the time his army in Yorktown was surrendering, he was sailing

Souvenirs of Surrender

Pewter uniform button
A button engraved with the intertwined letters "USA." Many Continental soldiers were in virtual rags by the end of the war.

U.S. flag carried at Yorktown
A flag bears an American bald eagle with a U.S. shield at its breast and arrows and a laurel branch in its talons.

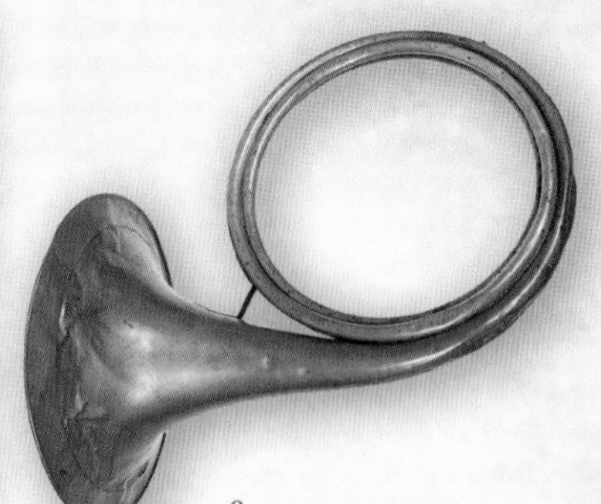

18th-century brass post horn
Light Cavalry, Light Infantry, and Hessian Jägers (mercenaries hired by the British) used this type of horn.

The German flag captured at Yorktown
A detail of a battle flag from the Ansbach-Bayreuth region

Cartridge box
This leather case held 25 tin cartridges. Loading and reloading was a time-consuming process in this era.

Mortar shell
A nine-inch French mortar shell found near Yorktown, Virginia. The allies kept up a relentless bombardment of the town during the siege.

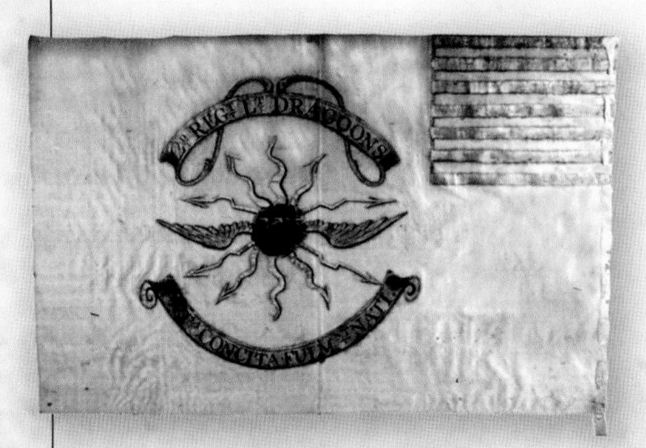

U.S. troop standard
The blue silk troop standard of the Second Continental Light Dragoons, a fast-moving cavalry unit

Hessian flagpole finial
A finial made of gilded iron with the cypher of Frederick II Landgrave of Hesse-Cassel

French cannon
A small French cannon used at the Battle of Yorktown

CHARLES CORNWALLIS (1738-1805)

Perhaps the British general of greatest note in the American Revolution, Charles Cornwallis fought in every major campaign of the war except for Saratoga. In many ways, it was appropriate that it was he and George Washington who faced off in the decisive battle that finally brought a conclusion to the protracted war for American independence. Since early in the conflict, the two commanders had sparred with each other—on Long Island and at Trenton, Brandywine, Germantown, Monmouth Court House, and at last Yorktown.

If by nature and inclination Cornwallis was a military man, by birth he was an aristocrat. He enjoyed a long and distinguished pedigree. One of his uncles had been Sir Robert Walpole, the first of Great Britain's chief ministers (what is now called prime minister), and another had been the Archbishop of Canterbury and as such head of the Church of England. His father had been the first Earl Cornwallis, and as eldest son, Charles assumed the title at his father's death. Cornwallis's own choice of a career in the army was not out of keeping with his high social rank, but most aristocrats did not bother to study war; he did, enrolling at the respected military academy in Turin, Italy. His first experience on the battlefield came soon after that in Germany during the Seven Years' War, where he fought valiantly and proved himself a leader in battle.

In 1762, at his father's death, the young lieutenant colonel returned home to take his place as the Second Earl Cornwallis in the House of Lords. Soon thereafter, America and Britain began their long disagreement over taxation, and Cornwallis frequently favored the American view, voting in Parliament against both the Stamp Act and the Declaratory Act. But when war actually broke out, Cornwallis, then 37, was quick to offer his services to king and country.

He sailed for America in 1776 as a major general in His Majesty's army and was involved in Gen. Henry Clinton's first unsuccessful attempt to take Charleston that year. As the war ground to an end, Cornwallis, the earl, found himself second in command under Clinton, whose title and skills were beneath Cornwallis's own. The tension between the two commanders hampered the British war effort, and their personal feud over who was responsible for the ultimate defeat went on long after the war was over. If Cornwallis's bravery and commitment as a commander were beyond reproach, his tactics were not. He was a by-the-book strategist, little match in the end for the desperate boldness that often characterized George Washington's tactics.

History remembers Cornwallis for the defeat at Yorktown and the loss of British America, but George III never lost confidence in the earl. In 1786 Cornwallis was appointed governor-general of India, where he performed admirably as a reformer, administrator, and, when necessary, military protector of the crown's interest—a performance that earned him the elevated title of marquess. After India, he assumed a similar role in Ireland, where he put down an Irish rebellion but also supported passage of a bill uniting the English and Irish parliaments.

Despite his lofty status, Cornwallis had married a commoner and often espoused the cause of justice over raw imperialism. Beneath his mantle of title, privilege, and duty, he may just have had an unrealized appreciation of democracy, a belief in America that he himself never fully understood. ■

from New York with a force of 5,000—the reinforcements Cornwallis had hoped would save him. The flotilla finally arrived off the Virginia Capes at the end of October, but it soon turned around again for New York.

When word of Cornwallis's surrender finally reached Britain and Lord North, George's minister of war for a dozen years, the lord understood its import and declared, "My God! All is over." Still, official peace would be a long time coming. Upon the fall of Yorktown, roughly 25,000 British troops were scattered through North America—about 14,000 in New York and the rest in the South—but they soon lost their fighting fervor. Some, like Benedict Arnold and Cornwallis, returned to Britain the following year. With his booty from the war in Virginia, Arnold was what he had always longed to be: a hero and "rich as a Nabob." Clinton, recalled from his command, returned too. And in halls of official London, the wheels of disentanglement began to turn. Early in 1782, the British quietly probed Benjamin Franklin in Paris, to see whether "America was disposed to enter into a separate treaty with Great Britain." If not, then Britain would continue the war "to the last man, and the last shilling, rather than be dictated to by France." Geopolitics being what they were, an alliance with the former colonies against the old enemy France was the most expedient path for Britain to take. Franklin, now a past master at diplomatic maneuvering, assured the British that America had no intention of "deserting a noble and general Friend [France] . . . for an unjust and cruel Enemy." In November, he confided to a British friend of his that he despaired of seeing the war "finished in my time. Your thirsty nation has not yet drank enough of our blood."

My God! All is over.

BRITISH MINISTER OF WAR LORD NORTH

THIS BRITISH POLITICAL CARTOON, *entitled "The American Rattlesnake," depicts the surrender at Yorktown by showing the British troops encircled by two coils of the American snake.*

Negotiating Peace

By March 1782, Lord North, who had been urging peace, was gone, and in April Franklin was approached again to negotiate a separate peace. Again he refused, though he did dangle one possible solution to war reparations: ceding Canada to America. Despite his public statements about the French-American alliance, Franklin well knew that a critical game was afoot among the superpowers—France, Britain, and Spain—and that game could cripple his young nation if negotiations were not handled deftly. America needed to lay claim to as much of the continent as possible, yet it was in the interests of all three European nations to bottle her up against the eastern seaboard instead. France was clearly dragging her own feet on ending the war, some thought to ensure American dependence on her, but the official reason given was Gibraltar. Spain, France's ally, was fighting Britain to gain back control of what John Adams called "that impenetrable Rock . . . And what is the importance of it? A mere point of honour! A trophy of insolence to England and of humiliation to Spain!" Adams was pushing back against France as well. From Holland he wrote to Franklin that he should not capitulate to the French, that they were more in America's debt than the reverse.

The game went on and on through the first half of 1782, with Franklin playing the lead in charting a course through the labyrinth of European politics that would secure America's future. That summer, Spain lost another military bid for Gibraltar, and from Russia, neutral up to that point, the sound of saber rattling grew as Catherine the Great eyed Crimea. France now saw a pressing need to escape the American obligation and to solidify new alliances. Vergennes, the wily foreign minister, finally freed the Americans to make their own peace. "You will treat for yourselves," he told Franklin, "and every one of the powers at war with England will make its own treaty. All that is necessary for our common security is that the treaties go hand in hand, and are signed on the same day."

The congress had appointed other peace commissioners to join Franklin, but, being the only one in Paris, Franklin remained the lead. In early July, he sent the British two lists: one with non-negotiable terms that America would not relinquish and another with "advisable" terms to consider. It was a starting point, at least. By fall, two other commissioners, John Adams and John Jay, had joined Franklin in Paris, but no love was lost among the three. The ever suspicious Adams wrote, "Between two as subtle spirits as any in this world, the one malicious [Franklin], the other I think honest [Jay], I shall have a delicate, a nice, a critical part to act. Franklin's cunning will be to divide us."

John Adams, Benjamin Franklin, *and John Jay represented the United States during the negotiation of the peace treaty between the United States, Britain, France, and Spain. The preliminary peace treaty was signed at Versailles, France, on January 20, 1783. Inset: The signature page of the Treaty of Paris, which finally brought peace in 1783*

But Franklin was old and ready for peace. He had no desire to combat his fellow commissioners, and by the end of November, preliminary articles of peace had been signed. They

The French celebrated *the news of peace by shooting off fireworks in front of the Hôtel de Ville in Paris.*

ensured that American boundaries would extend to the Mississippi River and that navigation rights on the river would be protected. At John Adams's insistence, they also granted fishing rights on the Grand Banks off Newfoundland—a great boon to New England fisherman; and they stipulated the settlement of certain debts—an issue that would create much political controversy in the United States later on.

Even as the Americans negotiated with the British, the French worked against the Americans through back channels. Vergennes told London that he was opposed to America's claims and wrote his ambassador in Philadelphia that France need not "sustain the pretentious ambitions" of America when it came to her boundaries or fishing rights. But America was no longer in thrall to the French, and Vergennes's ploys failed. "Let us now forgive and forget . . . ," Franklin wrote an old friend in Britain in March 1783. "America will, with God's blessing, become a great and happy country; and England, if she has at length gained wisdom, will have gained something more valuable . . . than all she has lost." A month later, the congress ratified the Preliminary Articles of Peace, and Washington issued orders that "all Acts of Hostility" be suspended. It would take almost half a year more, until September, for the Treaty of Paris to be formally signed. In its grand opening statement, it proclaimed that "Divine Providence" had disposed all the hearts of those in the long conflict "to forget

ON DECEMBER 4, 1783, *Gen. George Washington announced to his military officers that he would be resigning his commission and returning to private life at Mount Vernon. Witnesses say that Washington wept and embraced each individual officer as he said farewell.*

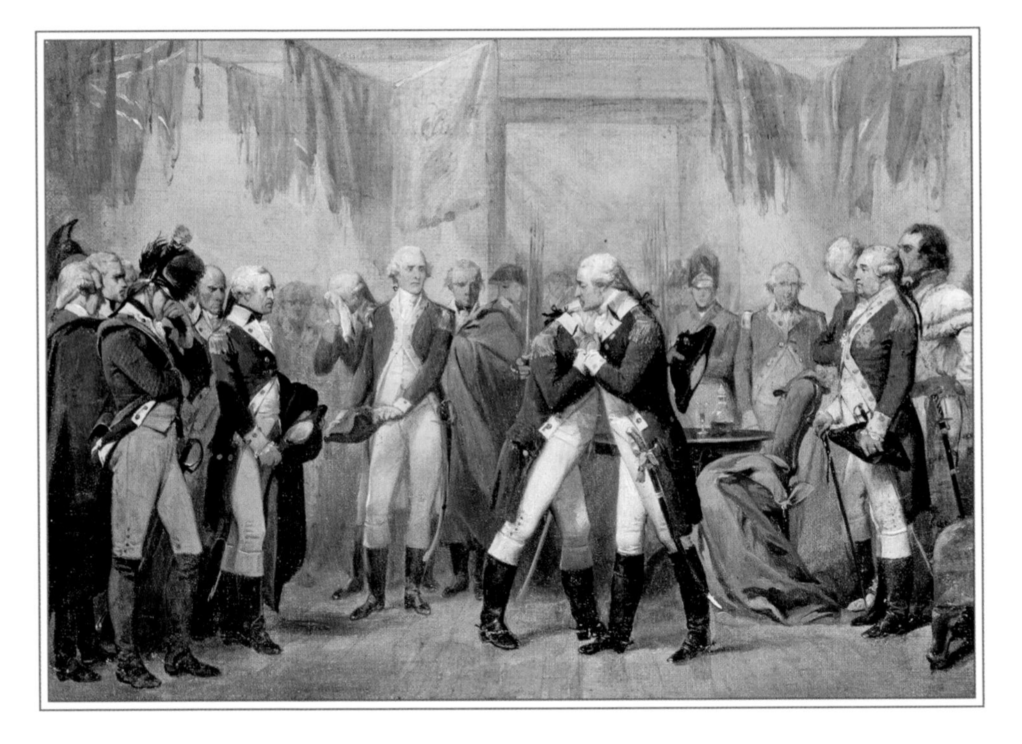

all past misunderstandings and differences that have unhappily interrupted the good correspondence and friendship which they mutually wish to restore, and to establish such a beneficial and satisfactory intercourse, between the two countries upon the ground of reciprocal advantages and mutual convenience as may promote and secure to both perpetual peace and harmony."

Finally, in late November 1783, British troops evacuated New York City, their bastion throughout the war. Washington was on hand to watch them leave. He had fought for this city fiercely in 1776, and he had lost it. Now it was American again. Washington then made his way to Annapolis, where the congress was waiting. Along his route, crowds turned out to see the man who had become the savior of a country. One Dutch visitor in Philadelphia wrote to his wife that he had seen "the greatest man who has ever appeared on the surface of this earth." It was characteristic of the kind of apotheosis Washington would endure for the rest of his life, but in those final cold days of 1783, he was intent on returning to his private life—Mount Vernon, Martha, his family. On December 23, having been feted for several days in Annapolis, he appeared before the congress. An official began the ceremonial proceedings and intoned to Washington, "Sir, the United States in Congress assembled are prepared to receive your communications." Washington rose and read his prepared statement as his hands trembled and his voice rasped. He asked "the indulgence of retiring from the Service of My Country" and commended "the Interests of our dearest Country to the protection of Almighty God." He closed by saying, "Having now finished the work assigned me, I retire from the great theatre of Action . . . and take my leave of all employments of public life."

Washington's Circular to the States, 1783

Head Quarters, Newburgh, June 8, 1783.

Sir:

The great object for which I had the honor to hold an appointment in the Service of my Country, being accomplished, I am now preparing to resign it into the hands of Congress, and to return to that domestic retirement, which, it is well known, I left with the greatest reluctance, a Retirement, for which I have never ceased to sigh through a long and painful absence, and in which (remote from the noise and trouble of the World) I meditate to pass the remainder of life in a state of undisturbed repose; But before I carry this resolution into effect, I think it a duty incumbent on me, to make this my last official communication, to congratulate you on the glorious events which Heaven has been pleased to produce in our favor, to offer my sentiments respecting some important subjects, which appear to me, to be intimately connected with the tranquility of the United States, to take my leave of your Excellency as a public Character, and to give my final blessing to that Country, in whose service I have spent the prime of my life, for whose sake I have consumed so many anxious days and watchfull nights, and whose happiness being extremely dear to me, will always constitute no inconsiderable part of my own . . .

George Washington resigns his commission before the congress on December 23, 1783.

The Citizens of America, placed in the most enviable condition, as the sole Lords and Proprietors of a vast Tract of Continent, comprehending all the various soils and climates of the World, and abounding with all the necessaries and conveniencies of life, are now by the late satisfactory pacification, acknowledged to be possessed of absolute freedom and Independency; They are, from this period, to be considered as the Actors on a most conspicuous Theatre, which seems to be peculiarly designated by Providence for the display of human greatness and felicity; Here, they are not only surrounded with every thing which can contribute to the completion of private and domestic enjoyment, but Heaven has crowned all its other blessings, by giving a fairer oppertunity for political happiness, than any other Nation has ever been favored with . . .

Such is our situation, and such are our prospects: but notwithstanding the cup of blessing is thus reached out to us . . . it appears to me there is an option still left to the United States of America, that it is in their choice, and depends upon their conduct, whether they will be respectable and prosperous, or contemptable and miserable as a Nation . . .

Alexander Hamilton
(1755/57-1804)

THE CHANGES IN THE HUMAN CONDITION ARE uncertain and frequent. Many, on whom fortune has bestowed her favours, may trace their family to a more unprosperous station; and many who are now in obscurity, may look back upon the affluence and exalted rank of their ancestors," Alexander Hamilton once observed, no doubt considering how fortune had intervened in his own life. He surely had been born into an unprosperous station: He was a "bastard child" whose parents never officially wed, his mother the estranged wife of another man, and the exact year of his birth is unknown. His childhood world was that of the British West Indies, a swashbuckling global crossroads where European merchants and seamen, pirates, slaves, and sugar barons mixed and melded against a backdrop of tropical languor. It was a very long way from the class-conscious aristocracy of Washington's or Jefferson's Virginia and even farther from the stolid, virtuous New England of Adams or Franklin. And so perhaps more than any other Founding Father, Hamilton understood the potential for American meritocracy, and he devoted his vast energies to ensuring it. The "bastard boy" from the West Indies became the great nation builder, the designer who created a grid of interconnected institutions that insured the smooth running of commerce and government.

ALEXANDER HAMILTON *(opposite)—war hero, political philosopher, and first secretary of the Treasury—riles up a crowd (above) for the cause of liberty from the steps of King's College (now Columbia University) in New York City in 1775.*

Hamilton's early life probably gave him the vision and the love of fame that he later used to build America's institutions. His boyhood had been changeable, unpredictable, and hard. His father, James Hamilton, the son of a wealthy Scottish laird, abandoned the family when Alexander was ten. His mother, who at one point had been briefly imprisoned by her first husband, died two years after Alexander's father left, and the cousin who succeeded her as Alexander's caregiver committed suicide soon after taking custody of the child and his slightly older brother. The two teen boys were left adrift and penniless—and it was then that fortune bestowed her "favours." Alexander took work as a merchant's clerk, and even at his young age—14—he began to take an interest in global commerce, market fluctuations, and the inherent potential of capitalism. At the same time, he was taken in by a prosperous merchant family on St. Croix, the Stevens.

Hamilton began to flourish in his new, more sedate circumstances. He had been given use of a private library earlier in his childhood and had consumed what it offered. Now he continued his self-education and improvement and found that he liked writing—poetry particularly—and his verse was good enough to be published in the local paper. But he could write prose as well, and when a hurricane devastated the island, he wrote a description of the destruction: "The roaring of the sea and wind—fiery meteors flying about in the air—the prodigious glare of almost perpetual lightning—the crash of the falling houses—and the ear-piercing shrieks of the distressed." But he also lambasted his fellow humans for their "boasted fortitude and resolution . . . arrogance and self-sufficiency . . . See thy wretched helpless state and learn to know thyself . . . Despise thyself and adore thy God."

As overwrought as it may now sound, Hamilton's hurricane missive struck a chord with those who read it or heard it read, and once again fortune bestowed her favors. A subscription fund was established to send the promising young writer to North America for an education, and in 1773, Hamilton arrived in New York, perhaps the most Loyalist-leaning city in America. He was there, studying at King's College, as tensions in Boston fueled the Tea Party, and he took the stage at a mass rally to denounce Parliament's unfair tax policies and to urge more civil disobedience against the crown lest "fraud, power, and the most odious oppression will rise triumphant over right justice, social happiness and freedom." It was a powerful performance that earned him the recognition he craved. In late 1774 he published a political pamphlet, "A Full Vindication of the Measures of the Congress," which again justified America's stance against Britain and again earned Hamilton fame. He continued his pamphleteering as tensions between the mother country and the American colonies came to a boil, and in February 1776 he announced with characteristic drama, "I am going into the army and perhaps ere long may be destined to seal with my blood the sentiments defended by my pen."

GEORGE WASHINGTON *was very impressed with Alexander Hamilton at their first meeting and personally invited the young officer to join his staff in 1777.*

The small, slight young man was made captain of an artillery company, and he took on the role with passion. He fought for supplies for his men, shared their hardships, and offered them leadership. His adopted city, New York, became contested ground later that year, and when Washington's army finally had to abandon it, Hamilton "was among the last of our army that left the city."

It was during this period, as the American forces retreated and regrouped on Harlem Heights, that Hamilton apparently came to the notice of George Washington. The following month, at White Plains, Hamilton, then 21, fought with the general's forces and distinguished himself by his bravery. His reputation continued to grow at Princeton in early 1777, when he again showed himself to be a brave, solid commander, his company "a model of discipline." People were often surprised that such a slight man could be so forceful. One observer who watched as Hamilton marched his company into Princeton after the battle described him as "a mere stripling, small, slender, almost delicate in frame, marching beside a piece of artillery . . . apparently lost in thought, with his hand resting on a cannon and every now and then patting it, as if it were a favorite horse."

Hamilton's superiors took note of his heroics and leadership, and in late January George Washington personally sent him a note, inviting Hamilton to be one of his aides-de-camp. It was a tremendous honor, yet Hamilton chafed at the possibility. He had wanted the command of an artillery regiment. In any case, Hamilton's better judgment prevailed, and he joined Washington's staff in early 1777. For the remainder

ELIZABETH SCHUYLER *(left), Alexander Hamilton's wife, was the second daughter of a rich and prominent New York family. Hamilton (right) wed her in 1780, and the two had eight children.*

of the war, he would be at the choke point of problems, decisions, defeats, politics, and power.

Along with Lafayette, Hamilton enjoyed Washington's confidences and affections in a way that few humans ever did. Washington seems almost to have considered the two young men the sons he never had. Yet while the French marquis returned the general's affections, Hamilton did not. Despite his loyalty, Hamilton harbored quiet doubts about Washington's military decisions and a deep resentment that he, Hamilton, had not been given a field command, though Washington entrusted him with other critical duties. Writing many of Washington's letters, the young aide learned to anticipate and virtually channel the general's thoughts and desires. He also undertook delicate meetings on Washington's behalf. In short, he eased Washington's burden as the army lurched from crisis to crisis.

Despite the trust Washington put in Hamilton, the general was known for his cool, exacting personality, and Hamilton, after all, was at his commander's beck and call. Finally, in February 1781, the young man had had enough. He resigned his position on Washington's staff, though the general urged him to return. He would not. Hamilton even confessed to a friend, "For three years past, I have felt no friendship for him [Washington] and have professed none. The truth is our own dispositions are the opposites of each other." On that score, Hamilton was surely correct. He was impetuous, volatile, and vain, but as Washington was none of those things, he held no grudge against Hamilton, and so, at Hamilton's repeated urging, Washington finally gave him the field position he had coveted for so long. At Yorktown, Hamilton's light infantry led the night bayonet charge on one of the two strategic British redoubts. "They made such a terrible yell and loud cheering that one believed the whole wild hunt had broken out," one Hessian remembered. It was a small but critical victory that soon led to the larger, final fall of the British at Yorktown.

During the war, Hamilton had married Elizabeth Schuyler, a daughter of Gen. Philip Schuyler, the New York poltroon who had been ousted, through political intrigue, from his command before the Battle of Saratoga. The marriage gave Hamilton solace, as well as social standing and some wealth, and after the war, he and Elizabeth returned to New York. Hamilton turned his galloping mind and ambition to the law and was soon a successful lawyer. But he did not give up public service, and the year after Yorktown, he was in Philadelphia as a member of the Confederation Congress, called to address the state, mostly woeful, of the fledging nation's affairs in the wake of war. Hamilton and others were keenly aware of how little true authority the federal government had without the ability to raise revenues, and Hamilton introduced a resolution for "the establishment of permanent and adequate funds to operate generally throughout the United States, *to be collected by Congress.*" It went nowhere, but it focused Hamilton's mind on the issues that eventually would be his causes célèbre: finance and federalism.

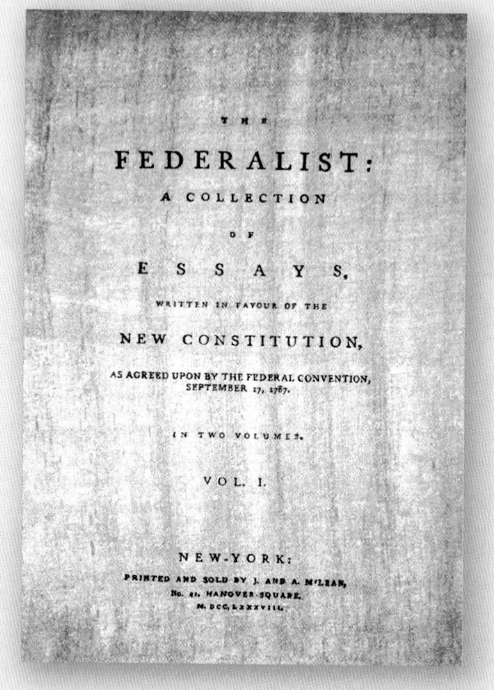

THE
FEDERALIST:
A COLLECTION
OF
ESSAYS,
WRITTEN IN FAVOUR OF THE
NEW CONSTITUTION,
AS AGREED UPON BY THE FEDERAL CONVENTION, SEPTEMBER 17, 1787.
IN TWO VOLUMES.
VOL. I.
NEW-YORK:
PRINTED AND SOLD BY J. AND A. M'LEAN,
No. 41, HANOVER-SQUARE.
M,DCC,LXXXVIII.

THE SERIES OF ESSAYS *now known to history as* The Federalist *were written anonymously by Alexander Hamilton and James Madison, with a few contributed by John Jay. Published over months in 1788, they argued for a strong federal government backed by the Constitution.*

In the next three years, the dapper young lawyer, then only in his early 30s, rose to great heights as the new country faltered and grappled with its own inadequacies and lack of definition. "I fear that we shall let slip the golden opportunity of rescuing the American empire from disunion, anarchy, and misery," he wrote to George Washington about this time, and he meant to do everything in his considerable powers to prevent that.

Hamilton believed in representative government, but he was also wary of the judgment of the common man, and he wanted checks on that. At the Constitutional Convention, Hamilton argued strongly for changes to what became the final draft. Even though his changes weren't incorporated, he fought mightily for the Constitution's ratification in his home state of New York. The weapon he chose was his pen, and in so doing, he left a legacy document that has not been surpassed: *The Federalist.*

According to Hamilton's wife, Eliza, the idea for these essays came to him on a sloop in the Hudson, and he soon enlisted the help of two other legal minds, Virginian James Madison and fellow New Yorker John Jay. Over the course of seven months, their essays explaining and defending the Constitution appeared in New York papers. Despite the pressures of his career, Hamilton wrote more than half of the essays—51 of 85—steaming through his arguments with grand eloquence and a speed born of necessity. But New York's political machine, under the powerful governor, George Clinton, remained immovable. New York was one of the last states to ratify the Constitution, and then only under the threat of isolation.

With a viable constitution at last in place, Hamilton began coaxing and cajoling Washington to take the reins of leadership yet again and stand for President. Washington was the only man, Hamilton felt, who had the character and public respect to save the fragile union. When at last John Adams entered the multicandidate field, Hamilton conspired to take votes away from Adams in order to ensure Washington's victory. Hamilton's backroom dealing made of Adams a permanent enemy—but Hamilton had a vast talent for that. In the coming years, as he took his place in Washington's cabinet as the first and probably most forceful secretary of the treasury—many believed he had overreaching and undue influence—Hamilton managed to alienate Thomas Jefferson, James Madison, James Monroe, and Aaron Burr. Yet in those same years he also created a strong federal government with a budget and tax system, a central bank, a funded debt, a customs service, and a coast guard.

It was the third Vice President, Aaron Burr, who dealt the final blow to Hamilton's energies and genius. Though the two had a friendly rivalry in their early days as lawyers in New York, the relationship hardened into hatred when Burr unseated Hamilton's father-in-law in the U.S. Senate. After the election of 1800, when Burr lost to Thomas Jefferson (thanks in part to more backroom cajoling by Hamilton), the tensions escalated into violence, and Burr ultimately challenged Hamilton to a duel. It was an honorable way for gentlemen to settle accounts in the early 19th century, and duels rarely ended in death. But on the morning of July 11, 1804, when the two faced off in the Hudson Palisades at Weehawken, New Jersey, Aaron Burr delivered a fatal shot. At 49, Alexander Hamilton was dead.

He had never had an easy relationship with life—he had devoured it. But his greatest passion had been the preservation of the union, and more than any other Founding Father, he knitted the union into a whole by giving it the institutions and the vitality to live on after he and all the other founders were gone.

ALEXANDER HAMILTON *and Aaron Burr had been friendly rivals throughout much of their political careers. The rivalry turned deadly, and the two fought a duel on July 11, 1804. Burr shot Hamilton on the dueling grounds in Weehawken, New Jersey, and Hamilton died the following day from his wound.*

CHAPTER 7

A little rebellion now and then is a good thing . . .
It is a medicine necessary for the sound health of government.

Thomas Jefferson

1784-1789
A More Perfect Union

Wars have a way of knitting factions into a tenuous whole, and the American Revolution had done that, bringing the 13 states into common union. But with the war over, factionalism and self-interest returned in force, and some questioned the need for a federal governing body at all. Jefferson, wondering whether the congress should be replaced by a committee, wrote from Europe, "The constant session of Congress cannot be necessary in times of peace." Henry Knox, the Revolution's great artillery commander, worried, "Our federal government is a name, a shadow, without power, or effect." From Mount Vernon, Washington declared, "We are either a United People, or we are not. If the former, let us in all matters of general concern act as a nation, which have national objects to promote, and a national character to support."

But were there national objects, and was there a national character? In the wake of war, the states had reverted to their old, self-interested ways, and with good reason. They had their own problems to deal with—enormous public debts and, with British ports closed to American merchants, languid trade prospects. Grabbing desperately for advantage, individual states established their own currencies, tariffs, duties, and trade barriers. The national government as it existed under the Articles of Confederation was toothless, and it received little respect from either the states or the foreign powers. Even the members of the Congress lost

After his decision *to withdraw from military life, George Washington wished to spend his life as a gentleman farmer on his Mount Vernon estate with his family. But debates over the best form of government for the new nation drew him back into public life. Preceding pages: Measuring 20 by 30 feet, this glorious painting of the signing of the Constitution hangs in the U.S. Capitol, above the east grand stairway of the House of Representatives.*

interest in a federal governing body, and attendance dropped so low in 1786 that the necessary quorums weren't reached.

Alarmed at what he saw, Washington watched the factionalism from the sidelines until he could stand it no longer. When Maryland and Virginia began fighting over navigation rights on the Potomac—a river that flowed through his own backyard and that he considered "the great avenue into the western country . . . which promises to afford a capacious asylum for the poor and persecuted of the earth"—he offered Mount Vernon as a setting for negotiations. There, on the banks above the contested Potomac, Maryland and Virginia resolved their differences with such success that it was an incentive for more such efforts.

Calling themselves *Commissioners to Remedy Defects of the Federal Government, a group of delegates from Virginia, New York, New Jersey, Pennsylvania, and Delaware met at the State House in Annapolis, Maryland, in September 1786.*

Eventually, September 11, 1786, was set for a meeting of national delegates to discuss commerce and other issues, but when it convened in Annapolis, Maryland, only a dozen representatives from five states—Virginia, New York, New Jersey, Pennsylvania, and Delaware—were on hand. The delegates called themselves Commissioners to Remedy Defects of the Federal Government, but they achieved very little in the way of remedies. Still, there were productive moments, and large thinkers emerged, among them Alexander Hamilton and James Madison, who quickly developed a strong affinity for each other. The Caribbean-born Hamilton represented New York, while Madison came from Virginia's planter aristocracy. The two men were both slight of build but were powerhouses of intellect and ideas about the new nation. It was clear to them that another meeting was necessary to "render the constitution of the Foederal Government adequate to the exigencies of the Union." The date for the next convention was set for May 1787, and following long precedent, Philadelphia was chosen as the gathering place.

The eight months between the Annapolis and Philadelphia conventions was a long time in a restive country where backcountry farmers, plagued by debt, were staging mini-insurrections. Local militia had quickly put down most of the uprisings, but in Massachusetts and other pockets of New England the protesters were not to be quelled. Many farmers there had served their country, often with little or no pay. Now they had returned home and begun the long process of reestablishing their farms and lives. But instead of helping them, Massachusetts had levied heavy poll and land taxes and had insisted the taxes be paid in gold and silver currency rather than in goods or produce. The payment was an impossibility for the hardscrabble farmers in the hill towns of central and western Massachusetts. As families watched, their grain, livestock, personal belongings, and even

lands were seized for back taxes. By the late summer of 1786, they had had enough, and they marched on the courthouse in Northampton, thus preventing the county court from sitting. As one farmer put it, "The great men are going to get all we have and I think it is time for us to rise and put a stop to it, and have no more courts, nor sheriffs, nor collectors nor lawyers."

In 1786, *during the short-lived New England uprising known as Shays's Rebellion, fighting between authorities and local farmers broke out at the courthouse in Springfield, Massachusetts.*

As the fall progressed, the protesters rallied behind 39-year-old Daniel Shays, who had distinguished himself as a captain in the Revolution; he had fought at Bunker Hill, Saratoga, and Stony Point. Like him, many of his Shaysites, as they came to be known, wore remnants

Washington to his former artillery commander, Bostonian Henry Knox, on Shays's Rebellion

Mount Vernon, December 26, 1786.

. . . I feel, my dear Genl. Knox, infinitely more than I can express to you, for the disorders which have arisen in these States. Good God! who besides a tory could have foreseen, or a Briton predicted them! were these people wiser than others, or did they judge of us from the corruption, and depravity of their own hearts? The latter I am persuaded was the case, and that notwithstanding the boasted virtue of America, we are far gone in every thing ignoble and bad . . . There are combustibles in every State, which a spark might set fire to. In this State, a perfect calm prevails at present, and a prompt disposition to support, and give energy to the foederal System is discovered, if the unlucky stirring of the dispute respecting the navigation of the Mississippi does not become a leaven that will ferment, and sour the mind of it . . .

In both your letters you intimate, that the men of reflection, principle and property in New England, feeling the inefficacy of their present government, are contemplating a change; but you are not explicit with respect to the nature of it. It has been supposed, that, the Constitution of the State of Massachusetts was amongst the most energetic in the Union; May not these disorders then be ascribed to an endulgent exercise of the powers of Administration? If your laws authorized, and your powers were adequate to the suppression of these tumults, in the first appearances of them, delay and temporizing expedients were, in my opinion improper . . .

Henry Knox, Secretary of War during Shays's Rebellion, went to Springfield, Massachusetts, to defend the federal armory from the rebels.

That G. B [Great Britain] will be an unconcerned Spectator of the present insurrections (if they continue) is not to be expected. That she is at this moment sowing the Seeds of jealousy and discontent among the various tribes of Indians on our frontier admits of no doubt, in my mind. And that she will improve every opportunity to foment the spirit of turbulence within the bowels of the United States, with a view of distracting our governments, and promoting divisions, is, with me, not less certain. Her first Manoeuvres will, no doubt, be covert, and may remain so till the period shall arrive when a decided line of conduct may avail her . . . Vigilance in watching, and vigour in acting, is, in my opinion, become indispensably necessary. If the powers are inadequate amend or alter them, but do not let us sink into the lowest state of humiliation and contempt, and become a byword in all the earth . . .

of their old Continental Army uniforms and a sprig of hemlock in their hats to distinguish themselves from the official militia called up to deal with them.

Appalled at the uprising, Benjamin Lincoln, the former Revolutionary general and a wealthy resident of eastern Massachusetts, wrote to his old comrade-in-arms, George Washington, "There doth not appear virtue enough among the people to preserve a perfect republican government." Washington wrote back, "What, gracious God, is man that there should be such inconsistency and perfidiousness in his conduct? It was but the other day that we were shedding blood to obtain the constitutions under which we now live,—constitutions of our own choice and making,—and now we are unsheathing the sword to overturn them!" Jefferson had another opinion altogether of the Shaysites' insurrection: "A little rebellion now and then is a good thing," he observed from his perch in Europe. "It is a medicine necessary for the sound health of government. God forbid that we should ever be twenty years without such a rebellion."

Shays's Rebellion was short-lived. It lasted only a few months, during which courts were disrupted and the federal armory in Springfield was seized. But brief as it was, the rebellion had profound political consequences: It left no doubt as to how weak the federal government truly was.

STATE DELEGATES GATHERED *at the Philadelphia statehouse from May to September 1787 to address growing problems among the states and suggest a new form of government for the new nation.*

The Philadelphia Convention

ALARMED AT THE REBELLION AND THE GENERAL STATE of the new nation, Washington succumbed to those urging him to leave retirement and agreed to attend the upcoming Philadelphia Convention. He was not a man who could make his way through the new country anonymously, and outside Philadelphia he was greeted by the usual fanfare—dignitaries, infantry, cannon blasts. In the city, church bells tolled his arrival and more admirers thronged the streets to cheer on their "old and faithful commander," as they had done so often during the war.

Virginia's delegates—including Washington; Gov. Edmund Randolph; James Madison; and George Mason, author of the Virginia Constitution—had arrived on time, but no others, except for Pennsylvania's representatives, were on hand on May 14, the designated starting date for the convention. While they waited, the Virginians put their time to good use and met "two or three hours every day in order to form a proper correspondence of sentiments." The four men were divided on the issue of federal versus states' and individual rights, with Washington and Madison in the federal camp and Mason and Randolph champions of individual and states' rights. It was a portent of conflicts to come, and yet the Virginians managed to reach some consensus. They agreed on a document with 15 articles of governance.

At last, on Friday, May 25, as rain soaked the city, delegates sent by seven of the thirteen states convened in the State House, site of so much Revolutionary foment. Almost immediately Pennsylvania delegate Robert Morris rose to propose George Washington as the convention's president. "The nomination came with particular grace from Penna. as Docr. Franklin alone could have been thought of as a competitor," James Madison wrote. But age and infirmity made Franklin far less viable than Washington, even on the opening day. "The Docr. was himself to have made the nomination of General Washington, but the state of the weather and of his health confined him to his house," Madison explained in his copious notes on the convention, which he believed would "decide forever the fate of republican government." In any case, Washington was unanimously elected president, and he took his place on a high-backed wooden chair ornamented by a rising sun and placed on a platform that lofted him above the fray. Wearing his old Continental uniform, Washington reigned like a silent, tempering angel.

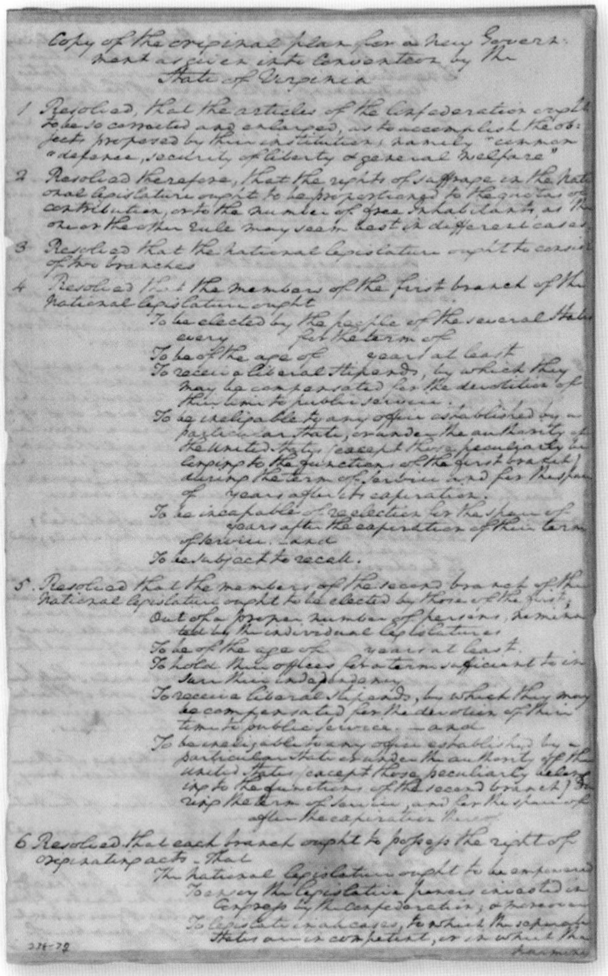

Once Washington was in place at their head, the delegates agreed on another item of pressing concern: secrecy. They wanted to hold the coming deliberations out of the public eye "lest our transactions get into the newspapers and disturb the public repose with premature speculations," Washington later explained. Many of the men present understood that they had met not simply to amend the Articles of Confederation but to write an altogether new document of governance. They surely had no idea on that rainy spring Friday that it would take them four months to do so.

The delegates met in the same paneled Assembly Room where the Declaration of Independence had been signed the previous decade. The 36-year-old Madison, self-appointed note taker, seated himself front and center, a "favorable position for hearing all that passed . . . I was not absent a single day, nor more than a casual fraction of an hour in any day, so that I could not have lost a single speech, unless a very short one."

GEORGE WASHINGTON'S *handwritten copy of the Virginia Plan (above), a set of 15 proposals drafted by James Madison to the Constitutional Convention. After much compromise and debate, the Virginia Plan provided the basic framework of the U.S. Constitution. Opposite: The delegates to the Constitutional Convention elected the nation's unassailable hero, George Washington, to serve as president of the proceedings.*

Madison, perhaps more than any other delegate, had hard-won experience in crafting public policy. He had recently been an active figure at the Annapolis convention, but he also had worked on the Virginia Constitution and had served on the Continental Congress, there too taking copious *Notes of Debates.* The organization of government was his forte, and earlier in the spring of 1787, he had shared his "outlines of a new system" with Washington, Jefferson, and Randolph: "Conceiving that an individual independence of the States is utterly irreconcileable with their aggregate sovereignty; and that a consolidation of the whole into one simple republic would be as inexpedient as it is unattainable, I have sought for some

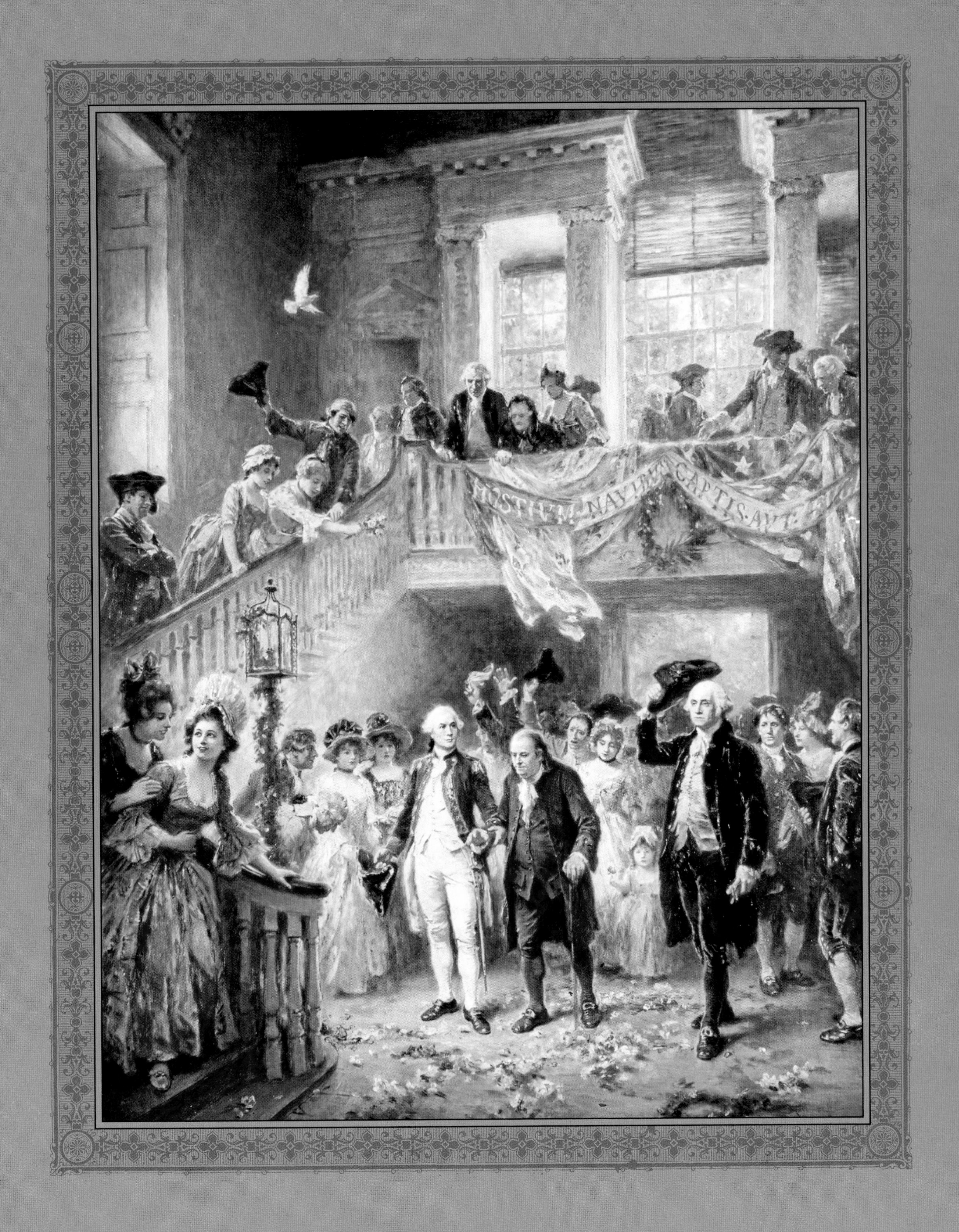
HOSTIVM
CAPTIS·AVT

middle ground, which may at once support a due supremacy of the national authority, and not exclude the local authorities wherever they can be subordinately useful." He had outlined a representative government that attempted to create checks and balances and to ensure that small states as well as larger ones were reasonably accommodated.

On the second day of the convention, Edmund Randolph stood to present Madison's modified outline. The so-called Virginia Plan called for three branches of government—executive, judicial, and legislative, the last to be bicameral. It also gave the federal government ultimate power over state authority. The Virginia Plan was more than a starting point for debate; it was a carefully considered template for governance. The great obstacle to its general acceptance among the convention delegates was not its organizational ideas but its subordination of state to federal authority. Knowing this, Randolph "concluded with an exhortation, not to suffer the present opportunity of establishing general peace, harmony, happiness and liberty in the U.S. to pass away unimproved."

All communities divide themselves into the few and the many.

Alexander Hamilton

May faded into June, and the delegates continued to meet as the heat and humidity climbed. The 81-year-old Ben Franklin attended whenever his health allowed. Gout and kidney stones so plagued him that he had to be carried to the meetings in a sedan chair borne by four convicts from the Walnut Street Jail. Still, he was elated by the gathering and called it "the most august and respectable assembly he was ever in in his life." He was also aware that his speaking abilities were far outstripped by firebrands like the young Alexander

Benjamin Franklin's advanced age *and ill health made attending the Convention a challenge for him. Rather than orate in the halls of the statehouse, he preferred to meet with other delegates, like Alexander Hamilton (shown here), in the outside courtyard.*

Hamilton, Pennsylvania's Gouverneur Morris, and Connecticut's Roger Sherman. Franklin preferred to hold private court under a mulberry tree in a courtyard.

Franklin had spent so much of the previous decades abroad that most Americans knew of him only by reputation. The convention was one of the few times in his later life when he attended to America's business in America. Though he was no public speaker, he had strong opinions about the form of governance he thought best for the country, and he let others present his ideas for him. After his long years living under the monarchies and aristocracies of Great Britain and France, he wanted to guard against "the two passions which have a powerful influence on the affairs of men . . . ambition and avarice: the love of power, and the love of money." With that in mind, he proposed that the executive branch receive no compensation at all. His motion "was treated with great respect, but rather for the author of it than from any apparent conviction of its expediency or practicality."

THIS SATIRICAL 18TH-CENTURY *engraving illustrates the major divisions between the Federalists and anti-Federalists on the eve of ratification of the U.S. Constitution. The artist clearly favors the Federalist cause.*

It was Alexander Hamilton who seconded Franklin's motion out of deference to the older statesman, but Hamilton had his own, almost diametrically opposed views on the executive branch. "All communities divide themselves into the few and the many," he pronounced. "The first are the rich and well born, the other the mass of the people . . . Give therefore to the first class a distinct, permanent share in the government. They will check the unsteadiness in the second, and . . . therefore will ever maintain good governance." Hamilton essentially wanted a constitutional monarchy, with a president and senators elected by special electors and thereafter serving for life. It was one of any number of ideas presented for the legislative and executive branches, and the debates on exactly how to structure them became circular and seemingly interminable.

As the summer wore on, the general enthusiasm for the work of the convention suffered a marked decline. Delegates grew weary of the proceedings, and some slipped away to tend to their homes, families, and businesses. Then, on July 16, a major hurdle was overcome when the small state/large state impasse that had threatened to derail the entire convention was settled—by a one-vote margin. The bicameral congress would comprise the House of Representatives, with seats assigned according to the proportion of a state's population, and the Senate, in which each state would have the same number of seats. At last, one solution to governance had been reached, and that reinvigorated the assembly, but it did little to

Reentering public life *at the urging of his colleagues, George Washington was inaugurated as the first President of the United States at Federal Hall in New York City on April 20, 1789. John Adams, who came in second in the election results, served as his Vice President.*

Delaware ratified the Constitution *in December 1787, making it the first state to do so; Rhode Island was the last, in May 1790. During this period, the borders of the original 13 states extended much farther west than they do today (opposite).*

point the way forward on the other great issues: suffrage, the disposition of new states as they joined the Union, commerce, taxation, separation of powers, states' versus federal rights, national security, foreign affairs, and that most polarizing of issues, slavery.

With all that to consider, the delegates bogged down on the nature of the executive branch. Should it be elected by popular vote, by Congress, or by some other body? The arguments morphed as the delegates themselves changed, some resigning and being replaced by new members. And through it all, the great little Madison hunched over his notes—with "a calm, penetrating blue eye . . . like a man thinking."

At the end of July, the delegates appointed the Committee of Detail to make sense of what had already been agreed to, and then the convention left the five-man committee to its work for a ten-day recess. When it reconvened on August 6, the committee presented its findings, inspiring another five weeks of sometimes rancorous debate. The issue of who would elect the President remained an unresolved hot spot. If it were left to Congress, a "legislative tyranny" could ensue, yet the majority of the convention delegates rejected the idea of a popular election. They seemed particularly concerned about the chaotic effects of "an excess of democracy."

Again, Roger Sherman, who had proposed the small state/large state solution, offered up an approach to the executive branch that all sides could live with: The President "shall hold his office during the term of four years, and together with the vice-President . . . be elected" by state electors, "the number of electors equal to the whole number of Senators and members of the House of Representatives, to which the State may be entitled in the Legislature." With that thorny issue finally laid to rest, the convention could move on to other issues of governance.

Finally, in mid-September, the Committee of Style presented a final draft of a constitution, crafted largely by Gouverneur Morris of Pennsylvania. It included seven sweeping articles, some divided into sections, and it dealt with all aspects of governance. Its ringing preamble proclaimed, "We the People of the United States, in Order to form a more perfect Union, establish Justice, insure domestic Tranquility, provide for the common defence, promote the general Welfare, and secure the Blessings of Liberty to ourselves and our Posterity, do ordain and establish this Constitution for the United States of America."

Despite the Constitution's elegance, the delegates immediately began to insist on changes and additions. A few were made, but not those championed by Virginia's George Mason, who argued for a bill of rights to protect the individual "if the Government should become oppressive, as he verily believed would be the case." His argument was quickly passed over in the clamor for other changes by other delegates.

Robert Morris

1734–1806

Born in Liverpool, England, Robert Morris moved to the colonies when he was 13 and eventually apprenticed at a financial firm in Philadelphia. Young Morris became one of the city's most prominent businessmen, specializing in shipping and real estate. He became involved in the early movements for independence, serving as a delegate to the Second Continental Congress. From 1781 to 1784 he was the superintendent of finance, a powerful position in which he controlled the purse strings of the new nation. Morris also loaned the struggling revolutionary effort money from his personal funds, and he earned his nickname, The Financier of the Revolution. After the Revolution, he served as a U.S. senator from Pennsylvania. Poor investments led to his bankruptcy in 1798 and a term in debtor's prison. After his release, he led a modest life in Philadelphia until his death eight years later.

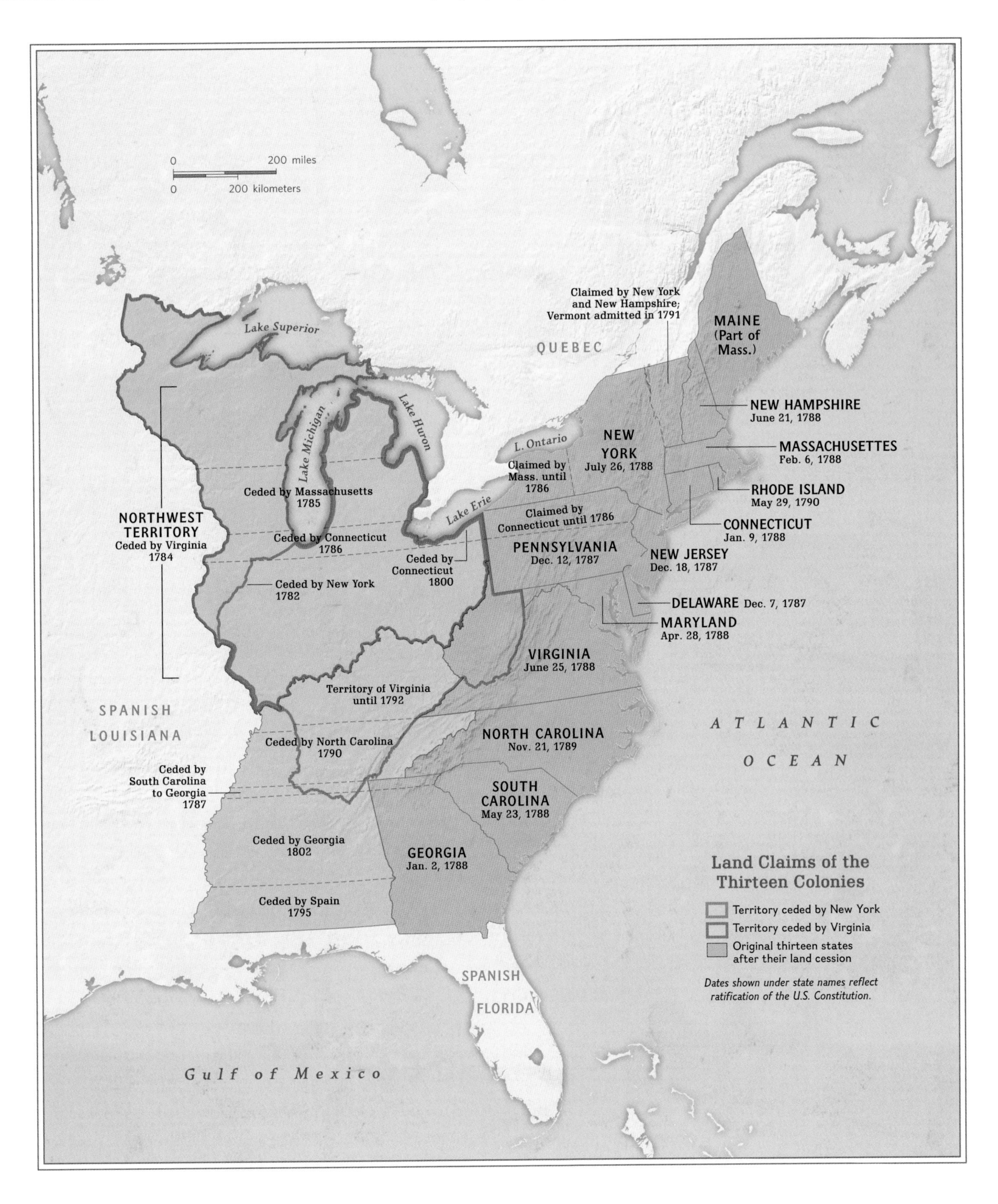

0
200 miles
0
200 kilometers
Lake Superior
Lake Michigan
Lake Huron
L. Ontario
Lake Erie
QUEBEC
Claimed by New York
and New Hampshire;
Vermont admitted in 1791
MAINE
(Part of
Mass.)
NEW HAMPSHIRE
June 21, 1788
MASSACHUSETTES
Feb. 6, 1788
RHODE ISLAND
May 29, 1790
CONNECTICUT
Jan. 9, 1788
NEW
YORK
July 26, 1788
Claimed by
Mass. until
1786
Claimed by
Connecticut until 1786
PENNSYLVANIA
Dec. 12, 1787
NEW JERSEY
Dec. 18, 1787
DELAWARE Dec. 7, 1787
MARYLAND
Apr. 28, 1788
VIRGINIA
June 25, 1788
NORTH CAROLINA
Nov. 21, 1789
SOUTH
CAROLINA
May 23, 1788
GEORGIA
Jan. 2, 1788
NORTHWEST
TERRITORY
Ceded by Virginia
1784
Ceded by Massachusetts
1785
Ceded by Connecticut
1786
Ceded by
Connecticut
1800
Ceded by New York
1782
Territory of Virginia
until 1792
Ceded by North Carolina
1790
Ceded by
South Carolina
to Georgia
1787
Ceded by Georgia
1802
Ceded by Spain
1795
SPANISH
LOUISIANA
SPANISH
FLORIDA
Gulf of Mexico
ATLANTIC
OCEAN
Land Claims of the
Thirteen Colonies
Territory ceded by New York
Territory ceded by Virginia
Original thirteen states
after their land cession
Dates shown under state names reflect
ratification of the U.S. Constitution.

Elbridge Gerry *(left), a delegate from Massachusetts, strenuously argued for the addition of a bill of rights to the U.S. Constitution. Roger Sherman (center), a delegate from Connecticut, co-wrote the Connecticut Compromise; Edmund Randolph (right), a delegate from Virginia, presented the Virginia Plan and advocated for a national judiciary.*

At the final session, on September 17, the ailing Franklin rose with a prepared speech in his hand but handed it to another delegate to read aloud:

> I confess that there are several parts of this constitution which I do not at present approve, but I am not sure I shall never approve them: For having lived long, I have experienced many instances of being obliged by better information, or fuller consideration, to change opinions even on important subjects, which I once thought right, but found to be otherwise. It is therefore that the older I grow, the more apt I am to doubt my own judgment, and to pay more respect to the judgment of others . . .
> On the whole, Sir, I can not help expressing a wish that every member of the Convention who may still have objections to it, would with me, on this occasion doubt a little of his own infallibility, and to make manifest our unanimity, put his name to this instrument.

With apologies to Dr. Franklin, Virginia's Edmund Randolph refused to sign. So did George Mason, and Elbridge Gerry of Massachusetts. But the other members present affixed their signatures, with Washington signing first. Franklin, the old sage, had the last word. He delivered a sort of informal benediction to the gathering: "I have often in the course of the session, and the vicissitudes of my hopes and fears as to its issue, looked at that behind the President without being able to tell whether it was rising or setting," he said, referring to the carved sun on Washington's chair. "But now at length I have the happiness to know that it is a rising and not a setting sun." Since 1754, when he had proposed his pre-Revolution Albany Plan, Franklin had wanted union. Now, there was a document that might bind the states into true nationhood.

For his part, Washington planned to wait and see. The day after the signing, in a letter to Lafayette, he called the Constitution "now a child of fortune, to be fostered by some and buffeted by others. What will be the general opinion on, or the reception of it, is not for me to decide, nor shall I say any thing for or against it. If it is good I suppose it will work its way good, if bad it will recoil on the framers."

Ratifying the Constitution

It was up to those framers to see that the nine states necessary for ratification be convinced of the document's good. And that would be no easy task. One New Englander declared flatly, "The vast continent of America cannot be long subjected to a democracy if consolidated into one government. You might as well attempt to rule Hell by prayer." The nation builders anticipated that the greatest opposition would come from the large states, Virginia and New York. Alexander Hamilton knew what an uphill battle it would be to win over his home state of New York, where Governor Clinton's anti-Federalists held powerful sway. In early October, Hamilton conceived a plan to go directly to the people with the merits of the Constitution. He determined to write a series of articles for the local newspapers to explain in detail why the document was good and necessary. Hamilton's wife, Eliza, later explained that he "wrote the outline of his papers in T*he Federalist* on board one of the North River sloops while on his way to Albany . . ." because "public business so filled up his time that he was compelled to do much of his studying and writing while traveling."

With his time so limited, Hamilton knew he needed collaborators, and he enlisted his friend James Madison, for whom he had developed a deep respect, and John Jay, who had served as President of the Continental Congress and had drafted the first New York State Constitution. Gouverneur Morris was asked to join the team as well but declined. That would be his loss, because *The Federalist* now ranks among the great American documents. Appearing from October 1787 to August 1788, its 85 essays totaled 175,000 words. They were submitted under the pseudonym Publius, evoking the first consul of the Roman Republic. Newspaper publishers and others, though, soon guessed who the real authors were. Hamilton wrote the majority of the papers, 51 in all, while Madison wrote 29, and Jay 5. As their name implied, the papers explained the need for ratification of the Constitution to ensure a strong federal government. In *Federalist* no. 51, Madison wrote persuasively, "The aim of every political constitution is, or ought to be, first to obtain for rulers men who possess most wisdom to discern, and most virtue to pursue, the common good of the society; and in the next place, to take the most effectual precautions for keeping them virtuous whilst they continue to hold their public trust."

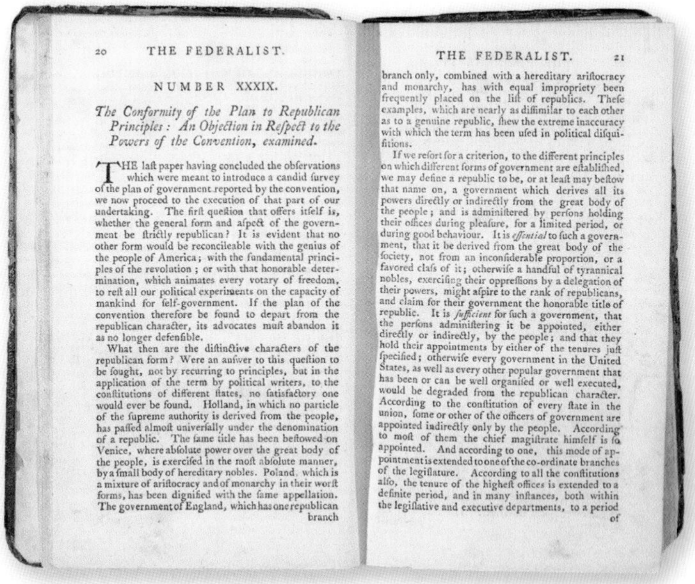

20 THE FEDERALIST.

NUMBER XXXIX.

The Conformity of the Plan to Republican Principles: An Objection in Reſpect to the Powers of the Convention, examined.

THE laſt paper having concluded the obſervations which were meant to introduce a candid ſurvey of the plan of government reported by the convention, we now proceed to the execution of that part of our undertaking. The firſt queſtion that offers itſelf is, whether the general form and aſpect of the government be ſtrictly republican? It is evident that no other form would be reconcileable with the genius of the people of America; with the fundamental principles of the revolution; or with that honorable determination, which animates every votary of freedom, to reſt all our political experiments on the capacity of mankind for ſelf-government. If the plan of the convention therefore be found to depart from the republican character, its advocates muſt abandon it as no longer defenſible.

What then are the diſtinctive characters of the republican form? Were an anſwer to this queſtion to be ſought, not by recurring to principles, but in the application of the term by political writers, to the conſtitutions of different ſtates, no ſatisfactory one would ever be found. Holland, in which no particle of the ſupreme authority is derived from the people, has paſſed almoſt univerſally under the denomination of a republic. The ſame title has been beſtowed on Venice, where abſolute power over the great body of the people, is exerciſed in the moſt abſolute manner, by a ſmall body of hereditary nobles. Poland, which is a mixture of ariſtocracy and of monarchy in their worſt forms, has been dignified with the ſame appellation. The government of England, which has one republican branch

THE FEDERALIST. 21

branch only, combined with a hereditary ariſtocracy and monarchy, has with equal impropriety been frequently placed on the liſt of republics. Theſe examples, which are nearly as diſſimilar to each other as to a genuine republic, ſhew the extreme inaccuracy with which the term has been uſed in political diſquiſitions.

If we reſort for a criterion, to the different principles on which different forms of government are eſtabliſhed, we may define a republic to be, or at leaſt may beſtow that name on, a government which derives all its powers directly or indirectly from the great body of the people; and is adminiſtered by perſons holding their offices during pleaſure, for a limited period, or during good behaviour. It is *eſſential* to ſuch a government, that it be derived from the great body of the ſociety, not from an inconſiderable proportion, or a favored claſs of it; otherwiſe a handful of tyrannical nobles, exerciſing their oppreſſions by a delegation of their powers, might aſpire to the rank of republicans, and claim for their government the honorable title of republic. It is *ſufficient* for ſuch a government, that the perſons adminiſtering it be appointed, either directly or indirectly, by the people; and that they hold their appointments by either of the tenures juſt ſpecified; otherwiſe every government in the United States, as well as every other popular government that has been or can be well organiſed or well executed, would be degraded from the republican character. According to the conſtitution of every ſtate in the union, ſome or other of the officers of government are appointed indirectly only by the people. According to moſt of them the chief magiſtrate himſelf is ſo appointed. And according to one, this mode of appointment is extended to one of the co-ordinate branches of the legiſlature. According to all the conſtitutions alſo, the tenure of the higheſt offices is extended to a definite period, and in many inſtances, both within the legiſlative and executive departments, to a period of

The Federalist *papers, published serially by newspapers over seven months in 1787–1788, was the brainchild of Alexander Hamilton, who wrote 51 of the 85 essays. Each presented different arguments for the ratification of the U.S. Constitution.*

As Hamilton and Madison were beginning the fight for New York, small Delaware swung into action and held the first ratifying convention on December 3. The state quickly rendered a unanimous vote in favor of the Constitution. Pennsylvania soon followed, then New Jersey and Georgia. By early February Connecticut and Massachusetts had signed on as well.

Then, suddenly, things bogged down. New Hampshire's convention refused to ratify, but its pro-Federalists managed to engineer an adjournment rather than an outright rejection, which is what Rhode Island delivered by popular referendum in March. That might have been predicted, because Rhode Island had not even bothered to send delegates to the Constitutional Convention. A month later, Maryland joined the six other states that had ratified. In late May, South Carolina became the eighth. Washington wrote prophetically to Lafayette, "The plot thickens fast. A few short weeks will determine the political fate of America for the present generation and probably produce no small influence on the happiness of society through a long succession of ages to come."

In mid-June the delegates in New Hampshire reconvened, and on June 21 it became the ninth state—the vital state—to vote for ratification. Virginia's Federalists had hoped and maneuvered for that honor after beginning deliberations on June 2, but the debates among delegates were contentious, and the vote was not held until more than three weeks later. Ratification won out, but only with a narrow ten-vote margin. In the end, Gov. Edmund Randolph, who had refused to sign the Constitution at the Philadelphia Convention the preceding September, voted in favor. But Virginia's ratification came with a recommendation that a bill of rights be added to the Constitution, along with a list of amendments.

When they voted, the Virginians believed they were the critical ninth state, because news of New Hampshire's ratification had not yet reached them. Though Virginia missed the honor of being ninth, it did play a pivotal role. When anti-Federalist New York heard that the Old Dominion had voted in favor of ratification, it followed suit—but only after a great deal of further wrangling and by an even narrower margin of 30 to 27. The two remaining states would take a longer time to come to the federal table—North Carolina in November 1789 and Rhode Island not until March 1790. But even without them, the Constitution was a fait accompli.

John Jay
1745–1829

John Jay was an American statesman with a long and distinguished career in public life. Born in New York, Jay began his career as a lawyer and then joined the patriot cause in 1774. He served as a New York delegate to the Continental Congress. During and after the Revolution he served as a diplomat and secretary of foreign affairs. One of Jay's most important contributions was his authorship of five of *The Federalist* papers. Jay was an advocate of strong, centralized government and worked with James Madison and Alexander Hamilton to promote this philosophy. But perhaps his most enduring contribution was his work as an opponent of slavery. During his term as governor of New York State he signed into law the 1799 Act, a law that ended slavery in the state through gradual emancipation.

Electing a President

In early February state electors from each of the 11 ratifying states were charged with casting their votes for the country's first President, as stipulated by the Constitution. The candidate with the most electoral votes would become President, and the runner-up would be Vice President. The field was full with ten candidates, but

most of the candidates—among them John Adams, John Jay, and the old general, Benjamin Lincoln—were generally interested in the Vice Presidency. Everyone understood that the new President would be George Washington. Yet he had needed some convincing to plunge back into leadership, and Hamilton, Madison, and a loving public obliged. Gouverneur Morris used a subtle logic on the childless Washington by assuring him that in becoming President, he would "become the father to more than three millions of children."

AFTER THE U.S. CONSTITUTION *was ratified in July 1788, a grand celebration was held in New York City, even though New York was an anti-Federalist stronghold.*

Washington's victory was unanimous, with each voting elector casting a ballot for him. John Adams, second in the count, would serve as Vice President. On April 30, 1789, when Washington stood on the balcony of New York's Federal Hall and took the oath of office, he little realized that he had eight more years of hard public service ahead of him. In that time, the fight over the nature of government in America would escalate, and large personalities such as Hamilton, Adams, Jefferson, and Madison would perpetuate the debate over the very meaning of the United States—which rights accrued to it, which belonged to the states, and which were reserved for the people.

Early on in that battle, some, like Madison, had worried that the Constitution would be enfeebled or even rethought. Throughout the fight for ratification, anti-Federalists

WELCOME
PRINCETON
MONMOUTH

A VARIETY OF BOATS *(preceding pages) escorted George Washington's ship to the Battery in New York City to welcome him to the city before his Inauguration in April 1789. Right: A document shows Thomas Jefferson's tally of the states' votes to ratify ten of the twelve amendments to the Constitution, collectively known as the Bill of Rights.*

Articles	Affirmative											Negative					
I.	N.H.		R.I.	N.Y.	N.J.	P.		M.	V.	N.C.	S.C.						D. postp.
II.							D.	M.	V.	N.C.	S.C.	N.H.		R.I. silent	N.Y.	N.J. silent	P. silent
III.	N.H.		R.I.	N.Y.	N.J.	P.	D.	M.	V.	N.C.	S.C.						
IV.	N.H.		R.I.	N.Y.	N.J.	P.	D.	M.	V.	N.C.	S.C.						
V.	N.H.		R.I.	N.Y.	N.J.	P.	D.	M.	V.	N.C.	S.C.						
VI.	N.H.		R.I.	N.Y.	N.J.	P.	D.	M.	V.	N.C.	S.C.						
VII.	N.H.		R.I.	N.Y.	N.J.	P.	D.	M.	V.	N.C.	S.C.						
VIII.	N.H.		R.I.	N.Y.	N.J.	P.	D.	M.	V.	N.C.	S.C.						
IX.	N.H.		R.I.	N.Y.	N.J.	P.	D.	M.	V.	N.C.	S.C.						
X.	N.H.		R.I.	N.Y.	N.J.	P.	D.	M.	V.	N.C.	S.C.						
XI.	N.H.		R.I.	N.Y.	N.J.	P.	D.	M.	V.	N.C.	S.C.						
XII.	N.H.		R.I.	N.Y.	N.J.	P.	D.	M.	V.	N.C.	S.C.						

had pressed for adding to the existing document a bill of rights—provisions that would protect "those essential rights of mankind without which liberty cannot exist." If such a rule of rights weren't established, what would keep a new tyranny from replacing the old tyranny of Britain? Madison himself had been gradually persuaded that a bill of rights, the very thing George Mason had championed at the Philadelphia Convention, was needed. Throughout the long constitutional ordeal, Madison had been corresponding with Jefferson, who was then in France, and Jefferson had often pushed for a bill of rights. And so, in June 1789, Madison, a newly elected member of the House of Representatives in the First Congress, offered a proposal to amend the Constitution.

Congress shall make no law respecting an establishment of religion . . . abridging the freedom of speech, or . . . press.

FIRST AMENDMENT TO THE U.S. CONSTITUTION

Madison's document began by acknowledging, "The Conventions of a number of the States, having at the time of their adopting the Constitution, expressed a desire, in order to prevent misconstruction or abuse of its powers, that further declaratory and restrictive clauses should be added . . ." The rest of the document addressed 12 areas in which an individual's rights would be protected against the excesses of government. Its language closely echoed the 1776 Virginia Declaration of Rights, written by George Mason at the height of Revolutionary fervor.

By that fall Congress had accepted Madison's 12 articles as amendments to the Constitution, and President Washington duly sent copies of the amendments to each state. It would take two years before ten of them were ratified by the necessary three-quarters of the states. Those ten live on now as the U.S. Bill of Rights, the first amendments to the Constitution. But the founders' debates over rights versus the need for governance go on, clear proof that America is still evolving, still searching for common ground, still trying to form a more perfect union.

ROBERT LIVINGSTON, *the Chancellor of New York, administered the Oath of Office to George Washington (opposite), who was sworn in using a Bible from St. John's Masonic Lodge No. 1. Washington and a number of other Founding Fathers were Masons.*

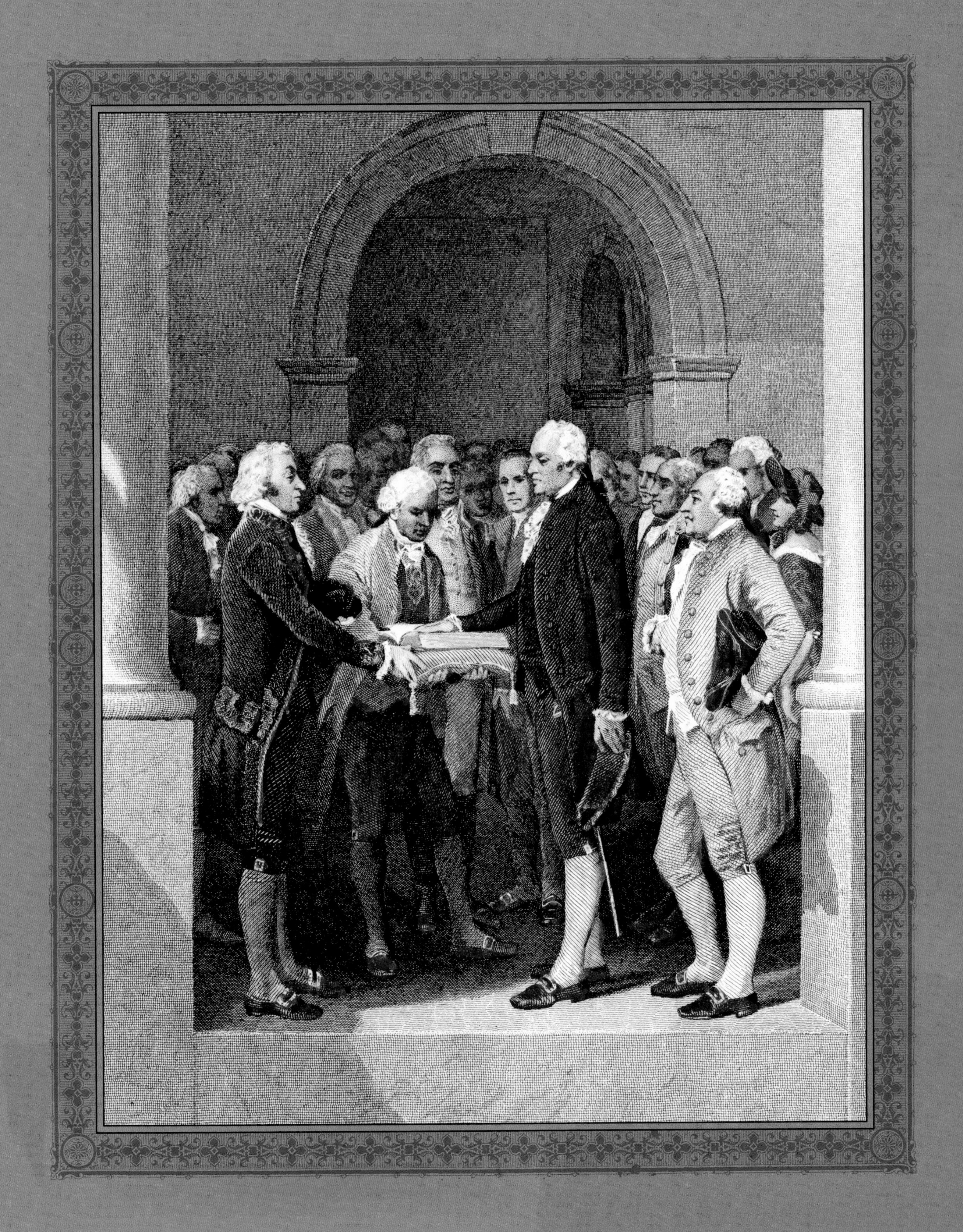

James Madison
(1751-1836)

In 1774, just after news of the Boston Tea Party galvanized the colonies, the man now called the Father of the Constitution wrote to a college friend. He briefly mentioned Boston and then breezily added, "But away with Politicks!" He was 22 at the time, two years out of the College of New Jersey (now Princeton University), and he had no idea what to do with his life.

James Madison had been born deep in the bosom of the Virginia aristocracy. His great-great-grandfather, a ship's carpenter, arrived in the mid-17th century a few decades after the colony was established. By the time James was born, the Madisons were wealthy planters, and as eldest son, James's fortunes were ensured. But the robust life of a planter, with its horse races, rounds of socializing, and attentions to a vast estate, were hardly conducive to a man whose "customary enjoyments" were "Solitude and Contemplation." Madison was scholarly, diminutive (five four), and sickly to the point of hypochondria. In fact, he decided not to go to the College of William and Mary in Williamsburg—the obvious choice—in part because the climate was said to be "unhealthy for persons going from a mountainous region." And besides, Williamsburg's student atmosphere, filled with drinking and card playing, was too boisterous for him.

Madison's college years in New Jersey were much to his liking, as they exposed him to the Enlightenment ideas he quickly embraced and to a world far beyond that of his home, Montpelier, and Virginia's planter society. But college did not point him to an occupation, and though he considered the law, he found the particular texts he attempted tedious. The other obvious occupation open to a man of his time and standing, the clergy, he found positively odious. And so he foundered. Even when patriotic fervor swept up other young men in their twenties, he was "restrained from entering into the military service by the unsettled state of his health and the discouraging feebleness of his constitution."

A miniature *of a young Madison at age 32 (above). Opposite: James Madison, the father of the Constitution and fourth President of the United Sates*

Then, in 1776, Madison found his true footing when he was elected to the Fifth Virginia Convention, charged with drafting a new government to replace the royal rule that was no more. That May he made his way to Williamsburg, and once there he felt his way carefully among the older, more seasoned men at the convention. George Mason, the chief architect of Virginia's new government, particularly impressed the shy young Madison, but he felt compelled to speak out on one of the issues Mason had woven into the Virginia Declaration of Rights, which the convention also produced. In the section dealing with religious freedom, Madison suggested that the wording "all men should enjoy the fullest toleration in the exercise of religion, according to the dictates of conscience . . ." be changed to "the full and free exercise of religion." In Virginia, where Anglicanism had long been the rule of the day, this was a subtle but radical step forward—to recognize an individual's liberty to choose his or her own faith.

In October Madison was back in Williamsburg as an elected member of the newly conceived Virginia House of Delegates, but he served only one year before losing his seat to a candidate who understood how necessary it was to entice voters to the polls with alcoholic libations on Election Day. It was a hard-won lesson that the ascetic Madison did not forget, and he obliged the voters in future races. In 1779, after serving on the Virginia Council of State, he was elected to the Continental Congress.

In Philadelphia Madison found himself in the midst of the dysfunctional, disunifying politics of the war years. He started taking careful notes of the congressional debates and served on numerous committees, giving him an intimate perspective on how threadbare the authority of Congress was—and, with it, the new Union. The experience led him to his life's work: He began to contemplate the issues of governance—what made it work, what worked against it, and what checks and balances it required.

Dolley Payne Madison *is one of the most beloved First Ladies in American history. She was a widow with a young son when she married James Madison, who was 17 years older than she, in 1794. By all accounts, their marriage was a very happy one.*

As the war drew to an end and members came and went, Madison continued on in the Confederation Congress, in which he had become a respected figure. He had no family commitments, business, farm, or other occupation to draw him away from public service. He could tend to the business of nation building. He stayed in Philadelphia for three and a half years before returning to Virginia, where he was soon back in the state legislature, which was as bankrupt and ineffective in its own way as the Continental Congress had been.

It was during this period that Madison conceived the idea of a federal convention to revisit the kind of governance the new nation would require if the states were truly to be bound together in union. A handful of other leaders also recognized the need for a meeting of national delegates, but would they come? Were the states committed enough to send them? Madison's fear that they weren't committed was born out when the poorly attended Annapolis Convention opened in September 1786 to reconsider commerce among the states. The 12 delegates from 5 states accomplished little, other than agreeing on the date for another convention to be held in Philadelphia the following spring. But in Annapolis, Madison found a group of compatriots as committed to nation building as he was, among them Alexander Hamilton.

The following spring Madison wrote his famous "Vices of the Political System of the United States," based on his experiences in state and federal government and on his own thinking. Chief among the vices were the "Failure of the States to comply with the Constitutional requisitions; Encroachments by the States on the federal authority; Violations of the law of nations and of treaties." He also began the outlines of a system of government he felt *would* work, and by May he was back in Philadelphia for what is now known as the Constitutional Convention. His original outline soon became the backbone of the Virginia Plan for national government, presented at the beginning of the convention. Many elements of the plan never made it into the Constitution, but Madison's overarching philosophy of governance did. Arguing forcefully against the complete independence of states, he said it would prove "utterly irreconcilable with the idea of an aggregate sovereignty." At the same time, he did not advocate

the dissolution of the states "into one simple republic." Instead, the "supremacy of national authority" had to be established, while the states maintained some integrity. It was a balancing act that the Constitution ultimately accomplished, and history attributes its paternity to Madison.

AN ADVOCATE *for a strong central government, James Madison put forth his views at the Virginia Constitutional Convention at Richmond in 1829.*

What Madison actually thought of the Constitution and its merits he set down in detail in the essays he contributed to Alexander Hamilton's project, *The Federalist.* Madison's masterpiece, *Federalist* no. 10, written in November 1787 "To the People of the State of New York," begins, "AMONG the numerous advantages promised by a well constructed Union, none deserves to be more accurately developed than its tendency to break and control the violence of faction . . . A republic, by which I mean a government in which the scheme of representation takes place, opens a different prospect, and promises the cure" to such factionalism. Madison concluded by assuring his readers that if they were truly republicans, they should join him "in cherishing the spirit and supporting the character of Federalists."

As 1788 opened, Madison was still a member of the Confederation Congress, operating under the Articles of Confederation, and he watched hopefully as state after state slowly but surely ratified the Constitution. He had tried mightily to turn New York sentiment toward the Constitution with his *Federalist* papers, and the following spring, he had to lobby for it just as hard at the Virginia ratifying convention, where the former Revolutionary firebrand, Patrick Henry, led the anti-Federalists in opposing ratification—or at the least requiring amendments to the existing document as a condition of ratification. Madison spoke out eloquently

THE WAR OF 1812 *was one of the major challenges Madison faced during his Presidency. This cartoon shows King George III of Britain wounded by James Madison, triumphant at the loss of British ships.*

at the convention in Richmond, and after weeks of debate, Virginia became the tenth state to ratify.

In the spring of 1789 Madison was back in New York as a newly elected member of the First Congress, after winning his seat over his opponent and friend, James Monroe. Madison knew what his first order of business had to be: He had to change the Constitution if he wanted to save it. The drumbeat for a new convention to reconsider it altogether had not died away, and the one remedy that might quell dissent was the addition of a bill of rights—something that Madison himself had opposed initially, since he believed that it was unnecessary and potentially dangerous. After all, he argued, "If an enumeration be made of our rights, will it not be implied, that every thing omitted, is given to the general government?" It was an intricate argument from the man who authored the U.S. Bill of Rights. They became the first ten amendments to the Constitution and part of Madison's abiding legacy.

Madison served in Congress until 1797, and during those years he and his old collaborator, Alexander Hamilton, became historic opponents, as Madison moved further and further from Hamilton's strong Federalist beliefs. In an era of nascent national politics, Madison became a consummate master of the game, and he and his longtime friend and political confidante, Thomas Jefferson, founded the Republican Party to counter the federal overreach they saw first in Hamilton's policies and then in John Adams's presidential administration.

In 1801 Thomas Jefferson succeeded Adams as third President, and during Jefferson's two terms, Madison was by his side as secretary of state, attempting to keep America neutral in the midst of the enveloping Napoleonic Wars. When Madison succeeded Jefferson as the nation's fourth President, those wars would sorely test his ideas of executive leadership. The Presidency was not a position to which Madison was well suited. He understood law, lawmaking, and legislation, but overt leadership had never been his strength. Now, as Britain and France tore at each other and threatened to engulf the fledgling United States in war, Madison foundered. His cabinet was weak and fractious, and the very factionalism he had always warned against had taken over Congress.

Even in the face of mounting hostilities with the old enemy, Britain—particularly British aggression against American ships and crews—Congress refused to adequately fund military preparedness. The situation looked bleak, with soldiers of the Revolution too old to fight again and the militias untrained and disorganized. Worse still, New England had no interest in fighting a war with Britain; Madison even worried that some of those states might secede from the Union and join British Canada. Yet, despite America's obvious weaknesses, on June 12, 1812, Madison signed a declaration of war with Britain.

The War of 1812 was an ignominious debacle for both sides, but particularly so for Madison, who stood by helpless as the British overran the new federal capital, Washington, and burned the President's House (White House) and the Capitol. If there was a hero, it was not Madison (though he did strap on pistols and ride out with the inexperienced militia). The romantic hero of the day was his wife, Dolley, the young widow he had married 20 years earlier. Mrs. Madison managed to save valuable papers and paintings by taking them with her as she fled.

When British soldiers *were poised to invade Washington, D.C., Dolley Madison saved many important documents (top), including the Declaration of Independence. On August 24, 1814, the British invaded Washington, D.C., and burned the White House (bottom), a low point during the short, inconclusive war.*

Madison's last duty to the nation was more tedious than exciting. In the years after he left the Presidency, he prepared for publication his notes on the Constitutional Convention. This remains the most complete record we have of the ideas and debates that created America.

Alexander Hamilton once said of Madison, his old collaborator turned opponent, that he was "uncorrupted and incorruptible." Hamilton also said that the fourth President was "very little acquainted with the world," and there was some truth to that. Madison lived all his days in the region between central Virginia and New York. He never went abroad, as he worried that such travel would compromise his fragile health. But if he was not bold or adventurous in his actions, he was daring in his intellect, in his exploration of a new way for people to govern themselves and to exist side by side in some harmony.

America's Founding Documents

The documents that now form the backbone of American thought were conceived in very different ways. The Declaration of Independence came mostly from the pen and mind of Thomas Jefferson and is infused with Enlightenment thinking. It was meant to be a philosophical statement about how humans and governments should interface. The Constitution, on the other hand, was intended to detail a system of laws that would make that interface fair and flexible. It took endless debates and many minds to create what, in the end, was a compromise document. To this day its meaning is interpreted in various, often conflicting ways. But the Founding Fathers themselves had never agreed, and that no doubt is the brilliance of the American way.

IN CONGRESS, JULY 4, 1776.

The unanimous Declaration of the thirteen united States of America,

When in the Course of human events, it becomes necessary for one people to dissolve the political bands which have connected them with another, and to assume among the powers of the earth, the separate and equal station to which the Laws of Nature and of Nature's God entitle them, a decent respect to the opinions of mankind requires that they should declare the causes which impel them to the separation. —— We hold these truths to be self-evident, that all men are created equal, that they are endowed by their Creator with certain unalienable Rights, that among these are Life, Liberty and the pursuit of Happiness. — That to secure these rights, Governments are instituted among Men, deriving their just powers from the consent of the governed, — That whenever any Form of Government becomes destructive of these ends, it is the Right of the People to alter or to abolish it, and to institute new Government, laying its foundation on such principles and organizing its powers in such form, as to them shall seem most likely to effect their Safety and Happiness. Prudence, indeed, will dictate that Governments long established should not be changed for light and transient causes; and accordingly all experience hath shewn, that mankind are more disposed to suffer, while evils are sufferable, than to right themselves by abolishing the forms to which they are accustomed. But when a long train of abuses and usurpations, pursuing invariably the same Object evinces a design to reduce them under absolute Despotism, it is their right, it is their duty, to throw off such Government, and to provide new Guards for their future security. — Such has been the patient sufferance of these Colonies; and such is now the necessity which constrains them to alter their former Systems of Government. The history of the present King of Great Britain is a history of repeated injuries and usurpations, all having in direct object the establishment of an absolute Tyranny over these States. To prove this, let Facts be submitted to a candid world. —— He has refused his Assent to Laws, the most wholesome and necessary for the public good. —— He has forbidden his Governors to pass Laws of immediate and pressing importance, unless suspended in their operation till his Assent should be obtained; and when so suspended, he has utterly neglected to attend to them. —— He has refused to pass other Laws for the accommodation of large districts of people, unless those people would relinquish the right of Representation in the Legislature, a right inestimable to them and formidable to tyrants only. —— He has called together legislative bodies at places unusual, uncomfortable, and distant from the depository of their public Records, for the sole purpose of fatiguing them into compliance with his measures. —— He has dissolved Representative Houses repeatedly, for opposing with manly firmness his invasions on the rights of the people. —— He has refused for a long time, after such dissolutions, to cause others to be elected; whereby the Legislative powers, incapable of Annihilation, have returned to the People at large for their exercise; the State remaining in the mean time exposed to all the dangers of invasion from without, and convulsions within. —— He has endeavoured to prevent the population of these States; for that purpose obstructing the Laws for Naturalization of Foreigners; refusing to pass others to encourage their migrations hither, and raising the conditions of new Appropriations of Lands. —— He has obstructed the Administration of Justice, by refusing his Assent to Laws for establishing Judiciary powers. —— He has made Judges dependent on his Will alone, for the tenure of their offices, and the amount and payment of their salaries. —— He has erected a multitude of New Offices, and sent hither swarms of Officers to harrass our people, and eat out their substance. —— He has kept among us, in times of peace, Standing Armies without the Consent of our legislatures. —— He has affected to render the Military independent of and superior to the Civil power. —— He has combined with others to subject us to a jurisdiction foreign to our constitution, and unacknowledged by our laws; giving his Assent to their Acts of pretended Legislation: — For Quartering large bodies of armed troops among us: — For protecting them, by a mock Trial, from punishment for any Murders which they should commit on the Inhabitants of these States: — For cutting off our Trade with all parts of the world: — For imposing Taxes on us without our Consent: — For depriving us in many cases, of the benefits of Trial by Jury: — For transporting us beyond Seas to be tried for pretended offences: — For abolishing the free System of English Laws in a neighbouring Province, establishing therein an Arbitrary government, and enlarging its Boundaries so as to render it at once an example and fit instrument for introducing the same absolute rule into these Colonies: — For taking away our Charters, abolishing our most valuable Laws, and altering fundamentally the Forms of our Governments: — For suspending our own Legislatures, and declaring themselves invested with power to legislate for us in all cases whatsoever. — He has abdicated Government here, by declaring us out of his Protection and waging War against us. —— He has plundered our seas, ravaged our Coasts, burnt our towns, and destroyed the lives of our people. —— He is at this time transporting large Armies of foreign Mercenaries to compleat the works of death, desolation and tyranny, already begun with circumstances of Cruelty & perfidy scarcely paralleled in the most barbarous ages, and totally unworthy the Head of a civilized nation. —— He has constrained our fellow Citizens taken Captive on the high Seas to bear Arms against their Country, to become the executioners of their friends and Brethren, or to fall themselves by their Hands. —— He has excited domestic insurrections amongst us, and has endeavoured to bring on the inhabitants of our frontiers, the merciless Indian Savages, whose known rule of warfare, is an undistinguished destruction of all ages, sexes and conditions. In every stage of these Oppressions We have Petitioned for Redress in the most humble terms: Our repeated Petitions have been answered only by repeated injury. A Prince, whose character is thus marked by every act which may define a Tyrant, is unfit to be the ruler of a free people. Nor have We been wanting in attentions to our Brittish brethren. We have warned them from time to time of attempts by their legislature to extend an unwarrantable jurisdiction over us. We have reminded them of the circumstances of our emigration and settlement here. We have appealed to their native justice and magnanimity, and we have conjured them by the ties of our common kindred to disavow these usurpations, which, would inevitably interrupt our connections and correspondence. They too have been deaf to the voice of justice and of consanguinity. We must, therefore, acquiesce in the necessity, which denounces our Separation, and hold them, as we hold the rest of mankind, Enemies in War, in Peace Friends. ——

We, therefore, the Representatives of the united States of America, in General Congress, Assembled, appealing to the Supreme Judge of the world for the rectitude of our intentions, do, in the Name, and by Authority of the good People of these Colonies, solemnly publish and declare, That these United Colonies are, and of Right ought to be Free and Independent States; that they are Absolved from all Allegiance to the British Crown, and that all political connection between them and the State of Great Britain, is and ought to be totally dissolved; and that as Free and Independent States, they have full Power to levy War, conclude Peace, contract Alliances, establish Commerce, and to do all other Acts and Things which Independent States may of right do. —— And for the support of this Declaration, with a firm reliance on the protection of divine Providence, we mutually pledge to each other our Lives, our Fortunes and our sacred Honor.

John Hancock

Button Gwinnett
Lyman Hall
Geo Walton.

Wm Hooper
Joseph Hewes,
John Penn

Edward Rutledge 1.

Thos Heyward Junr.
Thomas Lynch Junr.
Arthur Middleton

Samuel Chase
Wm Paca
Thos Stone
Charles Carroll of Carrollton

George Wythe
Richard Henry Lee
Th Jefferson
Benja Harrison
Thos Nelson jr.
Francis Lightfoot Lee
Carter Braxton

Robt Morris
Benjamin Rush
Benja Franklin
John Morton
Geo Clymer
Jas Smith
Geo. Taylor
James Wilson
Geo. Ross
Caesar Rodney
Geo Read
Tho M:Kean

Wm Floyd
Phil. Livingston
Frans Lewis
Lewis Morris

Richd Stockton
Jno Witherspoon
Fras Hopkinson
John Hart
Abra Clark

Josiah Bartlett
Wm Whipple
Saml Adams
John Adams
Robt Treat Paine
Elbridge Gerry
Step Hopkins
William Ellery
Roger Sherman
Saml Huntington
Wm Williams
Oliver Wolcott
Matthew Thornton

DECLARATION OF INDEPENDENCE

IN CONGRESS, JULY 4, 1776.

The unanimous Declaration of the thirteen united States of America,

When in the Course of human events, it becomes necessary for one people to dissolve the political bands which have connected them with another, and to assume among the powers of the earth, the separate and equal station to which the Laws of Nature and of Nature's God entitle them, a decent respect to the opinions of mankind requires that they should declare the causes which impel them to the separation.

We hold these truths to be self-evident, that all men are created equal, that they are endowed by their Creator with certain unalienable Rights, that among these are Life, Liberty and the pursuit of Happiness.—That to secure these rights, Governments are instituted among Men, deriving their just powers from the consent of the governed, —That whenever any Form of Government becomes destructive of these ends, it is the Right of the People to alter or to abolish it, and to institute new Government, laying its foundation on such principles and organizing its powers in such form, as to them shall seem most likely to effect their Safety and Happiness. Prudence, indeed, will dictate that Governments long established should not be changed for light and transient causes; and accordingly all experience hath shewn, that mankind are more disposed to suffer, while evils are sufferable, than to right themselves by abolishing the forms to which they are accustomed. But when a long train of abuses and usurpations, pursuing invariably the same Object evinces a design to reduce them under absolute Despotism, it is their right, it is their duty, to throw off such Government, and to provide new Guards for their future security.—Such has been the patient sufferance of these Colonies; and such is now the necessity which constrains them to alter their former Systems of Government. The history of the present King of Great Britain is a history of repeated injuries and usurpations, all having in direct object the establishment of an absolute Tyranny over these States. To prove this, let Facts be submitted to a candid world.

He has refused his Assent to Laws, the most wholesome and necessary for the public good. He has forbidden his Governors to pass Laws of immediate and pressing importance, unless suspended in their operation till his Assent should be obtained; and when so suspended, he has utterly neglected to attend to them. He has refused to pass other Laws for the accommodation of large districts of people, unless those people would relinquish the right of Representation in the Legislature, a right inestimable to them and formidable to tyrants only. He has called together legislative bodies at places unusual, uncomfortable, and distant from the depository of their public Records, for the sole purpose of fatiguing them into compliance with his measures. He has dissolved Representative Houses repeatedly, for opposing with manly firmness his invasions on the rights of the people. He has refused for a long time, after such dissolutions, to cause others to be elected; whereby the Legislative powers, incapable of Annihilation, have returned to the People at large for their exercise; the State remaining in the mean time exposed to all the dangers of invasion from without, and convulsions within. He has endeavoured to prevent the population of these States; for that purpose obstructing the Laws for Naturalization of Foreigners; refusing to pass others to encourage their migrations hither, and raising the conditions of new Appropriations of Lands. He has obstructed the Administration of Justice, by refusing his Assent to Laws for establishing Judiciary powers. He has made Judges dependent on his Will alone, for the tenure of their offices, and the amount and payment of their salaries. He has erected a multitude of New Offices, and sent hither swarms of Officers to harrass our people, and eat out their substance. He has kept among us, in times of peace, Standing Armies without the Consent of our legislatures. He has affected to render the Military independent of and superior to the Civil power. He has combined with others to subject us to a jurisdiction foreign to our constitution, and unacknowledged by our laws; giving his Assent to their Acts of pretended Legislation: For Quartering large bodies of armed troops among us: For protecting them, by a mock Trial, from punishment for any Murders which they should commit on the Inhabitants of these States: For cutting off our Trade with all parts of the world: For imposing Taxes on us without our Consent: For depriving us in many cases, of the benefits of Trial by Jury: For transporting us beyond Seas to be tried for pretended offences For abolishing the free System of English Laws in a neighbouring Province, establishing therein an Arbitrary government, and enlarging its Boundaries so as to render it at once an example and fit instrument for introducing the same absolute rule into these Colonies: For taking away our Charters, abolishing our most valuable Laws, and altering fundamentally the Forms of our Governments: For suspending our own Legislatures, and declaring themselves invested with power to legislate for us in all cases whatsoever. He has abdicated Government here, by declaring us out of his Protection and waging War against us. He has plundered our seas, ravaged our Coasts, burnt our towns, and destroyed the lives of our people. He is at this time transporting large Armies of foreign Mercenaries to compleat the works of death, desolation and tyranny, already begun with circumstances of Cruelty & perfidy scarcely paralleled in the most barbarous ages, and totally unworthy the Head of a civilized nation. He has constrained our fellow Citizens taken Captive on the high Seas to bear Arms against their Country, to become the executioners of their friends and Brethren, or to fall themselves by their Hands. He has excited domestic insurrections amongst us, and has endeavoured to bring on the inhabitants of our frontiers, the merciless Indian Savages, whose known rule of warfare, is an undistinguished destruction of all ages, sexes and conditions.

In every stage of these Oppressions We have Petitioned for Redress in the most humble terms: Our repeated Petitions have been answered only by repeated injury. A Prince whose character is thus marked by every act which may define a Tyrant, is unfit to be the ruler of a free people.

Nor have We been wanting in attentions to our Brittish brethren. We have warned them from time to time of attempts by their legislature to extend an unwarrantable jurisdiction over us. We have reminded them of the circumstances of our emigration and settlement here. We have appealed to their native justice and magnanimity, and we have conjured them by the ties of our common kindred to disavow these usurpations, which, would inevitably interrupt our connections and correspondence. They too have been deaf to the voice of justice and of consanguinity. We must, therefore, acquiesce in the necessity, which denounces our Separation, and hold them, as we hold the rest of mankind, Enemies in War, in Peace Friends.

We, therefore, the Representatives of the united States of America, in General Congress, Assembled, appealing to the Supreme Judge of the world for the rectitude of our intentions, do, in the Name, and by Authority of the good People of these Colonies, solemnly publish and declare, That these United Colonies are, and of Right ought to be Free and Independent States; that they are Absolved from all Allegiance to the British Crown, and that all political connection between them and the State of Great Britain, is and ought to be totally dissolved; and that as Free and Independent States, they have full Power to levy War, conclude Peace, contract Alliances, establish Commerce, and to do all other Acts and Things which Independent States may of right do. And for the support of this Declaration, with a firm reliance on the protection of divine Providence, we mutually pledge to each other our Lives, our Fortunes and our sacred Honor.

Original Constitution

Signed by Delegates to the Philadelphia Convention
September 17, 1787

We the People of the United States, in Order to form a more perfect Union, establish Justice, insure domestic Tranquility, provide for the common defence, promote the general Welfare, and secure the Blessings of Liberty to ourselves and our Posterity, do ordain and establish this Constitution for the United States of America.

Article. I.

Section. 1.

All legislative Powers herein granted shall be vested in a Congress of the United States, which shall consist of a Senate and House of Representatives.

Section. 2.

The House of Representatives shall be composed of Members chosen every second Year by the People of the several States, and the Electors in each State shall have the Qualifications requisite for Electors of the most numerous Branch of the State Legislature.

No Person shall be a Representative who shall not have attained to the Age of twenty five Years, and been seven Years a Citizen of the United States, and who shall not, when elected, be an Inhabitant of that State in which he shall be chosen.

Representatives and direct Taxes shall be apportioned among the several States which may be included within this Union, according to their respective Numbers, which shall be determined by adding to the whole Number of free Persons, including those bound to Service for a Term of Years, and excluding Indians not taxed, three fifths of all other Persons. The actual Enumeration shall be made within three Years after the first Meeting of the Congress of the United States, and within every subsequent Term of ten Years, in such Manner as they shall by Law direct. The Number of Representatives shall not exceed one for every thirty Thousand, but each State shall have at Least one Representative; and until such enumeration shall be made, the State of New Hampshire shall be entitled to chuse three, Massachusetts eight, Rhode-Island and Providence Plantations one, Connecticut five, New-York six, New Jersey four, Pennsylvania eight, Delaware one, Maryland six, Virginia ten, North Carolina five, South Carolina five, and Georgia three.

When vacancies happen in the Representation from any State, the Executive Authority thereof shall issue Writs of Election to fill such Vacancies.

The House of Representatives shall chuse their Speaker and other Officers; and shall have the sole Power of Impeachment.

Section. 3.

The Senate of the United States shall be composed of two Senators from each State, chosen by the Legislature thereof for six Years; and each Senator shall have one Vote.

Immediately after they shall be assembled in Consequence of the first Election, they shall be divided as equally as may be into three Classes. The Seats of the Senators of the first Class shall be vacated at the Expiration of the second Year, of the second Class at the Expiration of the fourth Year, and of the third Class at the Expiration of the sixth Year, so that one third may be chosen every second Year; and if Vacancies happen by Resignation, or otherwise, during the Recess of the Legislature of any State, the Executive thereof may make temporary Appointments until the next Meeting of the Legislature, which shall then fill such Vacancies.

No Person shall be a Senator who shall not have attained to the Age of thirty Years, and been nine Years a Citizen of the United States, and who shall not, when elected, be an Inhabitant of that State for which he shall be chosen.

The Vice President of the United States shall be President of the Senate, but shall have no Vote, unless they be equally divided.

The Senate shall chuse their other Officers, and also a President pro tempore, in the Absence of the Vice President, or when he shall exercise the Office of President of the United States.

The Senate shall have the sole Power to try all Impeachments. When sitting for that Purpose, they shall be on Oath or Affirmation. When the President of the United States is tried, the Chief Justice shall preside: And no Person shall be convicted without the Concurrence of two thirds of the Members present.

Judgment in Cases of Impeachment shall not extend further than to removal from Office, and disqualification to hold and enjoy any Office of honor, Trust or Profit under the United States: but the Party convicted shall nevertheless be liable and subject to Indictment, Trial, Judgment and Punishment, according to Law.

SECTION. 4.

The Times, Places and Manner of holding Elections for Senators and Representatives, shall be prescribed in each State by the Legislature thereof; but the Congress may at any time by Law make or alter such Regulations, except as to the Places of chusing Senators.

The Congress shall assemble at least once in every Year, and such Meeting shall be on the first Monday in December, unless they shall by Law appoint a different Day.

SECTION. 5.

Each House shall be the Judge of the Elections, Returns and Qualifications of its own Members, and a Majority of each shall constitute a Quorum to do Business; but a smaller Number may adjourn from day to day, and may be authorized to compel the Attendance of absent Members, in such Manner, and under such Penalties as each House may provide.

Each House may determine the Rules of its Proceedings, punish its Members for disorderly Behaviour, and, with the Concurrence of two thirds, expel a Member.

Each House shall keep a Journal of its Proceedings, and from time to time publish the same, excepting such Parts as may in their Judgment require Secrecy; and the Yeas and Nays of the Members of either House on any question shall, at the Desire of one fifth of those Present, be entered on the Journal.

Neither House, during the Session of Congress, shall, without the Consent of the other, adjourn for more than three days, nor to any other Place than that in which the two Houses shall be sitting.

SECTION. 6.

The Senators and Representatives shall receive a Compensation for their Services, to be ascertained by Law, and paid out of the Treasury of the United States. They shall in all Cases, except Treason, Felony and Breach of the Peace, be privileged from Arrest during their Attendance at the Session of their respective Houses, and in going to and returning from the same; and for any Speech or Debate in either House, they shall not be questioned in any other Place.

No Senator or Representative shall, during the Time for which he was elected, be appointed to any civil Office under the Authority of the United States, which shall have been created, or the Emoluments whereof shall have been encreased during such time; and no Person holding any Office under the United States, shall be a Member of either House during his Continuance in Office.

SECTION. 7.

All Bills for raising Revenue shall originate in the House of Representatives; but the Senate may propose or concur with Amendments as on other Bills.

Every Bill which shall have passed the House of Representatives and the Senate, shall, before it become a Law, be presented to the President of the United States: If he approve he shall sign it, but if not he shall return it, with his Objections to that House in which it shall have originated, who shall enter the Objections at large on their Journal, and proceed to reconsider it. If after such Reconsideration two thirds of that House shall agree to pass the Bill, it shall be sent, together with the Objections, to the other House, by which it shall likewise be reconsidered, and if approved by two thirds of that House, it shall become a Law. But in all such Cases the Votes of both Houses shall be determined by yeas and Nays, and the Names of the Persons voting for and against the Bill shall be entered on the Journal of each House respectively. If any Bill shall not be returned by the President within ten Days (Sundays excepted) after it shall have been presented to him, the Same shall be a Law, in like Manner as if he had signed it, unless the Congress by their Adjournment prevent its Return, in which Case it shall not be a Law.

Every Order, Resolution, or Vote to which the Concurrence of the Senate and House of Representatives may be necessary (except on a question of Adjournment) shall be presented to the President of the United States; and before the Same shall take Effect, shall be approved by him, or being disapproved by him, shall be repassed by two thirds of the Senate and House of Representatives, according to the Rules and Limitations prescribed in the Case of a Bill.

SECTION. 8.

The Congress shall have Power To lay and collect Taxes, Duties, Imposts and Excises, to pay the Debts and provide for the common Defence and general Welfare of the United States; but all Duties, Imposts and Excises shall be uniform throughout the United States;

To borrow Money on the credit of the United States;

To regulate Commerce with foreign Nations, and among the several States, and with the Indian Tribes;

To establish an uniform Rule of Naturalization, and uniform Laws on the subject of Bankruptcies throughout the United States;

To coin Money, regulate the Value thereof, and of foreign Coin, and fix the Standard of Weights and Measures;

To provide for the Punishment of counterfeiting the Securities and current Coin of the United States;

To establish Post Offices and post Roads;

To promote the Progress of Science and useful Arts, by securing for limited Times to Authors and Inventors the exclusive Right to their respective Writings and Discoveries;

To constitute Tribunals inferior to the supreme Court;

To define and punish Piracies and Felonies committed on the high Seas, and Offences against the Law of Nations;

To declare War, grant Letters of Marque and Reprisal, and make Rules concerning Captures on Land and Water;

To raise and support Armies, but no Appropriation of Money to that Use shall be for a longer Term than two Years;

To provide and maintain a Navy;

To make Rules for the Government and Regulation of the land and naval Forces;

To provide for calling forth the Militia to execute the Laws of the Union, suppress Insurrections and repel Invasions;

To provide for organizing, arming, and disciplining, the Militia, and for governing such Part of them as may be employed in the Service of the United States, reserving to the States respectively, the Appointment of the Officers, and the Authority of training the Militia according to the discipline prescribed by Congress;

To exercise exclusive Legislation in all Cases whatsoever, over such District (not exceeding ten Miles square) as may, by Cession of particular States, and the Acceptance of Congress, become the Seat of the Government of the United States, and to exercise like Authority over all Places purchased by the Consent of the Legislature of the State in which the Same shall be, for the Erection of Forts, Magazines, Arsenals, dock-Yards, and other needful Buildings;—And

To make all Laws which shall be necessary and proper for carrying into Execution the foregoing Powers, and all other Powers vested by this Constitution in the Government of the United States, or in any Department or Officer thereof.

SECTION. 9.

The Migration or Importation of such Persons as any of the States now existing shall think proper to admit, shall not be prohibited by the Congress prior to the Year one thousand eight hundred and eight, but a Tax or duty may be imposed on such Importation, not exceeding ten dollars for each Person.

The Privilege of the Writ of Habeas Corpus shall not be suspended, unless when in Cases of Rebellion or Invasion the public Safety may require it.

No Bill of Attainder or ex post facto Law shall be passed.

No Capitation, or other direct, Tax shall be laid, unless in Proportion to the Census or enumeration herein before directed to be taken.

No Tax or Duty shall be laid on Articles exported from any State.

No Preference shall be given by any Regulation of Commerce or Revenue to the Ports of one State over those of another; nor shall Vessels bound to, or from, one State, be obliged to enter, clear, or pay Duties in another.

No Money shall be drawn from the Treasury, but in Consequence of Appropriations made by Law; and a regular Statement and Account of the Receipts and Expenditures of all public Money shall be published from time to time.

No Title of Nobility shall be granted by the United States: And no Person holding any Office of Profit or Trust under them, shall, without the Consent of the Congress, accept of any present, Emolument, Office, or Title, of any kind whatever, from any King, Prince, or foreign State.

SECTION. 10.

No State shall enter into any Treaty, Alliance, or Confederation; grant Letters of Marque and Reprisal; coin Money; emit Bills of Credit; make any Thing but gold and silver Coin a Tender in Payment of Debts; pass any Bill of Attainder, ex post facto Law, or Law impairing the Obligation of Contracts, or grant any Title of Nobility.

No State shall, without the Consent of the Congress, lay any Imposts or Duties on Imports or Exports, except what may be absolutely necessary for executing it's inspection Laws: and the net Produce of all Duties and Imposts, laid by any State on Imports or Exports, shall be for the Use of the Treasury of the United States; and all such Laws shall be subject to the Revision and Controul of the Congress.

No State shall, without the Consent of Congress, lay any Duty of Tonnage, keep Troops, or Ships of War in time of Peace, enter into any Agreement or Compact with another State, or with a foreign Power, or engage in War, unless actually invaded, or in such imminent Danger as will not admit of delay.

ARTICLE. II.

SECTION. 1.

The executive Power shall be vested in a President of the United States of America. He shall hold his Office during the Term of four Years, and, together with the Vice President, chosen for the same Term, be elected, as follows:

Each State shall appoint, in such Manner as the Legislature thereof may direct, a Number of Electors, equal to the whole Number of Senators and Representatives to which the State may be entitled in the Congress: but no Senator or Representative, or Person holding an Office of Trust or Profit under the United States, shall be appointed an Elector.

The Electors shall meet in their respective States, and vote by Ballot for two Persons, of whom one at least shall not be an Inhabitant of the same State with themselves. And they shall make a List of all the Persons voted for, and of the Number of Votes for each; which List they shall sign and certify, and transmit sealed to the Seat of the Government of the United States, directed to the President of the Senate. The President of the Senate shall, in the Presence of the Senate and House of Representatives, open all the Certificates, and the Votes shall then be counted. The Person having the greatest Number of Votes shall be the President, if such Number be a Majority of the whole Number of Electors appointed; and if there be more than one who have such Majority, and have an equal Number of Votes, then the House of Representatives shall immediately chuse by Ballot one of them for President; and if no Person have a Majority, then from the five highest on the List the said House shall in like Manner chuse the President. But in chusing the President, the Votes shall be taken by States, the Representation from each State having one Vote; A quorum for this purpose shall consist of a Member or Members from two thirds of the States, and a Majority of all the States shall be necessary to a Choice. In every Case, after the Choice of the President, the Person having the greatest Number of Votes of the Electors shall be the Vice President. But if there should remain two or more who have equal Votes, the Senate shall chuse from them by Ballot the Vice President.

The Congress may determine the Time of chusing the Electors, and the Day on which they shall give their Votes; which Day shall be the same throughout the United States.

No Person except a natural born Citizen, or a Citizen of the United States, at the time of the Adoption of this Constitution, shall be eligible to the Office of President; neither shall any Person be eligible to that Office who shall not have attained to the Age of thirty five Years, and been fourteen Years a Resident within the United States.

In Case of the Removal of the President from Office, or of his Death, Resignation, or Inability to discharge the Powers and Duties of the said Office, the Same shall devolve on the Vice President, and the Congress may by Law provide for the Case of Removal, Death, Resignation or Inability, both of the President and Vice President, declaring what Officer shall then act as President, and such Officer shall act accordingly, until the Disability be removed, or a President shall be elected.

The President shall, at stated Times, receive for his Services, a Compensation, which shall neither be increased nor diminished during the Period for which he shall have been elected, and he shall not receive within that Period any other Emolument from the United States, or any of them.

Before he enter on the Execution of his Office, he shall take the following Oath or Affirmation:—"I do solemnly swear (or affirm) that I will faithfully execute the Office of President of the United States, and will to the best of my Ability, preserve, protect and defend the Constitution of the United States."

SECTION. 2.

The President shall be Commander in Chief of the Army and Navy of the United States, and of the Militia of the several States, when called into the actual Service of the United States; he may require the Opinion, in writing, of the principal Officer in each of the executive Departments, upon any Subject relating to the Duties of their respective Offices, and he shall have Power to grant Reprieves and Pardons for Offences against the United States, except in Cases of Impeachment.

He shall have Power, by and with the Advice and Consent of the Senate, to make Treaties, provided two thirds of the Senators present concur; and he shall nominate, and by and with the Advice and Consent of the Senate, shall appoint Ambassadors, other public Ministers and Consuls, Judges of the supreme Court, and all other Officers of the United States, whose Appointments are not herein otherwise provided for, and which shall be established by Law: but the Congress may by Law vest the Appointment of such inferior Officers, as they think proper, in the President alone, in the Courts of Law, or in the Heads of Departments.

The President shall have Power to fill up all Vacancies that may happen during the Recess of the Senate, by granting Commissions which shall expire at the End of their next Session.

SECTION. 3.

He shall from time to time give to the Congress Information of the State of the Union, and recommend to their Consideration such Measures as he shall judge necessary and expedient; he may, on extraordinary Occasions, convene both Houses, or either of them, and in Case of Disagreement between them, with Respect to the Time of Adjournment, he may adjourn them to such Time as he shall think proper; he shall receive Ambassadors and other public Ministers; he shall take Care that the Laws be faithfully executed, and shall Commission all the Officers of the United States.

SECTION. 4.

The President, Vice President and all civil Officers of the United States, shall be removed from Office on Impeachment for, and Conviction of, Treason, Bribery, or other high Crimes and Misdemeanors.

ARTICLE III.

SECTION. 1.

The judicial Power of the United States shall be vested in one supreme Court, and in such inferior Courts as the Congress may from time to time ordain and establish. The Judges, both of the supreme and inferior Courts, shall hold their Offices during good Behaviour, and shall, at stated Times, receive for their Services a Compensation, which shall not be diminished during their Continuance in Office.

SECTION. 2.

The judicial Power shall extend to all Cases, in Law and Equity, arising under this Constitution, the Laws of the United States, and Treaties made, or which shall be made, under their Authority;—to all Cases affecting Ambassadors, other public Ministers and Consuls;—to all Cases of admiralty and maritime Jurisdiction;—to Controversies to which the United States shall be a Party;—to Controversies between two or more States;—between a State and Citizens of another State,—between Citizens of different States,—between Citizens of the same State claiming Lands under Grants of different States, and between a State, or the Citizens thereof, and foreign States, Citizens or Subjects.

In all Cases affecting Ambassadors, other public Ministers and Consuls, and those in which a State shall be Party, the supreme Court shall have original Jurisdiction. In all the other Cases before mentioned, the supreme Court shall have appellate Jurisdiction, both as to Law and Fact, with such Exceptions, and under such Regulations as the Congress shall make.

The Trial of all Crimes, except in Cases of Impeachment, shall be by Jury; and such Trial shall be held in the State where the said Crimes shall have been committed; but when not committed within any State, the Trial shall be at such Place or Places as the Congress may by Law have directed.

Section. 3.

Treason against the United States, shall consist only in levying War against them, or in adhering to their Enemies, giving them Aid and Comfort. No Person shall be convicted of Treason unless on the Testimony of two Witnesses to the same overt Act, or on Confession in open Court.

The Congress shall have Power to declare the Punishment of Treason, but no Attainder of Treason shall work Corruption of Blood, or Forfeiture except during the Life of the Person attainted.

Article. IV.

Section. 1.

Full Faith and Credit shall be given in each State to the public Acts, Records, and judicial Proceedings of every other State. And the Congress may by general Laws prescribe the Manner in which such Acts, Records and Proceedings shall be proved, and the Effect thereof.

Section. 2.

The Citizens of each State shall be entitled to all Privileges and Immunities of Citizens in the several States.

A Person charged in any State with Treason, Felony, or other Crime, who shall flee from Justice, and be found in another State, shall on Demand of the executive Authority of the State from which he fled, be delivered up, to be removed to the State having Jurisdiction of the Crime.

No Person held to Service or Labour in one State, under the Laws thereof, escaping into another, shall, in Consequence of any Law or Regulation therein, be discharged from such Service or Labour, but shall be delivered up on Claim of the Party to whom such Service or Labour may be due.

Section. 3.

New States may be admitted by the Congress into this Union; but no new State shall be formed or erected within the Jurisdiction of any other State; nor any State be formed by the Junction of two or more States, or Parts of States, without the Consent of the Legislatures of the States concerned as well as of the Congress.

The Congress shall have Power to dispose of and make all needful Rules and Regulations respecting the Territory or other Property belonging to the United States; and nothing in this Constitution shall be so construed as to Prejudice any Claims of the United States, or of any particular State.

Section. 4.

The United States shall guarantee to every State in this Union a Republican Form of Government, and shall protect each of them against Invasion; and on Application of the Legislature, or of the Executive (when the Legislature cannot be convened), against domestic Violence.

Article. V.

The Congress, whenever two thirds of both Houses shall deem it necessary, shall propose Amendments to this Constitution, or, on the Application of the Legislatures of two thirds of the several States, shall call a Convention for proposing Amendments, which, in either Case, shall be valid to all Intents and Purposes, as Part of this Constitution, when ratified by the Legislatures of three fourths of the several States, or by Conventions in three fourths thereof, as the one or the other Mode of Ratification may be proposed by the Congress; Provided that no Amendment which may be made prior to the Year One thousand eight hundred and eight shall in any Manner affect the first and fourth Clauses in the Ninth Section of the first Article; and that no State, without its Consent, shall be deprived of its equal Suffrage in the Senate.

Article. VI.

All Debts contracted and Engagements entered into, before the Adoption of this Constitution, shall be as valid against the United States under this Constitution, as under the Confederation.

This Constitution, and the Laws of the United States which shall be made in Pursuance thereof; and all Treaties made, or which shall be made, under the Authority of the United States, shall be the supreme Law of the Land; and the Judges in every State shall be bound thereby, any Thing in the Constitution or Laws of any State to the Contrary notwithstanding.

The Senators and Representatives before mentioned, and the Members of the several State Legislatures, and all executive and judicial Officers, both of the United States and of the several States, shall be bound by Oath or Affirmation, to support this Constitution; but no religious Test shall ever be required as a Qualification to any Office or public Trust under the United States.

Article. VII.

The Ratification of the Conventions of nine States, shall be sufficient for the Establishment of this Constitution between the States so ratifying the Same.

The Word, "the," being interlined between the seventh and eighth Lines of the first Page, the Word "Thirty" being partly written on an Erazure in the fifteenth Line of the first Page, The Words "is tried" being interlined between the thirty second and thirty third Lines of the first Page and the Word "the" being interlined between the forty third and forty fourth Lines of the second Page.

Attest William Jackson Secretary

done in Convention by the Unanimous Consent of the States present the Seventeenth Day of September in the Year of our Lord one thousand seven hundred and Eighty seven and of the Independance of the United States of America the Twelfth In witness whereof We have hereunto subscribed our Names.

BILL OF RIGHTS

(AMENDMENTS I TO X TO THE CONSTITUTION)

Congress of the United States begun and held at the City of New-York, on Wednesday the fourth of March, one thousand seven hundred and eighty nine.

THE Conventions of a number of the States, having at the time of their adopting the Constitution, expressed a desire, in order to prevent misconstruction or abuse of its powers, that further declaratory and restrictive clauses should be added: And as extending the ground of public confidence in the Government, will best ensure the beneficent ends of its institution.

RESOLVED by the Senate and House of Representatives of the United States of America, in Congress assembled, two thirds of both Houses concurring, that the following Articles be proposed to the Legislatures of the several States, as amendments to the Constitution of the United States, all, or any of which Articles, when ratified by three fourths of the said Legislatures, to be valid to all intents and purposes, as part of the said Constitution; viz.

ARTICLES in addition to, and Amendment of the Constitution of the United States of America, proposed by Congress, and ratified by the Legislatures of the several States, pursuant to the fifth Article of the original Constitution.

Note: The following text is a transcription of the first ten amendments to the Constitution in their original form. These amendments were ratified December 15, 1791, and form what is known as the "Bill of Rights."

AMENDMENT I

Congress shall make no law respecting an establishment of religion, or prohibiting the free exercise thereof; or abridging the freedom of speech, or of the press; or the right of the people peaceably to assemble, and to petition the Government for a redress of grievances.

AMENDMENT II

A well regulated Militia, being necessary to the security of a free State, the right of the people to keep and bear Arms, shall not be infringed.

AMENDMENT III

No Soldier shall, in time of peace be quartered in any house, without the consent of the Owner, nor in time of war, but in a manner to be prescribed by law.

AMENDMENT IV

The right of the people to be secure in their persons, houses, papers, and effects, against unreasonable searches and seizures, shall not be violated, and no Warrants shall issue, but upon probable cause, supported by Oath or affirmation, and particularly describing the place to be searched, and the persons or things to be seized.

AMENDMENT V

No person shall be held to answer for a capital, or otherwise infamous crime, unless on a presentment or indictment of a Grand Jury, except in cases arising in the land or naval forces, or in the Militia, when in actual service in time of War or public danger; nor shall any person be subject for the same offence to be twice put in jeopardy of life or limb; nor shall be compelled in any criminal case to be a witness against himself, nor be deprived of life, liberty, or property, without due process of law; nor shall private property be taken for public use, without just compensation.

AMENDMENT VI

In all criminal prosecutions, the accused shall enjoy the right to a speedy and public trial, by an impartial jury of the State and district wherein the crime shall have been committed, which district shall have been previously ascertained by law, and to be informed of the nature and cause of the accusation; to be confronted with the witnesses against him; to have compulsory process for obtaining witnesses in his favor, and to have the Assistance of Counsel for his defence.

AMENDMENT VII

In Suits at common law, where the value in controversy shall exceed twenty dollars, the right of trial by jury shall be preserved, and no fact tried by a jury, shall be otherwise re-examined in any Court of the United States, than according to the rules of the common law.

AMENDMENT VIII

Excessive bail shall not be required, nor excessive fines imposed, nor cruel and unusual punishments inflicted.

AMENDMENT IX

The enumeration in the Constitution, of certain rights, shall not be construed to deny or disparage others retained by the people.

AMENDMENT X

The powers not delegated to the United States by the Constitution, nor prohibited by it to the States, are reserved to the States respectively, or to the people

TIME LINE OF SELECTED KEY DATES

1763

October 7 Royal Proclamation of 1763

1764

April 5 The Sugar Act

September 1 The Currency Act

1765

March 22 The Stamp Act

March 24 The Quartering Act of 1765

October 7–25 The Stamp Act Congress

1767

June 29 The Townshend Revenue Act

1770

March 5 The Boston Massacre

1773

December 16 The Boston Tea Party

1774

March 31–June 22 The so-called Intolerable Acts

September 5–October 26 The First Continental Congress meets in Philadelphia and executes the Declaration of Colonial Rights

1775

March 23 Patrick Henry's speech: "Give me liberty or give me death"

April 18 Paul Revere's ride

April 19 Clashes at Lexington and Concord

May 10 Benedict Arnold, Ethan Allen, and the Green Mountain Boys take Fort Ticonderoga

May 10 The Second Continental Congress meets in Philadelphia

June 17 Battles of Bunker and Breed's Hills

December 11 Patriots rout Loyalist troops and burn Norfolk, Virginia

1776

January 15 Thomas Paine's *Common Sense* published

March 17 The British evacuate Boston

March 18 Parliament repeals the Stamp Act

March 18 Adoption of the Declaratory Act

June 12 The Virginia Declaration of Rights

June 29 Virginia's first constitution adopted

June 28 Patriots defeat the British Navy at Fort Moultrie, South Carolina

July 4 Congress adopts the Declaration of Independence

August 27 Redcoats defeat Washington's army in the Battle of Long Island; Washington's army escapes at night

September 15 British occupy New York City

September 16 Generals George Washington, Nathanael Greene, and Israel Putnam hold their ground at the Battle of Harlem Heights

October 28 The Americans retreat from White Plains, New York, into New Jersey

November 16 Hessians capture Fort Washington, New York

November 20 Cornwallis's troops take Fort Lee, New Jersey, from Nathanael Greene

December 26 Washington crosses the Delaware and captures Trenton from Hessians

1777

September 11 British victorious at Brandywine, Pennsylvania

September 26 General Howe occupies Philadelphia

October 17 General Burgoyne surrenders to General Gates at Saratoga, New York

1778

February 6 The United States and France sign a treaty of alliance

June 18 British withdraw from Philadelphia and return to New York

June 19 Washington's forces leave Valley Forge

December 29 British occupy Savannah, Georgia

1779

June 21 Spain declares war on Great Britain

September 23 John Paul Jones, aboard the *Bonhomme Richard,* captures British man-of-war *Serapis*

September 28 The Tappan Massacre

November–June 23, 1780 Washington's second winter at Morristown, New Jersey

1780

September 23 Benedict Arnold's treason exposed

October 14 Nathanael Greene becomes commander of the Southern Army

1781

January 17 Gen. Daniel Morgan defeats Banastre Tarleton at Cowpens, South Carolina

March 2 Articles of Confederation adopted

September 15 French fleet drives British naval force from Chesapeake Bay

October 19 Cornwallis surrenders British forces at Yorktown, Virginia

1782

March 20 Lord North resigns as British prime minister

November 30 British and Americans sign Preliminary Articles of Peace

1783

September 3 The United States and Great Britain sign the Treaty of Paris

December 23 Washington resigns as commander in chief of the Continental Army

1787

May 25–September 17 Philadelphia Convention members craft the U.S. Constitution

1788

June 21 U.S. Constitution adopted

1789

April 30 George Washington sworn in as the first President of the United States

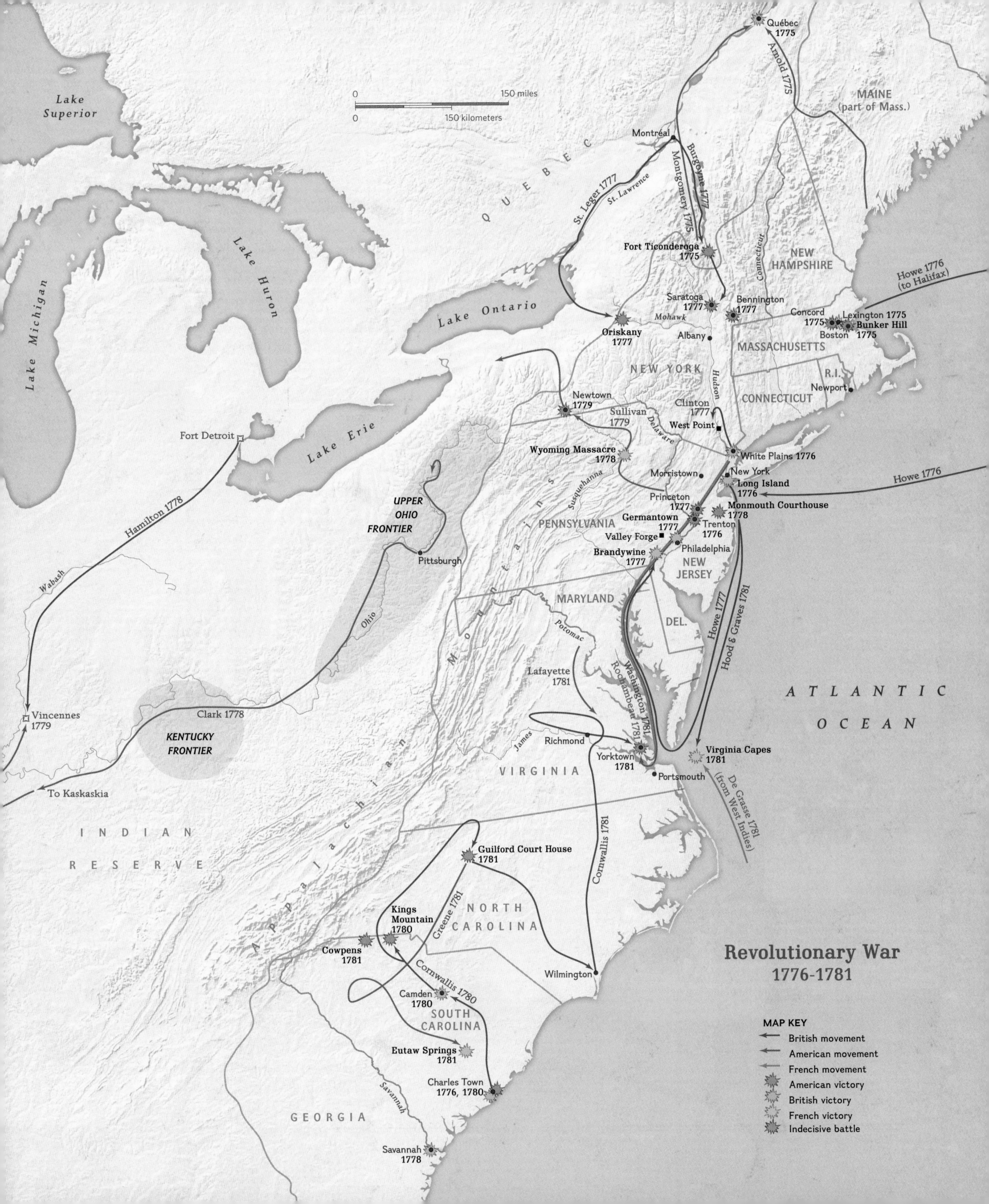

Revolutionary War
1776-1781
MAP KEY
British movement
American movement
French movement
American victory
British victory
French victory
Indecisive battle
0
150 miles
0
150 kilometers
Lake Superior
Lake Michigan
Lake Huron
Lake Ontario
Lake Erie
QUEBEC
MAINE (part of Mass.)
NEW HAMPSHIRE
MASSACHUSETTS
R.I.
CONNECTICUT
NEW YORK
PENNSYLVANIA
NEW JERSEY
MARYLAND
DEL.
VIRGINIA
NORTH CAROLINA
SOUTH CAROLINA
GEORGIA
INDIAN RESERVE
ATLANTIC OCEAN
UPPER OHIO FRONTIER
KENTUCKY FRONTIER
Appalachian Mountains
Québec 1775
Arnold 1775
Montréal
Burgoyne 1777
Montgomery 1775
St. Leger 1777
St. Lawrence
Fort Ticonderoga 1775
Connecticut
Saratoga 1777
Bennington 1777
Howe 1776 (to Halifax)
Concord 1775
Lexington 1775
Bunker Hill 1775
Boston
Mohawk
Oriskany 1777
Albany
Hudson
Newport
Newtown 1779
Sullivan 1779
Clinton 1777
West Point
Delaware
Wyoming Massacre 1778
White Plains 1776
Morristown
New York
Long Island 1776
Howe 1776
Susquehanna
Princeton 1777
Monmouth Courthouse 1778
Germantown 1777
Trenton 1776
Valley Forge
Philadelphia
Brandywine 1777
Fort Detroit
Hamilton 1778
Wabash
Pittsburgh
Ohio
Vincennes 1779
Clark 1778
To Kaskaskia
Potomac
Lafayette 1781
Washington 1781
Rochambeau 1781
Howe 1777
Hood & Graves 1781
James
Richmond
Yorktown 1781
Virginia Capes 1781
Portsmouth
De Grasse 1781 (from West Indies)
Cornwallis 1781
Guilford Court House 1781
Greene 1781
Kings Mountain 1780
Cowpens 1781
Wilmington
Cornwallis 1780
Camden 1780
Eutaw Springs 1781
Charles Town 1776, 1780
Savannah
Savannah 1778

Allen, Thomas B. *Tories: Fighting for the King in America's First Civil War.* New York: Harper, 2010.

Bailyn, Bernard. *The Ideological Origins of the American Revolution.* Cambridge, MA: Belknap Press, 1992.

Brands, H. W. *The First American: The Life and Times of Benjamin Franklin.* New York: Doubleday, 2000.

Buchanan, John. *The Road to Guilford Courthouse: The American Revolution in the Carolinas.* Hoboken, NJ: Wiley, 1997.

Chernow, Ron. *Alexander Hamilton.* New York: Penguin, 2004.

——. *Washington: A Life.* New York: Penguin, 2010.

Commager, Henry Steele, and Richard B. Morris, eds. *The Spirit of Seventy-Six: The Story of the American Revolution as Told by Participants.* Indianapolis: Bobbs-Merrill, 1958.

Davis, Burke. *The Campaign That Won America: The Story of Yorktown.* Newport News, VA: Daily Press, 1970.

Fenn, Elizabeth. *Pox Americana: The Great Smallpox Epidemic of 1775–82.* New York: Hill & Wang, 2002.

Ferling, John. *Almost a Miracle: The American Victory in the War of Independence.* New York: Oxford University Press, 2009.

——. *A Leap in the Dark: The Struggle to Create the American Republic.* New York: Oxford University Press, 2004.

Fischer, David Hackett. *Paul Revere's Ride.* New York: Oxford University Press, 1994.

——. *Washington's Crossing.* New York: Oxford University Press, 2004.

Franklin, Benjamin. *The Autobiography of Benjamin Franklin and Other Writings.* New York: Penguin, 1986.

Hamilton, Alexander, James Madison, and John Jay. *The Federalist Papers.* Edited by Richard Beeman. New York: Penguin, 2012.

Isaacson, Walter. *Benjamin Franklin: An American Life.* New York: Simon & Schuster, 2003.

Jefferson, Thomas. *The Portable Thomas Jefferson.* Edited by Merrill D. Peterson. New York: Penguin, 1977.

Malone, Dumas, and Merrill D. Peterson. *Thomas Jefferson: A Brief Biography.* Chapel Hill: University of North Carolina Press, 2001.

McCullough, David. *John Adams.* New York: Simon & Schuster, 2001.

——. *1776.* New York: Simon & Schuster, 2005.

Middlekauff, Robert. *The Glorious Cause: The American Revolution, 1763–1789.* New York: Oxford University Press, 2007.

Morgan, Edmund S. *The Birth of the Republic, 1763–89.* University of Chicago Press, 1993.

Nelson, Craig. *Thomas Paine: Enlightenment, Revolution, and the Birth of the Modern Nation.* New York: Viking, 2006.

Paine, Thomas. *Collected Writings.* CreateSpace Independent Publishing Platform, 2013.

Peterson, Merrill D. *Thomas Jefferson and the New Nation: A Biography.* New York: Oxford University Press, 1970.

Rakove, Jack. *Declaring Rights: A Brief History With Documents.* Boston: Bedford/St. Martin's, 1997.

——. *James Madison and the Creation of the American Republic.* New York: Library of America, 2006.

Rutland, Robert. *James Madison: The Founding Father.* New York: Atheneum, 1987.

Selby, John E. *Revolution in Virginia.* Williamsburg: University of Virginia Press, 2007.

Tarleton, Banastre. *A History of the Campaigns of 1780 and 1781, in the Southern Provinces of North America.* Dublin: 1787. babel.hathitrust.org/cgi/pt?id=mdp.39015063754298

Thomas, Evan. *John Paul Jones: Sailor, Hero, Father of the American Navy.* New York: Simon & Schuster, 2004.

Thompson, John. *The Revolutionary War.* Washington, DC: National Geographic, 2001.

Wiencek, Henry. *Master of the Mountain: Thomas Jefferson and His Slaves.* New York: Farrar, Straus and Giroux, 2012.

Wood, Gordon. *The American Revolution.* New York: Modern Library, 2003.

——. *The Radicalism of the American Revolution.* New York: Vintage, 1993.

Woolhouse, Roger. *Locke: A Biography.* New York: Cambridge University Press, 2007.

Map Sources

Barnes, Ian. *The Historical Atlas of the American Revolution.* New York: Routledge, 2000.

Esposito, Vincent J., ed. *The West Point Atlas of American Wars, Vol. 1 (1689–1900).* New York: Frederick A. Praeger, Publishers, 1959.

Kagan, Hilde Heun, ed. *The American Heritage Pictorial Atlas of United States History.* New York: American Heritage Publishing Co., 1966.

National Park Service, U.S. Department of the Interior. "American Revolution at a Glance."

National Park Service, U.S. Department of the Interior. Minute Man National Historical Park. "Lexington and Concord: A Legacy of Conflict." www.digitalhistory.uh.edu/active_learning/explorations/revolution/lexington_concord_lesson.pdf

National Geographic Society. *Historical Atlas of the United States* (revised edition). Washington, D.C., 1993.

Perry-Castañeda Library Map Collection. University of Texas Libraries, The University of Texas at Austin. www.lib.utexas.edu/maps/

United States Geological Survey, U.S. Department of the Interior. *The National Atlas of the United States of America.* Washington, D.C., 1970.

Ward, Sir Adolphus William, et al., eds. *The Cambridge Modern History Atlas.* London: Cambridge University Press, 1912.

Illustrations Credits

Front cover: (background map), Library of Congress, Geography and Map Division, G3764. B6S3 1775 .M61; (UP A), Engagement Between the *Bonhomme Richard* and the *Serapis* off Flamborough Head, 1779, Willis, Richard (Contemporary Artist)/Guardian Royal Exchange Insurance Collection/The Bridgeman Art Library; (UP B), Alexander Hamilton, ca 1804 (oil on canvas), Trumbull, John (1756–1843)/© Collection of the New-York Historical Society, USA/The Bridgeman Art Library; (UP C), Portrait of George Washington Taking the Salute at Trenton (oil on canvas), Faed, John (1820–1902)/Private Collection/Photo © Christie's Images/The Bridgeman Art Library; (UP D), Thomas Jefferson (1743–1826) (color litho), Peale, Rembrandt (1778–1860)/Private Collection/Peter Newark American Pictures/The Bridgeman Art Library; (LO A), Portrait of Benjamin Franklin (oil on canvas), Duplessis, Joseph Siffred (1725–1802)/Private Collection/Peter Newark American Pictures/The Bridgeman Art Library; (LO B), The Library of Virginia; (LO C), John Adams, 1860 (oil on canvas), Healy, George Peter Alexander (1808–94)/Corcoran Gallery of Art, Washington D.C., USA/Museum Purchase, Gallery Fund/Public Domain/The Bridgeman Art Library; (LO D), Samuel Adams (color litho), Copley, John Singleton (1738–1815)/Private Collection/Peter Newark American Pictures/The Bridgeman Art Library; 1, Military and Historical Image Bank; 2-3, Revolutionary War 1775–1783 (American War of Independence): George Washington riding in triumph through streets of Boston after 11-month siege ended with the withdrawal (evacuation) of British forces. Chromolithograph 1879/Universal History Archive/UIG/The Bridgeman Art Library; 4, Courtesy of Concord Museum, Concord, MA; 6, Library of Congress Prints & Photographs Division, LC-DIG-pga-03609 DLC; 8, American flag, ca 1781 (wool & cotton), American School (18th century)/© Collection of the New-York Historical Society, USA/The Bridgeman Art Library; 10-11, Colonists under Liberty Tree (color litho), American School (18th century)/Private Collection/Peter Newark American Pictures/The Bridgeman Art Library; 12, George III (1738–1820) (oil on canvas), Ramsay, Allan (1713–1784) (studio of)/Scottish National Portrait Gallery, Edinburgh, Scotland/The Bridgeman Art Library; 14, Treaty of Paris, ending the Seven Years' War, signed by France, Great Britain, & Spain on 10th February 1763 (pen & ink on paper), French School (18th century)/Archives du Ministère des Affaires Étrangères, Paris, France/Archives Charmet/The Bridgeman Art Library; 15, George III, ca 1781 (oil on canvas), Gainsborough, Thomas (1727–1788)/The Royal Collection © 2011 Her Majesty Queen Elizabeth II/The Bridgeman Art Library; 16, Architect of the Capitol; 18 (UP LE), Military and Historical Image Bank; 18 (UP CTR), Courtesy of the Mount Vernon Ladies' Association; 18 (UP RT), Military and Historical Image Bank; 18 (CTR LE), Military and Historical Image Bank; 18 (CTR RT), Teapot (silver), Revere, Paul (1735–1818)/Worcester Art Museum, Massachusetts, USA/The Bridgeman Art Library; 18 (LO LE), Military and Historical Image Bank; 18 (LO CTR), Military and Historical Image Bank; 18 (LO RT), Military and Historical Image Bank; 20-21, From *Historical Atlas* by William R. Shepherd, 1923/Courtesy the University of Texas at Austin; 22 (UP), Fotosearch/Getty Images; 22 (LO), Library of Congress, Prints & Photographs Division, #3g05315; 23, Colonel Isaac Barre, 1785 (oil on canvas), Stuart, Gilbert (1755–1828)/Brooklyn Museum of Art, New York, USA/Carl H. de Silver Fund/The Bridgeman Art Library; 24, the Philadelphia Museum of Art/Art Resource, NY; 25, © National Portrait Gallery, London; 26, House of Commons Interior before the fire of 1834, from Ackermann's *Microcosm of London,* Rowlandson, T. (1756–1827) & Pugin, A. C. (1762–1832)/British Library, London, UK/© British Library Board. All Rights Reserved/The Bridgeman Art Library; 27, Stapleton Collection/Corbis; 28-29, Library of Congress Prints & Photographs Division, ppmsca.05479; 31 (LO), Portrait of George Mason (oil on canvas), Guillaume, Louis Mathieu Didier (1816–92)/Virginia Historical Society, Richmond, Virginia, USA/The Bridgeman Art Library; 32, John Hancock, ca 1770–1772 (oil on canvas), Copley, John Singleton (1738–1815)/Private Collection/The Bridgeman Art Library; 33, Affray at Boston between the soldiers and rope-makers, 1770, illustration from *Cassell's Illustrated History of England* (engraving) (sepia photo), English School (20th century)/Private Collection/The Stapleton Collection/The Bridgeman Art Library; 34-35, A View of the Town of Boston in New England and British Ships of War Landing Their Troops, 1768, 1770 (engraving), Revere, Paul (1735-1818)/Gilder Lehrman Collection, New York, USA/The Bridgeman Art Library; 36, Burstein Collection/Corbis; 37, Drawing of the four coffins from the Boston massacre, printed in the *Boston Gazette,* 12th March 1770 (litho), Revere, Paul (1735–1818)/American Antiquarian Society, Worcester, Massachusetts, USA/The Bridgeman Art Library; 38, Thomas Hutchinson (1711–1780) 1741 (oil on canvas), Truman, Edward (18th century)/© Massachusetts Historical Society, Boston, MA, USA/The Bridgeman Art Library; 39, Destruction of the schooner *Gaspé* in the waters of Rhode Island, 1772, engraved by J. Rogers (engraving), McNevin, J. (19th century) (after)/Private Collection/Ken Welsh/The Bridgeman Art Library; 40, Christie's Images/Corbis; 41, Facsimile of the proclamation from the Philadelphia patriots to the Delaware pilots warning them not to deal with the British tea ship, 7 December 1773 (litho), American School/Private Collection/Peter Newark American Pictures/The Bridgeman Art Library; 42, Courtesy, American Antiquarian Society; 43, Benjamin Franklin Appearing before the Privy Council (oil on canvas), Schussele, Christian (ca 1824–1879)/Huntington Library and Art Gallery, San Marino, CA, USA/©The Huntington Library, Art Collections & Botanical Gardens/The Bridgeman Art Library; 44-45, Library of Congress Prints & Photographs Division, LC-USZC4-538; 46, Library of Congress Prints & Photographs Division, LC-DIG-ppmsca-19467; 47, Portrait of General Thomas Gage, ca 1768 (oil on canvas mounted on masonite), Copley, John Singleton (1738–1815)/Yale Center for British Art, Paul Mellon Collection, USA/The Bridgeman Art Library; 49, The First Continental Congress, Carpenter's Hall, Philadelphia in 1774, 1911 (oil on canvas), Deland, Clyde Osmer (1872–1947)/© Philadelphia History Museum at the Atwater Kent/Courtesy of Historical Society of Pennsylvania Collection/The Bridgeman Art Library; 50, Library of Congress Prints & Photographs Division, LC-DIG-ppmsca-31798; 51, The Granger Collection, NYC—All rights reserved; 52, Portrait of Benjamin Franklin (oil on canvas), Duplessis, Joseph Siffred (1725–1802)/Private Collection/Peter Newark American Pictures/The Bridgeman Art Library; 53, Library of Congress Prints & Photographs Division; 54, Portrait of Deborah Read Franklin, 1758–1759/Attributed to Benjamin Wilson/oil on canvas/41 1/2 x 36 inches/Courtesy of American Philosophical Society. 58.P.44; 55, The Philadelphia Museum of Art/Art Resource,

NY; 56, Benjamin Franklin, Printer, ca 1928 (oil on canvas), Dunsmore, John Ward (1856–1945) (after)/© Collection of the New-York Historical Society, USA/The Bridgeman Art Library; 57, National Museum of American History & Smithsonian Institution Archives; 58-59, Gift of Edgar William and Bernice Chrysler Garbisch, Photograph © Board of Trustees, National Gallery of Art, Washington; 60, The Granger Collection, NYC—All rights reserved; 62, Patrick Henry, 1851 (oil on canvas), Sully, Thomas (1783–1872)/Virginia Historical Society, Richmond, Virginia, USA/The Bridgeman Art Library; 63, SuperStock/Getty Images; 64, Paul Revere's famous ride on the night of 18 April 1775 (color litho), American School (19th century)/Private Collection/Peter Newark American Pictures/The Bridgeman Art Library; 65, Samuel Adams, ca 1770–1772 (oil on canvas), American School (18th century)/© Collection of the New-York Historical Society, USA/The Bridgeman Art Library; 67, The Granger Collection, NYC—All rights reserved; 68-69, Library of Congress Prints & Photographs Division, LC-USZC4-628; 72, Print Collection/Miriam and Ira D. Wallach Division of Art, Prints and Photographs/The New York Public Library, Astor, Lenox, and Tilden Foundations; 73, Portrait of John Murray, 1929 (oil on canvas), Harris, Charles Xavier (b. 1856)/Virginia Historical Society, Richmond, Virginia, USA/The Bridgeman Art Library; 74-75, Library of Congress, Geography and Map Division; 76, The capture of Fort Ticonderoga, 10 May 1775 (litho), American School (19th century)/Private Collection/Peter Newark American Pictures/The Bridgeman Art Library; 77, Fort Ticonderoga on Lake Champlain/Encyclopaedia Britannica/UIG/The Bridgeman Art Library; 78 (musket), Courtesy Fort Ticonderoga Museum, National Park Service; 78 (powder horn), courtesy Fort Ticonderoga Museum, National Park Service; 78 (musket balls), Military and Historical Image Bank; 78 (snare drum), Snare drum, said to have been captured at Bunker Hill/© Massachusetts Historical Society, Boston, MA, USA/The Bridgeman Art Library; 78 (pistol), Armed Forces History Division/National Museum of American History, Smithsonian Institution; 78 (cartridge box and belt), Military and Historical Image Bank; 78 (sword), Courtesy Fort Ticonderoga Museum, National Park Service; 79, The Honourable Sir William Howe, 1777 (color mezzotint), Purcell, Richard (ca 1736–ca 1766) (after)/Brown University Library, Providence, Rhode Island, USA/The Bridgeman Art Library; 80, Courtesy of the Mount Vernon Ladies' Association; 81, George Washington in the uniform of a Colonel of the Virginia Militia during the French & Indian War (1755–1763) (color litho), Peale, Charles Willson (1741–1827) (after)/Private Collection/Peter Newark American Pictures/The Bridgeman Art Library; 82, George Washington (1732–1799) taking command of the American Army at Cambridge, Massachusetts, 3 July 1775, 1876 (color litho), Currier, N. (1813–1888) and Ives, J. M. (1824–1895)/Private Collection/Peter Newark American Pictures/The Bridgeman Art Library; 84-85, Francis G. Mayer/Corbis; 86, Library of Congress Prints & Photographs Division, LC-USZC2-1256; 87, Library of Congress, Geography and Map Division, G3764.B6S3 1775. M61; 88, Library of Congress Prints & Photographs Division, LC-USZ62-54; 89, The Granger Collection, NYC—All rights reserved; 90, The Granger Collection, NYC—All rights reserved; 91, Portrait of John Locke (1632–1704) (see also 1419), Kneller, Sir Godfrey (1646–1723) (after)/Private Collection/Photo © Philip Mould Ltd, London/The Bridgeman Art Library; 92, Colonel Benedict Arnold, pub. London, 1776 (mezzotint), English School (18th century)/Brown University Library, Providence, Rhode Island, USA/The Bridgeman Art Library; 94, Death of General Richard Montgomery in Quebec, December 31, 1775, 1786, by John Trumbull (1756–1843), American War of Independence, Canada, 18th century/De Agostini Picture Library/The Bridgeman Art Library; 95, "Wha Wants Me," cartoon showing Tom Paine and the Rights of Man by Isaac Cruikshank (1756–1811/16)/British Library, London, UK/© British Library Board. All Rights Reserved/The Bridgeman Art Library; 96, National Portrait Gallery, London; 97, Bettmann/Corbis; 98, Thomas Paine's *Rights of Man*, 1792/Courtesy of the National Archives, TS 24-3-9; 99, "The Rights of Man, or Tommy Paine, the little American Taylor, taking the Measure of the Crown for a new Pair of Revolution-Breeches," published by Hannah Humphrey in 1791 (hand-colored etching), Gillray, James (1757–1815)/© Courtesy of the Warden and Scholars of New College, Oxford/The Bridgeman Art Library; 100, Courtesy of The Lewis Walpole Library, Yale University; 101, Library of Congress Rare Book and Special Collections Division; 102-103, Washington Crossing the Delaware River, 25th December 1776, 1851 (oil on canvas) (copy of an original painted in 1848), Leutze, Emanuel Gottlieb (1816–1868)/Metropolitan Museum of Art, New York, USA/The Bridgeman Art Library; 104, Engraving by Lambert/Getty Images; 106, Mercenaries embarking from Hesse to America, 1776/Photo © Tarker/The Bridgeman Art Library; 107, Henry Knox, ca 1805 (color litho), Stuart, Gilbert (1755–1828) (after)/Private Collection/Peter Newark American Pictures/The Bridgeman Art Library; 108, North Wind Picture Archives; 109, Anne S. K. Brown Military Collection/Brown University Library; 110, George Washington at Dorchester Heights, Massachusetts (color litho), Leutze, Emanuel Gottlieb (1816–1868) (after)/Private Collection/Peter Newark American Pictures/The Bridgeman Art Library; 112-113, Lord Howe organizes the British evacuation of Boston in March 1776 (color engraving), English School/Private Collection/Peter Newark Pictures/The Bridgeman Art Library; 114, Library of Congress Prints & Photographs Division, LC-USZC4-2135; 115 (UP LE), Military and Historical Image Bank; 115 (UP CTR LE), New-York Historical Society; 115 (UP CTR RT), Military and Historical Image Bank; 115 (UP RT), Collection of the New-York Historical Society; 115 (LE CTR), Military and Historical Image Bank; 115 (CTR), Connecticut State Library; 115 (RT CTR), Armed Forces History Division/National Museum of American History, Smithsonian Institution; 115 (LO LE and LO RT), Military and Historical Image Bank; 116, The Granger Collection, NYC—All rights reserved; 117, National Portrait Gallery, Smithsonian Institution/Art Resource, NY; 119, Writing the Declaration of Independence in 1776 (oil on canvas), Ferris, Jean Leon Gerome (1863–1930)/Virginia Historical Society, Richmond, Virginia, USA/The Bridgeman Art Library; 120, The U.S. National Archives and Records Administration; 121, Library of Congress Prints & Photographs Division, LC-DIG-ppmsca-17521; 122-123, Francis G. Mayer/Corbis; 124, The New York Public Library, Astor, Lenox, and Tilden Foundations; 125, Anne S. K. Brown Military Collection/Brown University Library; 126, National Guard Heritage Collection; 127, George Washington directing the retreat from Brooklyn Heights, 29 August 1776 (litho), American School (19th century)/Private Collection/Peter Newark American Pictures/The Bridgeman Art Library; 128, The Peace Conference on Staten Island, Interview between Lord Howe and the Committee of Congress, 11th September 1776 (engraving) (b&w photo), Chappel, Alonzo (1828–1887) (after)/Private Collection/The Bridgeman Art Library; 129, Sir William Howe, Commander in Chief of the British Army (1776–1778) in full dress dismounted (w/c on paper), Lefferts, Charles MacKubin (1873–1923)/© Collection of the New-York Historical Society, USA/The Bridgeman Art Library; 130, Franklin Urging the Claims of the American Colonies Before Louis XVI, ca 1847/by George Peter Alexander Healy/oil on canvas/32 x 44 inches/Courtesy of American Philosophical Society. 58.P.28; 132, Emmet Collection/Miriam and Ira D. Wallach Division of Art, Prints and Photographs/The New York Public Library, Astor, Lenox, and Tilden Foundations; 133, The Granger Collection, NYC—All rights reserved; 134-135, National Maritime Museum, Greenwich, London; 136, The Granger Collection, NYC—All rights reserved; 137, I. N. Phelps Stokes Collection/Miriam and Ira D. Wallach Division of Art, Prints and Photographs/The New York Public Library, Astor, Lenox, and Tilden Foundations; 138, Photo by Mansell/Time & Life Pictures/Getty Images; 140, Emmet Collection/Miriam and Ira D. Wallach Division of Art, Prints and Photographs/The New York Public Library, Astor, Lenox, and Tilden Foundations; 141, Emmet Collection/Miriam and Ira D. Wallach Divsion of Art, Prints and Photographs/The New York Public Library, Astor, Lenox, and Tilden Foundations; 142-143, Library of Congress; 143, Battle of Trenton, 26 December 1776 (color litho) (see also 332831), McBarron, H. Charles, Jr. (1902–1992) (after)/Private Collection/Peter Newark American Pictures/The Bridgeman Art Library; 145, Yale University Art Gallery/Art Resource, NY; 146, Portrait of Thomas Jefferson, 1805 (oil on canvas), Peale, Rembrandt (1778–1860)/© Collection of the New-York Historical Society, USA/The Bridgeman Art Library; 147, Library of Congress Prints & Photographs Division, LC-USZ62-128740; 148, Thomas Jefferson as U.S. Ambassador to France, 1786 (oil on canvas), Brown, Mather (1761–1831)/Private Collection/Peter Newark Pictures/The Bridgeman Art Library; 149 (LE), Library of Congress; 149 (RT), National Museum of American History, Smithsonian Institution; 150, Monticello: 2nd version (west elevation), recto, 1803 (pen & ink with w/c on paper), Mills, Robert (1781–1855)/© Massachusetts Historical Society, Boston, MA, USA/The Bridgeman Art Library; 151, A Philosophic Cock, 1804 (color litho), American School (19th century)/American Antiquarian Society, Worcester, Massachusetts, USA/The Bridgeman Art Library; 152-153, Princeton University Art Museum/Art Resource, NY; 154, © RMN-Grand Palais/Art Resource, NY; 156, Charles Cornwallis, 1st Marquis Cornwallis (color litho), Gainsborough, Thomas (1727–1788) (after)/Private Collection/Peter Newark American Pictures/The Bridgeman Art Library; 157, Battle of Princeton on 3rd January 1777 (oil on canvas), Mercer, William (ca 1773–ca 1850)/© Philadelphia History Museum at the Atwater Kent/Courtesy of Historical Society of Pennsylvania Collection/The Bridgeman Art Library; 158-159, Yale University Art Gallery/Art Resource, NY; 161, The Granger Collection, NYC—All rights reserved; 162, Betsy Ross (oil on canvas), Ferris, Jean Leon Gerome (1863–1930)/Private Collection/The Bridgeman Art Library; 163, Iberfoto/SuperStock; 164, Library of Congress, Geography and Map Division; 165, The Granger Collection, NYC—All rights reserved; 166, General John Stark at the Battle of Bennington, Vermont, 1902 (color litho), Yohn, Frederick Coffay (1875–1933) (after)/Private Collection/The Bridgeman Art Library; 167, General Gates at Saratoga, ca 1799 (oil on canvas), Peale, James the Elder (1749–1831)/Private Collection/Peter Newark American Pictures/The Bridgeman Art Library; 168-169, Fraunces Tavern® Museum, New York City; 171, Courtesy Fort Ticonderoga Museum, National Park Service; 172-173, Courtesy of the Tennessee Historical Society; 173, General John Burgoyne (color litho), Reynolds, Sir Joshua (1723–1792) (after)/Private Collection/Peter Newark American Pictures/The Bridgeman Art Library; 174, The Burial of General Simon Fraser (1729–1777) after the Battle of Saratoga in 1777, ca 1800 (oil on canvas), Graham, John (1754–1817) (after)/National Army Museum, London/The Bridgeman Art Library; 175, The Battle of Saratoga, the British General John Burgoyne surrendering to the American General, Horatio Gates, October 17, 1777, by John Trumbull (1756–1843), 1822, oil on canvas, American War of Independence, USA/De Agostini Picture Library/The Bridgeman Art Library; 176, Library of Congress Prints & Photographs Division, LC-USZC4-4526; 177, Alexander Hamilton (1757–1804) in the Uniform of the New York Artillery (oil on canvas), Chappel, Alonzo (1828–1887)/© Museum of the City of New York, USA/The Bridgeman Art Library; 178, West Jersey History Project; 179, The Granger Collection, NYC—All rights reserved; 180-181, The Battle of Germantown, 4th October 1777 (oil on canvas), Gatta, Saviero Xavier della (fl. 1777-1820)/Valley Forge Historical Society, USA/The Bridgeman Art Library; 182 (swords), Armed Forces History Division/National Museum of American History, Smithsonian Institution; 182 (fishing gear), Courtesy of the Mount Vernon Ladies' Association; 182 (drinking vessel), Courtesy of the Mount Vernon Ladies' Association; 182 (uniform), Armed Forces History Division/National Museum of American History, Smithsonian Institution; 182 (writing case), National Museum of American History, Smithsonian Institution, Behring Center; 182 (camp bed), Camp bed said to have been used by George Washington at Valley Forge, ca 1777–1785 (wood, canvas, and iron), American School (18th century)/© Collection of the New-York Historical Society, USA/The Bridgeman Art Library; 183, The Colonial Williamsburg Foundation. Gift of the Lasser Family; 184, Franklin at the court of France, 1778, receiving the homage of his genius and the recognition of his country's advent among the nations, 1853 (hand-colored mezzotint), Jolly, Baron (18th–19th century) (after)/© Boston Athenaeum, USA/The Bridgeman Art Library; 185, The U.S. National Archives and Records Administration; 186-187, George Washington at Valley Forge, preliminary sketch, 1854 (oil on canvas), Matteson, Tompkins Harrison (1813–1884)/Private Collection/Photo © Christie's Images/The Bridgeman Art Library; 188, The Granger Collection, NYC—All rights reserved; 189, Photo courtesy

Everett Collection, Inc.; 190, The Granger Collection, NYC—All rights reserved; 191, General Sir Henry Clinton (1730–1795) ca 1777 (w/c on ivory), Smart, John (1741–1811)/National Army Museum, London/The Bridgeman Art Library; 192-193, Battle of Monmouth, June 28, 1778, early 19th century (oil on canvas), American School (19th century)/© Chicago History Museum, USA/The Bridgeman Art Library; 194 (UP), Portrait of Charles Henri (1729–1794) Count of Estaing (oil on canvas), Franque, Jean Pierre (1774–1860)/Château de Versailles, France/Giraudon/The Bridgeman Art Library; 194 (LO), Image copyright © The Metropolitan Museum of Art. Image source: Art Resource, NY; 196-197, Library of Congress; 198, Library of Congress Rare Book and Special Collections Division, LC-USZ62-45270; 199, Library of Congress Prints & Photographs Division, LC-USZ62-34859; 200, George Washington (oil on canvas), Stuart, Gilbert (1755–1828)/Sterling & Francine Clark Art Institute, Williamstown, Massachusetts, USA/The Bridgeman Art Library; 201, Library of Congress Prints & Photographs Division, LC-USZC4-7247; 202, Library of Congress Prints & Photographs Division, LC-DIG-pga-03456; 203, Library of Congress Prints & Photographs Division, LC-DIG-pga-02796; 204 (UP), National Portrait Gallery, Smithsonian Institution/Art Resource, NY; 204 (LO), Courtesy of the Mount Vernon Ladies' Association; 205, George Washington (1732–1799) on his Mount Vernon estate with his black field workers in 1757, published in 1852 (color litho), Currier, Nathaniel (1813–1888)/Private Collection/Peter Newark American Pictures/The Bridgeman Art Library; 206-207, Engagement Between the *Bonhomme Richard* and the *Serapis* off Flamborough Head, 1779, Willis, Richard (Contemporary Artist)/ Guardian Royal Exchange Insurance Collection/The Bridgeman Art Library; 208, John Paul Jones (color litho), American School/Private Collection/Peter Newark American Pictures/The Bridgeman Art Library; 210, Bettmann/Corbis; 211 (BACK), Library of Congress, Geography and Map Division, G3791.S3 1779 .M3; 211 (INSET), Portrait of Ki-on-twog-ky, 1796 (oil on canvas), Bartoli, F. (fl. 1796)/© Collection of the New-York Historical Society, USA/The Bridgeman Art Library; 212, Photo by Mary Evans Picture Library/Everett Collection, Inc.; 213, H. Armstrong Roberts/Classicstock/Everett Collection, Inc.; 215, The Granger Collection, NYC—All rights reserved; 216, The Granger Collection, NYC—All rights reserved; 217, *An Historical Account of the Small-Pox inoculated in New England,* pamphlet published in London (ink on paper), English School (18th century)/Private Collection/Peter Newark Pictures/The Bridgeman Art Library; 218-219, Library of Congress; 219, Picture Collection/The New York Public Library, Astor, Lenox, and Tilden Foundations; 220, Captain Henry Clinton (1730–1795) First Regiment of Foot Guards, ca 1758 (oil on canvas), Saunders, M. L. (fl. 1730–1765) (attr. to)/American Museum, Bath, Avon, UK/Courtesy of the Director, National Army Museum, London, UK/The Bridgeman Art Library; 221 (UP LE), University of North Carolina at Chapel Hill, Wilson Library, Special Collection; 221 (UP RT), Military and Historical Image Bank; 221 (CTR LE), Military and Historical Image Bank; 221 (CTR RT), Military and Historical Image Bank; 221 (LO LE), Military and Historical Image Bank; 221 (LO RT Front and Back), North Carolina Collection Gallery, Wilson Library, University of North Carolina at Chapel Hill; 222, The Granger Collection, NYC—All rights reserved; 223, Universal Images Group/ SuperStock; 224-225, The Granger Collection, NYC—All rights reserved; 226, Emmet Collection/Miriam and Ira D. Wallach Division of Art, Prints and Photographs/The New York Public Library, Astor, Lenox, and Tilden Foundations; 227, Colonel Banastre Tarleton (1754–1833) 1782 (oil on canvas), Reynolds, Sir Joshua (1723–1792)/National Gallery, London, UK/ The Bridgeman Art Library; 228, A sketch of the operations before Charlestown, the capital of South Carolina, ca 1780 (color litho), DesBarres, Joseph Frederick Wallet (1721–1824)/Gilder Lehrman Collection, New York, USA/The Bridgeman Art Library; 229, British Library/Art Archive/Art Resource; 230, Emmet Collection/Miriam and Ira D. Wallach Division of Art, Prints and Photographs/The New York Public Library, Astor, Lenox, and Tilden Foundations; 231, Death of Major Ferguson at King's Mountain, 1863 (colored engraving), Chappel, Alonzo (1828–1887) (after)/Brown University Library, Providence, Rhode Island, USA/The Bridgeman Art Library; 233, Bettmann/Corbis; 234-235, The Meeting of Greene and Gates at Charlotte, N.C., from "The Story of the Revolution" by Henry Cabot Lodge (1850–1924) (oil on canvas), Pyle, Howard (1853–1911)/Delaware Art Museum, Wilmington, USA/Howard Pyle Collection/ The Bridgeman Art Library; 236, Marion crossing the Pedee, 1852 (colored engraving), Ranney, William Tylee (1813–1857) (after)/Brown University Library, Providence, Rhode Island, USA/ The Bridgeman Art Library; 237, Photo courtesy Everett Collection, Inc.; 238 (LE), Jim McKnight/AP; 238 (RT), The Granger Collection, NYC—All rights reserved; 239, The Granger Collection, NYC—All rights reserved; 240, Execution of Major John Andre (color litho), Hamilton (18th century) (after)/Private Collection/Peter Newark American Pictures/The Bridgeman Art Library; 242, Abigail Adams (1744–1818), American First Lady, Wife of President John Adams, Mother of President John Quincy Adams, Portrait, Mather Brown, 1785/J. T. Vintage/The Bridgeman Art Library; 243, Map of Rhode Island at the time of its occupation 1780–1781 by the French Army on the orders of Jean-Baptiste de Vimeur (1725–1807) Count of Rochambeau (color litho), French School (18th century)/Service Historique de la Marine, Vincennes, France/Archives Charmet/The Bridgeman Art Library; 244, Portrait of John Adams (oil on canvas), Stuart, Gilbert (1755–1828) (after)/Musée Franco-Américain, Blérancourt, Chauny, France/The Bridgeman Art Library; 245, Abigail Smith Adams, ca 1766 (pastel on paper), Blyth, Benjamin (fl. 1740–1787)/© Massachusetts Historical Society, Boston, MA, USA/The Bridgeman Art Library; 246, The Granger Collection, NYC—All rights reserved; 247, John Adams, after 1783 (oil on canvas), Copley, John Singleton (1738–1815) (after)/ Museum of Fine Arts, Boston, Massachusetts, USA/Seth K. Sweetser Fund/The Bridgeman Art Library; 248, John Adams (1735–1826) as the First American Ambassador to the English Court, presenting his credentials to King George III (1738–1820) (lithograph), American School (19th century)/Private Collection/Peter Newark American Pictures/The Bridgeman Art Library; 249, The birthplace of John Adams (1735–1826) in Braintree, now Quincy, Massachusetts (color litho), American School (19th century)/Private Collection/Peter Newark American Pictures/ The Bridgeman Art Library; 250-251, The Granger Collection, NYC—All rights reserved; 252, Image Asset Management Ltd./SuperStock; 254, The Granger Collection, NYC—All rights reserved; 255, The Granger Collection, NYC—All rights reserved; 256-257, Colonel William Washington at the Battle of Cowpens, South Carolina, 17th January, 1781 (oil on canvas), American School (18th century)/© Chicago History Museum, USA/The Bridgeman Art Library; 258, Portrait of Nathanael Greene (Warwick, 1742–Savannah, 1786), American general/De Agostini Picture Library/J. E. Bulloz/The Bridgeman Art Library; 259, The Granger Collection, NYC—All rights reserved; 260, Battle of Guilford Courthouse, 15 March 1781 (color litho), McBarron, H. Charles, Jr. (1902–1992)/Private Collection/Peter Newark American Pictures/The Bridgeman Art Library; 261, The Granger Collection, NYC—All rights reserved; 262-263, David Rumsey Historical Map Collection; 264, Library of Congress; 265, Library of Congress, Geography and Map Division, ar145100; 266, Jean-Baptiste de Vimeur (1725–1807) Count of Rochambeau (oil on canvas), Lariviere, Charles-Philippe (1798–1876)/Château de Versailles, France/Giraudon/The Bridgeman Art Library; 267, The Granger Collection, NYC—All rights reserved; 269, The Granger Collection, NYC—All rights reserved; 270-271, Courtesy of the U.S. Navy Art Collection, Washington, D.C.; 272, Library of Congress, Geography and Map Division, ar146100; 274, © RMN-Grand Palais/Art Resource, NY; 275, The Granger Collection, NYC—All rights reserved; 277, The Granger Collection, NYC—All rights reserved; 278-279, Library of Virginia/Courtesy of www.virginiamemory.com/shaping; 280, The Granger Collection, NYC—All rights reserved; 281, Library of Congress, Geography and Map Division, ct002284; 282, The British surrendering to George Washington after Battle of Yorktown in October 1781, by John Francis Renault, engraving, American War of Independence, United States, 18th century/De Agostini Picture Library/M. Seemuller/The Bridgeman Art Library; 284-285, The Granger Collection, NYC—All rights reserved; 286, *Important Intelligence!* (announcing the surrender of Cornwallis at Yorktown), small broadside printed by M. Willis, Boston, 26th October 1781 (litho), American School (18th century)/Gilder Lehrman Collection, New York, USA/The Bridgeman Art Library; 287 (UP LE), Colonial Williamsburg; 287 (UP CTR), American flag, ca 1781 (wool & cotton), American School (18th century)/© Collection of the New-York Historical Society, USA/The Bridgeman Art Library; 287 (UP RT), Military and Historical Image Bank; 287 (CTR LE), West Point Museum; 287 (CTR), National Park Service; 287 (CTR RT), Military and Historical Image Bank; 287 (LO LE), Military and Historical Image Bank; 287 (LO CTR), Military and Historical Image Bank; 287 (LO RT), © RMN-Grand Palais/Art Resource, NY; 288, Portrait of Charles, 1st Marquess of Cornwallis (oil on canvas), Home, Robert (1752–1834)/Private Collection/Photo © Philip Mould Ltd, London/The Bridgeman Art Library; 289, The Granger Collection, NYC—All rights reserved; 290 (UP), The U.S. National Archives and Records Administration; 290 (LO), The Granger Collection, NYC—All rights reserved; 291, Fireworks in front of the Hotel de Ville in Paris celebrating the Peace of Versailles, 1783 (colored engraving), French School (18th century)/ Bibliothèque Nationale, Paris, France/Giraudon/The Bridgeman Art Library; 292, Washington's Farewell to his Officers (oil on canvas), Chappel, Alonzo (1828-87)/© Chicago History Museum, USA/The Bridgeman Art Library; 293, The Resignation of George Washington on 23rd December 1783, ca 1822 (oil on canvas), Trumbull, John (1756–1843)/Yale University Art Gallery, New Haven, CT, USA/Photo © Boltin Picture Library/The Bridgeman Art Library; 294, Alexander Hamilton, ca 1804 (oil on canvas), Trumbull, John (1756–1843)/© Collection of the New-York Historical Society, USA/The Bridgeman Art Library; 295, The Granger Collection, NYC—All rights reserved; 296, Print Collection/Miriam and Ira D. Wallach Division of Art, Prints and Photographs/The New York Public Library, Astor, Lenox, and Tilden Foundations; 297 (LE), The Granger Collection, NYC—All rights reserved; 297 (RT), Print Collection/Miriam and Ira D. Wallach Division of Art, Prints and Photographs/The New York Public Library, Astor, Lenox, and Tilden Foundations; 298, The Granger Collection, NYC—All rights reserved; 299, The Granger Collection, NYC—All rights reserved; 300-301, The Signing of the Constitution of the United States in 1787, 1940 (oil on canvas), Christy, Howard Chandler (1873–1952)/Hall of Representatives, Washington D.C., USA/The Bridgeman Art Library; 302, Courtesy of the Mount Vernon Ladies' Association; 304, Library of Congress Prints & Photographs Division, LC-USZ62-7871; 305, The Granger Collection, NYC—All rights reserved; 306, The Granger Collection, NYC—All rights reserved; 307, Library of Congress Prints & Photographs Division, LC-DIG-ppmsca-30579; 308, The Library of Virginia; 309, Constitutional Convention (w/c on paper), Ferris, Jean Leon Gerome (1863–1930)/Private Collection/The Bridgeman Art Library; 310, North Wind Picture Archives; 311, Library of Congress Prints & Photographs Division, LC-DIG-ppmsca-17522; 312-313, The Granger Collection, NYC—All rights reserved; 314, Robert Morris (oil on canvas), Peale, Charles Willson (1741–1827)/Pennsylvania Academy of Fine Arts, Philadelphia, PA, USA/The Bridgeman Art Library; 316 (LE), The Granger Collection, NYC—All rights reserved; 316 (CTR), The Granger Collection, NYC—All rights reserved; 316 (RT), The Granger Collection, NYC—All rights reserved; 317, *The Federalist,* published in 1788 (print), American School (18th century)/ American Antiquarian Society, Worcester, Massachusetts, USA/The Bridgeman Art Library; 318, John Jay, 1786 (oil on canvas), Wright of Derby, Joseph (1734–1797)/© Collection of the New-York Historical Society, USA/The Bridgeman Art Library; 319, The Granger Collection, NYC—All rights reserved; 320-321, The Granger Collection, NYC—All rights reserved; 322, The Granger Collection, NYC—All rights reserved; 323, North Wind Picture Archives; 324, Burstein Collection/Corbis; 325, Bettmann/Corbis; 326, Corbis; 327, The Granger Collection, NYC—All rights reserved; 328, War of 1812 (Anglo-American War 1812–1815): "The Boxing Match, or Another Bloody Nose for John Bull." George III wounded by James Madison, triumphant at the loss of British ships. William Charles (1776–1820) Scottish-American/Universal History Archive/UIG/The Bridgeman Art Library; 329 (UP), PoodlesRock/PoodlesRock/ Corbis; 329 (LO), Corbis; 330, The U.S. National Archives and Records Administration.

Boldface indicates illustrations.

A

B

C

Founding Fathers
K. M. Kostyal

Published by the National Geographic Society
John M. Fahey, Chairman of the Board
and Chief Executive Officer
Declan Moore, Executive Vice President;
President, Publishing and Travel
Melina Gerosa Bellows, Executive Vice President;
Publisher and Chief Creative Officer, Books, Kids, and Family

Prepared by the Book Division
Hector Sierra, Senior Vice President and General Manager
Janet Goldstein, Senior Vice President and Editorial Director
Jonathan Halling, Creative Director
Marianne R. Koszorus, Design Director
Lisa Thomas, Senior Editor
R. Gary Colbert, Production Director
Jennifer A. Thornton, Director of Managing Editorial
Susan S. Blair, Director of Photography
Meredith C. Wilcox, Director, Administration and
Rights Clearance

Staff for This Book
Gail Spilsbury, Editor
Barbara Payne, Contributing Editor
Carol Farrar Norton, Art Director
Jane A. Martin, Illustrations Editor
Carl Mehler, Director of Maps
XNR Productions, Map Research and Production
Marshall Kiker, Associate Managing Editor
Judith Klein, Production Editor
Mike Horenstein, Production Manager
Galen Young, Rights Clearance Specialist
Katie Olsen, Production Design Assistant
Erin Greenhalgh, Stephanie Lynn Thomas, Editorial Interns

Production Services
Phillip L. Schlosser, Senior Vice President
Chris Brown, Vice President, NG Book Manufacturing
Nicole Elliott, Director of Production
George Bounelis, Senior Production Manager
Rachel Faulise, Manager
Robert L. Barr, Manager

The National Geographic Society is one of the world's largest nonprofit scientific and educational organizations. Its mission is to inspire people to care about the planet. Founded in 1888, the Society is member supported and offers a community for members to get closer to explorers, connect with other members, and help make a difference. The Society reaches more than 450 million people worldwide each month through *National Geographic* and other magazines; National Geographic Channel; television documentaries; music; radio; films; books; DVDs; maps; exhibitions; live events; school publishing programs; interactive media; and merchandise. National Geographic has funded more than 10,000 scientific research, conservation, and exploration projects and supports an education program promoting geography literacy. For more information, visit www.nationalgeographic.com.

National Geographic Society
1145 17th Street N.W.
Washington, D.C. 20036-4688 U.S.A.

For information about special discounts for bulk purchases, please contact National Geographic Books Special Sales: ngspecsales@ngs.org

For rights or permissions inquiries, please contact National Geographic Books Subsidiary Rights: ngbookrights@ngs.org

Library of Congress Cataloging-in-Publication Data
Kostyal, K. M., 1951-
Founding fathers : the fight for freedom and the birth of American Liberty / K.M. Kostyal.
p. cm.
Includes bibliographical references and index.
ISBN 978-1-4262-1175-1 (hardcover : alk. paper)
ISBN 978-1-4262-1398-4 (deluxe)
1. United States--History--Revolution, 1775-1783--Campaigns. 2. United States--History--Confederation, 1783-1789. 3. Washington, George, 1732-1799. 4. Political leadership--United States. 5. Founding Fathers of the United States. I. Title.
E208.K856 2014
973.3092'2--dc23
2013024559

Printed in the United States of America

14/RRDW-CML/1

Acknowledgments

My thanks first to the countless historians who have spent their lives uncovering, decoding, and preserving the story of America's conception. Special thanks particularly to Jack Rakove for his insightful guidance on this book, and to the historians and librarians at Colonial Williamsburg, Mount Vernon, and the University of Virginia.

Appreciative thanks as well to the committed staff of this book at National Geographic: Gail Spilsbury for her support and calm in spearheading the project; Jane Martin for amassing the superb collection of historic images; Carol Norton for bringing all the pieces together into a compelling package; and Lisa Thomas for entrusting me with telling the story of a grand moment in history.

—K.M.K.

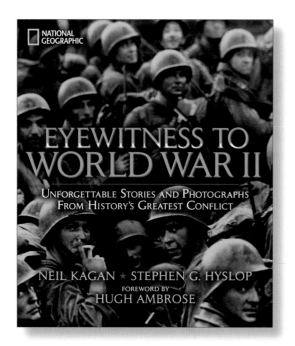

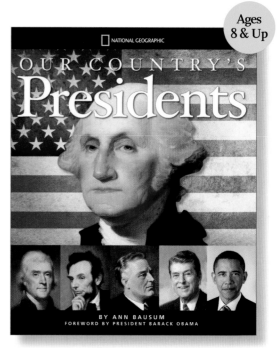

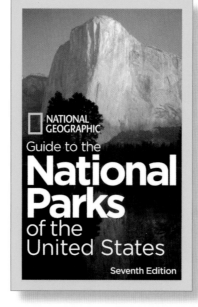